Respecting Persons in Theory and Practice

Essays on Moral and Political Philosophy

JAN NARVESON

ROWMAN & LITTLEFIELD PUBLISHERS, INC.
Lanham • Boulder • New York • Oxford

ROWMAN & LITTLEFIELD PUBLISHERS, INC.

Published in the United States of America
by Rowman & Littlefield Publishers, Inc.
4720 Boston Way, Lanham, Maryland 20706
www.rowmanlittlefield.com

12 Hid's Copse Road, Cumnor Hill, Oxford OX2 9JJ, England

British Library Cataloguing in Publication Information Available

ISBN 0-7425-1329-7 (cloth : alk. paper) ✓
ISBN 0-7425-1330-0 (pbk. : alk. paper)

Printed in the United States of America

♾™ The paper used in this publication meets the minimum requirements of American
National Standard for Information Sciences—Permanence of Paper for Printed Library
Materials, ANSI/NISO Z39.48-1992.

Contents

Preface

This selection from articles I have composed during nearly forty years was stimulated by an invitation from James Sterba, who was then philosophy editor at Rowman & Littlefield. The essays assembled here do not form a tightly connected set, though they are connected enough, in a looser way. One main principle of selection was that I still regarded the item as reasonably interesting; a secondary one was to present work from over my entire academic life. Thus one of my earliest papers, from the 1960s, opens the collection, followed by two from succeeding decades; most, however, were composed since 1990, and six of the sixteen here were not previously published. Most of them will surely be new to most readers, especially those who perchance have seen my most-anthologized article, about pacifism.[1] Those that were published elsewhere are here reproduced almost as they were, with only minor corrections and alterations to suit the stylistic requirements of Rowman & Littlefield.

Apart from the title of the first paper, none of these papers reflects my utilitarian period, as we might call it, which stretched from my graduate student days (at Harvard, 1956-61) to roughly the mid-1970s. As many readers will be aware, I no longer see much philosophical utility in Utilitarianism; but that is not the main reason for the exclusion. Rather, I felt that it would make more sense to collect together, in future, some of the many papers on that subject that I have composed over the years, both before and after my abandonment of that general view, into a volume devoted to an exploration of Utilitarianism, which, after all, remains a remarkably influential theory in the literature.

At that mid-1970s turning point, I came to realize, as I would now put it, that utilitarianism was a mistaken theory. What persuaded me of its error? The answer is easy to pinpoint: at a workshop on Contractarian Theory at the University of Toronto in June 1974, I heard and then read David Gauthier's seminal paper, "Reason and Maximization," which challenged the foundational theory I had supposed to be the right one. My foundational efforts were presented in the final chapter of *Morality and Utility*.[2] The persuasion was not instantaneous, but after the seeds of doubt were planted, they took rather firm root. This disaffection was further promoted at the end of that same year when I wrote a longish review of Robert Nozick's *Anarchy, State, and Utopia*, and while my treatment was still laced with utilitarianism, and I expressed many doubts about his book, in the end I think that Nozick appreciably influenced my subsequent thinking. In fact, after that my general view moved in the direction of accepting contractarian foundations and libertarian substance, both being fleshed out in my 1988-89 book, *The Libertarian Idea*.[3]

Readers may be a little surprised to find no papers here discussing, as such, the moral and political theory known as Libertarianism, the subject of one of my books and the label which, with perhaps a caveat or two, most nearly applies to the general view I am inclined toward in these matters. One reason, again, is that having written *The Libertarian Idea*, I thought perhaps it would be better not to discuss it head-on in a shorter essay, though I have of late produced some treatments of that type.[4] Since that time I have contemplated the need for "Son of Libertarian Idea," which would be a book of refinements, adjustments, restatements, and the like. That hasn't happened, but many of the essays in the present collection certainly reflect a libertarian viewpoint. I hoped, however, that they have some independent interest as well.

The pieces reflect a long-held view that philosophers are eligible to contribute both to very abstract studies of the concepts of ethics and to fairly concrete-level discussion of matters of current concern. Many of my essays of the latter type are to be found in my *Moral Matters*,[5] but the present collection contains several more. They are balanced fairly well between moral and political discussions, which indeed overlap to the point of near indiscernability. Essays 1 and 5 are the most nearly purely meta-ethical of these essays; but in fact, all are theoretical in a fairly straightforward sense of the term. Specialized or narrow issues in morals don't remain so; the need for a good answer to the question, "But why?" presses itself on intelligent people, who will not be satisfied with a shrug of the shoulders or an appeal to supposedly accepted social norms, or of course to religious views or to sheer assertion. My dealings with topics such as property rights, nondiscrimination, and the drug laws, as well as the several others explored here, are exercises in Casuistry, in the sense that they literally apply some quite general ideas to a range of fairly specific and quite concrete subjects. Those general ideas are to some degree developed and defended in context, and are certainly appealed to as having more weight than a purely intuitive appraisal of the matter in dispute could produce. Still, this is not a textbook or a monograph.

Finally, I note that few of these papers devote very much space to replies to critics, or to specific discussion of the many philosophers of the day with whose views, as will be obvious, I fairly sharply disagree. Academic hard disks, such as mine, are filled with discussions and replies that don't see print. Perhaps there is room for another book; in this one, only Rawls and Marx are treated at any appreciable length, while many others come in only for brief mention, or none. Noninclusion of the many others who deserve response is due not to lack of replies, or (usually) to not having read the relevant philosopher, but to lack of space.

Each essay has a note identifying publisher, or places it was read and worked on, or both, usually thanking members of audiences near and far, mostly anonymous, for helpful discussion. Beyond that, no one individual is owed specific thanks for this book, except James Sterba, with whom I have had many useful disagreements and to whom I am grateful, both for his good temper in responding to my criticisms over the years, and for the considerable stimulation his arguments provided. In a different vein, the efforts of longtime student and friend Jim Leger, and of my daughter Julia, helped considerably in making the text presentable to the reader.

Notes

1. "Pacifism: A Philosophical Analysis," *Ethics* 75, no. 4 (July 1965), 259-71.
2. Jan Narveson, *Morality and Utility* (Baltimore: Johns Hopkins University Press, 1967).
3. Jan Narveson, *The Libertarian Idea* (Philadelphia: Temple University Press, 1988); it is now republished (Peterborough, Ont.: Broadview, 2001).
4. "Contracting for Liberty," in T. R. Machan and D. B. Rasmussen, eds. *Libertarianism for the 21st Century*, (Lanham, Md.: Rowman & Littlefield, 1995), 19-40; and "Libertarianism," in Hugh LaFollette, ed., *The Blackwell Guide to Ethical Theory* (Oxford, UK: Blackwell, 2000), 306-324.
5. Jan Narveson, *Moral Matters* (Peterborough, Ont.: Broadview, 1999), 2d ed.

Introduction

Many of these chapters will be new to virtually all readers, and all will be new to many. Since the titles may not convey the basic idea of each, here is a short rundown, stating very briefly the theme of each chapter.

"Utilitarianism and Formalism" (1965) is not particularly about utilitarianism. It is, instead, an assault on the still very popular idea that there is a fundamental difference between two sorts of moral views, now usually known as "deontology" and "consequentialism." I show reason here why this simply can't be so, in any fundamental way.

"A Puzzle about Economic Justice in Rawls' Theory" (1976) refutes, I think, the claim, which again seems to be very widely held by current philosophers, that Rawls succeeds in finding a principled mean between the extremes of free-market libertarianism and out-and-out egalitarian communism.

"Marxism: Hollow at the Core" (1983) grew from the late 1960s and 1970s, when it became oddly popular to look to Marx as the great pundit of our time in social philosophy. The argument here is that if we look, not at what interpreters say he said, but simply at what Marx does actually say, we can find three basic arguments behind his general assault on capitalism. All of them are invalid, and in the third case, quite thoroughly incoherent. Marxism didn't fail because history proved too much for it: it was a failure from the start, at the conceptual level.

"On Recent Arguments for Egalitarianism" (1993) resulted from extensive talk with philosophers far and wide, and a perusal of the literature. Though egalitarianism is widely espoused, it is not often argued for, really. But I found about a half dozen sets of claims that seem reasonably regarded as arguments. They are, however, all wrong: either invalid, or with premises that just don't apply to the subject of the theory, namely society.

"Emotivism, Moral Realism, and Natural Law" (1996) takes up, if too briefly, a dispute still seething in the literature between proponents of a view that has come to be called "moral realism," according to which moral statements are true, when they are, in that they describe the world as it really is, and emotivism, according to which moral statements are basically expressions of the feelings or interests of the speakers in question. I argue that both views mistake the character of morals, which is essentially a set of rules (or virtues, either one) for adjusting interpersonal relations. The rules are man-made, indeed, but they have a perfectly reasonable basis, and can be argued for well or badly, and seen to be better or worse for the purpose.

"Justice as Pure Efficiency" (1996) denies an overwhelmingly popular view about justice, again more or less due to Rawls, namely that it has to go beyond efficiency in the sense, more or less assumed by economists, that its central concern is the prevention of harms to others, or more precisely the imposing of disutilities on others. I suggest that this view is coherent, but cannot be regarded as merely a minimum condition that one can or perhaps must "go beyond." Justice really does consist in rendering to each his or her due, which is to leave people in no worse shape than you found them. Better, of course, would be even better—but justice doesn't require that.

"Toward a Liberal Theory of Ideology—A Quasi-Marxian Exploration" (1992) really did pick up from reflection on Marx, even viewing part of his idea in this area with considerable enthusiasm. The thesis is that those with power in society can indeed find it in their interest to bamboozle their subjects, and when this is so, we should indeed be skeptical. However, Marx went too far: the fact that someone in power says that p isn't sufficient for the falsity or the meaninglessness of p, but merely a good reason to take it with several grains of salt.

"Property Rights: Original Acquisition and Lockean Provisos" (1999) examines several ideas about Locke's intended restriction on what people, acting on their own, may "take" from nature in the way of resources. All of these ideas are, I argue, baseless. Not baseless, however, is that we should respect the rights of those who got there before us, and not feel free to help ourselves to the proceeds of their labors.

"Deserving Profits" (1991) is a suitable sequel to the previous paper, in that it upholds the claim that, first, the concept of desert is a useful and acceptable one in all sorts of contexts, contrary to the apparent arguments of—once again!—Rawls; and, second, that people whose management of their investments or enterprises or other valued services made them money can and often do deserve their gains. Gains from free exchange are not ill-gotten, and the potential for making them works very greatly to the advantage of all of us, not merely to the capitalists.

"Fixing Democracy" (1991; retouched 1998 and 2001) draws attention to the obvious: democracy is rule by the people, which is not necessarily a good thing; in particular, it is far from identical with liberalism and offers very modest protection for liberal rights. These, it is suggested, are preferable, and the question is how if at all they can be cured.

"The Anarchist's Case" (1995) explores the case for the sort of anarchism—market anarchism, as it's often called—which, I argue, is the only sort that can be coherent. A lot of things would be very different without the State, but it appears that we could, in principle, have all the good things without it. It also appears that we are most unlikely to get to such a condition, any time soon, anyway.

"Have We a Right to Nondiscrimination?" (1977; pub. 1987) points to a fundamental problem hanging over the heads of all who think that there is some kind of basic injustice known as "discrimination." There are indeed injustices sometimes done in its name, but it is hard to see how it can itself be one such.

We all do all sorts of things that are obviously discriminatory, but few of us think these things in any way wrong. On the other hand, nondiscrimination principles are a fertile source of infringing and nullifying people's rights.

"Collective Rights?" (1991) proposes to make sense of collective rights despite the fact that the subjects of fundamental rights can only be individuals. Nevertheless, we can have plenty of rights to act in ways that stem from our group affiliations. Collective rights are really an application of Freedom of Association.

"The Drug Laws: More Nails in the Coffin of American Liberalism" (1995) is a complaint about one of the major trends in America in the past several decades: the trend to "make war on drugs." A liberal polity has no business doing this, it is argued, any more than it should be forcing us all to have a particular religion. The idea that people have a right to run their own lives, for better or worse, is surely far more promising than anything that can be said on behalf of drug laws, which in any case seem to stimulate the drug business far more than to curb it.

"Children and Rights" (2000) tries to make sense of the family in the context of liberalism. Children can't obviously be full subjects of liberal-type rights from the start; on the other hand, we can't consider them nothing but the property of their parents, either. A reasonable set of restrictions on what parents may and may not do to and with their children emerges, or so I hope.

"Natural Resources, Sustainability, and the Central Committee" (2001) is another public interest piece, really. It is widely thought that the world is facing a terrible crisis of scarcity of resources. That is all founded on misunderstanding of how resources work, what they are, and what our basic resources really are—namely, our human brains and spirits. Properly seen, these show that we have no reason to expect general scarcities of the type requiring all sorts of impositions on our various actions, over and above the restrictions we all face from our limited budgets. Sustainability isn't a problem: but people who think it is really *are* a problem.

The essays do share a general point of view, to be sure. Perhaps it can be summarized this way: that individual people have their own lives and interests, and should be credited, in the absence of strong evidence to the contrary, with not only that but some reason and common sense as well. Those things are enough to make many currently popular theories look rather arrogant. They impose tastes, preferences, and norms on people without any regard for what those people actually do care about. In my view, we are all in this life together, and we shouldn't have to put up with flummery, behind which, invariably, lies coercion, intended or otherwise.

Notes

1. "Pacifism: A Philosophical Analysis," *Ethics* 75, no. 4 (July 1965), 259-271.

2. Jan Narveson, *Morality and Utility* (Baltimore: Johns Hopkins University Press, 1967).

3. Jan Narveson, *The Libertarian Idea* (Philadelphia: Temple University Press, 1988); it is now republished (Peterborough, Ont.: Broadview, 2001).

4. "Contracting for Liberty," in T. R. Machan and D. B. Rasmussen, eds. *Libertarianism for the 21st Century*, (Lanham, Md.: Rowman & Littlefield, 1995), 19-40; and "Libertarianism," in Hugh LaFollette, ed., *The Blackwell Guide to Ethical Theory* (Oxford, UK: Blackwell, 2000), 306-324.

5. Jan Narveson, *Moral Matters* (Peterborough, Ont.: Broadview 1999), 2nd ed.

Chapter 1

Utilitarianism and Formalism

The Question

Is an act which is right, right on account of its intrinsic nature or on account of its consequences? Utilitarians (or other "teleological" theorists, with whom, however, I shall not be particularly concerned here) say that it is the latter, while Formalists contend that it is the former. In this chapter, I shall examine this popular characterization of a main division in ethical theory. I shall maintain that the *principium divisionis* does not in fact divide: each camp can and does hold that some right acts fall under each description.

Let me begin by explaining, for the sake of definiteness, whom I have in mind. My model utilitarian is anyone who holds what is in common to Sidgwick, Bentham, and Mill, viz., that the criterion of right and wrong is the tendency to promote the general interest or happiness (using the latter terms broadly enough so that they come to the same thing). My model formalist is W. D. Ross, and also such people as Price, Whewell, and at one time or another Broad, Carritt, and Ewing, to name a few. My model formalist contends that there are a number of independent but nonetheless ultimate ethical principles, most of which pick out a "type" of act and assert that acts are right (or wrong) insofar as they conform to that "type," where the description of the type in question is supposed to confine itself to "inherent" rather than "consequential" characteristics of the acts in question. Precisely what this means will, of course, be one of the principal subjects for inquiry below. Thus the "formalists" I have in mind are pluralistic, while the utilitarians are monistic: that is, the former hold that there are several ultimate criteria of right and wrong, while the latter hold that there is but one. An additional feature of this type of formalist is that he does not bank on the completeness of his list. He allows that there *might* be other features which make for right and wrong, so far as he knows.[1] Moreover, he does not have any one method for determining which of his independent principles is to take precedence in case of conflict; he holds that moral judgment involves a double process of intuition. We must (1) intuit the truth of various general principles, and (2) intuit which of them is to take precedence.

1

It is logically possible, of course, to hold that there is but one feature that makes for right or wrong, and nevertheless that it is nonconsequential. Some of my remarks below will apply to such theorists, while others will not; but I shall not be much concerned with such classificatory matters.

Intrinsic Rightness: Describing the Act

What does it mean, then, to say that an act is "intrinsically right," or "right of its own nature" and "apart from its consequences"? These phrases depend upon the phrase 'the nature of the act,' which authors of books on ethics treat as though it wore its meaning on its sleeve. But it decidedly doesn't. Consider the statement 'different acts have different natures': there is something terribly obvious about this, in a way, but it can also be meant very mysteriously. It can sound as though we could sit down and pick out some act, in our minds, and *then* try to decide what does and does not belong to its "nature." But of course, this can hardly be so. For "this" act is the one that has just "this" nature, and no other. To be able to say, then, that "this" act is right on account of "its" nature and not on account of "its" consequences, we must understand some description of "it," relative to which we can sort out various facts about the act into those which are part of its nature and those which are only its consequences.

And we now run into a difficulty. For as we all know, if we wish to talk about some individual act which has taken place at some time, there will be an indefinite number of ways in which we can describe that act. There will, that is to say, be an indefinite number of descriptions which are logically different from each other, and yet all of which hold true of the events in question. Thus, the following descriptions might all identify the same event:

'what Louie did on the night of March 3rd, 1962, at 8 p.m.'
'the time Louie shot Al'
'the time Louie fired his gun'
'the time Louie was playing poker with Al'
'the time Louie was over at Al's'
'when Louie shook the local Mafia to its roots'

Louie might have been over to Al's just once, played poker while there, fired his gun only once, shot Al that one time, and in consequence shook the Mafia to its roots; all this on the night of March 3rd. Moreover, he may or may not have shot Al in a rage because of Al's cheating at poker, he may or may not also have deeper motives, his wife may or may not have divorced him in consequence, Louie may or may not have been hanged for it; and so on. It would be absurd to try to say that some of these descriptions are "intrinsic" and some not, or that some of them state "the nature of the act" and some not. Every description either does or does not hold true of what happened that night, and of those which do, *all* of them describe "the nature of the act."

If, on the other hand, we pounce on some particular one of all of these true descriptions of what happened that night, and say, "this act is what I am talking about"—thus, suppose that 'Louie shot Al last night' is the descriptive sentence which we have in mind as describing "the event" or "the act"—then we can indeed say of all the other descriptions that they are, or that they are not, "part of the nature of the act." We can say that the fact that Al was playing poker with Louie at the time is *not* part of Louie's shooting Al, but that the fact that Louie whipped out his gun and pulled the trigger is part of Louie's shooting of Al.

In short, it does not make sense to say that this, that, or the other true description of an event is *the* description of the act, or states the nature of the act, if we are discussing some one actual happening; but it does make sense to say that this or that description (whether true or false) is or is not part of the nature of an act previously described in some other way. The phrase '*the* description of the act,' can only mean one of the following:

(1) That description in virtue of which what is being described is an act, i.e., the minimum description which can be taken as describing an act at all. This in turn is simply any specific set of descriptions which define something as an act. I suppose that the term 'act' just means 'what someone did'; and obviously, since we want to say that some acts are right and some are wrong, the 'intrinsic nature of an act' in this minimum sense is irrelevant here.

(2) The conjunction of *all* of the true descriptions of the particular act, where the "particular act" is defined by temporal and individual coordinates ('what Louie did on the night of the 3rd,' say.) Such a description, which we might call "the complete description" of any particular act, is obviously not available for putting into an ethical formula. Besides, in this sense *every* act would be either intrinsically right, intrinsically wrong, or intrinsically indifferent. For if we include all the descriptions which are true of the event, then those which state the "consequences" of the event must be there too, and since by definition there are no other descriptions of the act, then if "intrinsically right" means "right because of the intrinsic nature of the act," every act which is right at all must be right by virtue of its intrinsic nature.

(3) "The" description might be taken as that description of the act which the actor (agent) was operating under. This raises questions about the status of intentions, which I hope to take up in a future paper, but will not discuss here.

(4) Finally, "the" description can be simply that description which whoever is doing the describing wishes to use to pick out the act in question. This, clearly, is what we want. For we wish to discuss the status of universal statements asserting that all acts of a certain kind are right or wrong. For purposes of discussing any particular statement of that kind, the "intrinsic nature of the act" must be understood to be simply whatever is taken in by that description; which means, whatever the description *says*, plus (if one wishes to distinguish this) whatever it entails or logically implies.

I do not think we need to get into a lengthy discussion of the analytic versus the synthetic to establish the utility of this latter description. We can usually establish what is and what is not included in a description couched in ordinary language, with sufficient accuracy to make the discussion which depends upon it intelligible to all who know that language. There may come a point at which we have to be arbitrary; but when that juncture arrives in any of the discussions which occur below, the point I am trying to make will have been sufficiently well established, I believe.

Intrinsic Rightness: What It Is

The phrase 'the nature of the act', then, means 'whatever characteristics the act has in virtue of the description under which it is being referred to'. What, now, does it mean to say that an act is right (or wrong) "because of its intrinsic nature," that is, "intrinsically right" (or "wrong")?

The most obvious suggestion is simply that an act is intrinsically right (or wrong) if it follows from the description under which it is being referred to that it is right (or wrong). This clearly goes in the right direction, but as it stands, it will not quite do. The first reason it will not do has been well understood by my paradigm formalist, W. D. Ross. What we want to do is give some intelligible sense to such general statements as that "lying is wrong," say, or "benevolence is right." But as Ross was so quick to point out, we cannot say of all cases of lying that they are wrong, nor of all cases of benevolence that they are right. To be sure, some formalists had tried to maintain that untenable position—Kant being the most notable example. Kant, it will be remembered, tries to maintain that every case of lying is wrong, and indeed that every principle which is required by the Supreme Categorical Imperative is unlimitedly true in the same way; and, the reader will also no doubt recall, Kant gets into a frightful muddle when trying to defend his position that it would be wrong to mislead a would-be murderer about the location of his intended victim. I take it that no argument on my part is needed to show that general moral principles of the familiar type of "lying is wrong," and so forth, must be considered to be statements of what Ross called "prima facie duties" rather than duties, unqualified.

It makes no sense, of course, to say of a particular act that *it* is "prima facie" right: "prima facie rightness" is not a characteristic. But it does make perfectly good sense to say that if an act is an act of lying, then it is wrong, in the absence of any excusing conditions or overriding duties, and this is obviously what Ross had in mind. Kurt Baier has recently made a similar distinction, in very careful language, between "reasons prima facie" and "reasons on balance."[2] When we are considering a particular act, we should take into account all of those characteristics of it which tell in favor of doing it, all those which tell against it, and then make a decision as to whether the pro-considerations outbalance the con-considerations or vice versa.

It seems to me to be very close to what is meant by saying that a type of act is intrinsically right, that it is prima facie right, in the above sense. But this will not quite do either. For it now turns out that there will be classes of acts which are both intrinsically right and intrinsically wrong; for the logic of the phrase "prima facie" as applied to 'right' and 'wrong' is such that an act can have a characteristic that prima facie makes it right and another one that prima facie makes it wrong: for example, "misdirecting a murderer by lying to him about the location of his victim." This latter phrase picks out a certain class of acts which is both prima facie right and prima facie wrong, since it is wrong to lie, but right to prevent murders. And in general, for any two principles of the formalistic type, it would seem to be theoretically possible (though perhaps very difficult) to construct descriptions of acts in which they conflict, in the sense that the characteristic which one says is right-making is present together with the characteristic which the other says is wrong-making. Yet it does not sound sensible to say that acts which are described by any of these constructed descriptions are both intrinsically right and intrinsically wrong.

We might now try the following qualification: the formalist who contends that acts of type F are intrinsically right is saying that all acts of type F, *when they are right*, are intrinsically right. This certainly takes some steam out of his contention, but it does not trivialize it altogether. It does mean that the resulting statement can no longer be used to determine whether an act is right, for it must already be known whether *the act* is right in order to see whether it is intrinsically right, on this interpretation. Even thus weakened, however, it still will not do. For consider the principle that, say, Benevolence is intrinsically right: an act might be benevolent and right, and still not be right *because* it was benevolent. Thus, for example, Ross would probably argue that if I give money to the widow of the man I have driven to commit suicide, my act is indeed benevolent (since it does good for a person), but nevertheless that was not what made it right: what made it right is the fact that we have a duty to redress wrongs, and this was a redressing of a wrong.

What we would have to say in order to head off this last difficulty, it seems, is that those acts of type F are *intrinsically* right which (1) are right, and (2) are so *because* they are of type F. This formulation may impress the reader as being very trivial, and there is a sense in which it indeed is. Yet this does not make 'intrinsically right' a useless phrase, by any means. It does mean that such sentences as 'murder is intrinsically wrong' add nothing to saying that it is prima facie wrong, strictly speaking; but it does carry with it, so to speak, the suggestion that most acts of the description in question really are wrong, and that the description in question is an important one, one to be taken seriously. Thus the difference between 'prima facie right' and 'intrinsically right' is not essentially a descriptive one, it seems to me.

Formalism

Before going on to consider our main question directly, it might be worth making a remark or two about a view which is sometimes called 'formalism', and which is alluded to briefly above. I refer to the view that moral principles are universally true in the sense that they assert that all acts having a certain characteristic are right, not just prima facie but *on balance*. The view in question asserts of some characteristics, in other words, that the presence of one of them in act X is a sufficient condition for asserting act X to be right, without having to take anything else into account. But such a view is not properly called 'formalism'. If we take Ross as our standard formalist, which is surely just, then Ross was not a proponent of the view in question. For he explicitly denies that any general moral principles are other than prima facie.[3] This is one reason why we must always have another intuition in addition to the intuitions of general principles, according to Ross, when we judge particular cases, in order to assess the duty on balance. It is better to call the view in question 'rigorism'. As remarked above, Kant attempted to be a "rigorist" in this sense (and failed).

We are, however, using the word 'formalism' in this sense when, for example, we accuse policemen who give tickets for parking "offences" which, while indeed contrary to the letter of the rules, clearly do not do any of the kinds of harm which parking rules are intended to prevent, of being "formalists." Whether laws and regulations should be interpreted only as prima facie subject to general covering principles (such as the principle of utility) will not, however, be discussed here.

What I do wish to point out is that, oddly enough, while formalisms of Ross's type are not "rigoristic," utilitarianism *is*. For rigorism as presently understood holds that there are properties which are sufficient for attributing rightness or wrongness, even though they are not identical with rightness or wrongness. As seen above, Ross explicitly denies this. But utilitarianism, or at least the older "classical" versions, as I may call them, do assert precisely this.[4] They assert, namely, that if an act contributes maximally to the general happiness, then it is right. They explicitly deny that any other characteristic is relevant. It is, of course, perfectly true that it is difficult to determine whether an act has this characteristic or not; but nevertheless, it is intended that "contributes maximally to the general happiness," and others, should be properties that are not identical with being right, but which are nevertheless a sufficient (and in some versions, also a necessary) condition for being right. Strictly speaking, therefore, utilitarianism is rigoristic, whereas formalism is not. It does not of course follow that utilitarians are straightlaced, niggardly, narrow-minded, and fussy, characteristics which are identified with rigorism and formalism in the minds of some people. To be fair, one should say that there is no necessary connection between any of those characteristics and that of agreeing with Ross or with Mill on the theoretical issue just mentioned!

A Difference Evaporates

Thus far, we have been permitting any description whatsoever to count as specifying acts which might be regarded as "intrinsically right" or "intrinsically wrong." It is due to this liberal attitude that I have been able to conclude, in the preceding section, that utilitarianism is rigoristic and formalism is not, a conclusion which doubtless strikes some as paradoxical. They want to say that the "intrinsic nature" of an act which is specified in terms of its consequences is simply ignored. But the upshot of the foregoing reasoning is that this objection is unfounded, except perhaps on prejudice: the word 'intrinsic' cannot mean anything if not attached to a description, but does not of itself limit the range of descriptions to which we can apply it.

What we must say instead is that the issue we want to discuss when we consider whether utilitarianism countenances any acts as intrinsically right must be stated more narrowly than that. We must indicate some range of descriptions which are in question. For obviously, if we use the general criterion of 'intrinsically' specified in §2, it is clear that any ethical theory which holds any kind of acts to be right whatever, must hold that some acts are "intrinsically" right. If any acts are right at all, it must be because of their possession of some characteristics or other; and it is the business of a (substantive) ethical theory to say, in general, which are right and which wrong, or what comes to the same thing, how to go about finding out. (It comes to the same thing, because going about finding out whether an act is right consists in looking for right-making or wrong-making characteristics.) Thus we cannot distinguish any ethical theory from any other on this basis alone, with the degenerate exception of a theory which says that no acts are either right or wrong.

What then is this narrower range of descriptions which we need to discuss? At this point, another interesting fact about formalism crops up: namely, that "formalism" just isn't an ethical theory at all. If we adopt the characterization recommended in §1 above, we can see that the word 'formalist' is true of any of an indefinite number of possible ethical theories, namely, those which hold that there are several ultimate ethical principles. But calling a theory 'formalist' does not tell us just what the ultimate principles in question *are*. It is entirely possible to have two formalisms which do not overlap at all, although this is very unlikely in practice; and these nonoverlapping formalisms can be as mutually inconsistent as one wishes.

Why are they unlikely to be nonoverlapping or inconsistent "in practice"? It is, of course, because most of us do in fact agree to a very large measure on our ethical principles. It may well be that if a person claimed to live or to wish to live by principles which had no connection with our ethical principles, we should not call his principles "ethical." It is, for instance, very difficult to make sense of the statement "murder is right." As various ethicists have remarked, the purpose of ethical theory (even of the "substantive" type, which is what we are discussing here; that this is so of the purely analytical branch of ethical theory goes without saying) is mainly theoretical, a matter of the logical organization of the ethical principles which most or all of us already subscribe to. That ethical theory in this sense can and does affect "practice" as well seems to me incontestable. But in any case, this leaves us with an obvious source on which to draw for plausible principles which we can investigate in order to see whether what they state to be right or wrong is right or wrong on account of its "nature" or its "consequences."

The best we can do, therefore, is to consider some kinds of acts specified in certain typical ethical principles which formalists tend to say are right on account of their intrinsic natures rather than their consequences, and see whether the utilitarians could plausibly either (1) agree that they are right on account of their intrinsic natures rather than their consequences, or (2) argue that they are not really intrinsically right but are instead right on account of their consequences, or finally (3) argue that these principles are not after all true but that in so far as they are true, the acts they mention are only right in so far as they have consequences which utilitarians hold to be good. Clearly, we cannot examine all of the principles which formalism as such advocates, for as I pointed out previously, there is no end to the number of distinct principles which formalists *could* hold to be true in that way.

What I shall do, then, is to show (1) that utilitarians can distinguish between acts which are intrinsically right and those which are right on account of their consequences just as easily as the next theorist, however formalistic the latter, and (2) that the utilitarian's way of making this distinction does give a plausible account of many obvious moral principles.

Utilitarian Intrinsically Right Acts

There are, of course, several different theories which have been called 'utilitarian', not all of which have the same implications as to what is right and wrong. Consequently, some might be able to account for one principle while others may not. However, the method I will develop in this section for distinguishing between 'intrinsically right' and 'right on account of consequences' from the utilitarian point of view can be adopted by any form of utilitarianism whatever. For the present, therefore, I shall merely characterize utilitarianism schematically. A plausible schematized rendering would have the "principle of utility" saying simply that any act x is right if and only if x produces utility, and x is wrong if and only if x produces disutility, where 'utility' is understood as referring to some particular sort of consequence specified by some particular utilitarian theory, and 'disutility' its opposite.

If we take even so bare a formulation literally, however, it clearly is not what utilitarians have in mind. To see this, we need but reflect on the logic of the word 'produce'. Statements of the form 'x produces y' make no sense unless x is distinct from y. Now take, for example, an act of killing: it may be said to be part of the act of killing that someone or other ends up dead. So if we are to say what the act of killing *produces* in the way of consequences, the obvious candidates would be such things as grief on the part of the widow, confusion in the ranks, cessation of certain activities which required the victim's participation, and so forth. Clearly the utilitarian does not wish to say that the only considerations relevant to determining the rightness or wrongness of killing concern what it produces in that sense. Yet our formulation, it will be recalled, said that x was wrong if and *only* if x tended to produce disutility. Moreover, it will also follow from this formulation, if taken this way, that some acts are both right and not right. For again, consider some particular act, y: it may have been an act of pulling the trigger on some gun, which did indeed produce the consequences that somebody ended up dead, which is a disutility; but if described as an act of killing, it may have produced nothing of any interest whatever, in which case it would be indifferent. Yet both are descriptions of the same act.

To rectify this silly situation, we need to distinguish among the various levels at which an act, either one particular act or any act of a certain kind, may be described, and then invoke a sort of "principle of reducibility" to permit us to say what the utilitarian wants to say. Consider any description which characterizes acts. This description will sometimes entail that there is another description of the same act which is such that, relative to this second description, a certain thing has happened which is a consequence of a type which the utilitarian is interested in, i.e., the act as described by this second description *produces* utility or disutility. The second description might in turn entail that some third description applies, of which the same is true. Let me refer to all of these entailed descriptions as "infra-descriptions," and all of the things which are consequences relative to *them* "infra-consequences." Now, what the utilitarian obviously is saying is that in order to determine whether any act is right or wrong, we must take into account all of its consequences, *and* all of its infra-consequences. If, according to some formula which the utilitarian is supposed to have up his sleeve, the balance of these consequences favors utility, then the act is right, and if they favor disutility, then wrong.

We must carefully distinguish what I am calling 'infra-consequences' from consequences per se. Consequences are always logically distinct from what they are the consequences of, viz., the acts that produce them in this case. 'Infra-consequences', on the other hand, are part of the description, or entailed (if you prefer) by the description of the act relative to which they are infra-consequences: that is to say, the act could not be properly referred to by that description if the things called infra-consequences did not in fact take place. Thus, 'x murdered y' entails that y ended up dead in consequence of some action of x's; if x had pulled the trigger and missed or only wounded y, then we would have attempted murder rather than murder. When we are evaluating particular acts, of course, the utilitarian wants us to take all of the relevant consequences into account, as well as the 'infra-consequences' (the latter term's usability is, after all, only a function of the description by which we refer to the act in question). Now, if a certain type of act was such that it always had a certain consequence of a relevant kind for utilitarians, then that could be used as a reason for saying that that kind of act was wrong or right, I suppose. But in fact there seem to be no such invariable utilitarian consequences (as opposed to 'infra-consequences') of any *kind* of act. Utilitarians have tended, sometimes, to try to demonstrate the wrongness of ingratitude or lying, say, by reference to consequences which are generally produced by them. This is simply a mistake, in my view. It is hopeless to try to achieve the necessary universality of judgment in that way, if our purpose is to rebut formalisms.[5]

To take an obvious example, consider torture: if x tortures y, then it follows logically that x did something (and it might be any of a great range of things—'tortures' implies only that the infra-description be one of them, and not that it be this or that of them) which had the causal consequences that y suffered extreme pain, physical or mental. Obviously, this other thing was wrong. Hence we can say that if the act which consisted of x torturing y had no

U-consequences to outbalance this suffering which the infra-described act had, then it was wrong.

Now, clearly, this is precisely to say that torturing is *prima facie* wrong, from the utilitarian viewpoint, and hence to say that torture is intrinsically wrong, from that viewpoint.

On the other hand, there are plenty of acts which are not intrinsically wrong or right, but wrong or right on account of their consequences. Take, for instance, reading: 'x reads y' entails no infra-descriptions which refer to activities that produce utility or disutility: some people like to read, some don't; 'x reads y while Rome burns' describes, for many values of x, a wrong act; 'x reads y to the great pleasure of z' describes a right act (probably); and so forth.

I have shown, then, that according to utilitarians some acts are intrinsically wrong (or right) and some are only wrong (or right) on account of their consequences; though if we say "consequences or infra-consequences," then they hold that *all* acts are right or wrong on account of those.

In order to enable us to proceed in the analysis of moral principles vis-à-vis utilitarianism, it is essential to be able to decide which of these things I have called "infra-consequences" are, and which are not, entailed by the use of various descriptions of acts. And here we will come across the notorious difficulty that descriptions couched in ordinary language do not have very precise entailments. Let us take an example which I suppose some people will find a particularly difficult one for utilitarians, namely "killing." Can a utilitarian say that killing is wrong? Can he, that is, account for what we mean when we say that killing is wrong?

Now here, in part, is where we need clarification of the predicates 'utility' and 'disutility' which utilitarians employ. People have pointed out that if one wants to say that only acts which produce *pain* are wrong, then painless killing would not be wrong. But of course, Mill and Bentham did not mean to use the word 'pain' so narrowly. Suppose, instead, that we say that the utilitarian criterion for wrongness is that x is wrong if and only if x's consequences or infra-consequences are contrary to the interest of some person y. What now? Does 'x killed y' entail that some infra-consequence of what x did (namely, y ends up dead) is contrary to y's interest? One might argue that a man's death is always contrary to his interest; but it isn't, since there are suicides. Then one might argue that whenever x kills y, where x is not identical with y, y's death under the circumstances is contrary to y's interest. But this might not always be so either; y, for example, may have been unable to kill himself and persuaded x to do so.

At this point, however, we begin to see that the utilitarian's case is getting plausible. For the morality of suicide is not an open-and-shut question as yet among us. Some argue that men have a perfect right to commit suicide; bad as we may privately think it is, that too is still not wrong. And some may also go further and argue that if x kills y on y's request, then x hasn't done anything wrong provided that y really meant it: mercy killing is a case in point.

What we can all safely agree on is that in the *typical* case where x kills y, x's act is contrary to y's interest. This no one would dispute, except people who are playing with words or who are sour on the world. And I wish to suggest that the formalist could do no better than this. For if a person maintains that killing is inherently wrong, yet agrees that suicide and mercy killing are permissible, these latter are just the cases which the interest-criterion permits.

I would therefore suggest, as a general principle of operation in substantive moral analysis, that an act of a certain type is to be considered "inherently" or "intrinsically" wrong if the moral view under analysis implies that the typical case which is envisaged by the ordinary use of the expression picking out that type is wrong. There can then be important debate about the exceptional cases, of course: but it seems to me that the above is sufficient. It will give us the sort of precision which, as Aristotle says, is surely all we can expect in this kind of analysis, where vague and complicated language is necessarily employed.

I think it is easy to show that virtually all of the popular types of act which are said to be right or wrong turn out to be prima facie right or wrong in much the same way on the interest view of utilitarianism indicated above. To this there are two major exceptions: (1) there is the problem of showing that *intentions* may be morally judged as well as overt actions, and (2) there are the famous problems associated with the concept of justice which have led to various forms of rule-utilitarianism in recent years. These are large exceptions with which I cannot deal here.

Conclusion

To show whether utilitarianism is true or false, one must discover whether there are any acts which are right (or wrong) regardless of their consequences *or* infra-consequences. But this is impossible until we have a fairly precise specification from the utilitarian as to just which consequences or infra-consequences count. For, of course, any human action which anybody might want to say was right or wrong will have *some* infra-descriptions, hence *some* infra-consequences; and until we have a criterion for determining which of them are morally relevant and which are not, we can make no headway.

I wish to conclude by lodging a major complaint against certain types of ethical theory. Consider the type of "utilitarianism" advocated by Moore and Rashdall, for instance: "acts are right if they have good consequences, produce the more good on the whole than any alternative open to the agent at the time." Supposing, as is plainly reasonable, that they meant to include the act's infra-consequences as well as its consequences per se, it then follows that the "principle" of Ideal Utilitarianism is irrefutable. This is not because it is analytic (as Moore held it to be, in *Principia Ethica*), but rather because Moore and Rashdall were also intuitionists. Being intuitionists, they felt no logical responsibility[6] to produce criteria for deciding which consequences or infra-consequences count and which don't. But in the absence of such criteria, anything which anyone holds to be right or wrong can be held to be right or wrong on account of its consequences or infra-consequences, simply because all acts have some of the latter, and consequently the "Ideal Utilitarian" can always claim that these are what make the acts in question right or wrong.

The same goes for formalism, as such. If a man wishes to insist that there are *some* acts which are not right or wrong on account of their consequences or infra-consequences, on some particular interpretation of which of these are good and which bad, how can one prove him wrong? The reader will have noticed that it is a firm presupposition of this chapter that both "formalism" and utilitarianism are statements of what is right and wrong and *not* analyses of the meanings of the words 'right' and 'wrong'. Given that the principles which they respectively advocate are not analytic truths, then it is always logically possible for the formalist, whose position is simply the denial of the universal principle which the utilitarian advocates, to claim that there is some type of act which is right or wrong in a way inconsistent with utilitarianism. But until he is prepared to state examples, and also to state the reasons why (the characteristics on account of which) these examples *are* right or wrong, it will be impossible for anyone to argue intelligibly with him.

In short: formalism and "Ideal Utilitarianism" are not, as such, discussable theories. The utilitarianism of Sidgwick, Mill, and Bentham, on the other hand, though admittedly rather vague, was discussable. My purpose has been to show that the so-called controversy between formalism and utilitarianism simply cannot be carried on in the terms in which people have often done it in the past, since the issue "are acts right on account of their intrinsic natures or on account of their consequences?" does not distinguish between the two parties.

Notes

Jan Narveson, "Utilitarianism and Formalism," *Australasian Journal of Philosophy* 43, no. 2 (May 1965), 58-72, is reprinted by permission of Oxford University Press. Earlier versions were read at colloquia at the universities of Connecticut, Toronto, and Waterloo, among others. I wish to thank the members of those departments, and in particular, John Woods (then of Toronto), for valuable criticism and suggestions.

1. W. D. Ross, *The Right and the Good* (Oxford: Oxford University Press, 1930), 20. Ross says (27) "These seem to me to be, in principle, all the ways in which *prima facie* duties can arise," with the qualifier, ". . . without claiming completeness or finality for it . . ."

2. Kurt Baier, *The Moral Point of View* (Ithaca: Cornell University Press, 1958), 102-03.

3. Ross, *The Right and the Good,* 18-19.

4. On this matter, I am entirely in agreement with Ross who puts it just the same way: "The point at issue is whether there is any general characteristic that makes right acts right . . ." (Ross, *The Right and the Good,* 16).

5. Moore argues this in the grand manner in *Principia Ethica* (Cambridge: Cambridge University Press, 1954), 142-82.

6. Moore did, in fact, produce a list of the general kinds of things containing, as he thought, relatively large amounts of intrinsic value; but these were not produced on the basis of criteria, but rather as reports of intuition: as self-evident, as Moore says. See *Principia Ethica,* 142-44 and 188-89.

Chapter 2

A Puzzle about Economic Justice
in Rawls' Theory

The Rawlsian Thesis

Perhaps the most captivating feature of Rawls' *A Theory of Justice* to the contemporary western liberal is its apparently ingenious reconciliation of two conflicting demands, the demand for equality and the demand for inequality. That we have both of these is quite clear. On the one hand, we are inclined, in conscience, to believe that All Men Are Created Equal, and entitled to equality before the law, equality of opportunity, and so forth; and there is at least a nagging suspicion that this ought really to extend to equality of all socially distributable goods, including "material possessions" such as income and wealth. This demand is splendidly reflected in Rawls' "general conception of justice," which starts out by proclaiming, "All social values–liberty and opportunity, income and wealth, and the bases of self-respect–are to be distributed equally."[1] But on the other hand, we have very concrete desires for the sorts of things that money can buy, and a marked disinclination to follow Christ's advice to the rich man: "If you would be perfect, go, sell what you possess and give to the poor."[2] Indeed, we even must confess, on occasion, to having the desire to get ahead of our neighbor. In any case, we'd like very much to be able to keep what we have, even if it is more than others have and even if it's more than we need. And this is buttressed by a rather different set of "intuitions" about justice, namely, that some deserve, or are entitled to, more than others.[3] This part of our nature is appealed to by the remainder of Rawls' general conception quoted above, which goes on, "distributed equally, unless an unequal distribution of any, or all, of these values is to everyone's advantage."[4] Though "iffy," the clear intent is to allow inequalities to be accounted just, on occasion at least.

Rawls' "general conception" that I have been quoting underlies, of course, the "special conception" as we might call it in which there are two distinct principles, a principle of liberty, to the effect that "Each person is to have an equal right to the most extensive basic liberty compatible with a similar liberty for others,"[5] and a principle about "social and economic inequalities," to the effect that they "are to be arranged so that they are . . . reasonably expected to be

to everyone's advantage,"[6] which gets further refined into the famous "difference
principle," according to which "Social and economic inequalities are to be
arranged so that they are . . . to the greatest benefit of the least advantaged."[7]
(The second principle also invokes a requirement of equal opportunity and open
offices; this aspect of the principle does not concern us here.)[8] Further, there is
the famous requirement that the equal liberty principle is "lexically prior" to the
second, and the equal opportunity clause in the second lexically prior to the
difference principle. This requirement contributes still more to the alleged
reconciliation, for it specifies that liberty, which we by heritage hold dearest, is
to be absolutely equal before all else, while leaving the difference principle to
govern inequalities between them, be it noted, in such a way as to allow the
inequalities which we also hold dear, namely inequalities of wealth. I can now
state, in brief, the contention for which I will argue here: to wit, that this
reconciliation will not work. Either (1) it goes whole hog one way, leaving no
socially reinforced tendency toward equality in the distribution of wealth; or (2)
it goes all the way the other way, giving us Christ's injunction as a requirement
of justice—out and out communism in one understanding of the word; or (3) it
has theoretically indeterminate consequences which in fact leave us either with
no theory or with an entirely different theory. I proceed immediately to these
arguments, developing each horn of the trilemma in turn.

First Horn

Let us take seriously[9] the claim that the first principle is to be lexically ordered
with respect to the second. This means, in Rawls' words, that liberty "can be
restricted only for the sake of liberty."[10] And now let us suppose, as might be
expected, that this principle is designed, simply, to protect liberty, meaning our
doing what we wish without the interference of others.[11] If that is what is meant,
then the principle must include economic liberty as well. Now, economic
agents, of whom there are likely to be quite a few in any given
society—especially the society we are all members of–are people who are trying
to increase their own amount of wealth. They do so by buying and selling–
buying cheap and selling dear, preferably. The transactions by which they do so,
insofar as they take place in a *free* society, are voluntary. If Jones gets a low
wage and Smith a high one, that's just the way the ball bounces. Nobody is
preventing Jones from moving to a better-paying job, or one that offers other
compensations—self-employment for less money, for example—if he wants to
and can; and nobody is preventing a competitor from underselling Smith if he
wants to and can.

What is important about the liberty principle if applied to economic
matters is that it is not, to use Robert Nozick's useful terminology, a
"patterning" principle, but rather a procedural one. It imposes restrictions on the
ways in which individuals may acquire, but none on how much they can
acquire. By contrast, Rawls' difference principle is a patterning principle, and
apparently a very strong one, calling upon us to reduce as much as possible the

disparities between the bottom class and the rest, the extreme limit being, of course, no disparities at all. Nozick is only the most recent in a long series of theorists to point out that if we simply let people do what they want, then that is likely to upset any patterns we might want to realize in the distribution of goods.[12]

The point is, therefore, that if we really mean business with a liberty principle, then the inclusion of economic activities within its scope has the implication that we can simply jettison the second of Rawls' principles altogether. For there is no way to do anything toward socially weighting the distribution of wealth towards the least favored without infringing on economic liberty, for example, by redistributive taxation; but Rawls' strong priority of liberty would preclude using such measures, since it says that liberty may be infringed only for the sake of liberty and not for other economic or social gains. Of course, redistribution can be effected by voluntary means, in case enough people should happen to want to do it. But that we are allowed to give our money away if we like is not in question here. What is in question is whether there is a requirement of justice that redistribution in the direction of equality take place. To say that there is is to say that people may be required to promote equality, and not merely that they are permitted to. And this is to say that redistribution as a requirement of justice is incompatible with unlimited economic liberty; which is to say that if economic liberty is included in the scope of Rawls' apparently very strong first principle, then the difference principle cannot legitimately be institutionalized.

Certain criticisms of this argument should be mentioned here to dispel misunderstanding. It might, for instance, be argued that the income tax is not an infringement on economic liberty, on the ground that it does not prevent people from engaging in any particular sort of (legitimate) business or line of work, but only takes part of the proceeds from that activity, whatever it may be. Now, we may concede that this method would be much superior to Stalinism, say; nor need we agree with Nozick that taxing is equivalent to forced labor.[13] Nevertheless, it cannot be maintained that there is no infringement on economic liberty here. If I am engaged in a sequence of activities, aimed at realizing a particular result–such as my having a certain amount of money—and then at the final stage, you descend on me and take a third of what I have been working toward, without my permission, you have certainly interfered with my liberty of action, even if you left me entirely alone up to that point. Human activity is purposive, and interfering with purpose-fulfillment is interference with human activity.

Again, some will doubtless insist that free enterprise does not constitute economic liberty and is, indeed, not even compatible with it. Thus they will claim that a system in which economic roles are centrally and coercively allocated is actually in the interests of liberty. Space, unfortunately, precludes considering this claim at the length it deserves. I shall content myself with two pertinent observations. The first is that this is a thesis which could hardly be made out without redefining the term 'liberty'—which is a popular thing to do, but does not promote clear discussion *of* these matters. The most popular such redefinition is got by suggesting that if *A* isn't actually *assisting B* in doing x, then *A* is *holding B back.*[14]   With the assistance of this maneuver, we then justify coercing *A* into assisting *B* on the ground that we are merely rectifying an antecedent infringement of *B*'s liberty by the unhelpful *A*. In the process, of course, the very line which we require to define the notion of liberty as a distinctive value has been erased. If one's aim is to promote verbal chaos, this *is* admirable, but otherwise, it is difficult to see what the point is. After all, *if* one is in favor of coercive redistribution of wealth in order to promote the public welfare or the general good, why not say so? Why insist on stating one's aims in such a way as to foster the illusion that one is agreeing with the very people one is opposing?

The same comment applies to the argument, taken from the Rawlsian insistence[15] that the liberties must be viewed as a system and not taken in isolation, that the other liberties cannot be separated from economic considerations, and when we bear this in mind we will find that economic maldistribution interferes with the other liberties plainly intended to be equalized under the first principle. Thus if you are wealthy and own the local TV station, while I am either poor or have my money in something else, then you are infringing on my freedom of speech if you don't give me some time on your channel.

Certainly we must agree that what exactly constitutes "forcing" or "coercion" in economic matters is not an easy thing to decide. Thus, what of the successful entrepreneur who becomes a monopolist, not by unfair tactics but simply by offering a better product at a lower price, that is, being more efficient than his competitors? His competitors, it is now said, have been "forced" out of the market. But who "forces" them? The consumers in this market had their choice, and chose, overwhelmingly, to buy this entrepreneur's products rather than those of his competitor. If we now enact legislation requiring this firm to forego some of its market, or if we subsidize some less efficient competitor in order to keep the latter in the market—using tax money to do so—then it is clear enough that force is being used. But it is very unclear that the entrepreneur under consideration is using anything that can reasonably be called "force" or "coercion." Obviously, we can sometimes be forced by circumstances, or geography, or the weather, to do things, but these are not instances of social coercion as they stand. One might argue independently that each individual is entitled to some minimal share of the world's natural resources. Such a theory might lead to some kind of minimum wage as an equivalent for that share, for instance.[16]   However, this simply isn't Rawls' theory as we have it, and would not get us anywhere near the difference principle.

Finally, we must observe that whatever merit these other notions of liberty may have, they are not held by Rawls. Instead, he says:

> A final point. The inability to take advantage of one's rights and opportunities as a result of poverty and ignorance, and a lack of means generally, is sometimes counted among the constraints definitive of liberty. I shall not, however, say this, but rather I shall think of these things as affecting the worth of liberty, the value to individuals of the rights that the first principle defines.[17]

This terminology enables us to say clearly what we mean. And now a rather striking point about Rawls' system can be noted, namely that liberties in it are not *defended simply as such.* Having distinguished liberty and the worth of liberty, Rawls clearly opts for the latter as the proper goal of the social system, and not the former for its own sake. "Taking the two principles together, the basic structure is to be arranged to maximize the worth to the least advantaged of the complete scheme of equal liberty shared by all. This defines the end of social justice."[18] To the careful reader of Rawls, this will come as no surprise, actually, for the whole theory is anchored in the idea that individuals rationally concerned to maximize their own long-run satisfactions are constrained, by the concept of justice, to choose social principles with that motive intact,[19] but their individuality masked by the "veil of ignorance." Liberties and possessions will both, of course, be means to the same overall end, and so there can be no question of pursuing one to the exclusion of the other. And indeed, the general conception of justice, of which the two principles are a specification, applies to all primary goods, including both liberty and wealth, so that as far as it is concerned, "No restrictions are placed on exchanges of these goods and therefore a lesser liberty can be compensated for by greater social and economic benefits."[20] A special argument is required to separate these two types of goods and make them the object of separate principles, one of which has priority over the other—indeed, an argument which only holds in special circumstances, "favorable conditions."[21] It is a misunderstanding, then, to suppose that the lexical priority of liberty is ultimate and general.

Since this is so, Rawls can evade the first horn of my trilemma fairly easily. The first principle doesn't quite mean what it at first appears: it doesn't apply to liberty in general and as such, but rather to "basic liberties," the expression used in the fullest statement of the principles.[22] And whenever Rawls lists these liberties, we find only the standard civil liberties, the right of conscience, freedom of religion, speech, assembly, and so forth.

The closest we get to a purely economic liberty is "the right to hold (personal) property"[23]—note the specific exclusion of productive property. In brief, economic liberty in general simply isn't regarded as "basic." So Rawls evades the first horn of my trilemma by not counting economic liberty as one of the liberties intended to be covered by the first principle. This would be open to the charge of arbitrariness if the first principle were about liberty *as such.* But since it isn't, arguments can be given for including some liberties and not others in its scope, and indeed, the arguments are at length forthcoming. They consist of an assessment, from the point of view of the rational man, of the relative utility (or value, if you prefer) of liberty (meaning the other liberties) as compared with wealth. The rational chooser is said to "care very little, if anything, for what he might gain above the minimum stipend that he can, in fact, be sure of by following the maximin rule";[24] later, the preference is elaborated.[25] We shall not here pursue the further implication, that Rawls' system is, despite his ubiquitous professions to the contrary, utilitarian.[26] It is not my concern here to probe that deeply into the structure of his theory: instead, I aim only to raise some questions about the meaning and implications of the two principles as they stand. Obviously, it must be questioned how satisfactory a foundation Rawls' arguments provide for the stated principles. Most fundamentally, for instance, it may be questioned whether such assessments may legitimately be employed in the design of a social system at all. Less fundamentally, and perhaps more plausibly, we must query whether there can be any uniform assessment along these lines, as well as whether any uniform assessment is really needed.[27] All this can be left on one side at present. Having seen that Rawls can evade the first horn of my trilemma, at modest cost, we shall now turn to the second. There, if I am right, the difficulty will not be so easy to avoid.

Second Horn

The difference principle says that economic inequalities are to be permitted only if they are, in the long run, to "the greatest benefit of the least advantaged." The position of the least favored class is to be "maximized." Explicating this further, Rawls says:

> one should distinguish between two cases. The first case is that in which the expectations of the least advantaged are indeed maximized . . . No changes in the expectations of those better off can improve the situation of the worst off. The best arrangement obtains, what I shall call a perfectly just scheme. The second case is that in which the expectations of all those better off at least contribute to the welfare of the more unfortunate. That is, if their expectations were decreased, the prospects of the least advantaged would likewise fall.[28]

In brief, justice obtains when those at the bottom are as well-off as they can be. If allowing those above them to be still better off would also improve the prospects of those least well-off, then that is to be permitted; if, on the other hand, there is a situation of conflict with the poor, so that the more the rich get, the less the poor get, then the conflict is to be resolved in favor of the poor: the rich are to be taxed, or whatever, and redistribution effected until we reach either equality or a point where the conflict ceases and further diminishing the lot of the rich would no longer improve the lot of the poor.

What is the argument for this strongly equalitarian formula? As before, of course, the principle is to represent the choice of social principles by a rational chooser who is entirely ignorant of his own identity, and who, though self-interested, must therefore choose on the assumption that he might turn out to be just anybody. Under these circumstances, he will reason, according to Rawls, as follows:

> Since it is not reasonable for him to expect more than an equal share of social goods, and since it is not rational for him to agree to less, the sensible thing for him to do is to acknowledge as the first principle of justice one requiring an equal distribution. . . . But there is no reason why this acknowledgement should be final. If there are inequalities in the basic

structure that work to make everyone better off in comparison with the benchmark of equality, why not permit them?"[29]

It is interesting how readily Rawls' Principle has been accepted in the philosophical world, and one can only account for this acceptance on the assumption that people have supposed that the purported justification of inequality really does apply a lot of the time. Now, *given* the condition that inequalities might be necessary to make everyone better off than an equal distribution would make them, the justification may be agreed to follow readily enough. But would it ever be necessary? That they would have to be *necessary*, given the reasoning stated, is clear enough. For if an inequality were not necessary, and one could find an alternative way to improve the lot of everyone, then equality must clearly be preferred on the reasoning cited. Rawls' statement of the matter suggests that he sees no great difficulty in the condition required being realized. That, however, is what I shall now question.

We must begin by getting clear about the meaning of the term 'benchmark' here. Rawls' use of it might suggest to some that one could satisfy the principle by selecting some point in, say, the past of the society one winds up in, at which equality obtained and then permitting all developments which left no one any worse off than he was at the equal-distribution point. But this cannot be so. In the first place, it is notoriously impossible to select any such point in a nonarbitrary manner. Nor could sonic level of material development be nonarbitrarily selected such that equal distribution of the GNP at that time could be enacted for "benchmark" purposes in the way described. In the second place, and more fundamentally, there simply is no reason why a chooser behind the veil of ignorance should opt for any such scheme. Plainly what his reasoning, as depicted by Rawls, leads to is that things ought to be distributed equally—all things, at all times, unless the unequal distribution will benefit everyone more than an equal distribution of those things would have. What has to be understood by the suggestion that equality is the "benchmark" is that equal distribution is prima facie just, and inequalities require special justification of the kind stated. The question is how we are to understand the justification-condition proposed.

There is also an important ambiguity in the notion of "making everyone better off."[30] The two readings are as follows:

D1. 'Everyone is better off' = 'No one is worse off' (persons outside the transaction may be unaffected, compatibly with the requirement).

D2. 'Everyone is better off' = 'Each person's situation is improved by comparison with what it was before the transaction' (persons outside the transaction must be favorably affected, to meet the requirement).

Interpreting the difference principle along the lines of D1 would yield the result that any transaction between two parties which was to mutual benefit and had no detrimental effects on third parties would be permitted. In that case, of course, the difference principle would have ceased to be a patterning principle at all, and we would have the same result as in the first horn discussed above: no rectification of inequalities would be forthcoming so long as those inequalities were arrived at by voluntary transactions among individuals and not by force. Clearly, this cannot be meant. So D2 must be what is intended, and this immediately raises the question how much other parties must be benefited. Again, it would be possible to trivialize the principle by making the acceptable benefit level infinitesimal, or, for instance, by proposing that the sheer existence of society is a benefit or that any increase in wealth on anybody's part increases the amount of goods potentially obtainable by others and is therefore a benefit to everyone. Obviously, neither of these readings will do, either. Our rational chooser behind the veil of ignorance is in for a rude shock if he winds up a pauper in some society with nothing more than that as an explanation.

Now, the upper limit of benefits to those worst off is equality. And if all social goods ought, prima facie, to be distributed equally in the interests of justice, what sort of circumstances could justify us in claiming that we really must have an unequal distribution in order for those who thus come out with less to have more than they would under an equal distribution? The official answers are two: the need for savings, capital accumulation; and the need for incentives. Capital accumulation is necessary in any society which wishes to advance materially, and this requires that good investment decisions be made. But Jones might be better at making investment decisions than Smith, and so an inequality, putting Jones in a superior position for making such decisions, will be necessary. And incentives may be necessary in order to keep Jones contributing to the economy at a rate which will improve the lot of everyone, including Smith, who comes out with less. I shall now argue that neither of these answers will do.

The reason why the appeal to capital accumulation functions won't do is quite simple: it involves a confusion between capital "goods," which aren't really goods at all in Rawls' sense, with consumer goods, which are. Let us grant that the unequal distribution of talents will require, for efficiency's sake, that some persons have more managerial power than others, more say as to what should be produced and how. But none of this implies that the said managers must also have more to eat, bigger houses, nicer cars, and so forth. (It doesn't imply, either, that they must own the productive resources which they manage. All of this could be socialized.) In principle, then, the whole realm of capital can be separated from the realm of consumption goods, and different principles applied to each. There is no logical necessity that those who produce more must also get more of what is produced. And it is only consumption goods that are essentially in question here. Power, as Rawls has recently clarified, is not a primary good.[31] The correct distribution of power in a society, economically speaking, is whatever distribution will maximize production, subject, of course, to the constraints of respect for civil liberties. Production is for the sake of consumer goods. But what principle should govern distribution of the latter? That is what the difference principle is about, and so far, the indicated answer is that they should be distributed equally.

We turn, then, to the matter of incentives. The official view is as follows:

If, for example, these inequalities set up various incentives which succeed in eliciting more productive efforts, a person in the original position may look upon them as necessary to cover the costs of training and to encourage performance."[32]

We have already seen that covering the costs of training is beside the point, since those are capital costs. The question is whether medical students must be paid less than advanced specialists with years of practice behind them, and Rawls must explain why a "yes" to that question is in order. What counts, then, is incentive per se: the encouragement of performance by means of unequal reward.

Why should this be thought problematic for Rawls' theory? The answer is that incentives are psychological matters, which concern one's principles of action. If I hold out for, or accept, a greater payment for my services than someone else is getting for his, I am voluntarily consenting to an inequality. I cannot argue that this higher payment is "necessary," that I am *forced* to have more than you. Obviously, I could, if I wanted to, accept the same wage as everyone else. Alternatively, I can accept more, but then turn around and give the excess to those who have less. The question we are discussing is whether, in justice, I *ought* to do this. And to say that incentives are "necessary" for this purpose is to engage in confusion, or possibly even in self-deception.

Sometimes, conceivably, there will be laws of nature which make inequalities inevitable. Perhaps it will be impossible to give equal wealth to persons in distant deserts or tundras. But this is not the sort of justification we are considering. What we want to know is whether higher pay for some is literally necessary to extract more production from them. And on the face of it, the answer is surely that it is not. I *can* "sell all that I have, and give to the poor."

Will anyone seriously deny this? Perhaps those of Marxist persuasion will say, at this point, that it is a matter of "historical necessity" that people will not be willing to part with whatever their economic system happens to have given them. Or they might want to bring up the subject of historical determination of moral beliefs. Both would be red herrings, however. The first is irrelevant because our question is not what men will do, but what they conceivably could, if they chose. They often do not choose to give up their wealth, true. But it is quite another matter to insist that they don't even have that option. Anyway, can anyone seriously maintain that Karl Marx, who obviously could have been a successful lawyer or merchant, was somehow determined by his economic surroundings to become a social theorist instead? *Economically* determined? And the second is irrelevant because our question is not what men do think, nor what makes them think it; it is, merely, what follows from Rawlsian premises about what they ought to think.

We return, therefore, to the central question. If it is the case that socially distributable goods ought to be distributed equally unless an unequal distribution is required to improve the prospects of the worse off, and if we all have the option, if we so choose, of sharing equally with others, then does it not follow that if we don't take this option, we are being *unjust?* For in effect, my claim that I "need" more as an "incentive" is just a misleading way of saying that I *want* more and that I'm not willing to do as much if I don't get it. Or, to put it bluntly, it seems that in so acting, I am being voluntarily selfish. And it is hard to see how this would justify an inequality, if inequalities really need justifying along the lines Rawls proposes. It might excuse it, in some sense. Perhaps selfishness could be made out to be a sort of disease, which would excuse persons for insisting on higher salaries much as kleptomania might excuse a thief, or a bout with the flu a missed appointment. Even so, this would be an excuse and not a justification. But justification is what is in question. And it is not forthcoming.

The conclusion seems to be that if the difference principle is really the right principle for distributing economic goods, then any society manifesting any inequality other than what is naturally inescapable is to that extent unjust. Is this conclusion escapable in Rawls' system? Let us now consider a general line of objection to the above account which might be thought to get Rawls out of this problem, if a problem it is—some, of course, will cheerfully accept this result; but not, I think, Rawls. This general line of objection stems from Rawls' continued insistence that the primary subject of justice is the general structure of society—institutions and their workings, not individuals and theirs. So much is suggested in the very first sentence of the book: "Justice is the first virtue of social institutions, as truth is of systems of thought."[33] And the claim is frequently reiterated that these principles are not to be thought of as applying in detailed, individual cases. In general, such cases are supposed to be left to procedural justice to take care of. Thus he says:

> Now, as we have seen, the idea of justice as fairness is to use the notion of pure procedural justice to handle the contingencies of particular situations. The social system is to be designed so that the resulting distribution is just however things turn out. To achieve this end it is necessary to set the social and economic process within the surroundings of suitable political and legal institutions. Without the proper arrangement of these background institutions the outcome of the distributive process will not be just.[34]

Further, the proposal is that we look at the social system not from the point of view of individuals as such, but rather of "representative men." "In judging the social system we are to disregard our more specific interests and associations and look at our situation from the standpoint of these representative men."[35] Thus we have two contrasts related to each other: (1) that between procedural principles, which do not determine the shape of results but only the way in which they are attained, and patterning principles, which call for a particular shape of results, and (2) the "macro-micro" contrast, the difference between the "background institutions" and the individual case, the basic structure and the details. Why restrict ourselves thus? It would appear that what is supposed to justify invoking both contrasts in the theory is simplicity. "We cannot have a coherent and manageable theory if we must take such a multiplicity of positions into account. The assessment of so many competing claims is impossible."[36]

Finally, there is a general tendency to refer us back to the "circumstances of justice," the conditions which give rise to the whole subject. These are the circumstances depicted by Hume and others, and described by Rawls as follows:

> The circumstances of justice may be described as the normal conditions under which human cooperation is both possible and necessary. Thus . . . although a society is a cooperative venture for mutual advantage, it is typically marked by a conflict as well as an identity of interests. There is an identity of interests since social cooperation makes possible a better life for all than any would have if each were to try to live solely by his own efforts. There is a conflict of interests since men are not indifferent as to how the greater benefits produced by their collaboration are distributed, for in order to pursue their ends they each prefer a larger to a lesser share."

Having thus described the background conditions, Rawls feels justified in saying such things as this:

> One might think that ideally individuals should want to serve each other. But since the parties are assumed not to take an interest in one another's interests, their acceptance of these inequalities is only the acceptance of the relations in which men stand under circumstances of justice. They have no ground for complaining of one another's motives. A person in the original position would, therefore, concede the justice of these inequalities."

The emphasis on these themes certainly complicates the picture and the interpretation of Rawls' theory. But are they really of any avail in solving the problem which I have been describing?

Let us begin with the last point. Is it true that recognition of the circumstances of justice, including in particular the self-interested character of human motivation, leads to acceptance of inequalities of wealth? Will they really, for the reasons stated, have "no grounds for complaining of one another's motives?" No. In the original position, nobody knows who he is. All he knows is that whoever he turns out to be, he will want as much as he can get—it is, remember, precisely this knowledge that makes him reason in the peculiarly conservative manner described previously, leading to the difference principle. So we must ask what will and what will not be "accepted." Differences in ability, we will suppose, are simply natural and therefore must be accepted. But differences in material well-being are social. Prima facie, they will not be accepted. Will the existence of self-interested motivation be "accepted" in the sense that it is allowed as a reason for justifying differentials in social reward? Why would it? Surely not just because it is a motive. We condemn many motives, after all. Indeed, we condemn various forms of this one, under the names of 'greed', 'selfishness', 'avarice', and so on. Now, either self-interest is a contractible motive, or it is not. If it is, then surely the reasoning in the original position calls upon us to counteract it, by condemning it insofar as it leads to a lower level of well-being for ourselves, whoever we may turn out to be—that is, for the worst-off people, in case we turn out to be them. If it is contractible, then, it will not be accepted, and men will have grounds for complaining of one another's motives in this respect.

What if it is not contractible? It has been widely noted[39] that Rawls has a real problem with the subject of human nature in his theory. He postulates that men are disinterested in others, indeed rationally so, saying, for example, that "One feature of justice as fairness is to think of the parties in the initial situation as rational and mutually disinterested. This does not mean that they are egoists, that is, individuals with only certain kinds of interests, say in wealth, prestige, and domination. But they are conceived as not taking an interest in one another's interests."[40] Yet he has a theory which seems strongly non-self-interested in crucial respects. The upshot is that the assumptions of the theory make it hard to see how the results of the theory could ever be effective: why would men do what justice requires in those (many) cases where it requires foregoing a gain, if they are rational and rationality is essentially self-interested? If these critics are right, as I suspect they are, then either men behind the veil of ignorance will simply forget about the veil, foreseeing that nothing of interest can come of the venture; or they will carry on with it, knowing that what they come up with will call upon them to condemn a large percentage of the human race a large part of the time as unjust. This last option is certainly not unfamiliar, and my point is that it seems to be the one Rawls' theory will take him to. What recognition of these facts (if such they are) about human nature will not do is to enable us to interpret the difference principle as stated in such a way as to allow a degree of inequality somewhere between the free market and sheer equality. (Again, perhaps it will leave us with excused inequalities, on the ground that some things "exceed the capacities of human nature," to use a phrase which Rawls employs in another connection. But recognition of such an "excuse" is going to be mighty rubbery—failure to give away half of my income isn't like alcoholism or kleptomania, after all! And of course, again this would concede my point: that inequalities are not justified along these lines, but at best excused. They *need* excuse, because they *aren't* justified, if equality is the benchmark of justice.)

Nor can any headway be made by appealing, as Rawls frequently does, to the idea that justice must be indifferent as between particular differing conceptions of the good life, as typified in the following passage:

> Justice as fairness, however, . . . does not look behind the use which persons make of the rights and opportunities available to them in order to measure, much less to maximize, the satisfactions they achieve. Nor does it try to evaluate the relative merits of different conceptions of the good. . . Everyone is assured an equal liberty to pursue whatever plan of life he pleases as long as it does not violate what justice demands. Men share in primary goods on the principle that some can have more if they are acquired in ways which improve the situation of those who have less.[41]

This evades the problem, or begs the question before us. To start with, of course, it should be pointed out that anything whatever is just "so long as it does not violate what justice demands!" The question is, though, what *does* it demand? Nor is it in point to say that men are free to pursue whatever plan of life they may have, compatible with the constraints of justice. The trouble is that the constraint of the difference principle seems to limit the amount of wealth which anyone may have—limit it, prima facie, to the same amount as is had by others. It is no reply to this to say that they may spend what they do get in whatever way they please, provided it doesn't contravene the liberty principle. Again, we must remember that the difference principle is a patterning principle, *not* a procedural one.

Finally, and most fundamentally, let us turn to the macro–micro contrast. This is certainly a vague and slippery distinction to invoke in these contexts, as has been well argued by Nozick.[42] But I think we can go to the heart of the matter more satisfactorily simply by pointing out that the contrast, as used by Rawls, will not have the effect required to salvage justified inequalities of wealth. The reason for this is not merely that it is hard to see why people in the original position would accept as a constraint on choosable social principles that they stop short of applying to individual men and instead govern only institutions, if that is indeed a constraint; although, certainly, it is hard to see this. If one is allowed to assume only that one might be a member of the worst-off social class and chooses principles accordingly, only to wind up as one of the very badly off members of a generally well-cared-for worst-off social class, it isn't going to be much comfort to be told that "In any case we are to aggregate to some degree over the expectations of the worst-off,"[43] or, worse yet, that one does so in the interests of theoretical simplicity! And of course, Rawls does not postulate that one is so concerned about the prospects of one's social class generally that one would be quite willing to sacrifice one's own prospects for their sake. And why should he?[44] But we need not harp on that subject, for the facts about institutions are enough to make appeal to it in this context ineffective. The facts are two: first, that institutions *can* concern themselves with individuals in every sense relevant to this issue; and second, that institutions are *man-made*—as they must be in order for any principles to reach them anyway. Let us consider each, in the light of a suitable example.

Let us suppose, then, that one is a representative member of, say, the economically most favored class in some society. And let us suppose that some political party offers, as its platform, the proposal to establish as an entrenched constitutional right a guaranteed annual wage, to be set at the current national average and financed by an income tax which would confiscate all income in excess of this average and hand it by transfer payments to those below. (This might be a transitional mechanism, but that doesn't matter for present purposes. It also doesn't matter if there is no such party: for my argument will raise equally the question why any citizen should not proceed to do what he can to form one.)

Now we ask: given Rawlsian reasoning, ought our man to vote for this party? What does justice require of him when faced with such an option? Of course, if he ought to, then everyone ought to, since the principles here are the same for everyone. Of course also, the question of other means might arise. We are assuming that if everyone does vote for it, it will be done. But if others are disinclined to, obviously the question must arise whether violent means, by some small minority, shouldn't be used. But we ignore such problems here.

Two questions must be asked: (1) Would it be just, if it would work? And (2) Would it work? Now, I submit that on Rawls' reasoning, the answer to the first question must be a resounding affirmative. If it is possible to equalize income without, say, seriously diminishing the GNP in the process, then this must be the just thing to do, if justice requires the major institutions of society to maximize the position of the worst-off. And since the proposed measure would be a social institution, no macro-micro objection is reasonably invoked here. The issue therefore turns entirely on the second question—whether it would be likely to work.

Now, almost every reader will immediately answer that of course this scheme will not work. But if it wouldn't, why wouldn't it? And we all know the answer to this, too. David Hume and Nikita Khrushchev, not to mention many between, will join together in agreeing that

> however specious these ideas of perfect equality may seem, they are really, at bottom, impractical. . . . Render possessions ever so equal, men's different degrees of art, care, and industry will immediately break that equality. Or if you check these virtues, you must reduce society to the most extreme indigence; and instead of preventing want and beggary in a few, render it unavoidable to the whole community."

Men simply are not motivated by a concern for the welfare of their fellows to an extent which will keep them working as hard as before if required to share all proceeds equally with everyone. But suppose this is true, the question remains how we are to characterize this lack of concern, given a theory of the type we are considering. And the answer, I submit, remains that we must, on these principles, characterize this lack of concern as injustice. In being unwilling to lend their support to institutions which would certainly achieve the aim of economic justice, as defined on this theory, they are being prima facie unjust. And if the only reason why those institutions would not achieve that aim is that men won't willingly support them, then it cannot be said with a straight face that "Well, we are in favor of this in principle, but the trouble is, this just wouldn't work!"

In brief, there is nothing about the notion of an institution which prevents it from interfering in the market to the extent required to bring about economic equality, at the individual level. We have plenty of institutions which deal with individuals. Rawls' constraints on principles cannot prevent this, nor would it be coherent to do so. Imagine saying, "We agree that the unemployed, as a class, are entitled to relief, but of course that doesn't require us to help out any individual unemployed person!" They of course prevent institutions from being defined in terms of the way they treat Edwin T. Smith, but nothing of that sort is in question here. And there is nothing about the notion of an institution which blocks inferences to the duties of individuals. Again, it would be incoherent to maintain that there is, in any way general enough to defeat the present argument. People of course do say, "That's not my responsibility—let the Red Cross or the Health Insurance Commission or the Department of Indian Affairs do it." But can the person who doesn't give anything to the Red Cross, or who opposes public health insurance, or who doesn't think there should be any Department of Indian Affairs say such things? Obviously not. Either he doesn't accept the goals of these institutions, or he's being hypocritical or inconsistent. Similarly, a wealthy person who accepts Rawls' principles ought, so far as I can see, to favor establishment of a rigorous program of economic equalization. Most people, wealthy or not, do not favor such a program. But I suggest that most people, contrary to Rawls' claims about the intuitive support of his system, do not accept his principles; or if they claim to, it is because they have not clearly seen what follows from them about their commitments.[46]

I conclude that strict adherence to the difference principle will also require commitment to a perfectly equal division of wealth in nearly any society, including all societies of anything like our degree of material advancement. Then, and only then, could we honestly say that we have fulfilled the requirement of maximizing the welfare of the worst-off. Whether this is a welcome conclusion is, of course, another matter, about which I shall say a little in the closing section of this chapter. Meanwhile, let us move to the third horn of my trilemma.

Third Horn

So far, my argument has been that, depending on how you read Rawls' first principle, his second principle is either dispensable and gives no weight to economic equality, or it gives so much weight to it that only out-and-out equality will satisfy it. The thought naturally arises that perhaps what we need to do is find some kind of recipe for mixing the relevant claims in the right proportions, thus reestablishing the kind of reconciliation needed. For example, it might be proposed that the settlement point between equality and free market inequality is properly a matter of politics and should be left to the democratic process to work out. And indeed, this is probably what most people, other than extremists, do think about the matter. As a proposal within the Rawlsian framework, however, I shall argue that it won't do at all.

Let us begin by pointing out that the democratic principle sits rather uncomfortably with Rawls' first principle. As everyone well knows, if democracy is interpreted purely as majority rule, then it would have to be severely constrained to give us anything resembling our intuitions about human rights: obviously, a majority could decide to inflict any manner of evils on a hapless minority. Now, Rawls' liberty principle may readily enough be appealed to to supply many of those constraints. But what about the aim of economic equalization according to the difference principle? The situation remains unchanged. Either economic liberty is among the protected liberties, in which case majority rule is constrained by it as well as by the ordinary civil liberties; or it is not, so that the question arises whether the difference principle is also a constraint on majority rule. Either it is or it isn't, again. If it is, we have the same conclusion as before. If it is not, however, then we would seem to have the same conclusion as in part one above: for we will have whatever economic distribution the majority permits, and we may as well therefore dispense with the difference principle yet again.

Obviously, we cannot reasonably suggest that the constraints of the difference principle are *defined* by political procedures such as majority rule: as though the meaning of the phrase 'as well off as they can be' could be equated with 'as well off as the majority is willing to make them.' One reason why no such suggestion will do is that the principles of justice are supposed to provide *guidance* in this matter. People disagree about what ought to be done, in this case about what is just. Principles of justice are supposed to settle such disagreements, or at any rate provide the proper machinery for settling them. Now, the difference principle looks like such a principle. It is, as I have pointed out at various places above, a patterning principle. So if instead it is suggested that disagreements about the proper bases of distribution are to be left to the will of the majority, then that is to switch to a *different* principle, namely a procedural one. It is not to interpret the one we already have.

Or suppose it is said that the proper distribution is the one determined by weighing the motive of justice, which ideally calls for equality, against people's other motives in some politically acceptable mix. But now we have not only a different theory but, it would seem, an incoherent one. For this new suggestion apparently has it that the just thing to do is to effect the distribution which we get by mixing the motive of justice with other motives in some proportion. It seems absurd to call that a theory of justice; and in any case, it surely isn't Rawls' theory. Nor, of course, does it yield a determinate distribution—it could yield any distribution, including either of the two extremes we have been considering.

I conclude, then, that so long as we stay within Rawls' premises and the reasoning he offers us from those premises, there is no third option. It remains that either we have out–and–out free market distribution or, more likely, we have out-and-out equality as our model for distributive economic justice.

Concluding Note

I have characterized this as a "trilemma" for Rawls' theory, the implication being that all horns of it are unsatisfactory. And they are unsatisfactory for Rawls, at least, for if I am right, his theory cannot give him what he evidently wants, namely, an egalitarian–tending theory which nevertheless genuinely justifies a moderate amount of economic inequality. It is clear, however, that among the options provided, the main drift of Rawls' theory is toward the Charybdis of equality and away from the Scylla of the unbridled free market. The reason for this, as I pointed out, is that liberty as well as wealth get defended in his theory as utilities, at bottom, and Rawls' views about the utility of wealth are what make him opt for equality. Namely, Rawls assigns a strongly diminishing marginal utility to increased wealth. The rational chooser "cares very little, if anything, for what he might gain above the minimum stipend that he can, in fact, be sure of by following the maximin rule."[47]

One obvious way to fix things up, then, would be to adopt a less conservative view about the marginal utility of increments of wealth, be more forthrightly utilitarian than Rawls has been willing to allow, and replace the difference principle with a much weaker provision for the sort of minimum economic assistance which we are currently inclined to concede as what is due to those who have not done well by the market. But to work out the details of such an overhaul of Rawls' principles is not the task of this chapter.[48]

Meanwhile, what about the intuitiveness of the difference principle as it stands? I submit that as between the Scylla and the Charybdis in question, if we had to take our choice, surely Scylla would be much preferable as an account of these intuitions. If what we are concerned about is justice, rather than other moral qualities such as kindness, mercy, or sympathy for our fellows, then it is surely outrageous to propose that every time one person makes more than another from a mutually advantageous voluntary bargain, the former is being unjust to the latter—in any degree. Equality as a criterion of justice in the distribution of wealth, as such, is surely not just impractical, but wrong. Of course there are inequalities of treatment which are properly accounted injustices, and many of which will have economic ramifications, as when someone is prevented from seizing a certain economic opportunity on account of his or her race or religion. But the equality which Rawls is calling for is not limited to such contexts. From the lofty point of view of the original position, all differences—of natural ability, geography, parentage, and so on—get steamrolled as "morally arbitrary" and hence to be "compensated for." And this, as Nozick rightly objects,[49] is an outrageous inference. If Sally and Peter are accountants in a private firm which pays them for their services, and Sally gets far more done because she just happens by nature to be six times as adept at arithmetic as Peter, then she *deserves* a greater reward than he, and the fact that her ability is simply a gift of nature has no tendency whatever to upset this conclusion.

The point I am making here should not be misunderstood. De facto economic inequalities could, certainly, be a function of other features of the society which are genuinely unjust, and some economic equalization might well be justified under the aegis of rectificatory justice. And there could be other reasons for supporting the justice of a measure of economic equality, or measures which have that effect. It is one thing to say that economic equality simply is not as such one of the basic requirements of justice, and quite another to say that measures which tend to promote it, even by publicly coercive measures such as taxation, are on that account necessarily unjust. I am saying only the former, not the latter. It may very reasonably be argued, for instance, that people have a right to protect themselves from the uncertainties of the market by establishing programs of social insurance, unemployment compensation, a minimum wage, or whatever.[50] Or it might simply be argued that society is better off with a substantial degree of equality even if it is got at the expense of a fair amount of coercion, and that public interest in this outweighs the claims of freedom as they apply to the market. But for this, one does not need a theory which says that equality as such is an aim required by justice—that any society which does not recognize equality as a major aim is ipso facto unjust. That is what I am suggesting is outrageous, but it is apparently said by Rawls' principles. If so, something has gone seriously wrong.

Notes

This essay was published originally in *Social Theory and Practice* 4, no. 1 (1976), 1-27; reproduced here by permission of the editors. A paper to similar effect was presented at a meeting of the Society for Exact Philosophy at Wayne University, May 1976, and then (by mutual understanding with editors) published, together with other papers from that conference, under the title, "Rawls on Equal Distribution of Wealth," *Philosophia* 7, no. 2 (June 1978). However, the present version, which had been accepted for publication prior to that meeting, explores the issues more fully.

1. John Rawls, *A Theory of Justice* (Cambridge, Mass.: Harvard University Press, 1971), 62.

2. Matt. 19:21.

3. The substantial divergence between the concepts of entitlement and desert is no small matter for social theory. If I inherit my father's house and fortune though of wholly mediocre character and abilities, I am nevertheless entitled to them even though I may in no way deserve them. An injustice, in our usual way of thinking at any rate, is just as surely done me if you take them away under these circumstances as would be done if I had worked diligently and shrewdly and acquired these things on my own. See especially the essay "Justice and Personal Desert" by Joel Feinberg in his *Doing and Deserving* (Princeton, N.J.: Princeton University Press, 1970). Grounds for respecting both concepts is supplied, or at least strongly argued for, in Robert Nozick's *Anarchy, State, and Utopia* (New York: Basic Books, 1974). Nozick's book has had some influence on the main drift of this chapter, though not on its particular argument.

4. Rawls, *A Theory of Justice*, 62.

5. Rawls, *A Theory of Justice*, 60.

6. Rawls, *A Theory of Justice*, 60.

7. Rawls, *A Theory of Justice*, 83.

8. It should be emphasized, as Rawls recognizes, that the requirement that persons be given equality of opportunity and that desirable offices be open to all on a basis of fair competition is not part of a program of economic equality. On the contrary: it will bring greater rewards to the more talented, if people have native differences in such talents. There has been question whether this is the case, of course. But there is, in the present state of the subject, no reason to deny differences in native ability, of many kinds (there is, on the other hand, every reason to expect them). At the very least, the onus is on him who would cry injustice when another of obviously superior ability is preferred to him to prove that somebody or other has failed to equalize opportunity at some prior stage.

The concept of equal opportunity has been most usefully analyzed by Alistair MacLeod, in "Equality of Opportunity," in J. Narveson, ed., *Moral Issues* (Toronto: Oxford University Press, 1983), 370-78. MacLeod points out that there are three importantly different levels of application of equal opportunity principles: to talents however come by, to talents natively endowed, and to talents in principle equalizable by genetic engineering or whatever. Only the third—which is a brave new world category at present—would entail equality of wealth as a by-product.

9. There are very good reasons for not taking it very seriously. In the first place, Rawls agrees that lexical priority is not to be adhered to strictly until "circumstances favorable to justice" have been achieved; and prime among these is a certain level of economic advancement (151-52, 244-45, 542, among other places). There has been a good deal of discussion on this aspect of Rawls' theory. See, for instance, Brian Barry, *The Liberal Theory of Justice* (Oxford: Clarendon Press,

1973), ch. 7, and David Braybrooke's critical notice in *Canadian Journal of Philosophy* 3 (December 1973). Indeed, it could plausibly be argued that the priorities are the other way around. For a minimum degree of wealth is explicitly admitted to be the first goal, since liberty is admitted to be sacrificable to it until achieved; and once it is achieved, then it can reasonably be argued that you don't have to sacrifice wealth to achieve the liberty requirements anyway, so that priority of the difference principle will have no effect. (See Barry, 72.)

10. Rawls, *A Theory of Justice*, 302.

11. Rawls, *A Theory of Justice*, 202: "liberty can always be explained by a reference to three items: the agents who are free, the restrictions or limitations which they are free from, and what it is that they are free to do or not to do. . . constraints may range from duties and prohibitions defined by law to the coercive influences arising from public opinion and social pressure." Rawls does not count as a restriction on liberty the presence of neuroses in the individual, or native lack of ability, for example. His conception is "negative," in the classic liberal tradition.

12. See Nozick, *Anarchy, State, and Utopia,* especially 155.

13. Nozick, *Anarchy, State, and Utopia,* 169. A possible argument against this is found in my critical notice of Nozick's book, *Dialogue* 16 no. 2 (1977), 298-328 but it won't get us to Rawls' position either.

14. For a major case in point, consider C. B. McPherson who, in *Democratic Theory* (Oxford: Clarendon Press, 1973) seems to assimilate these throughout, especially in essays 5 and 7. Thus on 146 he argues that the sheer existence of a class with only its own labor to sell and another that has capital besides implies that the latter are *coercing* the former—never mind how those who own the capital came by it!

15. Rawls, *A Theory of Justice*, 203, for example.

16. Again, suggested in my discussion of the "Lockean proviso," in the notice cited in note 13 above. And see chapter 8 of this book. (Note added, 2001.)

17. Rawls, *A Theory of Justice*, 204.

18. Rawls, *A Theory of Justice*, 205.

19. For Rawls' theory of rationality, see *A Theory of Justice,* sections 61, 63, and 64 especially. That it is used behind the veil of ignorance is evident from the outset (see 13-14, for example): it is the imposition of the veil which does what a requirement of impartiality or benevolence would do in another theory. Some have supposed that the invoking of the "Aristotelian principle" alters matters, Rawls perhaps being one of them. Yet that principle, as explicitly stated in Rawls' text (426), says only that people enjoy the realization of their more complex capacities. It does not say that we are to engage in such realizations even if we don't enjoy it. It is a frankly psychological principle, one which may or may not be true but which other utility–maximizing theorists are free to accept. It does not alter the central conception of rationality.

20. Rawls, *A Theory of Justice,* 150.

21. Rawls, *A Theory of Justice,* 245.

22. Rawls, *A Theory of Justice,* 302.

23. Rawls, *A Theory of Justice,* 61.

24. Rawls, *A Theory of Justice,* 154.

25. Rawls, *A Theory of Justice,* 542.

26. My argument for this is fully elaborated in a paper, "Rawls and Utilitarianism" in H. Miller and W. Williams, eds., *The Limits of Utilitarianism* (Minneapolis: University of Minnesota Press, 1982), 128-43. (Note: That paper was not yet published at the time of writing of the present essay.)

27. Curiously, Rawls criticizes utilitarianism along these lines, saying for instance that "it seems impossible to justify the assumption that the social utility of a shift from one level to another is the same for all individuals." Yet the selection of the two principles depends upon the generalization that the desires of persons for material goods beyond a certain point "are not so compelling as to make it rational for the persons in the original position to agree to satisfy them by accepting a less than equal freedom." (543) Obviously, this requires the assumption that the relative utility of these goods for different rational persons is identical. It seems pretty obvious that they are not so in fact: and how is one to prove that the utility of something will be such-and-such for the rational person, if many apparently rational persons do not accord them that utility?

28. Rawls, *A Theory of Justice*, 78.

29. Rawls, *A Theory of Justice*, 150-51.

30. This ambiguity is important for assessing the argument against Rawls in the second paragraph of Nozick's footnote about envy, *Anarchy, State and Utopia*, 229. We are catering to envy if we insist that a distribution in which A has 10 and B 5 is worse than one in which A has 8 and B 5. A's move from 8 to 10 is permitted if moves which harm no one else are permitted; they are not if A must also positively benefit B before he is permitted to move.

31. See "Fairness to Goodness," *Philosophical Review* 84 (October 1975), where he says "that political and economic power is a primary good I never meant to say; if at certain points the text will bear this interpretation, it needs to be corrected." (note 8, 542-43). This should really have been evident all along. The reason for excluding power over others is the same as for excluding envy: for my having this good, if it were one, entails your not having it, insofar as the power I have is power over you. A maximizing theory applied to interpersonal situations can get nowhere with that kind of "good." Is this a good reason for excluding it from the list of primary goods? Not if the idea is to put all things on that list which really are useful to persons generally. But it is a splendid reason for excluding it from the list of things which will be socially divided, since it would tend to wreck the project.

32. Rawls, *A Theory of Justice*, 151.

33. Rawls, *A Theory of Justice*, 3.

34. Rawls, *A Theory of Justice*, 274-75.

35. Rawls, *A Theory of Justice*, 96-97.

36. Rawls, *A Theory of Justice*, 96.

37. Rawls, *A Theory of Justice*, 126.

38. Rawls, *A Theory of Justice*, 151.

39. Most especially, see David Gauthier, "Justice and Natural Endowment: Toward a Critique of Rawls' Ideological Framework," *Social Theory and Practice* 3 (Spring 1974); and John Marshall, "The Failure of Contract as Justification," *Social Theory and Practice* 4 (Fall 1975).

40. Rawls, *A Theory of Justice*, 12-13.

41. Rawls, *A Theory of Justice*, 94.

42. Nozick, *Anarchy, State, and Utopia*, especially 204 and following.

43. Rawls, *A Theory of Justice*, 98.

44. It is clear enough that in Rawls' theory, social classes are not objects of special concern to rational individuals, as such. But it is curious that this is regarded as an objectionable point by some Marxist–oriented critics. Milton Fiske, for example, in "History and Reason in Rawls' Moral Theory" in N. Daniels, ed., *Reading Rawls* (New York: Basic Books, 1974), argues, incredibly, that "If I were a member of a disadvantaged class, I would be able to recognize that such an

arrangement is a direct attack on the tendency of my class to throw off oppression (p. 72)." What makes this incredible is that the difference principle requires members of this allegedly "oppressed" class to be as well-off *as they can be*. Fiske's position, if seriously meant, would require him to hold that he, as a member of that class, would be rationally justified in overthrowing the upper classes even if his class was worse off as a result!

45. David Hume, *An Inquiry Concerning the Principles of Morals* (Indianapolis, Ind.: Bobbs–Merrill, Library of Liberal Arts, 1957), 25.

46. I am grateful to David Gauthier and Kenneth Arrow for pressing the objection to my argument along the lines I have been discussing here, having to do with the object of the theory's being institutions and not individuals, in discussions at an earlier presentation of it (Wayne State University, May 1976). I do not, however, know whether they would regard these rejoinders as adequate.

47. *A Theory of Justice*, Rawls, 154.

48. In particular, rectification of the havoc raised by the assumption noted in note 27 above would be the first order of business. Plainly, the person behind the veil of ignorance would opt for distribution in proportion to need, or utility, and not for equal distribution as such. The utilitarian's willingness to go into the details of particular cases is a strength here, not a weakness.

49. Nozick, *Anarchy, State, and Utopia*, especially 189-97.

50. On Nozick's view, they lack such a right; and on Rawls' view, others have the duty to provide for them even if they don't press for it. A theory on which this would be perfectly O.K. for people to do is provided by the more Hobbesian assumptions which require neither the veil of ignorance nor any constraints of Lockean natural rights. For the working out of this theory, see Gauthier's "Reason and Maximization," *Canadian Journal of Philosophy* 5 (March 1975); also the earlier part of my notice of Nozick mentioned in Note 6. (Note added in 2001: Since then, of course, one would refer readers to Gauthier's *Morals by Agreement* [Oxford: Oxford University Press, 1986].)

Chapter 3

Marxism: Hollow at the Core

Marxism or Marxisms?

In a recent volume of essays on Marx and Marxisms, G. H. R. Parkinson observes, commenting on the remark of one of the essayists to the effect that Marxism is a "historical movement," that "indeed it is. But it is a movement in the sense in which Christianity is a movement; one in which there are important *disagreements* as to what the message of the founder really was."[1] The comparison is certainly apt—in more than one respect, some would say. Writing on Marxism nowadays[2] is a frustrating business. It is scarcely possible to put forward any interpretation of Marx, or even any ascription to Marxism of any fundamental tenet, that will not be loudly (and abusively) disputed by some who claim to be Marxists. Accordingly, it is with some trepidation that I attempt in these few pages to put my finger on the core doctrines of Marx. Actually, I can be more restrictive than that. I shall concern myself only with those of Marx's major arguments that bear directly on the question of whether capitalism ought to be supplanted by socialism. This, I am sure, is the question of greatest interest to most readers, just as it is scarcely possible to doubt that it was the question of greatest interest to Marx and the one to which the major proportion of his vast output was devoted.

Even here one has to pause to note a particularly maddening feature of Marx's procedure, for it is very likely that Marx would have been quick to reject the formulation of the "question" with which, I have claimed, most of his work is concerned. For Marx almost never employs the language of 'ought', and he energetically denounces the practice of characterizing capitalism as "unjust." All such language, he held, is moralistic claptrap—"ideological nonsense about right and other trash so common among the democrats and French Socialists."[3] By and large, Marx instead argues that a transition from capitalism to socialism is "inevitable." He does not hold that there *ought* to be a revolution but that there *will* be. This would seem to make Marx's central claim a kind of open-ended prediction; and, of course, so viewed, his work invites, and has certainly received, criticism on such embarrassing questions as why, one hundred years and more later, the Revolution has not in fact taken place in the countries that one would have supposed were most distinctively eligible for it and just what the proposed time-modulus of the prediction was supposed to be. But I do not propose to add further to the quantities of ink already devoted to those questions. For, whatever Marx may have *said*, it is not only fairly plausible to suppose that he can hardly have meant to deny the legitimacy or relevance of questions of the form "Should we have a revolution or shouldn't we?" but, more important, his entire body of work becomes at best academic and at worst unintelligible if it is not relevant to such questions as that.

Reading Marx and his followers, we want to know which side we should be on. We want to know whether he has given us good reason for having serious doubts about the desirability of retaining the capitalist system (or those aspects of the current economic dispensation that fit that description). Nor can it seriously be doubted that Marxists do take his work as being relevant to those questions. When one tries to piece together how a revolution would be "inevitable" on his theories, especially when taken in conjunction with the fact that Marx also devoted a great deal of time to practical revolutionary activity, there can hardly be any reasonable doubt that the "mechanism" involved, just as we would expect, is the increasing sense on the part of a great many people (mostly members of the working classes, no doubt) that capitalism is an evil and should be replaced by a better system. I shall therefore not attempt further justification of my way of putting the central issue, except to point out that no deep-seated gap between "facts" and "values" is presupposed. On the contrary, as will be seen, my criticisms are largely on the "factual" side insofar as that is a "side."

Marx makes high-level claims about capitalism that are the basis of his critique of capitalism, and of such critiques by Marxists generally, and therefore the basis of his support for socialism. My thesis is that these claims rest, in Marx's own treatment, on identifiable arguments, proceeding from fairly definite premises, and that these arguments are invalid. That the criticisms are also independently false is another matter. I think they are, but with much reformulation they, or something very much like them, might be argued from quite different premises; and I do not here claim that all such reformulations also amount to nothing and that all such optional arguments are wrong. My claim is the narrower but still, I think, important one, that Marx's work is fundamentally based on fallacies. Subtle fallacies, perhaps, but not one whose status as fallacies is in any real doubt.

Many people who think Marxism in error think, I believe, along the following lines: Marx had an ingenious theoretical structure that led to certain general predictions about capitalism, and time has simply shown those predictions to be erroneous. And many Marxists think, I believe, that although it is surprising and worrisome that things haven't gone just the way one might have expected on the basis of Marx's writings, nevertheless his criticisms are fundamentally sound; and eventually history will after all prove him to have been right even if it is not entirely obvious so far. What I wish to argue here is that this is not the right way to look at Marx at all. My thesis is that Marx was wrong all along: not just in his predictions, but in his theoretical structure.

Marx argued from certain general features of capitalism that both he and his bourgeois opponents agreed about. Marx believed that those very features necessarily led to the demise of capitalism and to the necessity and desirability of a change to socialism. For my purposes, it does not matter whether he or anyone thinks that this change must or ought to be violent; for my argument is that his analysis is fundamentally faulty, faulty to the extent that it does not in fact give us good reason either for expecting or desiring the change at all, peaceful or otherwise. Marx was wrong, not in detail and not in incidentals, nor in excusable failure to see what the future held in store. He was wrong, I shall argue, at the core—wrong in *principle*. If, as I suspect, it is the particular doctrines on which he was in error that are almost universally assumed by modern as well as older Marxists in their criticisms of capitalism, then the implications for Marxism are serious. But given the previously alluded to difficulty of pinning any particular doctrines on absolutely all persons claiming to be Marxists, I shall not devote effort to showing that virtually all of them do in fact hold it. Can someone who disputes the divinity of Christ be accounted a Christian? I don't know. But I believe that the fundamentality of the doctrines I analyze below is such that one who rejected them but professed nevertheless to be a Marxist would be in just about the same boat.

The core doctrines of Marxism that will concern me here are two, closely related but distinguishable. They are: (1) that capitalism necessarily involves the "exploitation" of labor, in a sense of 'exploitation' that grounds a fundamental criticism of the system; and (2) that capitalism is a system that is founded on, and/or generates and reinforces, *class conflict*, in particular between owners and nonowners of the "means of production," the conflict being due to a fundamental conflict of interest between those classes. In the absence of doctrine (1), doctrine (2) would either make no sense or at least be reduced to a doctrine with no distinctive Marxian interest. The class conflict in question is due, fundamentally, to the exploitation asserted in (1). And, in the absence of (2), a socialist revolution—the essence of which is that it eliminates private ownership of the means of production, that is, the existence of a distinct capitalist class—would make no sense. Moreover, Marx's apocalyptic view that capitalism would ultimately destroy itself due to its internal "contradictions" is based on the exploitative "relations of production" that define capitalism.

I omit from this very short list many doctrines that could certainly, from various points of view, be regarded as "fundamental" to Marxism. One in particular whose omission perhaps requires a word of justification is the doctrine of Historical Materialism, this being one of the two theories mentioned by Engels in his speech by the graveside of Marx as being Marx's most significant "discoveries." The omission is intentional, however, for this famous but dark theory—the "law of development of human history," Engels calls it[4]—is far too general to supply what is needed for supporting a socialist revolution. The two doctrines I have selected are, in effect, the specific applications of Historical Materialism to the circumstances of the capitalist era. And it would, I should point out, be perfectly possible to accept Historical Materialism—assuming that very difficult doctrine actually has any clear meaning anyway[5]—and yet deny that the time is ripe for such a revolution.[6] The two doctrines I propose to examine here are the linchpins of Marxism as a revolutionary doctrine. Both, I shall point out, are arrived at by fallacious reasoning. The Marxian analysis is faulty at the crucial points. Let us consider each in turn.

Exploitation and Surplus Value

The Marxian theory of exploitation is rooted in the other of the two theories mentioned by Engels in the speech at Marx's grave side alluded to above: the "Theory of Surplus Value." The opening pages of the first volume of Marx's magnum opus, *Capital*, are devoted to the exposition of this theory and requisite background material. In Marx's pages, the theory is dependent upon—indeed, it is a straightforward deduction from—the Labor Theory of Value, a theory that is mired in problems. Not surprisingly, as we shall see, the Theory of Surplus Value, and in consequence the Marxian theory of exploitation, inherit these problems. To see how this all goes, we must, inevitably, briefly go into the Labor Theory of Value.

Marx opens his discussion by distinguishing between two sorts of 'value': use value, which is that about an object which makes it useful for whatever purposes the prospective purchaser, or the maker or finder, may have; and exchange value, or that about a transferable object which enables it to be exchanged for other things on a market, the market being the central institution of capitalism. Exchange value, in other words, is whatever it is that fundamentally accounts for price, since the price of an item is the money-expression of its capacity for exchange. And the Labor Theory of Value is the theory that exchange value is—at least "ultimately," or "fundamentally"—determined entirely by labor.

"Determined" how? Consider two identical shawls on adjacent stands in the local market. Shawl A was laboriously made by a little old lady who invested about fifty hours of work in it; shawl B was made by high-speed knitting machinery in Taiwan, with a total worker input of about five minutes. Shawl A will not, sentimental value apart, fetch six hundred times the price of shawl B; in fact, it may fetch merely the same price. Marx knew this, of course. His modification of the theory, which he accepted (having inherited it from his bourgeois predecessors), is to affirm that what is responsible for market values is not the actual "quantity" of labor embodied in any particular bit of goods, but rather this:

> The labor, however, that forms the substance of value is homogeneous human labor, expenditure of one uniform labor power. The total labor power of society, which is embodied in the sum total of the values of all commodities produced by that society, counts here as one homogeneous mass of human labor power, composed though it be of innumerable individual units. Each of these units is the same as any other, so far as it has the character of the average labor power of society, and takes effect as such; that is, so far as it requires for producing a commodity no more time than is necessary on average, no more than is socially necessary.[7]

From then on, we must presume that whenever Marx discusses the labor factor in production, the "units" of labor that figure in the various equations are these idealized units.

It is of considerable importance to appreciate that the theory in question is, and leads to, a theoretical quagmire—"of considerable importance" because Marxists tend to talk as though Marx had here come upon a fantastically brilliant insight that had settled all the problems of the labor theory. Like Marx—I believe—they want to cling to the theory because they think that it supplies powerful support for Marx's critique of capitalism and thus for a change to socialism. It needs to be seen that this is entirely wrong. There are three major points to make here, two of which I will make now; the third is best introduced after we have brought in the Theory of Surplus Value itself. In effect, the upshot of the first two criticisms is that the very claim that we have a definite theory here is an illusion. While trumpeted by Marx (and Marxists) as a "scientific" theory, its scientific purport turns out to be zero. The upshot of the third criticism will be that the theory, even if it was at least somewhat workable, would not have at all the effect that socialists, including Marx himself, might have supposed.

To begin with the first criticism: it will have been noticed that my statements of the Labor Theory of Value have included a parenthetical qualifier: market pricing is "(ultimately)" determined by labor. Why the qualifier? Marx was well aware that many other factors influence pricing in a market besides the labor inputs of the goods being sold. Some goods do not, in the usual understanding of the term, have a labor input at all: virgin land, for example. Sudden changes in demand will cause major changes in prices irrespective of labor inputs. All these are passed off as "incidental." But if these are incidental, then what is essential? The standard response to this is that what Marx is after is the determination of "equilibrium" prices: the prices achieved in a stable market when all variables have settled down—assuming, of course, a perfectly competitive market. In that case—if only it were possible to reply to the next objection, that is—prices would be proportional to labor inputs. But, if that is all the Labor Theory says, then it is exceedingly uninteresting. Nobody ever doubted that in the case of things produced by labor, labor costs are a significant factor in pricing. But Marx's claim is that it has a peculiarly fundamental significance—that it is, somehow, the *sole* factor that matters. Since both perfect competition and complete equilibrium are theoretical idealizations, akin to the perfect vacuum in physics, the upshot is that there is no actual case in which the central claim of the Labor Theory of Value is true. It began, bravely, by asserting that market prices are due entirely to labor; it ends by saying, meekly, that price is proportional solely to labor *when all else is held constant*—which is, for all practical purposes, never!

All this was assuming that we do, at least, have an empirically significant variable to work with in the Theory. But do we? Remember, it is no longer sufficient merely to measure the number of hours of labor put in by any, or even every, particular worker. For some "hours" are worth more than others! Thus in considering the case of skilled labor, Marx says, "Skilled labor counts only as simple labor intensified, or rather, as multiplied simple labor, a given quantity of skilled being considered equal to a greater quantity of simple labor. Experience shows that this reduction is constantly being made."[8] But how is it made? The sort of examples Marx uses in this connection confirm what any of us would say about it. In effect, we look at the effect on output of the different skill levels, on their different levels of training, and so forth. But mostly, in the end, we simply look at what we have to pay for different levels of skill! And it is really obvious, when one thinks about this, that there is no other theoretically possible way to do this. As soon as actual "labors" are nonhomogeneous, and we try to compare them in terms of their impact on production, we find we must employ the market in order to make the comparison. But of course the Labor Theory of Value says that market pricing is determined by quantity of labor! If the only possible way to measure the "labor" variable is in the light of antecedent market pricing activity, then the theory has become hopelessly circular. Of course this is not the "only possible way to measure" quantities of labor. We could just doggedly count up hours, no matter whose and no matter what is being done during those hours. But if we did, we would have a theory whose falsity was spectacularly obvious instead of a theory with a certain specious plausibility that turns out, as we have just seen, to be due to circularity.

With this background in mind, what about the famous Theory of Surplus Value? This theory is brought in to solve what appeared to be a serious problem. What motivates entrepreneurs in a market is the prospect of profit. Profits are made by selling things for more than the total cost of making and marketing them. But suppose we are convinced by the Labor Theory of Value? And suppose, as was assumed by Marx and his predecessors, that in a market things always exchange "at their values"—equals for equals. But if all value is labor value, then it seems that the amount of labor embodied in the goods bought by the consumer must be equal to the labor commanded by the money he pays for his purchase—so where does profit come from? To this Marx came up with a simple, ingenious, and elegant answer. We must, he points out, make a distinction when we come to the special case of that very important capitalist market commodity called labor power: a distinction between (a) the value that the laborer bestows on what he produces by laboring, and (b) the value that is "embodied in" the laborer himself! The appearance that there is a mystery about profit is due to the confusion between these two very different things. Quantity (a) is, of course, what determines the market value of the product, given the Labor Theory of Value. But quantity (a) is not what determines the value of the laborer's labor-power, even though all value is determined by labor. For quantity (b) is not the amount of time the laborer spends behind the machine or whatever. It is, instead, the amount of time spent by both himself and others in maintaining that laborer in a condition in which he can labor. Let us simplify the reference to "others" by assuming that all of the other costs are paid for by the laborer himself, on the average at any rate. Then we can say that there is a "quantity of labor" (labor-time, actually, but the reader will know what is meant) that determines the value of the laborer's wages, and so in that sense is "embodied in the laborer," and a different quantity embodied in what the laborer produces during his working hours. And, of course, if we look at it this way, it must follow that, if the firm is a profitable one, then on the average the quantity "embodied in the laborer" *must* be less than the amount embodied in the laborer's product. If all value is labor-value and there is profit, then that profit must embody labor, and (on the average, etc.) it must in fact embody some of the laborer's labor.

What the Theory of Surplus Value boils down to, if we have swallowed the background assumptions and followed out the logic of the argument, will certainly appear to be this: all profit is extracted from the hides of laborers. The temptation will be to say what Marx does say or obviously imply in many, many passages throughout his work, that profit is a sort of robbery and, what is more, the worst sort, since it consists in separating, as it were, a part of the very laborer himself from himself! In Marx's earlier writings, he tended to identify man's essence in terms of his work-activity. In the case of wage-work, the "form" of labor we have under capitalism, this "essence" is under the control of other men, the capitalists. The worker is "forced" under capitalism to sell himself to other people. This, of course, is dehumanizing, alienating and alienated, and so on.

On top of all this, Marx also tended to think of the Value of Labor as the minimum that could be expended in order to keep the laborer laboring; and he comes up with the famous "theory of immiseration," according to which wages under capitalism could be expected, by and large, to fall toward subsistence and, by and large, to remain there; or at least in the case of the wages of unskilled industrial workers, which were the main focus of his attention. (This tendency, it should be observed, emphasizes one of the two different components of the Marxian version of the Labor Theory of Value. That theory, recall, identifies the source of value as "socially necessary labor power," though it also identifies it with average labor power. 'Socially necessary' suggests the minimum of what is needed given the best current technology. On this understanding, the value of a laborer is the least it would take, given current methods of keeping someone alive, to keep that laborer alive. The independent problems with the "immiseration" theory will be gone into below.)

We can now explore the third criticism I have in mind. The laborer, on Marx's analysis, is necessarily exploited under capitalism. He is "exploited," to begin with, in one of the straightforwardly literal senses of that term, in that he is made use of, and of course, one would hope, made the best possible use of in the productive activities in which he is involved. And, second, he is "exploited" in a technical, Marxian sense deriving from what we have just been noting: exploited in that he is paid less than the value he confers on what he produces. All we need to do is to assume, as many people will naturally tend to do, that all of the work of a worker ought, after all, to belong to the worker—in short, that what he is worth is the entirety of that value. All workers, just by virtue of being workers, are necessarily underpaid! And thus, the allegedly "technical" sense of 'exploitation' takes on a third connotation that it also frequently has in ordinary usage, namely, the sense that to exploit someone is to do something unjust and wrong and to be criticized—a pejorative sense, in short.

Now the first of the two core doctrines of Marxism, I have said, is that workers are exploited in a sense of 'exploitation' that grounds a fundamental criticism of capitalism. Does the Marxian analysis in fact support such a criticism, so far as it goes? The answer to this, I suggest, is resoundingly in the negative. To see this, let us begin by pointing out that the entire framework of the Marxian analysis, rooted as it is in the Labor Theory of Value, is completely hopeless from the start, so that any theorems derived from it must thereby be suspect. For one example, just notice that, since there is no natural correspondence between a real hour of a real person's labor and the theoretical "unit of homogeneous socially necessary labor time" of the theory, you could never prove that any actual person was "exploited," even in Marx's technical sense, in the first place! The number of labor-theoretical hours embodied in Smith's wages might be far greater, rather than far less, than the number of actual hours he puts in. But never mind. Let us be extremely generous and suppose that some kind of sense can be given to the Surplus Value idea; still, what really matters is this: is the worker necessarily worse off by virtue of having some of "his" labor power "taken away from" him? Is the fact that profits are being made from his hide necessarily a bad thing from his point of view? A moment's reflection assures us that it is not.

To take a case that would be highly apropos in Marx's own time, consider the cottage worker with his hand loom, his own sheep, and so on. He is self-employed from start to finish, so there is no question of exploitation by a capitalist. Suppose he is able to produce one shirt a week from his efforts—of course he gets to keep 100 percent of whatever he can get for that shirt. Now consider his industrial colleague who labors, we shall hypothesize, the same number of hours a week (likely very high in both cases!); and suppose that the industrial worker produces, in effect, 100 shirts a week ("in effect" because, of course, this worker may never make a whole shirt; one must, say, divide the total output by the total number of workers in the shirt-producing sector of the factory to arrive at the relevant figure). Now even if the owner kept the equivalent of 95 of those shirts, the worker is left with five times the number of shirts he would have had in his cottage. If we measure his situation by his real income, that is, the volume of goods and services he commands by his efforts, then he would in this case be five times as well-off by virtue of being "exploited" as he would by being entirely his own master.

Obviously there is room to argue that the simple peasant's life he leads in his cottage is spiritually superior to the factory existence, and many socialists have, virtually, so argued. Such arguments do not sit very well with peasants, who know what their life is like, nor with typical industrial workers who are not much interested in returning to a steady diet of goat's milk and rough bread. Nor should they sit well with Marxists who, after all, profess to follow a man whose leading principle was that "mankind must first of all eat, drink, have shelter and clothing before it can pursue political science, art, religion, etc."[9] —or, we may add, appreciate the virtues of poverty and spiritual simplicity! But mainly, of course, socialists have leaned on Marx's apocalyptic assessment of capitalism, and in particular his belief that capitalism will necessarily lead to a growing "mass of misery, oppression, slavery, degradation, exploitation."[10] Insofar as that prediction is based on the simple theory of exploitation, it is, as we have seen, utterly unsupported. But perhaps, as Marxists will of course be quick to point out, it is not based only on that simple theory. Perhaps further social considerations will shore up the Marxian account? To follow Marx's technical argument to the end would involve endless labor, but fortunately we will find it unnecessary to do that. We shall instead turn to the claim about class interest and class conflict. Here, we shall find, the situation is not more favorable to the Marxist conclusion; if anything, it is less so.

Class Interests in the Capitalist Era

"Our epoch . . . has simplified the class antagonisms. Society as a whole is more and more splitting up into two great hostile camps, into two great classes directly facing each other: Bourgeoisie and Proletarian." [11]

William Leon McBryde remarks that he finds the claim above "intuitively highly plausible when applied to the most advanced industrial societies of Marx's day, but by the same token far less plausible when applied to most advanced contemporary societies." [12] Here again we see the tendency to suppose that it is only the facts that show Marx to have been wrong. But I shall again insist that the fault is not in the facts. Marx's premises, had he looked at them all with due care, would not have led him to the conclusion that the relationship between the two classes he identifies would be one of hostility. Hostility implies conflict of interests. But are the "classes" in capitalist society in conflict? Are their interests as classes opposed? I shall argue that they are not; or, more precisely, that there is nothing in the basic features of capitalism that imply this. Marx, of course, must (and did) hold that this conflict was absolutely fundamental. Let us see.

To begin with, let us get a clearer idea of the notion of 'class interest'. We should expect a class interest to be something that unifies its members, something that gives them reason to identify with one another and perhaps even to make some sacrifices on its behalf. A feeling that we all stand or fall together arises. And this will, of course, tend to be conjoined with perceptions that the other class or classes are (if "lower") to be kept in their places, or (if "higher") resented and envied. What must be emphasized is that anything worthy of being called a "class interest" has to be more than just the separate interests of its members. Possession of some common quality is not enough to make a social class.

Second, the new kinds of classes Marx envisages do not behave in the same way as the old ones exemplified by the Ancien Régime. The old-style classes were fixed subsets of the populace; mobility from one to the other was extremely rare, if not unheard of. The members of those classes did not have to do anything to be members: all you had to do was have the right parents. Since the membership in such classes was fixed, there was no problem identifying one's fellow members; and moreover, once a member, always a member. No problem about people sneaking across the lines.

Finally, let us bear in mind that Marx's argument is supposed to be purely economic. The idea is not that, by some kind of ill-understood chemistry, capitalists get together and so do proletarians. The interests of these classes are to arise directly from their "relationship to the means of production," namely, in that the capitalists own (have the official, socially sanctioned control over) those means while the proletarians do not and have nothing to sell but the sweat of their bodies.

The issue before us, then, is whether the "relations of production" in question do in fact yield a class interest or interests of the kind in question. In particular, of course, it is whether they yield an interest on the part of the working classes in eliminating the other class. (This sounds, and in frightening actual cases has been, rather apocalyptic. But, in fact, you eliminate this class not by eliminating its members but, rather, by changing the production relations, that is, by abolishing the private ownership of the means of production.) I shall argue that it does not.

What makes someone a capitalist, a member of the "bourgeoisie," is that he owns capital. And that is all. (Obviously the question "How much?" screams out for an answer, but we must neglect such important details here.) It has nothing, as such, to do with who your parents were—though there is a decent chance that, if they did well, then you would inherit some capital and hence find you have become a capitalist. Nor are there any laws saying that you, you, and you are forever barred from membership. Anyone can play, in one way or another; or, at any rate, anyone who is not literally earning at subsistence level (which Marx, of course, argued would be a lot of people; more about this below). In a purely market society, the laws protect people and their property: any kind of property, any person's property, so long as it was legitimately acquired. And, in fact, the membership of the "capitalist" class is unstable. It is also, of course, vague. (If you have a life insurance policy, as likely you do, would Marx consider you a capitalist? Or a retirement savings plan? If so, then almost all of us are capitalists!) Moreover, we have to bear in mind that, as things are, all sorts of noncapitalists make greater incomes than most capitalists. Nor, I hasten to add, were things all that different in Marx's day. The real wages of workers were, of course, much lower than now, but the substantial spread from low to high, with income derived from earnings on capital, wages, or a mix of both, was already there. This would make it a bit difficult for the aspiring member in good standing of the bourgeoisie to know who his friends were, and likewise a bit difficult for the workers to know who the enemy was. (Engels himself, for instance, was probably on the bourgeois side of the line, if anything—luckily for Marx, who survived for many years on frequent doles from the faithful Engels.) The Marxian class antagonisms, alas, do not have clearly separate and identifiable antagonists.

But never mind. Let us press on to the more fundamental question of why these "classes," supposing that we can identify them, are supposed to be at each other's throats. When we delve into the Marxian literature with this question in mind, we come upon a somewhat surprising fact: there doesn't seem to be any explicit argument for this. Evidently Marx, and Marxists following him, thought it required no argument. However, let us assume that what Marx thought was self-evident was not the proposition that classes in capitalism have inextricably opposed interests but, rather, that once you follow the argument in, say, *Capital*, it will then go without saying that they are so opposed. And on this, I fear, far too many readers have been taken in. But let us not be.

Let us give Marx the proposition that the interests of owners and workers within any particular enterprise are opposed, at least in the short run. Marx's capitalists operate in an economy characterized by considerable competition—perhaps "perfect" competition, but this needn't worry us here. And Marx is clear that even if the individual owner happened to be a benevolent fellow and would have preferred to pay his employees more, the forces of the market will deprive him of this luxury. Competition provides the motivation also for technological progress, which increases the productivity of labor (while, it will appear, depriving the thus displaced laborers of their livelihood). And large capitalism, with the nineteenth-century version of high technology, is what Marx has in mind. These features of the situation make for a general pressure toward lower wages.

So far, so good. But how does this prove what is to be shown? It certainly shows that each capitalist has a contrary interest to some workers. But what we need is the thesis that the capitalist *class* has, *as a class*, an interest in grinding down the proletariat to near-starvation levels of subsistence; and having, after all, "the control" over the means of production, presumably capitalists are in a position to bring this unhappy result about. Right?

Wrong! For we might try bearing in mind how our hypothetical capitalist makes his money, a point that Marx tends to sweep under the carpet. He makes it, ex hypothesi, by *selling*. Moreover, in the important cases he makes it by developing machinery of mass production. And who are the "masses" who will buy all this stuff? Well, given the Marxian scenario, we know what the answer would have to be. For, on his scheme, the bourgeoisie is a vanishing species. Polarization proceeds apace, with ever fewer richer capitalists at the top, and even more ever poorer proletarians at the bottom. Now, if this could happen at all, there would be a mystery indeed! For in a market society, the only way you can make a buck is to sell something, and you can only sell if someone buys. The conclusion stares us in the face: on Marx's premises, it must be the case, contrary to what Marx thunderously insists, that the proletariat is more or less steadily increasing in its purchasing power, rather than the reverse. It is *logically impossible* for the other tendencies to be realized if it does not. But more to the present point is the fact that capitalists have an interest in this being the case. The idea that they have, instead, an interest in the poverty of the working classes, and have it just by virtue of being members of the capitalist class, is sheer economic nonsense. And it is economics that is supposed to supply the premises for Marx's argument here.

It may be objected that, while the capitalists may, in some sense of 'interest', have the interest cited above, they are nevertheless powerless to do anything about it for reasons of the kind already mentioned. But this too rests on a fallacy. If capitalist A is able to reduce his costs by reducing wages, soon to be followed by B, C, and so on, the effect of all this in a competitive economy is that prices will go down. And this, so far as it goes, increases the real income of all who buy those goods, a fact that seems to escape Marx's myopic glare.

Understandably: for the upshot of all this is that when capitalists flourish, so in general does the "proletariat," with any luck at all. And one would have thought that that is not the way for inextricable, to-the-death, basic class conflicts to proceed.

There is a further small point concerning the class "solidarity" of the capitalists; viz., that insofar as they are capitalists, the people with whom they are most evidently in conflict are, in fact, the *other members of the class*. Far from expecting the members of this group to cleave together and support each other, we expect what we in fact find: that they are always on the lookout for ways to obtain a competitive advantage. This too is a very unsatisfactory basis for "class" interest. Why would members of a class so constituted want to make sacrifices for one another's welfare? Would they have any reason to do this that would not be an even better reason for supporting the welfare of noncapitalists—say, contributing to unemployment insurance and welfare funds?

All of this compresses a good deal of territory into a few pages, and it is only to be expected that any self-respecting Marxist will find epicycles to make the pronouncements of the Master square with his own basis of theory. Nor do I purport to have solutions to the pressing economic problems of advanced industrial societies today—a request for such being thought to be naturally forthcoming from the would-be Marxist. But my intention is not to shore up unlimited laissez-faire capitalism, nor to decry any need for social legislation; those are issues for another time. What I insist on here is simply that Marx does have fundamental theses, that these theses are highly influential, and that Marxian reasoning falls hopelessly short of supporting them. To any reasonably candid observer, history has, of course, shown Marx to be wrong in his main claims. For example, during the very decades that he labored away to "prove" that the proletariat must, under capitalism, sink deeper and deeper into misery, the real income of the English working class rose steadily. The point of this brief review is that this is what we should expect given the premises he was reasoning from rather than what he actually claims. The error is not happenstance. It is in the central logic of the theory. Marx may have made some contributions to economics. But his foundational ideas, the ones that form the main basis of his call for revolution, can only by fallacy lead in that direction. The core of Marxism turns out to be like the core of the onion rather than of the avocado: instead of the rich juicy pit of solid theory, the last peel leaves us with nothing.

Notes

This essay was published in *Free Inquiry* (Spring 1983), 29-35. Published by permission of *Free Inquiry*, the journal of the Council for Secular Humanism.

1. G. H. R. Parkinson, ed., *Marx and Marxisms*, Royal Institute of Philosophy Lecture Series No. 14 (Cambridge: Cambridge University Press, 1982), 2.

2. This was written in the period 1981-83.

3. Marx, "Critique of the Gotha Program," in D. McLellan, ed., *Karl Marx: Selected Writings* (Oxford: Oxford University Press, 1977), 564.

4. Engels, "Speech at the Graveside of Marx," in Robert C. Tucker, ed., *The Marx-Engels Reader* (New York: Norton, 1978), 681.

5. The major recent work on this is the brilliant study *Karl Marx's Theory of History*, by G. A. Cohen (in the United States, Princeton University Press, 1978). In the course of his analysis, he sets forth the problems of interpretation in this major area of Marx studies very nicely.

6. To see this, consider this excerpt from Marx's *Preface to The Critique of Political Economy*, the classic source for the theory of Historical Materialism: "No social order is ever destroyed before all the productive forces for which it is sufficient have been developed, and new, superior relations of production never replace older ones before the material conditions for their existence have matured within the framework of the old society" (International Publishers, 1970; 21). Clearly one could, at least as a logical possibility, accept the doctrine but claim that "all the productive forces for which it is sufficient" have *not* been developed.

7. Marx, *Capital, Vol. I*, in Robert C. Tucker, ed., *The Marx-Engels Reader* (New York: Norton, 1978), 310.

8. Marx, *Capital, Vol. I*, in Robert C. Tucker, ed., *The Marx-Engels Reader* (New York: Norton, 1978), 306.

9. Engels, "Speech at the Graveside of Marx," in Robert C. Tucker, ed., *The Marx-Engels Reader* (New York: Norton, 1978), 681.

10. Marx, *Capital, Vol. I*, in Robert C. Tucker, ed., *The Marx-Engels Reader* (New York: Norton, 1978), 438.

11. *Communist Manifesto*, in Robert C. Tucker, ed., *The Marx-Engels Reader* (New York: Norton, 1978), 474.

12. William Leon McBryde, *The Philosophy of Marx* (London: Hutchinson, 1978), 98.

Chapter 4

On Recent Arguments for Egalitarianism

Preliminary Definitions

Everybody agrees that morality in general, and justice in particular, has *some* connection with *some* sort of equality—that we ought to treat people somehow equally. But what connection, and what sort? This chapter concerns *Egalitarianism:* the view that justice requires that we attempt to bring it about that everyone has an equal (or, more nearly equal) and positive (nonzero) amount of some good that is not just formal. Familiar examples are welfare, income, wealth, resources, and opportunity. The egalitarian doesn't settle for the mere right to pursue one's welfare, income, or opportunities—he's insistent that we must all do what we can to provide these things, in equal measure, to all.[1] In short, egalitarian theories are programs of general positive rights. The good to which the positive right in question is a right has to be variable in degree, so that it makes sense to say that people have equal or unequal amounts of it. And the equality in question is not to be Aristotelian, in the sense of being variable though equally proportionated to, say, desert. (However, I will count distribution in proportion to need or desire, as opposed to desert, as falling within the range of the theories I'm concerned with here.)

What I mean by an *argument,* for present purposes, is the assembling of premises accepted by, or acceptable, on their own showing, to all parties to the argument about the matters under dispute, and the drawing of an inference from such premises to the effect that some normative view about those matters is the right one. Many arguments of this type utilize premises of a factual, empirical nature, and many of those are verifiable or refutable by known, familiar, and public procedures. Insofar as premises are of that kind, truth or well-confirmed stature are needed. *Moral* arguments are practical. Such arguments aim to induce one's dialectical discussant to adopt a certain (or confirm a preexisting) normative stance on the matters in question. Our premises incorporate propensities to act and to criticize the actions of others; a good argument induces those propensities on behalf of the indicated conclusions.

49

Admittedly, arguments for egalitarianism are rare; for the most part, egalitarians seem content simply to assert their views—they don't seem to think it *needs* any argument. But there have occasionally been what appears to have been intended as arguments, and it is of interest to examine those. That is the project of this chapter.

It's about Justice

I also take it that a requirement of *justice* is a moral duty in the strongest sense, in that it is enforceable: what is just may be secured by making laws, backed if need be by force, thus compelling everyone into line on the matter. Whether we ought to do the things in question, in short, is not to be a voluntary matter, such that some may do this, others do that, as they like or as their individual consciences dictate. We may compel people to refrain from murder, and threaten with serious punishment those who propose to do so; we may not compel people to wear sideburns, or to play Parcheesi. If egalitarianism is indeed a requirement of justice, then the law may impose taxes on us, or other costs, for the purpose of promoting equality of the type in question. If it is not, then, prima facie, it may not. The stakes, therefore, are high in this matter.

The Default Position

I shall take it to be common ground among us all that whatever else it may do, justice will prohibit the use of violence—force, fraud, coercion—against otherwise innocent persons to attain our ends. The reason, in my view and, I think, most people's view, is Hobbesian: the use of force creates a negative-sum game that can be played by almost everyone.[2] It is clearly in everyone's interests to subscribe to a principle generally forbidding the use of force to attain one's miscellaneous objectives, at least if such a principle can be effective.

Some degree of violence used on behalf of the enforcement of rules whose antecedent rationality is established is, of course, another matter. The question is whether there are any other such rules, of universal-society scope, besides the prohibition on violence itself. That's what the rest of this chapter is concerned with.

While there is an excellent case for prohibiting violence, it is not obvious that everyone has reason to subscribe to a society-wide, involuntary welfare-promoting scheme. My gain from refraining from hitting you is that you won't hit me. But what is A's gain from agreeing to respond to B's needs just because they *are* needs? Presumably it would be B's agreement, in turn, to respond to A's in similar fashion. But any number of things might make this a bad agreement from A's point of view. What if B's needs are much greater? Or what if A's power to cater to A's own needs is such that A sees little marginal benefit in B's being disposed to cater to them, and plenty of marginal loss, in view of the cost to A of catering to B's?

A good argument for egalitarianism is required to overcome this prima facie case against it. The arguments considered in this chapter are intended to do just that; or at any rate, I shall construe them as so intended.

Six (or So) Arguments

With this background in mind, let us turn our attention to some recent philosophical arguments in this field. Without pretending to completeness, I shall consider six arguments (or seven, depending on what you count as an "argument"). Here they are:

0. Appeal to Intuition, Direct Style
1. The Impartiality of Moral Principles
2. Veil of Ignorance Arguments
3. The Moral Arbitrariness of Desert
4. Conditions of Co-operation
5. Motivation by Counterfactual Interests
6. Equal Concern and Respect

The rest of the chapter examines these, seriatim.

Before Beginning: Appeals to Intuition

Here I need merely remind the reader that we are talking about *arguments* for equality, as distinct from sheer assertions of it. Appeals to "intuition"—that the commitment to equality is "moral bedrock," as I have heard it said—must, on the face of it, count in the latter category. As a device for supporting equality, this invites the response that, unfortunately, *my* "moral bedrock" might be something quite incompatible with the proponent's: say, that equality is a snare and a delusion. Strange bedrockfellows! So where would we go from there? If it's anywhere, it's going to have to be either back to arguments, or to non-rational or irrational activity, such as politics—waving flags, Bosnia, etc.

However, the proponent of intuition is likely to offer a sort of meta-argument: "Justification does come to an end. Perhaps the belief in egalitarianism is just such a belief. With it we can justify other moral beliefs, but it cannot itself be justified."[3] But does the end-point of moral arguments need to be some *moral* principle? Some of us deny it. On the right view of the foundations of morality, there are no moral bedrocks. Everything is arguable, and arguable by reference to considerations that have to be meaningful to those concerned, antecedently to the moral theory being put forward—namely their various values and preferences, whatever they may be, plus a variety of empirically manageable factual claims.

Here is a brief exposition.[4] The philosopher tries to propound, or at least inquire what it might be like to have, a rational morality. To do this one must, of course, have a view of rationality. Which rationality? And whose justice? The answer, programmatically, is: any thinking person's. What I think thinking persons think about practical matters, when they do, is that they cart around with them an assortment of preferences, more or less thought through, and they evaluate their actions in the light of their likelihood of, on the whole, promoting what they prefer (or, if you prefer, what they "value.")

How, then, do we evaluate a morality? The moralities we can evaluate are *possible de facto moralities*. Rational morality then, will be the set of proposable requirements on everyone's conduct that gets a suitably high rational rating. Here, we are saying, is a proposed rule for everyone's behavior, and to advocate this is to advocate its having effect upon all, including oneself. Now, one is oneself also a member of the tribe in question, and that's of considerable importance, just as so many moral philosophers have insisted it is. That is to say, there will be a problem about advocating a set of rules from which, you propose, you will yourself be exempt. This problem is *not*, however, that what one is proposing would then be literally *unintelligible*. If I say, "The rule is: you all have to do whatever *I* want, and meanwhile, I don't have to do anything you want," they *understand*, well enough, what I'm saying. The problem is that if this rule is to have any chance at all of being accepted by these people, they're going to have to be either very *peculiar* or else very *stupid*. The former is ruled out by the need for morality to be acceptable to all, not just to the peculiar. The morality we seek is to be the rules for any bunch of humans who interact, rather than of some particular bunch. The latter is ruled out by our terms: seeking a rational morality. 'X is rational' does not mean 'X is highly intelligent', to be sure. But X's being stupid *is* a matter of X's not doing what it would obviously be rational for X to do, in the case in question.

Rational moralities are rational by virtue of being supported from within rather than imposed from without. What rules do have a chance of rational acceptance? Answer: rules such that anyone in the community is, from her own point of view, better off given that set of rules than any other set, given that everyone else likewise is to accept them.

Meanwhile, on the Default position identified, we may note, enthusiasts for egalitarianism are welcome to use their own incomes—not just their intuitions— to promote equality. No one, I take it, is against the sheer impulse to share and share alike with one and all. But that isn't what is in question here, and is not what the egalitarianism we are investigating settles for. Instead, it asserts egalitarianism as a principle of justice. And the effect of holding such principles solely on the basis of intuition is to assert the lack of need to explain to the taxpayers or other cost-bearers of egalitarianism why they should allow you to cram your view down his or her throat. That is not argument.

First Argument: Impartiality of Morality

These arguments appeal to what is now, at least, common ground—so much so that there is temptation to turn it into a defining feature of morals: that its principles cannot arbitrarily favor one person (or class) over another, that we are all subject to uniform rules, rules for the common good rather than rules that would shore up the advantages of some person, elite class, race, or whatever. But this is beside the point in the present context, for what we are talking about here is not merely impartiality, but *egalitarianism*. And egalitarianism, which favors consumers over producers, looks to be *partial* rather than impartial. But what is uncontroversially central to morals is that its principles, and their administration, must be impartial. To infer from this uncontroversial specification that those principles must require each individual person to be *impartial as among possible recipients of whatever they can do for others* is simply fallacious. For a generally accepted example: all parents, impartially, have the right *to favor their own children over others*—an impartial right to be partial, *not* an impartial requirement to be impartial in that context. Indeed, egalitarianism itself may be accused of being *partial* at the highest level, by preferring consumers over producers. It says we may invade person A, though he has harmed no one, so as to improve the lot of person B, though B has done nothing to deserve this. The debate, as I say, is not whether morality is to be somehow equal, but over the respects in which it is to be so—equal *how*?, is the question. Egalitarianism is one (type of) view about this, but decidedly not the only one. It *needs* arguing.

Second Argument: The Veil of Ignorance

What I will loosely call Veil-of-Ignorance arguments suppose that it is a fundamental requirement of morality that it be impartial in the special sense that the principles of morals are to consist of principles we would only choose from a very special point of view, namely the one we would have if we had no idea who we were—the familiar Rawlsian idea. In fact, it is not really clear what this idea is, and in one interpretation it would be a mere *façon de parler* for the requirement that our principles do not load the dice in anyone's favor.[5] However, in another reading (probably more nearly the one actually intended by Rawls) the Veil does a lot more than that. For on this view, in requiring us to choose from such a special perspective, it also assures that the principles chosen will ignore individuals' interests in using their own powers for their own purposes, and instead have regard for persons only as beneficiaries of the exertions of collectivized powers by and for all. In choosing for "myself" when "I" don't know who I am and so don't *have* a self, I am necessarily choosing for Homogenized Anybody: I am assigning, say, the same probability to my being any actual person as to my being any other. Small wonder that it has a socialist (or at least utilitarian[6]) output.

But the Veil-of-Ignorance gambit has the problem that from the point of view of any real person, it is quite remarkably unclear why he should pay any attention to principles that could only appeal to people who didn't know who they were (or, of course, to people who would benefit from its output—not Everyperson, but Majorityperson, or Bureauperson!). As with the previous ideas, we just have to point out that the claim that the "moral point of view" is the one you'd have on *that* view of the veil is tendentious—hardly acceptable to all parties.

Third Argument: The Moral Arbitrariness of Desert

The most influential of all arguments for egalitarianism, I am sure, is this one, due in its modern form to Rawls, again. The basic idea is that we are all fundamentally entitled to equal ministrations because, roughly speaking, we are *not by nature fundamentally entitled to unequal ones*. The argument invokes what we may call the Transitivity of Nondesert: if you claim to deserve X by virtue of your having property F, then if your being F is not deserved, *neither is X*.

The idea is that *the differences between us that are due to our basic endowments from Nature are "morally irrelevant" or "arbitrary"* on the ground that we cannot be thought to *deserve* our natural assets—we are simply born with them; and the same goes for inherited wealth or other advantages. "No one deserves his greater natural capacity nor merits a more favorable starting place in society."[7] By Transitivity of Nondesert, then, we do not deserve whatever differential advantages we may try to lay claim to.

Once we appreciate what this is supposed to be an argument for, however, we shall see that this famous argument contains a fundamental fallacy. The conclusion of it, remember, is supposed to be that we all have the duty to utilize our personal powers so as to bring it about that everyone has a (roughly) equal amount of X [it doesn't presently matter what X is for this purpose]. Alternatively, the conclusion is that we are supposed to support political institutions which do that. Some think that's a difference that matters. I don't.[8] Yet the *premise* says only that nobody *deserves* any more X than anyone else— a purely negative premise. How are we supposed to get from it to the quite positive intended conclusion that everyone ought to get *some* X from us—an equal amount, as may be?

From the premise, 'Jones does not deserve X', does it or doesn't it follow that we *shouldn't give Jones any X?* On the "strong" version, it does: Jones deserves to get no X. The other is what we may call the "weak" version: *It is not the case that Jones deserves to get some X*. Which version does the proponent of the Differences-Are-Morally-Arbitrary view want to invoke? The "strong" version has it that Jones positively ought not to be given any X— giving him any would be wrong. Indeed, maybe it is our duty to take away what he has. But if an asset can't underwrite *differential* desert when it's not deserved, then how can *common* assets be able to do so? For after all, *they* aren't deserved either. If the strong version is offered, then, the conclusion would have to be, not the Egalitarian one, that everyone deserves an equal (nonzero) amount of something, but rather that *nobody ought to supply anything to anyone*. That's egalitarian, to be sure—but we may be sure that it isn't quite what the theorists we are considering have in mind.

Now, perhaps those theorists would want to back off and opt only for the *weak* version: it is not the case that anyone deserves anything from anyone; i.e., that *nobody is morally required to give anything to anyone*. In that case, however, the indicated conclusion is: so what? I shall then feel free to give Jones an X, should I happen to want to give him an X, or if I see some advantage in doing so, or if I think that Jones' having X would contribute to the value of the universe at large; and in doing so I would violate no moral injunctions of any kind. On this option, in short, we would then simply be right where, I think, we actually are: namely, with the need to construct a reasonable morality on the basis of our selves as the selves we actually are, shorn of arbitrary metaphysical baggage.[9] Which, I think, means settling for the nonviolence principle, with everything else by arrangement only—including what principles of desert for this or that undertaking we will employ.[10]

But there are no further alternatives. We could try backing off from the thesis that got us into this mess in the first place, namely, the transitivity thesis —that if B deserves X by virtue of having property F, and B did not deserve to have F, then B does not deserve X. But if you do that, then the back of this argument is broken. There are innumerable contexts in which the concept of desert is easy to wield: Louise, who makes beautiful sounds and stays on pitch, deserves the scholarship, while Jordan, who sounds like a rasp and is quite at sea about the location of C, does not. The only reason Rawls supplies for not being able to utilize such commonsense judgments is his thought that the desert-bases aren't deserved. If that is beside the point—which, of course, it is— then there's nothing left of his argument anyway.

The idea is also a bad one for egalitarians because proponents of equality are committed to denying that there is any *variable* property, F, such that anyone deserves a certain (equal) amount of good G by virtue of being F, because everyone has an equal amount of F. An example is found in a recent book which appeals to our "equal humanity" as a basis for distributive equality.[11] But humanity isn't a variable property in humans: either you are a human, or you aren't. (And claims that so-and-so's performance was "so human" or that this person is "a real mensch" and the like do not invoke judgments of a type that would lend themselves to claims about equality.) It makes no sense, then, to argue that since we are all "equally" human, it follows that we all deserve a certain equal amount of something that *is* variable, namely X. For example, it does not follow that we even deserve the minimum, whatever it is, necessary to *keep* us human, that is, keep us alive. That can only be inferred if we add the premise that what humans as such deserve from other humans is enough, from the rest of us, to enable them to remain human for some period or other (say, as long as possible). But where did *that* come from?

The other thing we should do is reject the premise that justice consists in giving people what they "deserve," unless we include the qualifier 'morally'. We could make it trivially true that justice consists in giving people what they morally deserve, if in turn we restrict morality to the part covered by justice. But that's surely not all of it, for one thing. And the idea that a great play by a hockey player "morally" deserves a rousing cheer, or the player himself a huge salary, seems to me silly. People with no interest in hockey owe nothing to any hockey players just for their merits as hockey players, however great those merits may be, and however much those players deserve their rewards from their head offices or from hockey enthusiasts. Similarly, the entrepreneur who makes available to us a great new product deserves, in the circumstances, to make a lot of money thereby. This hardly means that people who don't use that product owe him anything. Nor, however, has he done any disservice to those whose incomes are consequently much lower than his.

Fourth Argument: Conditions of Co-operation

This argument employs a more promising premise. Richard Norman is impressed with the idea of justice as co-operation: that the duties of justice are "appropriate to co-operative organizations, because they are principles on which everyone committed to such co-operation can agree."[12] He supposes (his only example) "a group of people coming together in some joint enterprise . . . [e.g.] who have decided to share a house."[13] He proposes that "two things follow from their commitment to co-operation. First, it will be a joint decision, not one imposed by some of them on the others."[14] The group will operate either by consensus, or at least by a procedure that gives everyone an equal vote, though "voting will not be used by a majority of the group to exploit a minority."[15] Second, he supposes, the joint *product* of this group would be divided among the members equally. There are, then, two "egalitarian principles of justice: (a) that power should be shared equally, and (b) that benefits and burdens should be so distributed that everyone benefits equally overall."[16]

Several questions need to be asked, both about these principles themselves and about their derivation. Norman's example is quite specific; generalizing it would require a characterization of co-operation, for starters. Norman supplies a "wide sense": "any interaction or association between a number of people producing a result which they could not have produced individually."[17] However, he later adds that "a co-operative community is contrasted with a coercive form of association."[18] That's well, since a group of slaves working with a cotton gin do co-operate in his "wide sense." It is essential, then, that a co-operative group be a *voluntary* group. And by this I take it, at a minimum, that anyone is free to leave if she doesn't like the way things are going.

Norman's group, however, contains people who, he says, are "fully committed to working together"; so, they don't ask "How can I get the others to organize things in the way that I want?", but rather "How shall *we* organize things?", attributing this way of thinking to Rousseau.[19] But for one thing, it is not true that if A belongs, voluntarily, to co-operating group G, then A necessarily thinks in this "Rousseauian" way about G. He can continue to think solely of his own good. Co-investors in a mutual fund think this way; so does the person seeking salvation for her soul by joining the (*non*-democratic) Roman Catholic Church. Nor is it necessarily true that their output will be divided equally. Norman's argument works *only* if his co-operators enter into their co-operative enterprise on terms of *antecedent* equality. If they don't, then they won't accept merely equal distributions of the benefits. Those who bring more, as well as those who do more, will doubtless get more, and should.

In any case, society is *not* a voluntarily co-operating group—it's just a whole lot of people who happen to bump into each other. Norman might insist that it *ought* to be a voluntarily co-operating group.[20] But he would need a case for that which does not presuppose that our group already is co-operative; and what could that possibly be, if not mutual benefit?

There is a plausible distributive principle for co-operative enterprises, worked out by David Gauthier, who points out that, in the first place, each person entering into co-operation must expect to get at least what she could get in her best alternative (she being, remember, free to leave any time, and motivated to make the best life for herself that she can). Then with regard to the "co-operative surplus," as Gauthier calls it, the rule will be that each gets an equal *proportion* of her maximal marginal claim. That principle does not afford a basis for a general social reinforcement of equality in the distribution of anything in particular.[21]

What about the equality of *political* power which Norman thinks is so basic? Well, suppose that it was brought into effect to prevent the more productive from doing something, even though what they did was advantageous to those who took them up on it? The principle of equal political power would now fall into conflict with the other principle—which, indeed, is what happens in every democratic society, so far as I can see: people use their equal political power to prevent all sorts of efficient reallocations of resources, despite the fact that those reallocations are beneficial to some and costly to none (except, of course, the bureaucrats supervising the reallocations). But plainly those contemplating joining an association and knowing that this could eventuate would have ample reason for thinking twice about doing so. They would want strong constraints *against* such uses of equal political power—constraints *against* egalitarianism.

Norman himself insists that the use of democracy would have to be constrained by a provision against exploitation of the minority by the majority. Of course, if political power is so constrained that no majority could ever overrule anyone, unless explicitly authorized to do so by all concerned, then we would have a society with *no* politics at all. Everything would be done by arrangements among the parties concerned, with due care that third parties not be negatively affected, and that would be that. So, I agree with Norman: political power should indeed be equally distributed. The correct share for each is exactly the same: zero. But again, this isn't quite what he wants. In the end, then, the appeal to co-operation yields no argument at all for general social equality of the interesting, substantive kinds we are asking about.

Fifth Argument: Motivation by Counterfactual

There is a central argument from R. M. Hare[22] purporting to establish the rationality of granting an equality of one of the types we are discussing here:

namely, that we morally must grant equal weight to the equally intense *desires* of all sentient beings. This indeed would not, one would think, yield equality of most of the familiar kinds, since people's desires differ enormously in intensity as well as in kind. Nevertheless, it would be very important if it could be demonstrated that I, for instance, must weight *your* desire for X just the same as *mine* when it comes to making up my mind what to do. So let us see.

Hare invites us to consider the relation between two sorts of propositions, namely propositions of the form

(1) "I now prefer with strength S that if I were in that situation x should happen rather than not"; and
(2) "If I were in that situation, I would prefer with strength S that x should happen rather than not."[23]

He claims that the first of these follows from the second. The intended effect of this maneuver is to get us to agree that, as a rational being, I ought to cater to the desires I would have if I were in C as if they were here and now my own: "it suffices for our argument that I cannot know the extent and quality of others' sufferings, and, in general, motivations and preferences without having equal motivations with regard to what should happen to me, were I in their places, with their motivations and preferences."[24] "In so far as I know what it is like to be the other person, I have already acquired motivations, equal to his, with regard to the hypothetical case in which I should be in his position."[25]

Many philosophers are inclined to take issue with the logical claim that (2) entails (1), evidently supposing that to accept this inference is to open the flood-gates (just as Hare evidently thinks it does).[26] But they needn't worry. Let us suppose that the entailment holds: my realizing that if I were you, I would desire that p, is tantamount to my having the *desire*, here and now, that *if I were you, then p*. But do these desires have any motivational force? Hare supposes they do. But wrongly, as we shall now see.

Consider what a rational agent does with desires concerning *unlikely* situations. Plainly he does not give them as much weight as he does to those of his desires regarding situations he is likely or certain to be in. Here a remark of Bernard Williams seems entirely in point:

> This claim seems hard to accept even if the I of the hypothetical situation is straightforwardly me, as in cases of buying insurance. I indeed know, for instance, that if my house caught fire, I would prefer, with the greatest possible intensity, that my family and I should get out of it. Since I am a moderately rational agent, I take some action now to make sure that we could do that if the situation arose, and that action comes of course from a preference I have now. But there is no sense at all in which that present prudential preference is of the same strength as the preference I would have if the house were actually on fire (driving almost every other consideration from my mind), and it is not rational that it should be.[27]

And if the situations in question are impossible? Then they will have *no* weight —they won't motivate him to do anything at all! The rational agent admits any and all of her desires to her practical decision-making base, indeed; but being concerned to *satisfy* them, she ignores or suppresses those, if any, requiring impossible conditions for their realization. Where the probability of p is zero, the desire to do x in the case that p is so thin that most of us would not bother to call them "desires" at all. My desire not to be shot, were I a rabbit, deters me not at all from pulling the trigger on the one currently before me, for my chances of being that, or any, rabbit are zero. Zero times a very intense desire = zero, rather than the same as the rabbit's! Any desires of this sort, then, are fancies, whims, or capricious hankerings—but not the sort of thing that people need take their time cultivating or dwelling upon. And this, needless to say, is not quite the result that Hare was looking for here.

Sixth Argument: Equal Concern and Respect

The thesis that a society owes its members equality of resources has been advocated by Ronald Dworkin.[28] I conclude by saying a little more than what I have already said in print[29] in response to his proposal. In Dworkin's view, governments have this duty because of a general responsibility to treat their subjects with "equality of concern and respect." This raises three questions: (1) What *constitutes* "concern and respect?" (2) *How much* concern and respect? And finally, (3) *Why*? Why must I *vote for that government*, anyway?

Dworkin's conclusion of a right to equal resources, as stemming from his principle of equal concern and respect, was presumably intended to have the implication that those who supply the resources end up having to hand over a considerable percentage of them to those who would otherwise have little or none. Now we may ask: does this show equal respect for all? There is the sort of question raised by Nozick: what is the equal respect of which we speak if the program issuing it sanctions use of force against some simply in order to shore up the resources of others? Is equal concern even *compatible* with equal respect? Perhaps not. You might reasonably take the view that I would respect you best by keeping my "concern" for you out of it; my equal respect for A might require that I concern myself very little, if at all, for A, who is frankly not interested in my attentions.

In any case, we are normally, and very properly, more concerned about those close to us; basic respect for all will ask us to allow people this inequality of concern, which is, after all, of the very essence of their lives in so many cases. If we ask, how much concern do we owe *everyone*, the most plausible answer is: Very Little, or perhaps None. And Dworkin, I think, agrees with this; he denies that his principle applies to us as individuals.[30] He thinks of the concern and respect of which he makes so much as being essentially political. Indeed, he supports the idea with an "abstract egalitarian thesis," which he states as follows: "From the standpoint of politics, the interests of the members of the community matter, and matter equally."[31] It isn't that *we owe each other* a whole lot of equal concern and respect, but that political institutions do.

Political institutions are human creations. So the question arises why we should *create* an institution incorporating such a principle if we don't think it applies to us, independently of those institutions. In any case, the abstract principle invites the same questions that I raised above: what is it for people's interests to "matter," how much do those interests matter, and why do they matter? For present purposes, indeed, we may simply ask whether those interests can be catered to without violating other interests of individuals— notably, without trampling upon their basic interest in pursuing the good life as they see it. Perhaps we would show still greater concern and respect for all by not turning a powerful government loose on them at all.

Note on Frank

I have not discussed in this chapter the intriguing findings and arguments of the economist Robert Frank.[32] Frank points out that distributions of rewards, such as incomes, in innumerable human associations, tend to be very much narrower in their spread from top to bottom than one would expect on the basis of the marginal products of the persons concerned. This is true not only in associations within the public sector, but also in fully private firms, including business organizations. Why is this? Frank surmises that it is because those in the upper brackets are willing to make sacrifices to keep those at the bottom in the organization—they choose the right pond. This is a good deal for both parties: the topmost, who retain beneath them suitable inferiors to look down upon, and those beneath, who are paid much more than they would get on a fully open market not influenced by such considerations. I don't discuss Frank's argument in the main body of this chapter, however, because it is not and does not purport to be an argument for egalitarianism. A moral duty to share or distribute anything unequally isn't the conclusion indicated by Frank's premises; a distribution differently structured, and in particular much narrower in span from top to bottom, than what one might expect from the principle of marginal contribution, is what we find instead. This shows something about human attitudes, but certainly doesn't demonstrate a case for egalitarianism.

Conclusion

These are not all the arguments there could conceivably be for equality, no doubt; but they are the main ones I have encountered in recent literature. All fail, crucially, to support their conclusions, and I think we should regard this as significant evidence that those conclusions are not to be accepted, especially given the very good reasons for rejecting them that are familiar to everyone. We shouldn't accept any moral hypothesis this strong without compelling reason, and such reason does not, so far as I can presently see, exist. This is not to deny that in many specific contexts there are good reasons for treating people, in certain respects, equally. Whenever there is a good reason for treating everyone in some class in a certain way, then we have a case for a sort of equality of treatment: insofar as people have the characteristic taken to constitute that good reason, then a given person will get whatever degree of treatment possession of that characteristic is supposed to call for. And whenever we owe the members of some class generally the duty of maximizing some benefit for them, then when that benefit is scarce, the distributive question of how to allocate it will arise, and prima facie equality may be indicated. But these conclusions are *very much weaker* than the theorists we have been looking at think to establish. In short: egalitarianism needs, but lacks, good arguments.

Notes

This essay was presented at the Canadian Philosophical Association meetings, Carleton University, Ottawa, June 1993. A skeletal version appears as part of "Liberty, Equality, and Distributive Justice," in *Liberty, Equality, and Plurality*, ed. by Larry May, Christine Sistare, and Jonathan Schonsheck (University Press of Kansas, 1997), 15-37. My thanks to the editors and that press for permission to reprint.

1. 'Opportunity' here is used in the sense in which we have to create and provide opportunities, not in the liberal sense of merely not interfering with the opportunities created by the agent or voluntarily offered him or her by others. Minimum wage laws, for example, interfere with opportunity by preventing people from offering work at lower wages; winter works programs provide it. To be sure, winter works program, supported by taxation do so at public expense, and to that extent they reduce opportunity on the part of the taxpayer.

2. I except from the present discussion the very interesting problem of what to do about and with young children; for present purposes, I will assume that we are dealing only with adults.

3. Kai Nielsen, *Equality and Liberty* (Lanham, Md.: Rowman and Allanheld, 1985), 38. It must be pointed out that Nielsen hopes that other arguments offered by him are persuasive; he does not intend simply to rest his case on intuition.

4. For a longer one, see, e.g., the middle section of my *The Libertarian Idea* (Philadelphia: Temple, 1988; now Broadview Press, 2001), or the introductory chapter in my *Moral Matters*—2nd ed., Broadview, 1999, 1-38.

5. One who has argued thus is G. E. Pence, "Fair Contracts and Beautiful Intuitions," *New Essays on Contract Theory*—*Canadian Journal of Philosophy* Supplementary Volume 3, ed. Kai Nielsen and Roger Shiner (1977), 137-52. Gauthier's *Morals by Agreement* offers another such interpretation (ch. 10, "The Archimedean Point," 233-67).

6. Rawls denies the utilitarian implication, and many have gone along with him on this, to be sure. I suspect that is due to the confusion of interpretation mentioned. See Narveson, "Rawls and Utilitarianism," in H. Miller and W. Williams, eds., *The Limits of Utilitarianism* (Minneapolis: University of Minnesota Press, 1982), 128-43.

7. John Rawls, *A Theory of Justice* (Cambridge, Mass.: Harvard University Press, 1971), 102.

8. For the reason why, see the last section, about Dworkin.

9. This is a somewhat different restatement of my argument in "Equality vs. Liberty: Advantage, Liberty," *Social Philosophy and Policy* 2, no. 1 (Autumn

1984), 33-60. Rawls' construction of choosers operating behind a veil of ignorance is my main target here. Michael Sandel explores various views about how to interpret this construction in *Liberalism and the Limits of Justice* (New York: Cambridge University Press, 1982); Rawls' talk does invite such conundrums, which I believe to be quite avoidable. See my *Critical Notice: Michael Sandel, Liberalism and the Limits of Justice, Canadian Journal of Philosophy* 17, no. 1 (March 1987), 227-34. I should also acknowledge a general debt to Nozick's treatment of Rawls in the second part of ch. 6, *Anarchy, State, and Utopia* (New York: Basic Books, 1974), 120-48.

10. I discuss the subject of desert at length in chapter 9.

11. Carol Gould, *Rethinking Democracy* (New York: Cambridge University Press, 1988).

12. Richard Norman, *Free and Equal* (Oxford, U.K.: Oxford University Press, 1987).

13. Norman, *Free and Equal*, 69.

14. Norman, *Free and Equal*, 69.

15. Norman, *Free and Equal*, 70.

16. Norman, *Free and Equal*, 73.

17. Norman, *Free and Equal*, 74.

18. Norman, *Free and Equal*, 74.

19. Norman, *Free and Equal*, 70.

20. Norman, *Free and Equal*, 90.

21. See David Gauthier, *Morals by Agreement* (Oxford, U.K.: Oxford University Press, 1986), ch. 5, 113-56.

22. R. M. Hare, *Moral Thinking* (Oxford, U.K.: Oxford University Press, 1981).

23. Hare, *Moral Thinking*, 95.

24. Hare, *Moral Thinking*, 96.

25. Hare, *Moral Thinking*, 99.

26. Hare, *Moral Thinking*, 113.

27. Bernard Williams, *Ethics and the Limits of Philosophy* (Cambridge, Mass.: Harvard University Press, 1985), 90.

28. Ronald Dworkin, "What Is Equality?" in two parts, *Philosophy and Public Affairs* 10, nos. 3 and 4. Part 1, "Equality of Welfare," no. 3 (Summer 1981), 185-246; part 2, "Equality of Resources," no. 4 (Autumn 1981), 283-346.

29. Jan Narveson, "On Dworkinian Equality," and "Reply to Dworkin," *Social Philosophy and Policy* 1, no. 1 (Autumn 1983), 1-23, 41-44.

30. Dworkin, "In Defense of Equality," *Social Philosophy and Policy* 1, no. 1 (Autumn 1983), 31.

31. Dworkin, "In Defense of Equality," *Social Philosophy and Policy* 1, no. 1 (Autumn 1983), 24.

32. Robert Frank, *Choosing the Right Pond* (New York: Oxford University Press, 1985).

Chapter 5

Moral Realism, Emotivism, and Natural Law

Thesis?

Jeremy Waldron's "The Irrelevance of Moral Objectivity,"[1] issues a general challenge to all natural-law type theorists in the field. Natural law theory, as Waldron affirms, is normally treated as ontological or metaphysical: the claim that x is right or wrong is somehow reflective of, due to, real facts in the world. Moral realism, in particular, asserts that moral truths are so by asserting the existence of "moral facts," which, somehow, just are "out there," independently of anyone's tendency to note or fail to note or respond to them. But if emotivists are right, then it seems that there isn't anything for moral disputes to be disputes *about*, and therefore no sense to the idea that someone is right, someone else wrong about them. Moral realists think that their view helps on an important aspect of morals—but does it? No, says Waldron. For people can disagree about these alleged "moral facts" and "moral realities" just as much as they disagree in their emotive utterances. What's to prevent it, after all? Thus in the legal context, where emotivism has the judge ultimately enforcing his own attitudes, moral realism has him asserting his own moral *beliefs*—but they are equally uncertifiable. So the supposed improvements offered by realism are illusory.

Waldron's argument is a strong one. So long as we dispute about matters lacking any epistemological criteria for resolving disputes about the subject matter in question, in ways that are acknowledged to be regulative by all concerned, what difference does it make whether our dispute is "emotive" or not? If I believe that the world is F and that therefore I am right about some practical proposal, Q, and you believe that the world is not F but G, and therefore that you are right in affirming the opposite of Q, then in the absence of any method recognized by us both for figuring out whether the world is F or G, we might as well be saying, about Q, "I'm for it!" and "I'm agin' it!" That is not a happy result, one would think, for the would-be realist.

63

Antithesis?

Michael Moore, a stalwart natural law proponent, thinks that Waldron's argument breaks down at an important point.

> Waldron's emotivist theorist cannot even start this argument. For the emotivist, there is no question to ask about whether a court or a legislature is better equipped to describe the rights persons actually possess because, for the emotivist, people don't actually possess any rights.[2]

But as Waldron would be quick to point out, and in fact already has in the very article to which Moore is responding,[3] the claim that people have no rights is normally itself a *moral* claim, being itself the expression of an attitude, and one with which most emotivists we know would disagree. Since the upholder of rights does actually have that attitude, she will obviously take issue with Moore's attribution to her of the view that there are "no rights." Emotivist metaethics certainly doesn't consist in substantively denying all sorts of moral statements that we often do make; instead, it is an attempt to arrive at a good account of our tendency to make such statements.

What's more, as Waldron points out, all realist theories are made uncomfortable by the very thing that is the central strength of emotivism: if right and wrong are just facts out there, why can't we be *indifferent* to them? On the emotivist account, we can't, because the "fact" being asserted by a moral statement expresses an attitude. We can lie, or put on an act, or be hypocrites, publicly purporting to condemn X while going right out and doing it ourselves when we get the chance. But those maneuvers must be seen to be such, for what we purport to do in pronouncing X to be right is approving of it, not just recognizing the existence of some intrinsically ignorable fact. Emotivism explains why such hypocrisy is inconsistent, whereas moral realism seems hard put to do so. For if the wrongness of X is simply one more objective fact about it, wherein lies any inconsistency whatever in the behavior of one who agrees entirely that there is this fact, and then engages in X? At *some* point, the *attitudes* of the realist are going to have to get engaged, and at just that point, his theory has come a cropper.

The Epistemic Challenge

What Waldron's argument turns on, however, is the matter of epistemology, broadly construed. He agrees that science is not a simple matter, and questions of fact can be difficult or even, for long periods at any rate, impossible to resolve. But still, the situation contrasts starkly with that in ethics:

> Still, our conception of reality in science is associated with the whole complex apparatus of methodology, heuristic, observation, and experimentation. We know how to proceed in the face of disagreement. The point is that there is nothing equivalent in morals, nothing that even

begins to connect the idea of there being a fact of the matter with the idea of there being some way to proceed when people disagree.[4]

This is crucial to his argument. Clearly, if there is such a way, then what is apparently at issue between emotivists and realists would make a difference, and that difference would seem to tell strongly against emotivism.

Or would it? In the following pages, I shall argue that Waldron is wrong in his epistemological claim regarding this issue—but then, so are those who call themselves "realists." Waldron utterly ignores the general point of view in these disputes known as contractarianism. He probably thinks that people are free to disagree about its merits just as much as they are about any other historically asserted or logically possible theory in this field; but I shall argue that he is wrong about that, too: whatever else you may say about it, you certainly can't say *that*. But since it is also by no means clear that contractarianism is incompatible with emotivism, as depicted by its proponents or more sympathetic students—though not, of course, by its caricaturists—the argument takes on a very different aspect when we look at it more carefully.

Taking Account of Facts about Attitudes

The charge that realism founders on the connection between objective facts and human behavior looks plausible at first. That plausibility underlies the centuries-long concern about the Naturalistic Fallacy. Examine willful murder, as Hume[5] invites us to: how far did the knife go in, how many units of blood emerged onto the carpet? All this can be understood down to the last detail, and yet the "fact" that murder is wrong won't be found anywhere on the scene.

Next, enter G. E. Moore. But he sees only half the problem. For his proposed solution, metaphysical intuitionism, subverts his own strongest argument. "Do, pray, act so, because the word 'good' is generally used to denote actions of this nature": such, on this view, would be the substance of their teaching"[6]—says Moore, thinking to have scored a *reductio* against the naturalist. But "Do, pray, act so, because the result would have a non-natural quality!" does no better. In general, any ethical theory, any moral theory, any political theory, and any legal theory that severs the subjects of good and bad, right and wrong, or legal and illegal from the interests of the human beings whose conduct moral, political, and legal theory purport to regulate, is utterly pointless. If moral realism is defined by the assertion that moral truths depict facts that are "independent of *anyone's* beliefs about the matters in question,"[7] then moral realism is, in a word, unreal.

In the long history of the subject from Hume onwards, the thesis of a fact-value split has been effective because the *range* of facts implicitly envisaged as "objective" is misleadingly restricted. Consider the phrase 'independent of anyone's beliefs about the matters in question' as definitive of "objective" facts. Well—*anyone's*?

In the case of murder, Hume considered facts about the action of the murderer and the effects on his victim (among many others). But what about the very sentiments in the human breasts of the onlooker and, especially, of the person making that moral judgment, to which in Hume's view we must turn if we are to locate right and wrong? Plainly they are facts, and hardly "irrelevant"—indeed, their essential relevance to the subject is exactly what Hume was emphasizing. My judgment that this was cold-blooded murder is my judgment that this was a killing and that it was wrong. It is a fact about me that I have made that judgment, and that I feel the way I do about this act. Now, the emotivist says, in effect, that these are not two facts, but one: for me to say or judge that it was wrong *is* for me to express my feelings about the crime. This is no doubt an overstatement, but there is a grain of truth to it. Morals is a matter of how we feel about each other; those feelings, we think, can be reasoned about, but feelings they are.

The issue between naturalism and emotivism was this: how much difference is there, really, between a "belief" and an attitude, if the "belief" is, say, "Sally is an angel" or "this thing tastes awful!"? More precisely, all these subjects are closely connected to states of mind that we can perfectly reasonably call "beliefs," and it would be crazy to think that the truths about *these* matters exist "independent of anyone's beliefs." 'I am angry at Bob,' 'I believe that I am angry at Bob', and 'damn Bob, anyway!' certainly aren't independent of each other.

Waldron points to a side issue about attitudes that is of considerable interest in this discussion, and of which we should take due note here. Critics of emotivism have tended to infer from it that moral judgments are a matter of whim. But while some of our emotions are indeed matters of whim, others, and in normal people most others, are not. People's aversion to pain, for example, can hardly be described as "whimsical"; and the love of parents for their children, while unquestionably a feeling, is one that endures, typically for our whole lives after our births. As Waldron says, "(Does anybody think that one's emotional attachment to one's child is best captured by 'Hooray for Sam!'?)"[8] Yet while this is right, and important, the thought that maybe morals is what it is because we have a certain very deep and enduring attitude really doesn't wash either. If we discover that the judge has pronounced Sam guilty because he, the judge, has a firm, long-held, and very deep attitude of disapproval toward people with noses like Sam's, we will have found something that undermines, rather than confirming, his pronouncement.

Emotivism impressed us in the philosophical world by denying that expressions of emotion were "factual." If I say, "Hooray!", they tell us, I am not simply reporting the fact that I am in a certain state of enthusiasm. True. Yet if I *am* in a certain state of enthusiasm at time t, and I report this fact, then if I don't do so with evident enthusiasm, the listener is entitled to have his doubts about just how enthusiastic I really am. If my approval of x implies an attitudinal inclination about doing x, then when I express that approval in words, what I say can be taken seriously only if I am in fact so inclined. The emotivist separation of expression from statement has the problem that in general, if it is true that person A is in emotional state E, then A's expressions of E will also be emotional. Why not? What I say about myself is true only if I am in the state reported or implied. It does not matter much for this purpose whether I say "it hurts!" or "ouch!" Either is believable, or sincere, only if it does hurt.

Now consider the moral realist's claim that, say, killing innocent people is wrong. We shall, to put it mildly, doubt that he means it if we find the theorist in question quite willing to kill his enemies without the slightest compunction. And if the theorist goes on to explain that his theory about the wrongness of killing wasn't meant to use 'wrong' in the "imprecise" way that we normal people use it, we shall infer that he doesn't know what he's talking about. Any theory of ethics having that feature is a nonstarter.

Emotions and Morals

Now to connect this discussion with moral theory, it is essential to do what most recent theorists in this field refuse to do—define our terms. Philosophers now shrink from this on the ground, apparently, that definitions don't really matter or that the things we are talking about aren't mere matters of definition, and other Quinean complaints of that general sort. Such complaints have done much to obscure the field. For there is a remarkably obvious and uncontroversial defining feature in this area, one that everybody agrees about: morals, law, and politics purport to regulate social behavior—not just the behavior of the utterer. That's where Waldron's thesis, and almost every critic's, goes wrong. Your attitude toward fish sticks, or Mozart symphonies, or for that matter anything, doesn't necessarily matter a fig to others, as such. No wonder, then, that it isn't definitive of anything in this field. But your claim that not only you, but I, indeed everybody, ought to do something, does matter.

Why? Because if we agree with you, then we are undertaking a commitment about our own behavior, and one that we might well not want to undertake, or at least not in the conditions you have in mind. If I am of murderous inclination, my coming to accept that murder is wrong is no small matter to me—nor to my potential victims. The subject matter of morals matters because that subject matter is *us* and the sort of lives we can lead if this, that, or the other moral theory is accepted. The idea that in accepting or rejecting such a theory I make no factual commitments of any sort—that there is *no* epistemic question about this acceptance or rejection—is simply incredible.

Practical Reason

To see why, let's have a brief review of the Theory of Practical Reason, to use a highfalutin phrase for something utterly familiar. When we describe someone as engaging in "practical reasoning" or practical deliberation, what are we saying about him?[9] The answer is helpfully provided, in essence, by Aristotle, who supplies this famous example:

> The one opinion is universal, the other is concerned with the particular facts, and here we come to something within the sphere of perception; when a single opinion results from the two, the soul must in one type of case [fn:

"i.e., in scientific reasoning"] affirm the conclusion, while in the case of opinions concerned with production it must immediately act (e.g., if everything sweet ought to be tasted, and this is sweet, in the sense of being one of the particular sweet things, then the man who can act and is not prevented must at the same time actually act accordingly).[10]

So how are we to get prescriptions from descriptions? Practical reasoning divides into three phases: (1) a premise asserting some kind of value, end, purpose, aim, object, or desire—asserting in the sense of entailing that it is *actually held* by the agent in question; (2) a premise that some outcome attainable by the agent would (probably) realize the value, achieve the aim, satisfy the desire in question; and (3) an appropriate action or tendency to act, as issuing from the combination of the two sorts of premises. What makes the "syllogism" in question *practical* is the character of the conclusion aimed at: an act, not another proposition, insofar as those are distinguishable. We may formulate the practical conclusion, the resulting impulse to action, in words—but what makes it practical is its bearing on, and its issuing in, action. The assertion in premise (1) is essential because without it we would have no basis for action. We would not be "doing" anything if there was no description under which our bodily motions amount to the attempt to bring about something or other, even if only a movement of our limbs for no further reason. But we could not be said to have engaged in any reasoning whatever if we did not have a premise of type (2): we must think that what we do will somehow achieve what is set out in (1). And if the action isn't forthcoming, the whole thing has failed to be practical and so is not an exercise of practical reasoning.

We should point out that the action needn't be at the moment. Aristotle says that the soul "must immediately act," but his case was choosing your breakfast cereal, where the time is indeed almost simultaneous with the deliberation—here are the cereal boxes, and you are hungry *now*. But we can deliberate about whether to have a child, or to enter graduate school, or to throw over all we have done and become a mendicant friar. The act is 'appropriate'—but not always (or usually) right now. What immediately issues from deliberation is a resolution to act, a tendency or disposition to do so. This relates to action in whatever way is relevant. If the issue is what to do right now, an action issues; if what to do over the course of a lifetime, then a disposition is what is in question. But dispositions to act are practical.

Practical Reason and Morals

All that is about practical reasoning, but it is not yet about morals, or law or politics, because morals and politics and law are not just any old practical subject—even though the possible subjects affected by them are indeed universal: a law or a moral finding might affect *any* behavior by anybody, conceivably. Nevertheless, if our subject is deliberating about his choice of breakfast cereals, he simply is not *as such* engaged in moral deliberation. To get morals into the picture, his premises must be more complicated: they must contain a rule or directive addressing "everybody" (that is, the relevant set of persons, which needs implicit or explicit specification). All are to do such-and-such or try to achieve so-and-so, and A's practical conclusion concerning his own behavior must be under the aspect of this generalization. No generalization, no morals.[11]

Now, there is what I want other people to do, which is one thing, but then there is what they, from their point of view, have any reason to do, which, perhaps unfortunately, is quite another. And that is why emotivism, carelessly stated, looks absurd as an account of morals. It is absurd to say that what's wrong with murder is that I don't like it. The obvious response is: "So?" The reason it is the obvious response is that if we are out to regulate the behavior of people in general by suggesting a rule for their deliberate action, then the plausibility of our effort is zero if it turns out that all my proposal has going for it is that I want it or would like it. Who, indeed, cares? Until I can explain why others should care, my proposal will be irrelevant to them. And if it isn't directed to them, we're wasting their time.

Which is the trouble with the current discussions of this matter. If you assimilate all practical judgments, of all sorts, to chocolate vs. vanilla, or even Mozart's vs. Beethoven's Quintet for Piano and Winds, then the lack of a uniform decision procedure, or any, will be appropriately seen to be a crucial problem, and the difference between emotivism and a "realist" view as currently conceived will come to nothing. But in morals, and law and politics, other people *are* involved; there our project is to bring about things that matter to those concerned, since if they won't, they won't be done. What "counts" for and against various proposals is considerably constrained in this area, precisely because we aren't just free to blow off any sort of steam we like—indeed, the charge that we are doing only that will also torpedo our proposal, if it can be made to stick. Yet what would make it stick is a suitable investigation—we are not devoid of epistemic constraints here.

This is in no way to repudiate the area of what we may call one-person ethics, or prudence, or the "philosophy of life," as a genuine subject of evaluative concern. It is, however, to set it aside as not what theories of law, politics, and morals are directly about. The fundamental fact about law, politics, and morals is that they are social, and this means that the output of our deliberations affects people with independent interests and ideas, life experiences and situations, and above all with minds of their own. A rule that is to have any chance of being reasonable must appeal to the *reasons* of the different people for whom it is intended. The question 'why should Jones do x?' is the question, "Why, given his interests and situation, *would* Jones do x, if she took account of the relevant facts?" There is no "gap" here of the is-ought type. Practical agents reason, well or badly, and which it is, is in general a subject on which there are tight constraints. The agent can make genuine errors in logic, whose relevance can be made plain to all, including himself. Again, it is possible, and frequent, to make mistakes of fact—practical controversies more often concern our minor premises than our major ones. And even when we get to the major ones, it will be characteristically possible to show to a fellow rational agent that he's overlooked something that, on his own account, must surely matter to him—that he's made a mistake, in fact. The claim that we are "nowhere near" to having a relevant epistemology in this area is just wrong—made, most likely, in a moment of philosophical enthusiasm.

But is the perception that there can be mistakes conducive to "moral realism"? Let's turn to that now.

Moral Realism?

We don't always appeal to reason. Sometimes we will just bash ahead on our own, and may even perhaps succeed despite absence of any sort of principled basis for our relations to others who may be involved. Sometimes—but not often. The rest of the time we had better be prepared to *appeal* to (their) reason(s) as well as our own: to explain to those concerned that what we're doing passes muster in some relevant way. Aunt Hettie is a testy elderly lady and we had better not ruffle her feelings, whereas friend Matilda won't be the least bit upset—such are propositions that can be brought to bear on practical problems; there's no question of just letting off steam here, even though feelings are certainly relevant.

When in general will a proposal be reasonable *for* a certain set of people? The very general answer to this is that it will be so when it serves each person's interest well enough, and at least as well as any other obviously available proposal. That is the general thesis of contractarianism in morals. A great deal has been said about it, of course, and very much more than could possibly be said in this chapter. What we should note here is simply that because the social contract is a function of interaction, of the workings of each person's practical reason as it affects each other's, there is ample room for facts and reasoning here despite each person's major premises being, effectively, emotive. Jones has a major premise to the effect that such-and-such is good; but Smith, sizing up Jones, merely notes that Jones is in favor of such-and-such, and asks how Jones's consequent behavior affects things that matter to Smith. How they do is a matter of fact, given Smith's interests; but of course, one of Jones's options is to try to persuade Smith to some other disposition. It is, then, plainly wrong to say that there are no epistemic constraints. But it is also wrong to classify the view as subjectivist, relativist, nihilist, or indeed, in the sense excoriated by theorists, emotivist.[12]

What, now, should we say about "Realism" in morals? The first thing to say has to be that until we identify one of the reasonably clear ideas about what this might mean, we can plainly get nowhere. Let's start with a characterization offered by Michael Moore:

> Realists believe that the various features of our moral experience—our willingness to reason about moral questions, our expectation that moral judgments are backed by reasons, our sense that moral judgment gives reasons for belief as well as for actions . . . are *best explained by* the realist thesis that a mind-independent moral reality exists . . . make *better sense of* the experience most of us at various times experience.[13] [my emphases]

This locates the issue quite precisely—quite a lot more precisely, perhaps, than Professor Moore supposed. For it locates why he is demonstrably in error. The tendencies he mentions, and which we do indeed want to explain, are *not* best explained by the proposal that all these things concern a "mind-independent moral reality." Quite the contrary, such an "explanation" renders these phenomena unintelligible. The tendencies in question are ubiquitous, and their ubiquity is part of what has to be explained. But you don't do that by invoking something as weird as a "mind-independent moral reality." Morality is definable: rules, principles for the regulation of the general behavior of the group whose morality it purports to be. The reason we would all be interested in and concerned about that is that we all have a lot to gain or lose, in terms of various things that matter to the individual persons in it, and matter a lot. Mind-independent moral realities just aren't on that list: we have no idea what that would be anyway, and even if we did, we wouldn't care. What we *do* care about, and care a lot, is that our kids turn out well, that we have food on the table tomorrow, that we not have to do a lot of boring things, and so on. The only concept of morals that is relevant to everybody is one recognizing the capacity of others to make our lives better or worse than they would otherwise be, and the crucial role of behavior-controls in bringing it about that how people act is as desirable, on balance, as one can reasonably hope—especially that they act on the whole better, in relation to us, rather than worse.

Why is there a problem that morals can help solve? Because in all sorts of human contexts, it will be possible to gain by cheating: by lying, by poisoning someone, by taking the money and running, and any number of other things. What we all know about these tendencies is that they are understandably attractive to those who engage in them. But we also know, perfectly well, that if those tendencies are unchecked, life is going to be worse for us all. We want to be able to depend on those around us to refrain from killing, maiming, injuring, duping, and otherwise ill-using us, and we know that it will not be reasonable for those other people to so refrain unless we do too. That is the inexorable logic of the Social Contract. Morals requires internalized dispositions to do what at a superficial glance may appear to be the worse course, but what on second look is quite otherwise. Behavior that invites cooperation is an investment on the part of the morally good person, and a very good investment it is—in almost all cases, the very best investment, among all the possible life investments, that he or she could make, and one that that person will have reason to be very unhappy with his parents and peers if they have not succeeded, early on, in inducing those dispositions in him.

Politics and law are in the same very general arena. Both purport to enable us to do better in life, in the one case by exercising political power, in the other by developing and enforcing a very complex set of generally applicable but still fairly specific, elaborated rules and rulings, knowable and followable by all. But morals is the basic one, for our informal understandings of and demands on each other's behavior underlie all else.

For our purposes, the interesting claim is that law (in the "legal" sense) depends on morals, and that morals is natural in the sense that it depends on, stems from, the way things are. Both of these claims are extremely interesting and, I think, correct. A legal law not compatible with moral law is a fraud, and bound to cause trouble. Perhaps communities should put up with bad laws for awhile—rebellion may be even worse—but that law can *be* bad and is so because it conflicts with morals is sound.[14]

Natural Law

But what about the natural law theory of morals? This now brings us to the central issue, which is that, after all, science, commonsense and otherwise, is descriptive, while the laws of morals are prescriptive. Stones tell no tales; neither does the Law of Gravity. So how are we to get prescriptions from descriptions? What sense is to be made of the idea of "natural law" in moral theory?

There is a reasonable answer. The idea that morality is "natural" may be pursued along three lines–two false leads, and one true one.

(1) One bad way is by so-called "moral realism", which is pointless and has no explanatory power.

(2) Another, suggested by passages in Aquinas and very popular in its own right, is that conscience is somehow natural—the problem being that it apparently isn't, and in any case consciences seem to differ way too much to do the job. When I say that it "seems to be" false, I mean to allow for the possibility that somehow an idea along this line might be made to work, with enough qualifications, complications, and deepenings. Thus it could be suggested that the sociopaths among us somehow have their normal course of development blocked, perhaps by bad parenting—the exercise of inconsistent discipline and insufficient parental affection, say. There is something attractive about this line of investigation, to be sure. However, it seems to me that it is not capable of giving us what we need, namely a fundamental explanation of morality. Natural conscience theory tells us that we just do react to this and that behavior in certain ways, and uniform ways. But why do we react that way? What's the point? And of course, once we get conscientious disagreement, as we surely do, how can we possibly sort things out? After all, Jones and Smith might, equally spontaneously, come up with quite contrary intuitions about the same sort of act. Not good![15]

(3) Finally, the right way: a proposed morality might be natural in the sense that it is that set of general rules (or other directives, such as models of virtues) for the direction of everyone's behavior that does best for each agent in question against the background of the facts about himself, about other people, his environment, and all interactions among those.

A rational individual will come up with certain general rules, and not with others, for this purpose. He may or may not be preequipped, either genetically or, more likely, by processes of social reinforcement, with various tendencies to approve or disapprove, react favorably or negatively. But a given set of reactions will be the appropriate, relevant ones only if they are called for by his interests, taken in relation to the interests and powers of those around him, in the prevailing circumstances. These interests can easily call for the adoption of rules greatly restricting the area of free operation of a given individual's pursuit of his or her various life plans.

Now, the circumstances, and the interests and powers of others, are indeed "independent realities," as the specification of realism calls for. But they are not "moral realities"—that idea is simply a red herring. The realities that we need to make our peace with are just plain old social and physical facts about what's going on around us: psychological, physical, and environmental. People are built in various familiar ways; they don't last long in the absence of food, water, and ambient temperatures falling within a fairly narrow span; they have desires, interests, imaginations, reasoning capabilities, and a battery of skills and powers, innate and (mostly) otherwise. These are the familiar facts of life, to be supplemented with the possibly quite unfamiliar facts that science reveals to us. Our practical job in life is to do the best we can in light of all this; and our job for morals in particular is to come up with that set of behavior-modifying principles and practices that will enable each of us to do best considering the way the rest of us are.

We can certainly have precepts that relate ourselves to nature, without addressing the presence of other people. Robinson Crusoe can find that some habits modifying his initial tendencies pay dividends, while others lead to disease or broken limbs, or frustration, and so on. Those may be said to be "natural"—but we should expect that the content of such sets of precepts is going to vary considerably from one individual to another. Those prudential values feed into but simply cannot be identified with morality, which is the set of principles to use in dealing with our fellow humans—thinking, practically deliberative, but highly varied humans, at whose hands we have so much to gain or to lose.

We get nowhere by just trying to soldier along with our own feelings, our own desires, our own passions, in the absence of any modification in light of what others can and are likely to do. When we see how others are, what they can and can't do, and more generally what they are like, we will discover that we are headed for trouble if we ignore them. So we back off, provided that others do likewise. We are then in a position to develop genuine moral rules—"precepts," as Hobbes and Aquinas call them, which advise us to do or refrain from this or that thing that we might, given our druthers, have wanted and intended to do. Seeing that these have good results, we solidify these perceptions, and we abandon others. The result is confirmed, "corresponds with" social and natural reality, by realizing our various ends as well as possible.

To claim that morality is simply "conventional" is either just plain wrong or uninteresting. We don't create moral rules out of thin air: they are, instead, rooted in our interests, and those are not just fancies or whims, changeable with the morning linen. There is nothing conventional about the undesirableness of being murdered or having one's limbs broken. There is something conventional involved in lies, fraud, and theft, to be sure. But again, language matters because information matters, and information matters because without it we cannot relate our interests to our actions. That its misuse can cause us to go over the cliff, or catch fire, or die a slow death of poisoning, ought to be sufficient to make the point that conventions are only means to ends, not (in general) ends in themselves. That people sometimes play games, charades, and the like shows that in special areas of life something closer to pure conventions also has its place: but the specialness of these shows us why and that convention just isn't where morals is at.

Coordination phenomena illustrate that conventions in another sense can be very useful indeed. When we all need to act together, but what matters is that it be the same way, among many equally desirable possibilities, then convention in the strong sense is what we need—organized, coordinated action based on the tendency of others somehow to come to do the same thing. But coordination is also a fairly limited aspect of social (and individual) life. Because of the prominence awarded it by one eminent thinker in the Natural Law tradition—John Finnis—let's pause briefly to consider its claims.

Finnis on Coordination

Coordination issues arise when the relevant actors have common interests in acting in a uniform way, but no common interest in which particular way it is: we all want to be at some place at time t, but don't much care which place; but some of us, on our own, would go to p1, some to p2, and so the desired uniform behavior wouldn't take place. And there might be some matters of that kind affecting a whole neighborhood, or village, or even city or country. Devices for resolving those are needed, and a few principles of the broad type we are considering will answer to coordination questions.

The rule of the road—to stick all to the left, or to the right as the case may be—is an excellent and instructive example, as are some other traffic directing devices. We all want to avoid crashes, and building multilane expressways is far beyond the budgets that there is any point in allocating to many roads. If we all keep left, as in the U.K., that's fine; if we all kept right, as in North America or the Continent, that's fine too. However, if some do one and some the other, things go badly for all concerned.

But while coordination is doubtless of great importance, it is hardly the only, or even the standard, case to which moral or legal rules are directed. Much more frequent will be out-and-out conflicts of interest, where Jones really prefers to do X, and Smith really prefers to do Y, but Jones's doing X precludes Smith's doing Y. Now some authors, including most conspicuously Professor Finnis, insist that practical judgments to the effect that one course of action is on the whole better than another must proceed by balancing what are in fact "incommensurable" goods, "the incommensurability of the goods (and reasons) at stake in alternative options available for morally significant choice in any context."[16] This incommensurability is "the absence of any *rationally* identified metric for measuring, or scale for 'weighing' the goods and bads in issue"[17] and is, he thinks, a ubiquitous feature of the human situation:

One meets incommensurability in humble contexts, such as having to choose between going to a lecture, reading a good book, going to the cinema, and talking to friends. One meets it in relation to grand social choices, such as whether to reject or renounce a nuclear deterrent: exploring such a choice will amply illustrate the impotence of all forms of aggregative reasoning towards morally significant choice. "

But here Finnis makes the same mistake I have ascribed to most of my fellow theorists in these matters. Utilitarians, indeed, may claim that social decisions are aggregative ones, but their idea can only work by being mistaken for, or better, subtly reinterpreted as, quite a different one, namely by implying that really the proposed policy will be best *for all.*

'Best for all' is not an open-ended, irresoluble somewhat. Best for all is best from each person's point of view, given the impingement of the others. What each individual person *thinks* is best in his case is, so far as it concerns others interested in securing that person's voluntary cooperation, what *is* best in his case, unless or until he is persuaded otherwise. And the project of finding general principles for adjusting our dealings with each other is so highly constrained by these facts that very few genuinely and substantially differing basic proposals have ever been or ever will be brought forward. Principles requiring all to refrain from molesting their fellows in various quite recognizable ways, for example, are simply inescapable, and they are so because they are rational for everyone, once you take note of the fact that there are other people around and that they too are rational, independent agents who can act in ways that affect your own situation and that matter to you. And they do not require commensuration of the sort Finnis appears to have in mind. Nor do they require mere coordination.

The claim that our personal decisions involve the weighing of incommensurables is not easy to evaluate. Individuals must choose among these things, and in so doing often decide, reasonably, that one option is better than others, or even the best among them. In so choosing, they do operationally "commensurate": they judge that on the whole, this option will be more satisfying, more interesting, etc., than that, upon reflection. Where Finnis is certainly right is that others may decide differently. And he is certainly right if he meant to imply that one person's choices do not rationally determine or lay down a rule for another's. Again, that is why we need morals, which is a set of rules by which all may reasonably be guided. And those rules, as we know from long experience, are mainly of the sort that each may do as he or she pleases, in her own place, her own time, her own sphere; and that sphere is to be determined especially by sheer existential factors. This body is Joan's, not Bob's, and is so because it is inextricably attached to Joan's mind, not Bob's—and for no further reason. (Not, for example, because it is so *nice* that this particular body should be under the control of this particular mind.) This parcel of land is Smith's, not Robinson's, and is so because Smith has been on it for decades whereas Robinson only recently arrived. And so on. Those rules involve no attempt to aggregate individually incommensurable items. Publicly commensurating the incommensurable cannot serve the common good; it can only put down some people in the interests of others. Finnis himself holds that properly framed moral proscriptions can be fully adhered to by all, avoiding conflict among persons—no incommensurabilities need apply. That is rather optimistic, but the basic idea is right—that we can pry people off each other in an orderly fashion, thus making real community, by voluntarily acting individuals, possible.

Morals Generalized

Of much greater importance are the prisoner's dilemma, chicken games, and still more complicated problems, which need to be addressed in society by clear rules, strongly and generally enforced by all. But the desirability of such enforcement is demonstrable—there is nothing problematic, nothing dubious, and certainly nothing epistemologically hopeless about it. If we are going to get anywhere, we must be able to make agreements we can rely on, trust others not to stab us in the back, know which one of these is John's and which is mine, and many more things of that kind.

The fundamental rules of morals are few and specific: do not kill, injure, disable, or inflict physical pain or disease on any others who have observed this same restriction in relation to others; do not lie, cheat, steal from anyone, with the same qualification; and be helpful, to some degree. For a rational, universal morality, the latter injunction must be applied cautiously: we are all different people, we don't necessarily like each other very much, and the temptation to violate the moral restrictions on some people out of the very urge to be helpful to others is frequent and sometimes very strong. Every one of these is grounded on obvious, pervasive properties of human beings all over. There is every reason to say that those basic rules are "natural" if by this we mean that they are obviously called for by reflection on the way things generally are and the way we ourselves are. And perhaps that is what is meant by those who have talked of the "natural law" or even of "moral realism." But it is hardly a matter of spotting metaphysical somewhats beneath the surface of ordinary life.

This is not, of course, a complete treatise. But I hope to have made it clear why and that morality can be said to be "natural" in contrast to the other options concerning its nature that have been popular among some theorists. That morality is simply the say-so of some mighty pooh-bah, that it is just a bunch of games people play, that it is an inscrutable deliverance of some profound but unknowable reality—all such theories are just off the mark. The materials leading to the need for and possibility of morality are pretty plain to see, and they have been seen with considerable clarity and insight by the likes of Hobbes, Hume, and Kant, as well as by ordinary people everywhere. The usefulness of rules of the moral type, which constrain us from doing what, in social circumstances, is going to lead to what anyone can see to be obvious evils, is undeniable, and is certainly due to empirically ascertainable facts about people and their relations to each other and the world around them. That, surely, is all we need to make it reasonable to affirm, in a quite straightforward sense, that morality is natural.

Notes

This paper was not previously published. It was presented at several philosophical colloquia and meetings, including the Ontario Philosophical Society in Guelph, Ontario, 1999, the University of Bristol, U.K., and Corpus Christi College, Oxford, 2000. I thank many discussants at those sessions for helpful suggestions.

1. Robert P. George, ed., *Natural Law Theory* (New York: Oxford University Press, 1992).

2. George, *Natural Law Theory*, 231.

3. George, *Natural Law Theory*, 159.

4. George, *Natural Law Theory*, 173.

5. David Hume, *Treatise of Human Nature* (London: Oxford University Press, 1955), 468-69.

6. G. E. Moore, *Principia Ethica* (Cambridge: Cambridge University Press, 1954), 12.

7. Waldron quotes this (George, *Natural Law Theory*, 159) from Ralph Walker, *The Coherence Theory of Truth* (London: Routledge, 1989), 3.

8. George, *Natural Law Theory*, 169.

9. See Narveson, "Morality: Force and Reason," delivered at the Ontario Philosophical Society meetings, Kingston, Ontario, October 1997.

10. *Nichomachean Ethics*, Bk. 7, ch. 3—1147a 30. Richard McKeon, ed., *Basic Works of Aristotle* (News York: Random House, 1941), 1041.

11. Jonathan Dancy's denial of generalization in morals is paradoxical in the sense of unintelligible, until one finds out that he has other fish to fry. See his *Moral Reasons* (Oxford: Blackwell, 1993), especially 111-16.

12. The classic modern exposition is, of course, David Gauthier's *Morals by Agreement* (New York: Oxford University Press, 1986).

13. George, *Natural Law Theory*, 228.

14. This goes back to Aquinas, of course. Aquinas is ready to contemplate rebellion in extreme cases: "However, tyrannical government is unjust for the same reason: it is directed not to the common good but to the private good of the ruler. To overthrow this kind of government, then, does not have the character of sedition, unless done so badly that society suffers more from the disorder than it did from the tyrant." (*Summa Theologia*, Second Part of Part II, 42. My modification of the translation by William P. Baumgarth and Richard J. Regan, S.J., in *Saint Thomas Aquinas on Law, Morality, and Politics* [Indianapolis, Ind.: Hacket Publishing Company, 1988], 231.)

15. This charge raises issues too large to deal with here, of course. That people around the world have had very differing and contrary consciences, and occasionally, at least apparently, even no conscience at all is, however, common-place.

16. George, *Natural Law Theory*, 145.

17. George, *Natural Law Theory*, 146.

18. George, *Natural Law Theory*, 146.

Chapter 6

Justice as Pure Efficiency

Pareto Efficiency, Justice, and the Free Market—A Pure Efficiency Conception of Justice

Introduction: Paretian Concepts

The term 'efficiency' has, in the twentieth century, acquired a special use in social studies from the work of Vilfredo Pareto. A social state of affairs, according to this definition, is "efficient" or "optimal" if one cannot improve the situation of anyone in it without worsening the situation of someone else. A related (indeed, component) notion is that of Pareto-*improvements*: a social state of affairs, S2, is said to be such an improvement on another such state, S1, if and only if at least one person is better off and no person worse off in S2 than in S1. Such an alteration is said to be "Pareto-superior" to S1. An apparently still weaker concept says merely that no one is worse off, though possibly no one is better off either. Alterations in either sense are said to be Pareto-efficient, and that is the familiar sense of 'efficiency' in which I use the term here.

To lend a sense of verisimilitude to this discussion, let's first look at a good contemporary example of a professional economist's writing on this matter. This author, Nicholas Barr,[1] defines 'economic efficiency' thus:

> Economic efficiency [Barr's note 4: "Referred to synonymously as Pareto efficiency, Pareto Optimality, allocative efficiency, or external efficiency"] is about making the best use of limited resources given people's tastes. It involves the choice of an *output bundle*: $X^* = (X1, X2, \ldots Xn)$ (where Xi is the output of the ith good) with the property that any deviations from these quantities will make at least one person worse off . . . [T]he optimal quantity of any good, *ceteris paribus*, is that at which the value placed by society on the marginal unit equals its marginal social cost.[2]

79

Like the definition supplied in my opening paragraph, the definition just given is formal and indeterminate in certain crucial respects as it stands. Before it can be applied to real states of affairs, we must render the concept determinate, and this requires us to make decisions along two dimensions. In the first place, we must ask which conception of value we are to use. But this being for social application, this question might as well, for all practical purposes, be taken to be the question, *whose* conception, or criteria, of value we are to use, that is, whose judgments of value we are to accept as definitive for the purposes at hand. Professor Barr's characterization commits us to accepting that it is people's "tastes" that are in question. This is something many philosophers would quarrel with, but as we shall see below, I propose, essentially, to accept that view. And in the second place, we need a conception of that kind such that it is both logically and realistically possible for the criterion to be both applied and met: possible, that is, for it ever to be true, and capable of being known to be true, that someone *is* "better off" and no one else "worse off" in some situation or configuration, as compared with some other, for the purpose of assessing efficiency. Barr's discussion, referring us to "the value placed by society" on the marginal unit, clearly requires that we attach some definite significance to that idea if we are to apply the notion of efficiency. This question will occupy us shortly below.

Meanwhile, however, the reader may certainly wonder why these are said to be concepts of "efficiency" at all—it seems a bit of a stretch. But there is, I think, a good reason, and the idea is important. Efficiency in the most general ordinary sense has to do with the ratio between input and output in the context of production of some kind: the more output for a given input, the more efficient. It is, of course, most at home in mechanical devices, especially those powered by fuels such as gasoline, where the input is a continuously measurable quantity, such as gallons, while the output can be understood, at least in one major respect, as miles traveled, thus making it easy to get neat figures such as X miles per gallon. Other contexts are more difficult. A more efficient worker will be one who accomplishes more than the comparison worker of the desired task in the same time, perhaps, or with the same amount of effort. We can measure time easily enough, but effort is more difficult. Of course, as soon as there are multiple tasks and multiple products, it becomes very difficult indeed to quantify output. Here the role of money comes to the fore, along with market exchange. In other contexts, we carry on somehow, and eventually we might talk about aesthetic efficiency, legal efficiency, and so on. What enables us to do so in each case is some idea of inputs and outputs.

Thus Barr, in developing the notion of efficiency, proposes as the first of three conditions of social economic efficiency that of *Productive efficiency*:

> *Productive efficiency* means that activity should be organized to obtain the maximum output from given inputs. . . . It is about building a hospital to a specified standard with as few workers as possible standing around waiting for something to do.[3]

But it could and presumably would also be about minimizing costs of production, which could, for example, include using vehicles that got more miles to the gallon. And where does it end? If a manager could improve the performance of his firm still further by working 13-hour days instead of 12-hour days, is it, then, "inefficient" if he foregoes this opportunity? Suppose he foregoes it at the request of his wife and family—does that count? One thing, at any rate, is clear: maximizing this kind of efficiency lies beyond the reach of economics. The best one can do with this aspect of the notion is to specify that each aspect of a productive process be "as efficient as possible" given the technology, management know-how, and so forth, of the day. And that is more like a wished-for ideal than a condition an economist, or anybody, could stipulate. Moreover, it is, as I shall point out below, dramatically contrary to a reasonable construal of the Pareto idea.

In any case, it is, as Barr notes, allocative efficiency that is more nearly what we would be after in talk of optimal social welfare. His next condition is *Efficiency in product mix*—"the optimal combination of goods should be produced given existing production technology and consumer tastes." And what is that? As economists will do, Barr here says that "production is . . . at the specific point . . . at which the ratio of marginal production costs . . . is equal to the ratio of marginal rates of substitution in consumption."[4] And how do we know when that point is reached? Here we go to the free activity of individual consumers, normally. And that is going to lead to a problem.

Efficiency in consumption, Barr's third condition, "means that consumers should allocate their income in a way which maximizes their utility, given their incomes and the prices of the goods they buy—in formal terms, the marginal rate of substitution must be equal for all individuals."[5] Barr draws the familiar Edgeworth box[6] for illustration, but we need not resort to such things for present purposes. We need only point out that there is a horrendous problem involved in applying the notion of utility-maximization for this purpose. Is it a fact about Sheila that she has "maximized her utility" when she buys Brand X rather than Brand Y, or for that matter when she decides not to bother with skincream at all, or when she decides to throw over her previous way of life and go into a convent? Will a professional economist be able to criticize her, in the latter event, for failing to do her duty and maximize her economic utility? The short answer is, of course, no. And the longer answer will be in the negative too, as I shall argue below. The concept that the rates of substitution for all consumers is equal is not verifiable.

Social Efficiency?

But what about societies—"social systems" as they might, rather misleadingly, be called? What shall we say are "inputs" and what "outputs"? That question is closely enmeshed with fundamental questions of political philosophy, of course. However, on any view of the matter, there needs to be some sort of concept of social good, enabling us to say that some societies or some social institutions in a given society are better than others. And a notion of good will also give us some handle on an idea of costs. The costs may be described as "evils," or less moralistically, simply referred to as costs. In any case, they are what you want to avoid, and if you can't avoid them, then at least minimize them.

What makes the Pareto notions of special interest is that we are here focusing on the social aspect of society, on society *as such*. Each individual will have goals, purposes, ideals, and will have a corresponding notion of costs. But when we get to interindividual relations, notoriously, the situation gets tricky. For one individual does not share another individual's consciousness, his purposes, his capabilities, or his values. At best, he has a similar goal or purpose. But in general, a cost for Smith is not *necessarily* a cost for Jones.

The idea of Pareto efficiency can now be explained as follows. *Social* efficiency—the doing-well of society as such—is a matter of how much interpersonal cost there is: to what extent do our actions impede each other, thus lowering our achievement of our various goals? In an inefficient engine, some fuel is expended merely in heating the engine rather than driving pistons; this impedes the operation of the engine somewhat, for it requires using still more energy to counteract the unfortunate effects of the heating. Fuel burnt with those effects is "wasted"; all we want out of it is forward motion of the vehicle. Somewhat similarly, a more Pareto-efficient society will be one in which people do better in relation to their expenditures of time and effort on trying to achieve whatever they want to achieve, insofar as they are less or not at all impeded in their pursuits *by* the impositions of others. And the presence of some who impede others creates a need for still others to spend time and energy combating the initial set of impeders. This idea fits somewhat, then, with ordinary efficiency. It is not an ideal fit, because a society could be perfectly efficient in the Pareto sense, and no machine, or indeed any individual human, can be that. (Let's agree that in both cases it's enormously unlikely anyway!) Moreover, it will surely be insisted, by many philosophers and probably by ordinary people, that it would be nice to have a corresponding notion about *benefit* to each other, and not just our non-harm to each other. We'll say more about that below.

Why?

Why think Paretian? On the face of it, it sounds a plausible principle. That is because it looks to be a social application of a rudimentary principle of practical rationality. If we can have our choice between two bundles of goods, {G1} and {G1, G2}, the second bundle containing everything that the first one does plus one more good thing, and no bad side effects, then surely it is rational to choose the second? But that would be misleading. The status of the Pareto Principle is actually a matter of considerable controversy and some misunderstanding. What is being advocated in these pages is by no means a truism, by no means self-evident, and certainly widely denied. Even so, I think it a powerful principle. To see why it is hardly self-evident, let us distinguish three quite distinguishable ideas about it.

(1) Those who think the principle self-evident are perhaps thinking that it is a straight dominance principle: if x differs from y in being in some way better and in no way worse, then x is better than y. Whether we should say that that is self-evident or not I don't know. But whatever there is to be said for this plausible view, it is by no means enough to support the Pareto Principle, as will be made clear in the next two points.

(2) As it stands, the principle means that we are not to do evil to person A in order to benefit person B. There is nothing logically self-evident about this, and it is not morally so either: to accept it, no matter how you understand the evaluations involved, is to go quite far out on a moral limb. It appears to deny, in particular, that the way to deal with A and B is to do what is "on the whole best" for them, just like that. For it says that if just one of the two, say A, is, on the whole, worsened *at all* by our doing x, then we are not justified in doing x even if it benefits B a great deal. As such, it behaves rather like what Nozick calls "side constraints."[7] That is clearly controversial. Moreover, no one who has ever advocated the principle, I think, means it to be totally sharp-edged. If we can benefit B a lot by imposing a quite trivial cost on A, most of us will do it. But then, in doing so, most of us rely on A's being a benevolent enough person that he would be happy to pay the trifling cost if asked. And in the face of utter disasters, we will all suspend side constraints to greater or lesser extent. That is an important fact. Still, we have not yet arrived at the fully liberal version of the Pareto Principle. As it stands, the principle still depends for its application on our idea of what is good, what bad, for individuals.

(3) The liberal version of the principle says that we are to act in such a way that all affected persons *see themselves* to be no worse off, on the whole, in consequence of our having acted that way than in the status quo ante. Moreover, this is intended to imply that if consent, or approval, by A, of something involving A only, is forthcoming, then that is sufficient for presuming better-offness in the intended sense.

The requirement that at least one person's situation be actually bettered, and not merely not worsened, may be treated in either of two ways. We may eliminate it, and insist merely that no one be worse off; or we may simply *assume* that an agent always acts for something he takes to be good, so that the weaker requirement is superfluous. An agent, we assume, normally tries to achieve what she regards as a benefit, either for herself or for someone that *she* chooses to benefit in some way. She tries, in other words, to bring about what she takes to be some desirable effect on something or someone else; and so the requirement is pleonastically met by all rationally acting agents. At least, it is met in intention: we may fail to achieve the hoped-for benefit, but it is what we were *trying* to do, anyway. For this reason, then, we need not concern ourselves about a distinction between the weaker and the weakest formulation of Pareto improvements: everyone is always doing what betters things, in that agent's view, relative to some other available choices.

Liberalism

In making decisions of the kind I have pointed to the need for, we inevitably engage in normative social philosophizing. It is too often said that talking in Paretian terms purports to be "value-free." But in any context of policy decisions, that is obviously false, to the point that this brief denial really ought to be unnecessary. Though the Pareto criterion is used rather often for explanatory purposes in the social sciences, and there is still a perfectly reasonable, and much more than residual, reluctance to accept values as entering into explanation, my purpose here is not primarily explanatory, except in the sense of clarifying and explicating certain options in normative theory: I propose to identify a type, or rather, a portion, of normative theory and spell out some insufficiently recognized implications of what is widely, though not universally, agreed to be an important and plausible idea. And I propose to be quite forthright and self-conscious in making the value-judgments in question.

The two decisions I shall adopt for these purposes are, I think, in the first case straightforward and in the second case crucial to this or any coherent project that accepts the first. First, then, I shall identify the relevant assessments of better- or worse-offness with the *preferences of the individuals in question*— what Professor Barr counts as "tastes." Alice will be declared to be "better off" for purposes of this theory if she prefers her new situation to the previous one, that is, if *she* believes that she is better off in it, whatever anyone else may think. And secondly, we will exclude *negatively tuistic* evaluations from our database of acceptable evaluations. This is a morally loaded move, not an arbitrary stipulation. It says that if a given policy, p, would benefit someone, A, by worsening the situation of some other person B who was the object of A's hatred or resentment, say, then society may not account it a point in favor of policy P that it satisfies a desire of that kind. Suppose, for example, that Jane is envious of Alice, so that when Alice is better off in some non-other-regarding respect, Jane is ipso facto, in her own view, worse off: if we accept malevolent values as determinative of what is acceptable and unacceptable for social purposes, liberalism is impossible. For in that case, the occurrence of just *one* individual with a certain profile of values could make it impossible for *any* Pareto improvements to occur. Justice requires that we unhook individuals from each other, except in respects in which both such individuals agree to be hooked.

Suppose, for instance, that one individual is a "radical" egalitarian: she judges herself to be worse off if *anybody* is better off than *anybody else*; thus, only if that person's situation is improved simultaneously and equally with the situation of everyone else in the society will she withhold her disapproval. If there are any persons with such profiles, that effectively renders it impossible for any Pareto-efficient changes to take place, since the condition is for all practical purposes impossible to meet. Liberalism, however, will account an improvement in one person's situation in any respect that is *independent* of anyone else's as genuinely an improvement for the purposes at hand, without regard to the attitudes of others toward that improvement as such. Of course people may attach great weight to their nonindependent desires, including ones that are negatively tuistic. But the point of Paretianism is that such desires are problematic in social contexts. As they stand, they can hardly provide a basis for the common good which, I hold—along with Aquinas and so many others—must be the basis of all reasonable law.

Between them, these two interpretations are, I believe, definitive of the normative outlook known as *Liberalism*.¹ Injustice consists in worsening the situation of one or more others in respects in which those persons' levels of well-being or utility are intrinsically independent of those levels in others, or in which any other who are objects of the desires in question are not averse to being so; on the other hand, any situation that does not worsen anyone else's is acceptable on the score of justice, and in that sense, it is just. (As Hobbes says: "whatsoever is not unjust, is *just*."⁹)

What this means, specifically, is that we do not as such have any positive duties toward others in general—that is, we may not properly be forced to make positive contributions to the welfare of others. For to do so is to worsen one person's situation in order to improve another's.

Justice

Recall that our inquiry here is into justice in particular, and not into any and all normative assessments. What, then, is justice? The theory of justice is the theory of what society may do "in the way of compulsion and control," as Mill puts it.¹⁰ To say that a person's action is unjust is to say that those actions are of a kind that society should, or at least may, coercively intervene to prevent or punish, that is, to override the individual's own preferences in that instance. That someone else doesn't like the new situation so far as the situations of others are concerned has, on the liberal view of the matter, no bearing on its justice or injustice. For to allow that is to put control over the lives of the others into the hands of the person with those attitudes. We may say that such persons have an "attitude problem"—their attitudes are malevolent, or at least unvirtuous. But on the liberal view, we may not take them into account in making our assessments regarding Pareto improvements or the reverse.

Since we are here doing only what has come to be called "ideal theory," we ignore the necessary refinements for dealing with the need to rectify or prevent injustices, which would no doubt be very difficult in principle. However, there is no reason to expect a fundamental divergence from our results from that quarter. If force of law is used only to prevent or to rectify the previous use of force against innocents, then one can reasonably say that it does not really impose on person and property at all.

Rawls on the Supposed Inadequacy of Efficiency

It has become commonplace over the years to say, along with Rawls, that efficiency is inadequate to "account for" justice. Those who say this tell us, as if by way of mere reminder, that there are many different but equally efficient configurations or distributions of, say, a society's assets which nevertheless differ, they claim, in the justness of those configurations. Consider this passage from Rawls:

> It is not difficult to see, however, that . . . this principle . . . is an inadequate conception of justice. There are presumably many arrangements of an institution and of the basic structure which are optimal in this sense. There may also be many arrangements which are optimal with respect to existing conditions, and so many reforms which would be improvements by this principle. If so, how is one to choose between them? It is impossible to say that the many optimal arrangements are equally just, and the choice between them a matter of indifference, since efficient institutions allow extremely wide variations in the pattern of distributive shares.[11]

To be sure, it is not quite clear just which principle Rawls is there referring to. And, too, he talks of "Optimality," which is related to but not identical to efficiency as discussed. An arrangement is optimal if no rearrangement *can* be made which is better for someone and worse for no one. Thus the situation in which one person is dictator to all others is the sort of situation that those who speak this way claim to be Pareto optimal. And if we assume that the dictator does not, in dictating, make others worse off, and that satisfying the dictator's desire to dictate counts in favor of others doing what he dictates, then what he says is certainly right.

Rawls' claim, then, is that the theory of justice in the contemporary sense of the term is underdetermined by Pareto Optimality. But it is not entirely clear how Rawls wishes to advance this criticism. Is he claiming that no conception of justice confining itself to Pareto efficiency can be coherently expounded? Or is he asserting a certain view about justice, as against other, rival views, claiming in effect that Paretian views are inadequate or implausible? There is some reason to think that it is the latter rather than the former. Be that as it may, theorists often hope to advance a view of that kind by showing that the alternative views really don't make sense, don't add up. My concern in this chapter is to rebut that criticism, by arguing not only that a pure efficiency view does in fact make sense, but also that the claim of nonuniqueness which seems to be being advanced by Rawls in that passage is false.

His view, if interpreted in this latter way, involves, I shall argue, either a misunderstanding or a partisan view, or more likely both.

I shall now argue that there is exactly one view determined by taking Paretianism seriously, if advanced under the aegis of liberalism—that all alternatives require its violation in some respect or other. Whether the view in question is also the right view is another matter, of course; though I am inclined to believe it is, that is not argued for here. For present purposes, it is enough to show that the claim that the pure efficiency view of justice is an "inadequate" view cannot be held on purely conceptual grounds, though it is surely reasonable to suggest that violations of Paretian efficiency are indeed prima facie objectionable, as Rawls himself implies.

It will be noted that Rawls talks of different specific "arrangements," selection among which is not a matter of indifference. The reason, he says, for doubting that different optimal arrangements are equally just is that "efficient institutions allow extremely wide variations in the pattern of distributive shares." Is this a good reason? It is, of course, *if* justice does indeed allow such wide variations. But what if it does not?

This question, in turn, leads to a related one: what does Rawls mean by an 'arrangement'? From context, one gathers that he means by it, simply, a configuration or pattern of the components, which in this case is human actions, *no matter how it is brought about*. If that is what he means, though, then there is indeed reason to deny the implicit claim that the justness of a distribution is incompatible with "wide variations" in the resulting pattern of holdings of valued things.

To see this, consider a very rudimentary example, one that Rawls himself is unlikely to disavow, and that very few readers would disavow unless they are already in the grip of a quite remarkable theory. Suppose you have some good, say a certain amount of purchasing power. Any amount will do—we needn't be talking about distributions of huge sums here: $5 will do nicely. Now, suppose you elect to spend this money on some good, perhaps a box of breakfast cereal of a certain sort which you happen to like, or a movie at a modestly priced theater. In doing this, you leave one firm with 100 percent of your $5 and all the other people in the world with 0 percent of it. This is surely an unequal distribution pattern—all for one, none for the rest. It is not clear how one could get a more unequal distributional pattern, if patterns are in question. But it is very commonly, indeed ubiquitously, instanced. Whenever you spend money, you confer all of it on some very tiny selection of firms or persons, and none of it on the rest—repeating the distributionally unequal pattern. Nicholas Barr observes,

> Natural-rights libertarians have little to say about the optimal distribution of goods. If the initial distribution is at c, then any point on the contract curve between d and e is optimal, provided that c accords with Nozick's idea of justice in holdings, and that the movement from c to the contract curve is the result of individual utility maximization through voluntary trading in a competitive market system. More generally, depending on the initial distribution, *any* point on the contract curve can be an optimum.[12]

Well, does that result indeed depend on embracing some philosophical system, such as Nozick's? Is it really true that whether a set of voluntary trades resulting in some particular, assume unequal, distribution is just is a matter of serious dispute? If Paretianism is assumed, then the answer would seem to be that if it is, that can only be because there was something wrong with that "initial distribution." Only if there was something wrong with it could there be said to be something wrong with a voluntary trade by persons in that system subsequent to the establishment of the initial distribution. We will return to that below.

Meanwhile, let's also appreciate that one could take any number of noneconomic examples to the same effect. If you choose a spouse, you devote a great deal of love and affection to that one person, and none (of that particular kind) to anybody else, instead of distributing it equally among some very large number of potential recipients. Yet Rawls, I am sure, is not going to object to that, either.

Why not, though? His answer in the case of the monetary example could perhaps be that you have, after all, already paid your dues to society, your taxes, and so what is left is really yours, to spend as you like. This answer won't do. If justice is allergic to inequitable patterns of distribution, then there is no inherent reason why it should tolerate them in the posttax distribution as compared with a pretax one. Here was a good, capable of being distributed; here was a distribution that showed no regard whatsoever for patterns. But if justice is a matter of patterns, then why wasn't it unjust, too? Most readers, along with this author and Rawls himself, will undoubtedly think that the example looks ridiculous—since, after all, it is ridiculous. But if it is, that establishes the point in question here: justice is perfectly compatible with wildly varying patterns of distribution of desirable things. No injustice is necessarily effected *merely* by distributing goods one way rather than another. Something has been left out.

This returns us to the question about 'arrangements'. According to Rawls, "different arrangements" are compatible with Pareto Optimality. In the sense of 'arrangements' in which what results from distributing any good in one way rather than another counts as an "arrangement," this is perfectly true. When you go forth with your $5, or your $N, there are innumerable possible recipients, *none* of whom will be made worse off by your employment of that money. You could, of course, use it to buy poison which you then put into someone's coffee, or bullets which you then put into his brain. But if so, it won't be the purchase, as such, that effects this violation of Pareto: it will, instead, be the use to which you put it. Obviously there are uses to which you can put resources that will cause violations of Pareto's principle. (That, as Hobbes pointed out, is true right down to the minimal level of one's bodily resources alone.) But we are here talking of distributions of *goods*, not of *evils*; voluntarily inflicted evils are, of course, violations of the principle, which, after all, says no more than that we are not to do evil to some person or persons in order to bring about what we suppose to be good for some other or others. Your expenditure of money, however, is, so far as it goes, the transfer of a *good*, from yourself to someone else—not of an evil.

Someone might, of course, regard worldly goods as inherently evil, to be sure. You presumably couldn't give such a person anything without violating Pareto, it seems. However, Pareto's idea is irrelevant to such attitudes. Paretianism, coupled with the liberalism that economists and most of us assume here, takes the (self-regarding) interests of the persons in question as definitive of what is good or evil in their cases.

Otherwise, as we have already seen, a set of "arrangements" in which someone or some very few persons get all of a good, and everyone else gets none, is perfectly compatible with justice, on the face of it.

Suppose, on the other hand, that a social philosopher of the familiar Rawlsian stripe comes along and, noting his disaffection with some pattern of distribution resulting from your employment of a set of goods, proposes to "rearrange" them. His way of rearranging them, though, is to deprive you, forcibly, of some or all of those goods and effect some distribution of them different from the one you would have brought about had you had your choice in the matter. If so, you are now worse off. Someone has been made better off, indeed—but at the expense of making you worse off. Paretian efficiency has therefore been violated.

But Rawls, remember, was arguing that Pareto was "inadequate"—not that it was *wrong*. He talked, that is, as though a theory of justice needs to choose among the *alternative* distributions *compatible* with Pareto Optimality. Yet how is he going to defend a redistributive theory on such a basis? For after all, it is perfectly possible to hold that any of the patterns consistent with voluntary action by all concerned would be just. "Don't rearrange things by force" is the relevant principle; innumerable specific patterns are compatible with it. The reach of the Pareto Principle is very deep indeed.

This forces us to reconsider the subject of "arrangements" or "distributions," insofar as they are examples of possible theories of justice. Characterizations of justice in Rawls are quite vague, to be sure. They are said to have to do with the "basic structure" of society, for instance.[13] But this vagueness is also misleading. When does a society have one "structure," in the relevant respect, as opposed to another? Rawls would presumably not count a society almost all of whose members are chess addicts and never have picnics as having a different "structure" from a society in which no one at all plays chess but lots of people have picnics. For that matter, he also would not count one society as having a different structure from another if the first was considerably populated by coal miners while in the other, not a single coal miner was to be found. What, then, is the kind of difference that the term "structure" is meant to convey? In fact, it is quite easy to answer. Certain of its legal and political features are what we must point to.

But which? The answer here is also not so difficult, although not quite so quick. A law *imposes* an order. All sorts of different orders are compatible with a given law, but if there is a law, the order you have as compared with the one you would otherwise have differs precisely in that the one you have as a result of the law has been, or at least may be, enforced, imposed. (Of course, the libertarian theorist will claim that what is "imposed" is really only restoring or helping to ensure a natural order—what it imposes is, we might say, non-imposition. True: but the apprehended thief has nevertheless been forced to restore the order he upsets.) More generally, in fact, justice is the rightful use of force, or more precisely, the principles concerning how it may rightfully be used.

If this is so, then let us go back to the choice among Pareto-optimal "arrangements." As we have seen, these have nothing, as such, to do with justice. Justice comes on the scene when we do or should intervene, using force to bring about one distribution rather than another. Had a given distribution come about with no use of force at all, nor any threat of it, it would not differ in respects relevant to justice, though it might differ greatly in its patterns. The difference between one society and another, the first of which had many coal miners and the second none, or the first many chess players, the second devoid of them, is a great difference of pattern, but no difference at all in respect of justice. The social system, in the sense of the system determined by a given set of laws, could perfectly well be identical as between them. And the same could be true of two societies, one of which displayed great variation in income, the other substantial equality in that respect.

Consider, then, the claim that Pareto efficiency is "inadequate" as a guide to justice. We now see that this claim is misleading. It is possible to have a system of justice in which Paretian efficiency is enforced.

The Uniqueness of Paretianism

Now we can make the point I am concerned with here. I wish to suggest that there is, actually, one and only one system of justice that is efficient in the relevant sense, one and only one system that is concerned exclusively with efficiency in the Pareto sense. That is a system in which force and fraud are the only things which force may legitimately be used to rectify. As for any other variations in "patterns," so long as they result exclusively from the voluntary interaction of people, no forcible intervention would be permitted to alter them. They would all be reckoned to be just. This is, of course, a pure market system —indeed, that is the definition of a pure market system. (Some deny this; I will discuss their claim below.)

Rawls' claim, then, that Pareto efficiency is "inadequate" is misleading in a quite fundamental way. For he makes it sound as though the further principles of justice that he proposes are meant to affect the choice of distributions compatible with Pareto efficiency. But that isn't so. By definition, any other principle of justice would require people to do some things they do not want to do, or refrain from things that they want to do, *other* than actions taken to counter or correct Pareto suboptimal actions. For examples, the introduction of principles requiring equal opportunity, the forced social provision of minimal levels of income, and many other things, all advocated by Rawls and by most contemporary social philosophers, are incompatible with pure Paretianism. They are *not* selections of patterns of distribution, each compatible with that criterion, some of which are more just than others.

In other words: if we accept Paretianism as a principle of justice, and allow that we worsen people's situations when we force them to do what they do not want to do, unless what they want to do would in turn worsen the situation of others, then it crowds out all contrary views of that subject.

I am inclined, myself, to support the system in which Paretianism is enforced, in the sense discussed, as against all of its rivals. But my point here is not to do that; it is, rather, to correct a misconception inherent in, and very extensively fostered by, Rawls' extremely influential writings. It is disarming to begin in the way he does, for if indeed all of the various systems he discusses were literally compatible with Paretian efficiency, what would there be to complain of? None of the different systems would have been exacted at the expense of anybody! Of course this is false, and indeed quite spectacularly so.

The different systems are systems in which some are made better off by making others worse off (the favored subjects being those "better off"). In only one of them is that not so, in principle: the pure free market system.

The "Ideal Market"

Mention of free markets makes it useful to add a brief note about one further possible misconception. There is a famous thesis to the effect that only a society with a so-called "ideal market" would result in a "Pareto Optimal equilibrium state." Barr, for example, adopts this view.[14] Such so-called ideal markets have many extraordinary features: each participant has perfect information and is perfectly rational, transaction costs are nonexistent, and there is "perfect competition" in the sense that nobody is in a position to unilaterally affect the price of anything.[15] While this proof is of some intrinsic interest, it has little to do with the argument of this chapter, which in no way depends on the exotic conditions mentioned. One might suggest, indeed, that it has little to do with reality. But certainly the just society is not efficient in the sense that no conceivable trades could be made that would improve someone's condition without making someone else's worse. It is, rather, optimal in the sense that the only transactions that are *permitted*, apart from rectifications, are transactions that *impose no costs*, so far as any relevant persons can see, on other parties. How many and which of the infinity of mutually advantageous exchanges that could conceivably be made are actually made is irrelevant to justice. All permitted trades are presumptively Pareto superior to the status quo, because they are made between parties who, upon consulting their respective preferences and information bases, voluntarily engage in those trades. Liberalism takes that to be sufficient for supposing that those agents regard the aimed-at situation as superior to the one they are already in. But any proposed "improvement" brought about by force would automatically violate this condition. It is in that sense that the free market society is the only one that is efficient, despite not being at all likely to be in the optimal state meant by the theorem. For any other principles proposed as principles of justice would require imposing conditions on unwilling parties, thus effecting whatever improvements they make to some people, if any, at the expense of others.

If you abandon liberalism, of course, you can help yourself to plenty of forcible interventions to make social improvements. You might even claim not to have abandoned it, insisting that when you take 25 percent of Smith's income to pay for Medicare for all, you're getting Smith what he really wanted all along, however much he protests. But Rawls and others who have accepted his claims about this matter claim to be liberals. Perhaps some who are persuaded by the foregoing sketch will also regard it as a reductio of that outlook. We'll have to leave that for another day.

Professor Barr holds that the imperfections of real-world markets are such as to justify a variety of interventions; and I presume that he speaks for a majority of his colleagues in the economics area these days. It is interesting to see how he proceeds on this matter. Take, as an example, rectification regarding imperfect information.

> Simple theory assumes that consumers know what goods are available and their nature. The assumption can fail because economic agents may have imperfect knowledge of the *quality* of goods or their *prices*. The literature thus has two strands. The first analyses the effects of imperfect information about quality: consumers might be badly informed (e.g., about the quality of an automobile), so might producers (e.g. about the riskiness of an applicant for insurance). The resulting literature investigates such topics as 'lemons' and signaling. The second strand, imperfect information about prices, embraces search theory and reservations wages.[16]

Such failures, he supposes, could justify regulation in some cases, e.g., where "information is seriously deficient."[17] Note that the question of *how* the consumer, or the producer, came to be in this condition of deficiency is not really addressed. But surely that makes all the difference. You can be poorly informed, for example, because I have deliberately misinformed you. In that case, I do you a hurt, and have violated the Pareto restriction, attempting to improve my own situation at the expense of you. But suppose your sorry state of information is in no way my fault, or perhaps anyone's. What right, then, would regulators have to intervene and "correct" the situation? Indeed, how did they know? And how can the criteria of efficiency Barr introduces enable us to judge that the situation in which some people buy products for bad reasons that are not the fault of others label the resulting situations as "inefficient"? On the contrary, it would seem that if I force you to do something that you think to be best, even though I think you are in error in so thinking it, I have done something wrong. Or if not, it might be a case in which your ignorance is indeed your fault, and I in friendship or sympathy act to correct it. But this correction can hardly be at the expense of third parties in no way involved.

It is hard to see, in short, that the consumer is entitled to be in some or other state of information. He is entitled not to be in a state of misinformation caused by the deliberate actions of those with whom he interacts, indeed. But what else?

Barr does agree that sometimes misinformation can be corrected by market action. An example, I presume, is that people are willing to pay a good deal for education, with a view to improving their general state of information. But it is, to put it contentiously, not obvious that we all owe each other an education. To be sure, typical academics today *do* find that obvious. After all, we make our livings providing this great good. Not surprisingly, we are happy to have someone else pay for our efforts, thus improving the market for education. But this is no longer a free market we're talking about. Free markets, one would think, are based on freedom.

Real-World Paretianism

Two possibly important notes should be added here. The abstract idea that we are not to harm Peter in order to help Paul requires, as we saw, two things to complete it. First, we need to know what constitutes help and harm. Our answer to this is that it helps Peter to put him in a state that he prefers, and harms Paul to put him in a state that he prefers not to be in. But going ahead and applying the Pareto Principle on those interpretations is subject to the important restriction that the people in question be relevantly innocent, that is, that they themselves are not in turn guilty of the sort of aggression that the Pareto Principle prohibits. Those who are thus guilty are not automatically eligible for the treatment that the innocent are. On the other hand, being guilty of some small violation does not automatically deprive one of all the protections of morality. It means that you owe somebody something and need to pay it; it does not mean that you owe everybody everything.

Moreover, as we have seen, when we help Paula by doing something that in her view benefits another individual, say Johnny, we assume that Johnny is not unhappy with the arrangement. In the case where Johnny is a small child, applying this criterion may not be easy. It is, indeed, difficult enough that we will leave it for another essay.[18]

Restricting ourselves, then, to the somewhat easier case of ordinary people, we should note that, in the first place, the individuals we come in contact with are usually, if not always, "innocent" in the sense important for these purposes. In general, Paretianism applies to the *relevantly* innocent. However, I am claiming that we may in turn use Paretianism to identify who is innocent and who isn't. The criterion is intended to be reiterative in its application. The innocent are those who in turn have not worsened the situations of any other innocents. And where would this end? Presumably with those who have harmed no one at all. But why not?

Tricky questions can indeed be raised about this. Suppose that C. Milquetoast has been perfectly civil and nonviolent toward certain evil persons whom he might have been able to help bring to justice. I don't have a simple answer to that, but prima facie am doubtful that we in general have a duty to bring miscreants to justice, though it is certainly something we should do if we can.

Second, and more important: presumably it is by no means unusual to inflict very tiny harms on other people. These may be of either of two sorts. First, we may raise by some vanishingly small amount the probability that someone will experience a certain sort of worsening. Or, second, there may have been actual worsenings, but again, vanishingly small.

In both cases, there is a fairly straightforward criterion to bring into play. It has two points. First: if the person allegedly harmed simply pronounces that he doesn't care, that's that. And second, if his situation is *unnoticeably* worsened, in that sense that our supposed victim can't even distinguish between the new situation and the old one, then we shall again ignore this particular supposed objection to our action. We deal, then, only with significant harms as seen by the persons affected.

There is a very interesting question, indeed, concerning applications at the other end of the spectrum—catastrophe, lifeboat situations, and the like. Hume argued that the restrictions of justice are simply inapplicable when no matter what we do, the greater number will perish.[19] I do not attempt to deal with this problem here, but only to recognize that it is one, and that it is in real need of a solid theory. But certainly, for starters, Paretianism runs out of scope for application when it is impossible to avoid harm for all or most of those concerned, in particular for the agent himself. Generally speaking, morals is framed by the potential for all to benefit, or at least not be harmed, in the course of social interaction. That is the basis of the Social Contract approach to morals, one or another version of which is ubiquitous among those who think morality to have any foundation at all.

Meanwhile, there is also concern in many quarters with the supposed injustice in initial conditions, from reasons other than violence. In a sense this raises a large issue. But how large? It is not plausible to think that my fellow men are to blame for my lack of athletic ability or pianistic prowess, either of which I would be glad to be possessed of. It is not believable that I am allowed to invade my neighbor in order to rectify these disparities, even if that were possible. And it is obvious that innumerable differences among people will result from differing climates, available resources, and the particular interests, abilities, and proclivities of those around them. But in this there is no evident complaint of justice, which is all we are investigating here.

Conclusion

I conclude that it is a mistake to suppose that there are lots of different views about justice that are *equally efficient*. There are not. So far as I can see, there is only one such view, though the range of specific types of social states compatible with this view, e.g., specific "patterns" of enjoyments or holdings of goods, could vary wildly. All of them, however, would exemplify one and only one theory of justice, one principle of justice. That principle, in effect, is that justice consists in using force only on behalf of, literally, the common good, liberally conceived in the Paretian spirit. Rival theories may differ in all sorts of interesting ways, but all of them, rather than exemplifying the Pareto Principle plus further features, violate it in some area or other. Justice as pure efficiency is, I would contend, not only a viable conception, but an eminently plausible one; in any case, however, it is, contrary to the almost universally shared view of Rawls, a unique one.

Notes

Versions of this paper have been read at the University of Georgia in 1996, among others, and at the Canadian section of the International Society for Social and Legal

Philosophy (IVR); it was to be published in the now-defunct *On-line Journal of Social Philosophy*, and has benefited from many comments, most of them adverse. I am indebted to Alistair MacLeod for much, in my view, erroneous but instructive criticism, and to Jan Lester, whose criticisms were not erroneous at all.

1. Nicholas Barr, *The Economics of the Welfare State* (Stanford, Calif.: Stanford University Press, 3rd ed., 1998).

2. Barr, *The Economics of the Welfare State*, 70.

3. Barr, *The Economics of the Welfare State*, 70.

4. Barr, *The Economics of the Welfare State*, 71.

5. Barr, *The Economics of the Welfare State*, 71.

6. Barr, *The Economics of the Welfare State*, 72.

7. Robert Nozick, *Anarchy, State, and Utopia* (New York: Basic Books, 1974), 28-30 and ensuing discussion.

8. The criterion is further discussed and argued for in Jan Narveson, "Liberal/Conservative: The Real Controversy," *Journal of Value Inquiry*, 2000, special issue on Liberalism, guest-edited by Jan Narveson and Susan Dimock, vol. 34 nos. 2-3, 167-88.

9. Thomas Hobbes, *Leviathan* (New York: E. P. Dutton, Everyman Library, 1950), 119.

10. John Stuart Mill, *On Liberty*, chapter 1. Also *Utilitarianism*, chapter 5.

11. Rawls, "Distributive Justice," in Peter Laslett and W. G. Runciman, eds., *Philosophy, Politics, and Society*, Third Series (Oxford: Blackwell, 1967), 65.

12. Barr, *The Economics of the Welfare State*, 74.

13. John Rawls, *A Theory of Justice* (Cambridge, Mass.: Harvard University Press, 1971), 7.

14. Barr, *The Economics of the Welfare State*, 78.

15. I employ the description of the argument in Allen Buchanan's well-known *Ethics, Efficiency, and the Market* (Totowa, N. J.: Rowman & Allanheld, 1985), 14-15.

16. Barr, *The Economics of the Welfare State*, 82.

17. Barr, *The Economics of the Welfare State*, 82.

18. See chapter 15 for an attempt in this direction.

19. David Hume, *An Inquiry Concerning the Principles of Morals* (Indianapolis, Ind.: Bobbs–Merrill, Library of Liberal Arts, 1957), 17.

Chapter 7

Toward a Liberal Theory of Ideology
A Quasi-Marxian Exploration

Introduction

One of the more suggestive but not very satisfactory components of Marx's general theory was his theory of "ideology." As he expounded it, the ethics, religion, and philosophy (and maybe some other things) of a given "era" were part of a sort of conspiracy by the "ruling class," which he and his followers called the "bourgeoisie" and identified with the "capitalist" class. The effect of this conspiracy was to keep the masses in their place, construed somehow (but with an implication that the place was, economically speaking, in the basement). Along with this went an implication that ideas used for this purpose were either false or perhaps meaningless: being part of the ideology undermined their status as independent claims to truth. This seems to have led to Marx's tendency to reject ethics and ethical theory as meaningless shams, among many other things. Perhaps most unsatisfactorily of all, the scope of his claims was such that Marxism itself looks rather like one of the things that ought to have been undermined by his theory—surely an embarrassment for any self-respecting social theory.

The theory sketched here is not put forward essentially as an interpretation of Marx, though it does owe much of its inspiration to him; hence the subtitle 'quasi-Marxian'. I shall, at any rate, be concerned to indicate where the proposal is and where it is not in agreement with (what I understand to be) Marx's version. It is, however, put forward in its own right. Nothing that follows should be understood to depend conceptually on anything's having been said or thought by Marx.[1] (Since, as will be evident, I have no use whatever for Marx's economics or for his socialist political theories, the latter caveat is no doubt a welcome one to some.)

My discussion here has two aims. First, there's the aim of generalizing the idea: making it independent of Marx's critique of capitalism, for instance, and in principle applicable to any number of specific social configurations and economic arrangements. The second aim is to develop a modest but, I think, reasonably important application to our own day. There is ample room to suggest that a substantial ideological component affects, as a quite inherent side effect of our political system, the politics (and thus the economics) of the liberal-democratic societies that are dominant in our era.

Ideology Theory: Basics

The essential components of an ideology theory would seem to be these:

(1) a "ruling class" (which we'll call 'R', for 'rulers'), distinguishable from a "ruled class" (call it 'C', for 'citizens');
(2) a recognizable set of interests of R, *in conflict with* the interests of C, such that R is interested in its being the case that C has certain beliefs, which
(3) are either false or meaningless, and which
(4) R has the power to induce C to believe

The central claim of the theory, then, is that in the political systems in question, rulers have an interest in, and the power to, bamboozle their subjects on matters of importance to the latter; and that, because they do, there is an appreciable probability that the ideas and information disseminated by those rulers on those matters is both open to suspicion and likely to be worthwhile suspecting on the part of the citizens.

Let me caution that it need *not* be part of the burden of an ideology theory that the phenomena captured by it be all-pervasive or irresistible or even merely overwhelmingly dominant. In particular, for instance, nothing requires that *all* of the ideas which R would like C to believe are either false or contrary to C's interest. What is required, for an ideological theory to have scope, is only that *some* have those characteristics. Moreover, it is not flatly assumed that ideology is unjustifiable, overall. Perhaps in the grand perspective of all things, Plato's Big Lie might be benign after all? What is argued is only that the phenomenon of ideology in the sense we hope to capture here is important, and affords, so far as it goes, a prima facie significant kind of criticism of the operation of any polity in which it is a significant factor.

Ideology and Conflicting Interests

The leading idea of any such theory is that ideas are *used as tools on behalf of the interests of the rulers*, and are so used in such a way as to go *against* the interests of the ruled—or at least against their interests as *they* conceive them. Of course, when we say that "ideas" are so used, what we mean is that their *propagation* is so used. The reason why A tries to induce B to believe p is not because A *believes* p (or not only because of that; we must allow for the—rather important, I think—cases in which A also believes it), nor that it would be *useful to B* to believe p, but rather that it is *useful to A to have B believe p*.

Thus, to make the theory plausible, we need to show that the rulers whose behavior we are considering do have such an interest and that it is indeed contrary to the interest of subjects. The latter is essential, for, to remind the reader, it is by no means maintained that *all* ideas circulated by rulers involve this kind of conflict. If that were so, things would be far worse than they are; indeed, it is reasonable to suggest that they would be downright impossible. (How do you run a post office if *everything* the clerk tells the user is false or meaningless?) It's just that where the interests of R and C are at one with respect to p, and p is true, then we don't have "ideology"—we simply have education, enlightenment. One could use the term 'ideology' more broadly, shorn of any requirement that the ideas in question be either false or contrary to the interest of the subordinate class, but that seems rather pointless.

In saying such things, we imply that there is, in the cases in question, a conflict of interests between R and C. In attributing such conflicts, we have to be cautious about the sort of interests we have in mind, and the sort of evaluations being made.

First, we had better distinguish between a person's interests, generically, and her self-interest. We may be, and usually are, interested in all sorts of things, typically including various other people. When I am (positively) interested in you, then the fact that you do well, in the respects I am interested in, serves my interest as well, so far as it goes. It does so by serving this particular other-regarding interest in you.

There is an extremely important, and very difficult, question whether my interest in you must at some point or other be based on your self-interest. The thesis that they must would say, for instance, that if I claim to be positively interested in your welfare, then what I am interested in is that certain states of you obtain which are in your interest *tout court*: e.g., my interest that you be well fed is an interest in a state of you that can be defined independently of my interest. Of course, there could also be negative other-regarding interests: if I am a sadist, I might be interested in you starving or being tortured to death.

There can also be other-regarding interests whose objects are definable independently of the interests of the persons in whom the interest is taken. I could be interested in your having a characteristic about which you simply don't care, one way or the other.

Is it conceivable that I should have an interest in an irreducible relation between me and you, not definable independently of either of us? Some have talked as though some important personal relations, such as love, are like that. But—luckily—we need not pursue this further here. What matters is that for purposes of making good claims about ideology, we must specify interests of the ruled in a plausible, recognizable way, such that the range of ideas focused on in the claim works contrary to their interest, in the sense that acceptance of them will motivate action (or inaction) on the part of C that is suboptimal from C's point of view.

Conflict of interest between one person and another obtains when what is in one person's interest is such that if it is realized, then the resulting state of affairs would be against the other's interest. In a straight zero-sum game, A's gain is B's loss, and vice versa. In most of the situations of interest to political philosophy, though, this special case isn't what's going on. Rather, it's that if x is done, then the result is worse for B and better for A, whether or not A actually *identified* his interest with B's loss. One not only hopes, but really supposes, and plausibly so, that modern "rulers" in the liberal democracies do not positively hate their subjects.

Establishing Motivation

This requirement that the theory be able to characterize the opposed interests in a plausible way is an important one, for one of the main responsibilities of a theory of ideology is to provide plausible accounts of the motivations of the actors. Absent this, its purported explanation of the phenomena it considers would not be plausible. In Marx's case, for example, his theory is unable to explain why capitalists are supposed to be "interested" in doing down the proletariat, for that is an aim that makes no inherent sense in capitalist society, especially at the "class" level.

This point is an extremely important one, and it is worth pausing for a moment to consider the failure of Marx's own theory in regard to the motivational question. Marx supposed that there was a general conflict of interests between owners and workers, a conflict leading the owners to "exploit" their workers by paying extremely low wages. Now, owners do, of course, have an interest in minimizing their costs, which include wage costs. True. But on the other hand, they also have an interest in selling to as many people as possible. The latter interest requires that those people, the potential buyers, have enough income to buy the goods that the owners wish to sell to them. So which of these two interests is the greater? It doesn't take a lot of insight to see that the latter interest is the greater, by far. If nobody can afford his goods, the capitalist will go out of business no matter how badly he treats his own employees. But if everybody can afford them, on the other hand, then he will be able to afford to pay his employees well and still make money. A Marxian could counter this by claiming that capitalists were too shortsighted to see this, but if one takes that line, it goes counter to his insight that we should be talking about *objective* interests. Besides, Marx's standard case (rightly) was that of *mass* production. A mass producer who doesn't see the wisdom of having millions of ready buyers able to buy has to have quite a lot less savvy than even Marx's theory can feel comfortable positing.

To put the point more generally, while we might try crediting people with a general interest in dominating others for its own sake, this does not seem a plausible view. What makes a lot more sense is when the domination in question results in some *independently specifiable* gain for the dominator. Thus the holdup man may or may not want simply to dominate his victim, but if he's picked the right victim, then the result of his domination will be a considerable increase in the dominator's disposable income. And that does make sense. Almost no matter who the dominator is, it is understandable that he would be interested in increasing his disposable income—the class of potential dominators is very large indeed if that is the motive.

Note that there is no intention, and no need, to elevate pecuniary motivation to the status of an a priori truth. What makes money a plausible object of desire is precisely that it is *not* intrinsically valuable. Rather, it's that it can be exchanged for almost anything, and so its *ex*trinsic value is extraordinarily widely based. It was reasonable for Rawls to have classified income and wealth as "primary goods." For him to so classify domination, on the other hand, would have been, I think, bizarre. Such a hypothesis would have to be defended by resorting to spelunking in the murky caverns of depth psychology—not a move to be commended to the aspiring social theorist.

Liberalism and Ideology

Another point of importance here is: who evaluates people's situations? Clearly it is possible for A to think that x is good for B when B does not himself think so. This could happen either because A believes some matter of fact that B doesn't, though such that if B did know it, then B would come to agree that x was good for B; *or* it could be due to a "basic value disagreement" between them. Suppose—to take an example dear to this writer's heart—they disagree about the intrinsic value of Mozart's quartets. A might think that B was better off listening to Mozart even if B manifestly hated it. But while he could think this, he has, according to the liberal, no business acting on that view. In the liberal view, the view about A's interests that is definitive for social purposes is A's. Each person is taken to be the ultimate authority on his or her own interests. (This must be distinguished from the claim that a person is the "best" judge of them. There is room for reasonable, as well as unreasonable, disagreement about that.)

I shall, then, be advancing a Liberal theory of Ideology. The theory is that some people, the "ruling class(es)," tend to propagate half-truths and untruths to the ruled, who in consequence act so as to solidify, expand, and/or enhance the private interests of the rulers. Like all ideology theories, this one is Thrasymachean, except that Thrasymachus insisted on *defining* justice as 'the interest of the stronger party'—or anyway, so Plato's translators have him saying. That's silly. Of course what is in the interest of the stronger party isn't by definition just; but the rulers do it anyway. This is not necessarily because they are evil but merely because they are *people*, and thus can be expected to have a natural bias toward their own interests. In the theory being expounded here, the rulers propound as "just" various ideas and bits of information which are in fact either vacuous or false, and do so because it serves their interests as private persons that those things be generally believed, and are able to get people to accept them precisely because they are the rulers. From the liberal point of view, of course, this is a *misuse* of the ruling power. But conservatives could hold otherwise, in various ways that we needn't detail here.

An interesting further question is whether we should suppose that people have an interest in the truth, so that anyone attempting to induce someone to believe a false proposition is thereby working against that person's interest. If we were Plato, of course, we could just posit this. But—being liberals—we aren't, so we need an explanation. However, for present purposes we need only point out that what the class being bamboozled is being bamboozled *about* are things in which they have (other) interests. An intrinsic interest in knowing, for its own sake, while not altogether implausible, is fortunately unnecessary.

Ideology and Truth

We may distinguish, for present purposes, three theses concerning the relation between ideological employment and truth that have been associated—rightly or wrongly—with Marxian ideology theory.

(a) Crucial to ideology theory is the general idea that the use of ideas for "ideological" purposes *calls their truth into question*. (Or it may call their meaningfulness into question, but this has the same effect: if a sentence is meaningless, it is certainly not true, whatever else it may be.)

Two further theses are, I shall argue, not crucial to it, but certainly have been major components of the Marxian versions. They are

(b) that certain *kinds* of ideas—notably moral ones—are *inherently* "ideological."

If we combine these two theses, and add that the prevailing ideas of an epoch are put into circulation by its rulers, then we arrive at the conclusion

(c) that all normative ideas, or more precisely all normative moral and political ideas, are *inherently false or meaningless*, owing to their being hopelessly "ideological."

My proposal is that we should basically accept the first thesis, but, with some qualifications, reject the second and third.

The fact that A's conveying of thesis p to person B has that motivation on A's part is certainly *ground for suspicion* about p. But it is not in general a *sufficient* ground, and certainly not a logically sufficient ground for convicting p either of falsehood or meaninglessness. If A's *only* reason for saying something to B is to put B at some sort of disadvantage, then A is saying this for reasons having nothing to do with its truth. In this case, then, *his saying it* provides *no presumptive evidence for* its truth. This is important, for ordinarily when someone sincerely says something, this *does* provide such evidence. Obviously, it does not provide conclusive evidence. No one is infallible, people make mistakes, and so on. Nevertheless, people normally talk about things they know something about, and speak with a view to conveying information. And very often, the fact that some person whose motives we have no particular reason to suspect has said something is just about the only "evidence" the hearer has to go by. In the cases we have in mind, however—cases which include the ideological ones with which this chapter is concerned—the truth is *randomly* correlated with the spontaneous statements of the "ideologist," that is, with those whose motive in speaking is, say, private profit or the promotion of some cause rather than the supplying of information.

Even so, though, that simply doesn't prove that p is false, nor that it is meaningless. It isn't just that the monkeys-typing-the-encyclopedia scenario is logically possible, but rather the fact that our inherent conceptual organization as information managers is strongly enough oriented toward truth that it's just not plausible to suppose that everything said by an ideologist would be false. All it shows is that there is genuine reason for suspicion. Given the character of our information source, p might very well be false, and we therefore should not rely on A as a source of information about the matters p is concerned with. Independent verification is recommended.

In fact, as we all know, there are many kinds of statements that can lead us astray. There is, for example, the famous trilogy of "lies, damn lies, and statistics." In fact, the typical case in the modern world for the sort of theory I am sketching lies in the third class. More broadly, this is the class of "half-truths"[2]—characteristically much harder to detect than outright lies. Not always, to be sure—it depends a lot on how gullible B is and how much perceived ideological authority B is inclined to attribute to A. Hume's simple fisher folk or unlearned peasantry will swallow stories of miracles that a more discerning individual would attach no credence to. Outright lies had better be addressed to those in a state of, as we may put it, epistemological destitution, or to those who are strongly motivated to believe *some* story and ill equipped to check it out in the time available.

As to "damn lies," we might, for the sake of elegance, classify outright mystification in this category—things like religion, or Hegel's theory of the State. Being propositions that make no evident sense, though somehow imparting an uncomfortable feeling of profundity, they are obviously useful to the aspiring tyrant. What's more, because of their obscurity, they intrigue the scholarly and the philosophical so much that it is likely to be quite some time before the basically empty character of these propositions emerges in the light of rational reflection.

Statistics, however, are another matter. They are the new growth industry for the aspiring tyrant. The field is rife with possibilities. Ordinary people, even those with considerable education, don't understand statistical reasoning very well, and are easily led to believe what is false when it is presented in statistical guise. This remains true even—indeed, especially—when the "statistical" claims are expressed in nonstatistical terms. For example, high on the current list are claims to the effect that substance x is "dangerous," or "can lead to" such familiar evils as cancer, heart disease, etc. Indeed, the terms 'true' and 'false' become misleading in the area of statistics, where half-truths and tenth-truths are the problem, rather than simple "untruths." The false proposition that the Ruler, in the mouth of his agent, the civil servant, wishes to leave the public persuaded of is "this stuff is so dangerous as to constitute a good reason why *we* [that is, the government] should do something about it." Meanwhile, the true propositions that are all he has going for him are such as "this stuff leads to death in about one case in two hundred million." If the cost of the proposed program to deal with the stuff is the equivalent of, say, ten deaths in two hundred million, then it is not in the interest of the public to support that program. But who in the government is going to appreciate that point, subversive as it is to the (well-paid) involvement of the rulers?

A significant part of what I take to be the Marxian program that I do accept here, then, is the assumption that the particular purveyor of p need not be "lying" at all. He may be quite sincere in supposing that p is true. Yet the fact that he says it, given his interests, is nevertheless ground for caution. As the Marxists put it, this is a matter of the objective situations of the persons concerned, and not necessarily or primarily a matter of their phenomenological surface motivations. The fact that your believing p would be in the purveyor's interests is an important point about the situation, and gives you reason to check it out. When the scientist dutifully reports that there is a serious problem about x, the public looks at his scientific credentials—but not the fact that he only gets his research grants if it seems that there *is* a "serious problem about x." Needless to say, the number of "serious problems" will skyrocket under these conditions. Yet the scientist may be perfectly serious when he says this.

A part of the Marxian program that I emphatically reject, however—if indeed it was his, which may be debatable—is the one that got him into most trouble: namely, the idea that the occurrence of an idea, especially a normative one, in these contexts ipso facto demonstrates either its falsity, or its lack of independent meaning. This is just a mistake, so far as I can see, but it is a very serious one. *Some* of the ideas that occur in these contexts may well be meaningless, in some suitably garden-variety sense of 'meaning': religious views, for instance.[3] But I assume that typical normative assertions, for instance, are meaningful, and their use in such contexts has no tendency to show that they are not. To repeat: their occurrence in these contexts is merely ground for suspicion, not for outright rejection.

However, the suspicions thus engendered can only be checked out if there are independent grounds for doing so. If, somehow, the very meaning of what you say is *totally* contingent on the context in which it is functioning as "ideology," then perhaps that renders it meaningless; at least it would seem to render it hopelessly untestable. An example might be afforded by the case of preachers and mystics who get people under their power by sheer force of animal magnetism, personal charisma. The person who succumbs to this power might find it impossible to explain what 'p' is supposed to mean, and might insist that either you take it or you leave it, for no independent check is possible, even in principle. ("I *know* that my Redeemer liveth—but don't ask me how I know it!") Cases like this are important for normative political purposes. Their main importance is that an enormous number of people do have beliefs of just that kind, and those beliefs characteristically imply (so he thinks) positions on public policy matters.

I take it to be clear that no public policy should ever be founded on claims having only that status; yet democracy, especially, provides no check whatever on the voter whose vote is subservient to his religious interests. This last is itself a normative claim, of course. But then, that normative claims in general, and political and moral ones in particular, are (that is, can perfectly well be) meaningful and susceptible to rational analysis and discussion independently of their occurrence in any ideological contexts, is a general presumption of my proposal, in marked contrast (at least apparently) to the Marxian version of the theory.

In fact, I suggest, there is no more reason why ethical or other normative propositions should figure as values of p for ideological purposes than factual, scientific, or even logical or mathematical ones. This is by no means to marry ethical naturalism. Let's grant that at the bottom of any practical argument we must have some normative premises. But those are just the *major* premises; the minor ones, as Aristotle noted, are and indeed must be of a factual character—for if they weren't, we would lose all connection of the basic value premises with outputs to action. Now, what matters to A, our aspiring ideologue, is only that A can bamboozle B to the *practical* effects he wants by means of making the particular claim in question, and nowadays ideas with a "scientific" ring to them are at the top of the list. Marx's own shabby economic analysis, indeed, is, in my view, a fine example of the point. Its claim to be "scientific," in contrast to the hopelessly "utopian" theories of its rivals, was a major source of its remarkable power to bamboozle, and they were in fact used to induce millions of people to act in ways that were deleterious to those people, though highly conducive to putting and keeping the rulers, such as the members of the Communist Party, in power.

Specifying the "Rulers"

This brings us naturally to the question of just who is the "ruling class." Here we need to make a distinction between what we may call the *general* and the *special* forms of our theory. The general form doesn't have to be specific about this. It merely says that the ruling class are whatever people rule in the sense of 'rule' that the theory has to explicate. Having the power to make people do things, and in particular, enough to make it possible for them to get away with bamboozling people, in particular the power to make it quite probable that when they tell people that p, those people will believe p, is of course essential if the thing is going to work. Just which people the latter are is a matter for detailed empirical investigation. But the formal power to "make people do things," as I put it, is of course possessed by the government, by definition. Whoever is in the ruling class, one may suppose, the rulers themselves should be.

Special instances of the theory would then need to supply specific values for the ruling-class variable, claiming that this or that group is in fact the ruling class, whether or not it looks like it. Marx, notoriously, proposed that the "capitalist" class was the culprit, by virtue of "owning the means of production." The special theory briefly sketched in this chapter rejects Marx's analysis as not only completely off base but as being itself ideological, in the sense relevant to theories of this type. Specifically, his version is (1) independently wrong—its arguments fallacious, its assumptions either false or meaningless, and quite unsubstantiated by the evidence, if evidence is allowed to be considered; and yet (2) very much in the interests of a certain class, to wit the class of leaders and bureaucrats that would be spawned in systems formed under the influence of advocates of his views—and (3) against the interests of the people—specifically of the class of producers, broadly speaking, by which I mean to include, as Plato does, *both* the "proletariat" *and* the "bourgeoisie," even though ostensibly out to serve those interests. Whether Marxists deceived themselves is, on the construal developed here, beside the point; that they deceived those over whom they came to have so much power is central.

Liberalism—A Primer

It is fashionable these days to suppose that any and all questions, including what used to be regarded as sheer questions of definition, are deep and dark, requiring elaborate, evasive, and "iffy" answers. Certainly liberalism is among the topics so treated. Nevertheless, I shall offer a thumbnail sketch of the basics of liberalism, in its most general sense.

There are two defining features. First, and obviously necessary but, definitely not sufficient, is that the *sole* purpose of government is to *serve the governed*. Government exists *exclusively* for their good. Members of government are, of course, people, and inter alia, good government, if that is possible, would serve their interests along with everyone else's. However, that is not to be from the claim of Thrasymachus, that the smart ruler exploits his position to the maximal advantage of himself.

It must, of course, since it is concerned with *all* the people, aim to promote the *common* good, not the good of any particular class.

The other condition is the differentia of liberalism. According to it, the good of the people is determined *by* those people themselves. More precisely, the good of any individual, for political purposes, is a matter on which that individual himself is the *ultimate authority*. Others may advise, suggest, attempt to persuade, even reprimand, but when it comes to identifying A's good, we must in the end consult A, not anyone else.

Condition (1) may now be beefed up. The ruler needn't be Thrasymachus. He may instead be Plato, in some version or other—equipped with a political outlook, a view of human nature, ideas of what life is all about. But Liberalism says that when he acts as a ruler, these views of his have *no special status*. He may not formulate government policy on their basis any more than on the basis of his own pecuniary interests. The government, must, as the modern theorists put it, be neutral as between any and all such views or theories: it may attend only to the interests of all individuals.

In so saying, the liberal is, of course, putting forth a theory himself. But it is not a theory of the same type—not a theory of how each person should live his life, but rather, a theory about how an agency entrusted with power over all ought to use that power, on the basis entirely of the interests of those they exercise it over in their ongoing relations with each other.

Naturally there is disagreement about just how the liberal idea is to be realized. But what has been said is sufficient for identifying what is objectionable about Ideology in government.

Liberal Ideology Theory

In the version put forth here, then, the culprit class consists, in the first instance, literally of the rulers, that is, the holders of political power. Of course, in a democracy, these rulers are supposed to be, and in a quite straightforward sense really are, "the people," though at any given time, of course, only the majority or perhaps even more likely, a plurality. However, the set concerned may be reasonably expected to be rather larger than that. Just as Marx had to distinguish between the capitalists and their lackeys and dupes in order to accommodate the apparently extensive number of persons not officially capitalists whom yet he would have wanted to count as serving their interests, so we make here a similar distinction. Specifically, we mention the following:

(a) officials, elected or otherwise (but especially otherwise), and the subordinates in their bureaucratic domains, who may be viewed as one sort of "lackey" class;

(b) the majority voters, who give them their power, and so may be accounted among the primary conspirators, in one sense, even though they (along with the rest) are also ultimately fellow members of the bamboozled class. And finally, we have

(c) the set of persons who in one way or another benefit by being aligned with the former classes: educators in publicly owned school or university systems, welfare recipients, trade unions benefiting from legislation entrenching their positions, journalists, and so on.

In a democratic election, the voters vote for some or other policy in the expectation that if they get their way, the rest of the people will be obliged to pay for some privilege or benefit collected by those who voted for it. This makes them the primary culprits, in a weak sense. As a refinement, however, we can identify, within the majority in question,

(b1) the class of immediate beneficiaries of the proposed policy, which is not likely to be an outright majority nor even necessarily a majority of the majority who voted in the legislators (who in turn make the hoped-for policy a reality) but who have a strong interest in bamboozling the rest of the voters into accepting the ideological basis for this beneficiary class's preferment by the proposed policy; and

(b2) the rest of the majority that ends up supporting them.

Together, this class—which in a democracy is the ultimate ruling class, of course—sustains and empowers the (a) class, which in its turn may usefully be divided into

(a1) a small class of elected *legislators* and, in some systems, elected highest administrators or judges who enact, enforce, or interpret the "laws"; and

(a2) the rather large class of appointed officials who administer the policies in question at the lowest, middle, and next-to-highest levels, that is, the *bureaucracy*.

It is especially this latter class, a2, in whose interest it is to propagandize for the causes allegedly served by the policies in question. Bureaucratic imperialism holds sway. Ministers want larger ministries, their underlings want more secretaries and gofers, and all want job security, which is much promoted by convincing the public that they are Doing Good. And, indeed, convincing themselves while they're at it—who wants a civil servant who is insincere, after all?

A further effect should be noted. In a democratic system, the legislators are elected. But everybody gets the vote—both the civil servants and the rest of the populace. So once the civil servant class gets very large, a very large fraction of the populace owes its living to The System. If we assume that people vote in their own perceived interests, we get the result that the legislature will be elected to a large extent by the very people who benefit from the sort of legislation that entrenches and expands the civil servant class. Even if civil servants are not in a majority, yet if they vote as a block, their influence on the election will often be decisive. Where they are an absolute majority, as is readily conceivable (and probably true right now in Canada, for instance), their hold on the system will amount to an unbreakable hammerlock. Big Government in a democracy is thus self-perpetuating, regardless—within very wide limits—of its real contribution to the public good.

Sources of Ideological Control

Finally, if we ask why this class is very likely to succeed, the short answer is that even though in liberal democracies there is a free press, yet the government's power to influence is quite enormous. As time goes by, of course, because of the last point made above, they will largely be preaching to the converted. Few bureaucrats are of the view that we should greatly reduce employment in *other* parts of the bureaucracy. And if, say, the universities are all financed entirely by the State, it will not be surprising if policies involving an expansion of State power are very popular, and if many of them are readily brought to agree that the State is a doer of great good for the public, which would—of course!—suffer if left to their own devices. So people pointing to embarrassing counterexamples or the lack of any real evidence for proposed policies are readily shunted aside as voices crying in the wilderness. "Political Correctness" prevails, and considerations of independently confirmable truth are largely shunted aside.

Fleshing out such a theory on the empirical side would involve further detailing of the methods by which the ruling class in a democracy has scope and power to mislead the citizens in its own interests. We are here, of course, only setting forth broad outlines, within the confines of a modest book chapter.

Summary

This brief presentation is intended only to show how the general idea of ideology can be taken out of its original Marxian setting, where it did not fare very well, and used to analyze political situations of the kind that Marxists did much to bring about, as well as the familiar more or less liberal democracies that predominate in today's world. The conclusion drawn in the latter case is that democracy offers great scope for the operation of ideological factors in affecting the shape of policy and the design of institutions—and that it is not going to be easy to rectify the results, for the same reasons. Liberal democracy can be expected to give us a society much poorer, and a great deal less liberal, than people might have hoped, or indeed still imagine.

Notes

This essay was originally presented at the annual meetings of the Canadian Philosophical Association, at the University of Prince Edward Island, Charlottetown, P.E.I., in June 1992. Thanks are due for helpful comments from anonymous readers and discussants. It was later published in *Reason Papers* 20 (Fall 1995), 22-34. My thanks are due to the editor for permission to reprint it here.

1. A reasonable, and short, exposition and discussion of Marx on these matters is found in Henry B. Mayo, *Introduction to Marxist Theory* (New York: Oxford University Press, 1960), ch. 3, 63-91. For a much more subtle and extensive analysis, see G. A. Cohen, *Karl Marx's Theory of History: A Defense* (Princeton, N.J.: Princeton University Press, 1978). Ideology is a prominent theme in that work; see Cohen's index for many references to it.

2. I thank an anonymous reader for the Canadian Philosophical Association, to which this chapter was first presented, for the suggestion that I increase the amount of attention paid to the category of half-truths. That, indeed, is where the main action is.

3. Lest I be thought to be displaying an antireligious bias here, I point out that the "suitably garden-variety sense" in which religious claims are meaningless is the one needed for public affairs: *public* confirmability, on the basis of *publicly* observable evidence. Perhaps we get some insight into Marxian "materialism" in this respect if we think of it as calling for a "show-me" attitude when flummery is in the sociopolitical offing.

Chapter 8

Property Rights
Original Acquisition and Lockean Provisos

Introduction

Many writers in the liberal tradition have agreed that at least some sort of "first appropriation" reasonably supports ownership by an individual, but have insisted that it does so only if that individual's appropriation leaves, in the words of Locke, "enough and as good for others," a condition that has come to be known as the "Lockean Proviso." Interest in that proviso among philosophers was greatly stimulated by Robert Nozick's discussion,[1] followed by many others. But my interest in this investigation is neither to catalog their views[2] nor to arrive at the definitive interpretation of Locke. My thesis is twofold. First, I point out that "the" Proviso is subject to a number of conspicuously different interpretations—five, in my analysis, with two importantly different variants of one. Second, one of these is also the right one—not as an interpretation of Locke, but as a view about just property holding. The view I shall advocate is simpler and clearer than any of the others, avoids the conundrums to which they give rise, and provides a credible view that also has the merit of reflecting actual practice among individuals, if that is regarded as a merit. Indeed, I argue, it is the only view that really makes sense. But it conspicuously fails to do what most interpreters seem to think the right doctrine *should* do: justify the imposition by the State of more or less severe restrictions on the extent of legitimate ownership of natural things in the world by particular individuals or groups.

Liberalism

Throughout, I shall be considering only theories that, at least provisionally, accept certain very general claims distinctive of the political and moral outlook of liberalism. For present purposes, there are four such claims:

111

(1) The sole legitimate purpose of the State is to promote the good, in the sense just stated, of people other than the rulers themselves, rulers being included only insofar as they are citizens, not rulers.

(2) The assessment of that good is to be made from the point of view of the individuals concerned: value, for political and social purposes, is what satisfies their preferences—not what realizes somebody else's view of what they ought to prefer.

(3) Paretianism: If S1 is a social situation alternative to S2, and in S1 at least one (innocent) person is better off and no one worse off than in S2, then liberalism calls for preferring S1 to S2—provided that S2 is not itself defective in respect of justice, in some way that can be specifically rectified.

(4) The general thesis of self-ownership, which prohibits all utilization of people without their own uncoerced consent, which implies everyone's negative right to "life, health, or liberty," as Locke's "Law of Nature" has it.[3] Locke famously adds 'property' to that list, but we must omit it here, since the point of our inquiry is to determine whether there is such a right and if so, why. In effect, our question is whether a good case can be made for including property in Locke's list on the basis of the others, especially liberty.

Obviously I cannot undertake a full-scale defense of liberalism here. But many would, I think, accept these four components even if they wouldn't identify them as 'liberalism'; and those who disagree may still find the present argument of interest, for it claims that liberalism as so characterized supports property rights without incoherence; if successful, it removes one source of support for nonliberal theories.

The subject of our discussion is whether and why full property rights may be acquired by individuals or groups of voluntarily acting individuals. We can shelve the question of the *extent* of individually owned property. In some primitive tribes, there is very little of it; and in any society much is owned by a number of persons rather than a single individual. Yet the tribes that forbid privatization to individual members declare areas of forest or land the collective domain of the group, to the exclusion of all others—privatization enough for our purposes. Moreover, their presence in the area before others came by is taken by them to justify their continued presence and exclusion of outsiders. Whether prohibitions by the tribe on privatization by individuals within it might be valid we leave open here. Our primary focus is on activities familiar in largely agrarian and industrial societies such as our own. Within such societies, property is typically acquired by exchange. Those activities are part and parcel of property rights, but they require that at some point property was acquired in some other fashion. If there is no initial acquisition, there is no acquisition.

The Proviso: The General Thesis

The passage containing the famous phrase goes as follows:

For this *Labor* being the unquestionable Property of the Laborer, no Man
but he can have a right to what that is once joyned to, at least where there is
enough, and as good left in common for others.[4]

Some profess to deny the whole idea of a right to property. But even they often
trace their misgivings to the "proviso." At the least, there is a general sense that
without it, liberalism is incoherent. Robert Nozick generalizes this concern,
suggesting that "any adequate theory of justice" will have to contain a proviso
to this general effect:

A process normally giving rise to a permanent bequeathable property right
in a previously unowned thing will not do so if the position of others no
longer at liberty to use the thing is thereby worsened.[5]

Let's call this the "General Version" of the Proviso on Acquisition. It is general
in that 'worsened' is unspecified. Made worse *how*? In *what respect*? And what
measures worsening? Theories differ. Liberalism, however, provides the general
premises for an answer. If we can show that individual A's appropriation of
previously unowned item x does not, by liberal standards, worsen the situation
of any other individual, then the liberal must agree that A has the right to x in
the circumstances in question. That won't resolve every difficulty about
particular cases, but it will show what is at issue in such disputes.

Five Interpretations

There is considerable divergence about the meaning to be attributed to the
proviso as Locke states it. Here are quick descriptions of what I take to be the
five options about what the relevant sort of worsening might consist in:

(1) Unrestricted worsening.
(2) Worsening in respect of B's use of x itself.
(3) Type-Worsening: worsening in respect of B's ability to command
similar resources (such as other pieces of land).
(4) Utility-Worsening: reducing B's level of utility.
(5) Worsening in respect of B's previously-acquired possessions.

In the following discussion, I examine the first four interpretations in
enough detail to show why we cannot rationally accept them, given Liberalism.
I remind the reader that these are not mainly offered as interpretation of Locke,
but rather of the idea I take Locke to be trying to explain. I conclude that the
fifth is the correct option, not just because it is the only one left, but on the
basis of further direct arguments as well.

1. Unrestricted Worsenings: Excluding Nonliberal Desires

On the first view, A's initial appropriation must not worsen B's situation in *any way at all*. Even if what B finds wrong with A's proposed appropriation is that B simply dislikes A's having x, A's appropriation of x is forbidden. This view is essentially a straw man, but one whose errors are important to be clear about. If A's right to do something is subject to reversal at the hands of its negative impact on just *any* desires that *anyone* else may have, then every version of liberalism is impossible—along with every possible theory of whatever kind. For whatever anyone wants to do, somebody, somewhere, won't like it—antiliberal theorists, for example. Liberalism requires that desires by B that F be true of A, simply as such, cannot be counted in support of publicly imposed restrictions on A's actions.

Restricting us to "nontuistic" desires, allowing only desires directed at states of the agent herself that can be characterized nonrelationally, would no doubt fulfill this requirement. But it would be extremely restrictive, and certainly far more so than we need. It is enough that no authoritative imposition of restrictions on A, by government or society at large, may be made merely on the basis of B's preferences regarding A as such. Preferences of such kinds, if they are to have any weight, must be supported by B's *independently* specified interests. For example, the fact that B doesn't like A's taste in paintings is irrelevant, but the fact that A's painting is being hung in B's living room is not. Or again, if the fact that x would benefit C—A's child, say—is taken by A to be a strong point in favor of x, then we will account x as a benefit to A as well, and certainly not as a point against doing x.

2. Using and Excluding

The next three versions cover the mainstream options. All assume that the deprivation of B's capability of freely using x in the future constitutes at least a prima facie worsening, relevant for assessing proviso restrictions, but they differ considerably in how they do it. On the second version, B is worsened in respect of his ability to use that very thing, x *itself*, where 'x' ranges over *particular* things. That B, owing to A's appropriation, can no longer use x is sufficient, as it stands, to make A's appropriation of x at least prima facie wrongful. Should we accept this? No. To do so would restrict legitimate appropriations to no cases at all. To begin with, many uses will destroy x, say by consuming it: if A eats the whole apple, then B doesn't. In those cases, (2) is obviously impossible.

It may be suggested that they should share. But this rather natural idea, entertained by so many of communist persuasion, misfires in two ways. First, n people sharing an apple, or any material object, given large enough n, will satisfy no one. We can always find a group, G, large enough that trying to share x among all members of G will reduce the share of any given member below the level at which that person would find it worthwhile to bother with x at all. In the case of eating an apple, n is perhaps a dozen. In the case of an acre of land, x will vary greatly, depending on what they want to do with it. But then, that is part of the point: people will want to do different things, and for each envisaged use there will be a value of n meeting the above condition. It will very often be just two: person A will want to do something with it that *cannot* be done by more than one person.

As a major type of case in point, consider the use of x as a means of production. This inherently excludes persons other than the producers. If Jones hammers *now*, with *this* hammer, then Smith does not. Going to cooperative uses may widen the scope a little, but will never expand the user-group to include everyone. Cooperative hammering at time t by all members of group G is either impossible or so ineffective that no member of G would have found it sensible to join G for that purpose. A group of women cooperatively washing linen in the creek excludes others when there would be too many for the creek, or not enough linen for the newcomers. Nonsharability beyond some threshold number n is the normal situation, not the exception. Moreover, n is usually very low—often just one. To require sharing, across the board, is self-defeating. True commons illustrate rather than deny this point. In a true commons, the number who participate is small, and nonmembers are decidedly unwelcome.[6]

We may add that social ownership and management usually *decreases* access, rather than increasing it. A man who simply owns a hammer can lend it to someone without further ado; but if it is controlled by the Central Committee, the process of securing permission to use it is likely to be so daunting as to render the hammer effectively inaccessible to virtually all, apart from those with political connections, or the temerity and dexterity necessary to proceed without benefit of official approval.

Second, and more basically, prohibition of exclusive use violates liberalism. For liberalism must be neutral as between different innocent[7] preferences: so long as A's proposed use of x can be accomplished without damage to others, liberalism requires acceptance of that as a legitimate use. Of course, damage to others, as we have seen in discussing version (1), must be assessed in non-question-beggingly specified respects. Whatever x may be, *any* use of x is going to frustrate the desires of those who didn't want the user to use it, and will frustrate those who wanted to do something that required nonuse of x in that way at that time.

3. Qualitative Equivalence

The third version is the most obvious reading. Here x is understood to be appropriated by A only as an instance of a type, F, such as land, which ranges fairly narrowly over things suitably *like* x. If B cannot have x, then she must instead be allowed to have some other instance of F, call it y, which is to be "just as good"—an equally fertile area of land, for example. Proposal (3) tries to assure person B, excluded from x by A's acquisition of it, that she was in effect not really excluded after all. B's exclusion from x is no problem, for B can have another instance of the same *kind* of thing as A.

This natural reading of Locke's words, at first glance, seems a marked improvement. But only at first glance. There is, for one thing, the obvious point that the world may not meet the condition anyway: there may not be "enough" left of that kind of thing. Should we disallow private appropriation of the few instances of F that there happen to be, then? Why? Is it better that all starve than that only some do? Paretianism says it is not.

Further, there is the horrendous problem of specifying the relevant kind to the satisfaction of all possible comers. Is the land down the road "as good"? Even if its soil is identical, perhaps the sun doesn't shine as well on it, or the shade trees along its borders are less numerous, or it's farther from town. In the end, this version of the proviso has the same implications as before, for large populations, and still more so if we include potential users in the future.[8]

Restricting relevant users may help: only wheat farmers need apply, say. But how can we do that and remain faithful to liberalism? All sorts of things can typically be done with any given bit of real estate or minerals, or any natural stuff. Why should those who wish to do one thing with it be preferred to those who wish to do something else? And what about 'enough'? Does it mean 'enough to get them what they want'? Or should we talk instead of getting them only what they "need"? But that again abandons liberalism, overruling some preferences in favor of others. Nor will it work anyway: just as there is no limit to wants, so there is no limit to needs, especially self-assessed needs. So view (3) is really just as hopeless as version (2).

As a general comment on both (2) and (3), I note that if the set of natural resources available for possible use is insufficient relative to a particular type of demand, then that use for those people involves them in a zero-sum game: if some get all they want to use in that way, others necessarily do not. There cannot be a universal principle giving it to *everybody*; thus it is pointless to say that all are "entitled" to it. Nor is there any use in trying to divide x up equally, giving no one enough instead of enough to some few. This most popular and natural understanding of Locke's proviso, then, comes a complete cropper—a lesson that has not been sufficiently learned by theorists.

4. Equal-Value Theories

So we move to another natural thought: perhaps what must be left for others should be "as good as" A's x, without imposing the impossible requirement that it be of the same *kind* as x. Obviously the next question is how we are to reckon equivalents for this purpose. One answer springs to mind: in a liberal theory, to be good for person A is to satisfy A, that is, to have utility for A. 'Enough and as good' will be enough, not necessarily of more F, but of some H having as much utility for A as x. This compensates B for loss of opportunity to use x. The first question for such a view is how we are to measure utility for this purpose. There are two available views: either we resort to interpersonally comparable cardinal measures, or we don't.

4a. Cardinal, Interpersonally Comparable Utility

This concept gets us into murky waters, since there is, to put it mildly, no agreement on the commensurability of utility, let alone just how we are to do it. But that is only one problem. The more basic one is that there is no inherent reason in liberalism why person A should regard person B's utility as equal in any way to her own, or even as having any value at all. Classical Utilitarianism, the standard-bearer of interpersonally comparable utility, has a fatal problem: few actually *want* the maximal sum of cardinal utility for all which it proclaims as the supreme end of action.

4b. Preferences and Bargaining Baselines

The other variant rejects that requirement. Abandoning interpersonal comparisons, it simply says that what we offer person B in return for A's exclusive possession of x should be some y such that B will be indifferent between x and y. This prima facie offers a workable criterion. But we must now confront the question of motivation. Version (4b) enables us to get to the nub of the matter: why should A be required to do any such thing? There is one classic answer: that the world, prior to society, is a Commons. If so, all are entitled to it, and so B has as a baseline for bargaining her natural share of the world—a stockholder's vote in the World Corporation.

The "Commons"

Locke supposed that the world had been "given to men in common" by God. 'Belongs to mankind in common' isn't exactly pellucid, to be sure, but on the face of it, it says that the world is literally a *commons*. And many seem to have taken that claim as axiomatic—as though a "state of nature" must, as such, be a commons. It is nothing of the sort.

To see this, we must distinguish two senses of 'commons'. One sense designates a stretch of territory over which no rights are defined. Obviously natural things prior to ownership are common in that sense. But it supplies no support for the Lockean idea. The other idea, however, is indeed relevant. In this sense, a commons is a specialized case of joint ownership, each owner having specific rights to the use of the commons property, with many correlated exclusions. No member of the commons-using group may privatize any of it. All members get to graze, or whatever, at will—within the limits prescribed by the commons owners collectively. If all of nature is such a system, all persons being members of the commons corporation, then, as Locke saw,[9] we would have to ask *everybody* for permission to use *anything*.

Real commons systems are incapable of being universal in that way. Participants in real commons systems deny others access to their "means of production." The claim that the world is such a commons is not just dubious but utterly arbitrary, and the inference intended, that all have an equal claim to access, is incoherent. Commons, like other forms of ownership and use, provide certain benefits for members and exclude others. *Everyone's* having a share is simply impossible.

Locke himself invokes a theological story that many appear to find congenial. They shouldn't. In the first place, no one can have any reason for thinking that the creator, if there is one, would necessarily "give" nature to mankind in general, rather than some favored group—the "Chosen people," say—or even to no one. In any case, we must reject theology for these purposes. Theology is not publicly provable from common sense and science; to use it at all discriminates against those with different religious views, or none. To base laws for all on the religion of some, or even on the denial of religion, flouts the Law of Nature.

Once we understand that the world was not made by anybody, for anyone or any purpose in particular, then we must confront the fact that the world is just stuff, devoid of moral qualities and not owned by anyone, let alone by everyone. It is therefore wrong to suppose that the "state of nature" situation is one in which individual B has as his bargaining chip the status of "Commons," so that he is in a position to say to A: "Here, you get to keep x provided that the rest of us are reckoned to be the exclusive members of the Commons Corporation, and we've decided that you have to pay such-and-such a rent." But *that* isn't the situation facing people. What we do face is, simply, each other, with our various interests and powers.

This moves us to a more fundamental level of moral theory. The State of Nature is not naturally equipped with any rules whatever, about anything. The question is whether we can improve on that state of affairs by accepting some set of rules, and if so, which ones. That is what moral and political philosophy is about. Now, that situation is necessarily one in which each person asks what his best bargain is, given the situations of himself and others. The Hobbesian thesis about this is that the cause of the problems in this state is our possession and retention of the liberty to use all means whatever, including force, to achieve our ends. The Hobbesian solution is for all of us to give up the right to use force, as asserted in his First Law of Nature:

> That every man, ought to endeavor Peace, as farre as he has hope of obtaining it; and when he cannot obtain it, that he may seek, and use, all helps, and advantages of Warre.[10]

We do not follow Hobbes in his further proposal that we require a political Sovereign. Hobbes held that the sovereign would have complete say in these matters:

> Seventhly, is annexed to the Sovereign, the whole power of prescribing the Rules, whereby every man may know, what Goods he may enjoy and what Actions he may do, without being molested by any of his fellow Subjects: And this is it men call *Property*.[11]

This "solution" has it that whatever the government says is right *is* right. How could anyone believe that? But in any case, it obviously can't tell us which rules the Sovereign *ought* to propose. Invoking Sovereignty here is useless.

To that question—which rules are good rules?—there is only one credible answer: those which provide each person's best option, given rational compliance by all. That is the classic question of the Social Contract. Hobbes's Laws of Nature suggest the answer that what each receives in return for surrendering his liberty to use force is, simply, the like surrender of all others, yielding a social world in which each may do and get whatever he can *by peaceable means*, that is, without molesting others. Hobbes's Second Law of Nature has it "That a man be willing, when others are so too, as far-forth, as for Peace, and defense of himself he shall think it necessary, to lay down this right to all things; and be contented with so much liberty against other men, as he would allow other men against himself."[12] Hobbes is right: that is the *best* bargain we can make at so general a level. But accepting a right to use force against nonharmful persons for certain purposes—even that of having enough to eat—is not a good bargain.

Why not? This is a large issue, but, briefly, the trouble is that it is much too good for the unproductive, who are its beneficiaries, and much too bad for the productive, on whom it imposes the duty to support the rest. For without the efforts of productive people, the very food that the unproductive are begging for wouldn't exist. It is not rational, then, for all to grant them a claim in justice to it. Real indigents, assuming them otherwise innocent, must either offer their services in return for sustenance, or appeal to the sentiments of the productive. Doing so, fortunately, will provide them with outcomes greatly superior to those proffered by well-meaning proponents of commons rights.

Finders (First Users), Keepers

What can we say about property, then, if peace and liberty is to be our guide? The answer is that we should accept the right of first users—"finders, keepers"—a principle recognized by the classic writers on these matters, such as Pufendorf, Hobbes, and Kant, as well as Locke. More precisely, the principle is that of *first use*. She who gets there first *and* commences to use it, in ways that require ongoing access to it, may use it so long as she wants. No one else may use it without her say-so, until such point as she either sells or gives it to somebody, dies without leaving a will, or ceases to care. A more abstract contemporary formulation is David Gauthier's "Lockean Proviso" which "prohibits bettering one's situation through interaction that worsens the situation of another."[13] What constitutes "one's situation," to be sure, is what is largely at issue. The essence of the proposal is that one's situation consists of oneself and those elements of the environment over which one has exerted and continues intentionally to exert control. It does not include the indefinite array of opportunities that one has as yet done nothing to realize.

Of course it will not always be easy to decide just what a given user is using and how his use extends into the future. But it is obviously wrong to appeal simply to the first user's desires or intentions, by themselves; his intended further activities regarding x must be quite realistically focused *on x* and not, for example, on the entirety of North America. Use is *use*—not pie-in-the-sky. Others coming on the scene must be able to have publicly ascertainable evidence of the first-user's presence and activities. But that is typically available. Further clarification will often be needed, requiring discussion and negotiation. Nevertheless, those negotiations proceed from a baseline that is not arbitrary. Human activities of using this or that are identifiable, to a large extent, prior to determinations by judges or onlookers. Our proposal makes these prior initial activities the baseline from which such discussions must proceed.

Why this rule and not some other? For example, why not "second come, first serve," or "all comers, no matter when, get equal control"? The answer is that second-comers *intervene* in first-comer's uses, and thus violate the general liberty principle. They prevent continuation of a commenced activity, one which harmed no one when initiated, and in which the initiator invests effort, on the results of which he forms expectations and plans. If you lock me in my room, thus preventing me from bicycling to the next town if I should want to do so, you interfere with my liberty. Your actually muscling me off my bicycle, bundling me into the room and locking it interferes still more. In general, stopping people from doing what they are doing is our paradigm of interference. Telling them (authoritatively, with one's authority backed by force) that they can't do what they are realistically planning to do comes next. But telling them that they can't do what they would never have dreamed of doing anyway, and have done nothing to initiate, counts for nothing. I do not deprive you of the moon by pointing out that nothing you do is likely to get it for you, nor of the land down the road that you might like to have, yet never knew of.

Any other rule than the rule of first use conflicts with the liberty principle. If it gives the use to some designated other persons, it is no longer *general*, for it makes some people subordinate to others, arbitrarily preferring those others. If we give that use, as such, to B whom we claim to be "more productive," then we arbitrarily suppress A's activity, by deciding what counts as productive and how much is enough. The injunction not to take things because you must instead share them with others is, as we saw, absurd. The rule of first use uniquely respects the liberty principle.

Rights for first-users ensure optimal use from the social point of view. If Jones must wait to use x until the Central Committee decides it's O.K., the resource lies unused meanwhile. And when the Committee does decide, it will arbitrarily block some in favor of others, contrary to Liberalism. But if Jones need only clear it with those on whom his labor impinges, he's in a position to get a lot more done. In the rare case where he's in unoccupied land, this implies that he need seek no one's approval—in diametric contrast to the Commons view, which in principle, as Locke saw, requires that he clear it with *everyone*. The difference in administrative cost is astronomical.

5. The Status Quo

This clears the way for our remaining interpretation. According to it, the only legitimate restriction on our activities is that we not interfere with what others *already have*. The fact that in doing so appropriators deprive the others of the opportunity to do with x any of the things that are incompatible with initial users' uses of x is irrelevant. There are innumerable mutually incompatible uses of anything. Someone's realizing one of them rather than any of the indefinitely many others that consequently go unrealized cannot, just as such, count as an interference with anyone's liberty. That would be like saying that I interfere with you by virtue of your not being me.

In the abstract, the relation among us in regard to our sheer desires for particular objects and activities looks to be zero-sum. If it were, that would put an end to social philosophy, for it is logically impossible to have a social rule, valid for all and willed by all, declaring that in zero-sum games, party A should win. However, once time enters the picture, the appearance of zero-sum ceases. Given time, someone can get there first. His use competes with no others at that time. Yet from then on, until he yields it up, anyone else's attempting to use it requires a disruption of the first-comer's actions.

The first-use rule leaves "enough and as good" for others only in the sense that one leaves them in uncoerced possession of *what they have* and whatever they go on to acquire without trampling on the previous possessions of others. If, in their view, they do not have "enough" in the way of specific useful possessions, then they, like everyone else, have their work cut out for them: find or make some more, being subject, in the process, only to the restriction that they not damage what others have—may not, that is, interfere with what those others are already doing. If all their efforts fail, they are thrown upon the mercy of others. Another popular Lockean idea says that one's neighbor should have a "sufficiency," which the better-off should if necessary help them to achieve. But the unproductive are not *owed* anything as compensation for the sheer fact that they didn't get to x first. That fact would be strictly uncompensable anyway, were there any reason to think it a ground for compensation. But there isn't. For in taking something from the "state of nature," we are not taking anything from anyone, since it belongs to no one. There are no valid claims to compensation.

We should realize, though, that what is really enough and as good is liberty—noninvasion. We are adequately compensated for loss of the liberty to use force—which is a real loss, not a fanciful one—by others' surrender of the same liberty, thus yielding a social world in which peaceful exchanges and transfers are possible. That is the sole and sufficient basis of private property in things outside our own bodies. Such property can, of course, be jointly owned by many (voluntary) participants, as in genuine commons arrangements,[14] but anything else will interfere with activities legitimately undertaken.

Now, consider what those who allege that we also need compensation for something we have supposedly lost by someone's appropriation of some natural object are asserting. What they lose is opportunities. And it is indeed possible for people in some cases to have a claim to compensation for loss of opportunity. If A deprives B of some important resource, such as pianist B's fingers, then A certainly owes B a great deal in the way of compensation. But this is not because he has appropriated something affording opportunities that the other person has thereby lost in the absence of any specific antecedent claim to those opportunities. It is because the other person already *has* a special claim on those items. B's claim to those particular fingers is that they are parts of the very body that constitutes B. He had use of them in the status quo ante and now has not; A, then, has deprived B of something he previously had. But that is never true in regard to things one has done nothing to commence use of, however much one would *like* to have them. Morals, and the state, cannot be in the business of giving people what they want just because they want it. For that can only be done at the expense of others who produce or discover the things in question. And they may have no reason to devote them to such purposes.

In special cases, there are equal claims to something, as when A and B arrive at x simultaneously. In such cases, they must resolve their claims by negotiation. They might try a partnership, or one buy out the other. The price is a function of opportunity costs, indeed; but it is the equality of claims grounded in antecedent activities that matters. In state-of-nature appropriation, of course, this will be rare: Jones and Smith might work from opposite ends of the same mineral vein, meeting, to their surprise, in the middle. But to talk as though such cases are the norm, as though we are all "there first," is unintelligible. There is no way to make the appropriate measurements to restore the satisfaction that persons not in on particular appropriations thereby lose. To repeat: you cannot restore what someone never had in the first place.

Circularity?

It is common to think that the legitimizing of private ownership through first-use is somehow question-begging. Grunebaum, for instance, objects to Nozick's theory of original appropriation in respect of 'previously unowned' items, complaining that if 'previously unowned' means that nobody has previously become the owner *within* a system of private ownership, then "the argument already presupposes private ownership as the form of ownership in which the appropriation takes place and thus is obviously question begging."[15] As it would indeed, if the argument did presuppose that. But it doesn't.

In the first place, the *explication* of the theory doesn't presuppose anything. It specifies certain acts—people grasping things, walking on surfaces, and so on—that are describable without reference to any system of ownership. A can grasp x whether or not A owns x or ever heard of ownership. The theory then proposes—not *pre*supposes—that those who perform those acts, in the conditions the theory specifies as sufficient, are to be taken as thereby entitled to use the thing in question in the future. Of course the theorist owes us an explanation *why* we should accept that theory rather than some other.[16] But it is not one of the reasons why we shouldn't accept it that it somehow "presupposes" itself.

Nozick got us worrying about the Proviso by distinguishing two interpretations of Locke: "First, by losing the opportunity to improve his situation by a particular appropriation or any one; and second, by no longer being able to use freely (without appropriation) what he previously could."[17] The first is wrong because any given opportunity may be taken by only one or some few persons, and whoever gets it thereby excludes others; no principle *can* protect a general right to opportunity. What about the second and, as he claimed, weaker option?

Nozick says, "With the weaker requirement, . . . though person Z [the first person for whom there is not "enough and as good" left to appropriate] can no longer *appropriate*, there may remain some for him to *use* as before."[18] Does this help? No. For ownership simply *is* the right to use. If B has not appropriated x, or been given x by some previous owner, then x *isn't* B's to use as he will,[19] and that status isn't available to B as a bargaining chip against A who wants to appropriate x to B's exclusion. What B already has, he of course has the right to continue to use; but what he doesn't have, and has been taken by others, he has no claim on, nor did he ever. To repeat: given liberalism, we do not primordially own the world—only ourselves. And even that isn't primordial. We must argue even for that. But Hobbes, I believe, has provided such an argument. In the absence of the general right not to be molested by others for their own purposes, life for ourselves is bound to be worse. But we get that general right only from others, by mutual recognition.

Circularity of the Commons Hypothesis

Reflection shows that all views of the types I have found wanting, apparently including both of those distinguished by Nozick, make a mistake of the same fundamental kind. For in claiming that the appropriation of pieces of the world for the exclusive use of the appropriator restricts the liberty of others, they subtly assume that we have a prior *positive* right to use all those things. Such a right requires others to see to it that the rightholder gets it, if he is not able to do so on his own. Before ever coming near the place—indeed, before even being born, so these theories say—we all had some kind of claim or hold on the world, such that others proposing to go forth and use bits of it must make sure that we get some too, if we happen to want some; and therefore those others are required to justify their appropriations by arranging, in advance as it were, that we are adequately "compensated" for being no longer able to acquire them ourselves. But compensated for what? Not for what we have done, since we haven't done anything, by hypothesis; nor for damage to our products, since there are no such products. We are, it seems, to be "compensated" merely for *existing*—and at others' expense. But there is no such thing as a claim on the world, as such: worlds know naught of claims. Claims are against some (or all) other *person*(s). The only intelligible meaning to be assigned to notions of claims on things is that they are claims against other people *about* those things. To have a claim on, say, an "equal share" of Nature is to have a claim against other people regarding how it is to be used, or who uses it. But what would be its basis?

Our examination has shown us the options. If it's the claim that we must be allowed to use whatever we can that is still waiting to be used, then that is equivalent to claim (5), which I defend here. But it gives us no positive antecedent claim on bits of nature. Rather, the general right of liberty, which we negotiate in the pre-ownership "state of nature," says that we are free to use hitherto unused things, provided we not molest anyone else's efforts to use other things.

The contrary view needs to explain why it should be thought that we somehow already own the place, and thus get to charge for anybody else's use of it, despite having done nothing to come by it. No support has been provided for that claim, and as a supposed complaint against the liberty principle, it is beside the point. Critics of private property often point with special derision to those who got wealth by inheritance, the criticism being that they didn't do anything to deserve it.[20] Yet that is precisely the complaint against a priori claims to social ownership. The difference is that in the cases these critics have in mind, such as inheritance from wealthy parents, those parents *did* do something to acquire that wealth, or got it from others who did; and having done so, what they wanted to do with it next, as it turns out, was to give it to the inheritors. What is ours is what we may do as we wish with, and giving it to someone else is one of those things; thus general liberty gives us the right to do it. But no such intelligible explanation is forthcoming in common-ownership theories. Having jettisoned theological stories, for the reasons given, the question how we all came to be part-owners of the place, and thus to have a general obligation to "distribute" the material world to other claimants, becomes unanswerable. The "commons" theory is not really rival theory to ours: it has, rather, *no* theory, unless we count sheer assertion as theory.

The Prospects of Others

It is one of the important paradoxes of moral theory that sometimes restrictions on our behavior, even quite harsh ones, nevertheless conduce to our good. The point certainly applies resoundingly to the present subject. The right to acquire without fear of expropriation by others, even needy others, enables a society to increase its wealth to the point where there will be few if any needy, and make what few needy there are quite easy to cater to. Writers from Aristotle through Locke, Adam Smith to Hayek, David Schmidtz and others have made the case. The "secret" of wealth is no secret at all: it lies in intelligent hard work plus respect for other people's productive activities. That respect consists in a general and reliable disposition to refrain from forcibly depriving others of the results of their work. The more general and reliable such respect is, the greater the wealth of the society in question.

Reflecting on the spirit of Locke's Proviso, the rightness of the interpretation supported in this chapter is due, at bottom, to a fact that is inadequately appreciated by social thinkers: wealth comes from human effort, not nature's.[21] Locke noted that a small area of well-cared-for land in the England of his day had a thousand times the value of a similar area in the "wilds of America." He was thinking mainly of its capacity to yield food for humans, with then-current agricultural technology. Today we look to the conditions for the production of high-definition TVs, fast-preparable Thai dinners, air-conditioned off-road vehicles, Lyrca running suits, performances of *The Ring of the Nibelungs*, aspirin, and thousands of other useful products and services, none of which existed in a state of nature. The land on which stand the factories, retail stores, and opera houses for producing and distributing these things has several million times the value of similar-sized areas of sheer wilderness. Virtually all of this fabulous collection of goods was unheard of by people of earlier times, and none comes from unaltered nature, except the wilderness preserves whose aesthetic and recreational value rests on their unavailability for the production of other goods.

These points lead to a fundamental reflection. The value of anything lies in what we can do with it, and that is a function of our and other people's cognitive efforts relating to it. How would one ensure that there is "enough and as good left for others" when one formulates a new scientific theory or a plan for an improved microchip? The very question seems absurd. Ideas use no material resources, thus ensuring no reduction of such resources "left for others." The creative work of Newton, Beethoven, or Steve Jobs does not subtract from a pre-existing mass of something provided by nature. If we broaden our sights from symphonies to better mousetraps and superior grades of winter wheat, then what people do along such lines is essential to all wealth, not just intellectual and spiritual wealth. We have what we have, material or otherwise, because a great number of people have applied their ingenuity to specific problems relevant to the satisfaction of human interests, ranging from hunger to sheer curiosity. The idea that wealth consists in the accumulation of a large mass of natural stuff is utterly wrong. It is astonishing that that model should still be dominating discussions of this subject.

What makes particular bits of wealth available to other people is trade. Above all, there is the exchange of labor for goods or for other services between those who can provide the one and make use of the other, to the benefit of both. Only the Lockean Proviso in our last form can maximize benefits from such interactions. Exchanges of capital are really reconfigurations of productive capability, whose profitability is a function of their catering to voluntarily acting consumers at the end of the line. Consumers, in turn, can afford to buy because they are also producers, able to exchange their work with others who see potential benefit from it.

The result of all this is the general and, given peace and decent health, continual improvement in the well-being of all participants. Improvement is not necessarily for nonparticipants; providing for them is a matter of sympathy, love, or general human concern, rather than justice. The condition on which anything can be done for the unproductive is the previous activity of the productive—usually the same persons earlier in life. Locke's Proviso has nothing to do with the unproductive: his concern that there be enough and as good in the way of usable natural resources for others applies only to those who can produce. And rightly so. In society production comes first.

There has been quite a ferment of concern among recent writers, including philosophers, that the supposedly high consumption patterns of people in modern industrial countries will exhaust the earth's resources: "sustainable development" is asserted to be a serious problem for us now and in the future. Previously, this was a concern that human population would "outstrip its food supply," a claim completely falsified by now. Per capita consumption of food has increased along with human population around the world—not decreased, as the Malthusian view had it.[22] But the source of the Malthusian error has been resolutely ignored, it would seem, by most contemporary writers. The error is the same: failure to see that wealth consists in what we make of nature, not in nature itself. The desire to do better impels ingenious people to find better and better ways to use what is on hand. We recycle, reuse, and devise ways to make use of materials that exist in inexhaustible supply instead of ones that become scarce, or require trivial amounts of natural resources in the first place. Cumulative human knowledge solves problem after problem; less and less yields more and more; and issues of natural resource exhaustion fade into irrelevance.[23]

Thus the original intent of Locke's Proviso is met, in spades, by the on-going process of human production stimulated by individuals' interests, protected by property rights. What is "left" for others is, overwhelmingly, the opportunity to avail themselves of the production of their fellows. As society becomes more complex in its differentiation of products and skills, we are increasingly dependent on propensities to exchange on the part of their fellows, who meanwhile become reliable producers and exchangers. Thus what's left for others is not merely "as good," but much better from the start, and as time goes on incomparably better, to the point where the opportunity to appropriate bits of land suitable for agriculture or mining, say, equipped with primitive know-how, is looked on with contempt by all. Much better to leave the farming to others equipped with state-of-the-art agricultural technology. In the United States today, far more people are employed serving food in restaurants than on the farms that produce the food in the first place; waiters and waitresses, cooks and cashiers—all are better off than they could ever have been on any primitive farm.[24]

The most important kind of property we can have is, broadly speaking, intellectual rather than material, including knowledge of processes, formulas, and the like, as well as academic and literary writings. Here our thesis amounts to the view that one is entitled to something like copyright on one's ideas, so long as they are original. It is absurd to think of intellectual workers as drawing upon a quantifiable set of preexisting resources, with a possibility of not leaving "enough and as good for others." Ideas are as good as the thinker makes them, and the only interpretation of Locke's Proviso that makes sense in their case is that proposed in this chapter. Prohibition on plagiarism, entitling creators to the free use of their own ideas, suffices. There is ample room for controversy here: who thought of it first, and what exactly "it" is, are analogous to problems of identifying the limits of acquired material resources, entailing the same need for means of negotiating disputes on these matters. It is also obvious that virtually all intellectual work is heavily dependent on the work of predecessors—this chapter being an example. Rewards for such productions should be, and usually are, bestowed on individuals with a lively sense of obligation to their predecessors. Still, the point is that there isn't any sense to the idea that there is a great stock of preformed ideas lying about, such that one could unfairly help oneself to too many of them, leaving insufficient for others. Beethoven is a hard act to follow, but plenty of composers have managed, and in any case, there is no way to declare the field unfairly exhausted by Beethoven, who thus cheated the rest by walking away with the best ideas for himself.

Really, the models provided by the composer and the novelist, along with those of the technologist, the scientist, and the tinkerer, are more appropriate for understanding human wealth than those provided by hunting deer and coconuts. The entrepreneur has ideas about how to do things better, enabling more people to derive more benefit from the same fundamental range of natural resources. There is no limit to the supply of good ideas, hence no purchase for the distribution-limiting interpretations of the Lockean Proviso regarding them. And since they are the real source of wealth, there is also no rational application of distribution-limiting interpretations, even in their original area of application—natural resources.

Conclusions and Restrictions

Once we reject the adventitious theological components of Locke's theorizing about natural resources, we are left with no reason to think that later-comers are owed compensation for first-comers' acquisition of natural resources. But there is strong support, only sketchily asserted here, for the liberty principle as a premise for our inquiry. The most natural understanding of that principle implies a general right of acquisition of previously unowned resources of the general sort Locke asserted: the right to use bits of nature for our purposes, as we will, "without asking the consent of anyone," provided only that we respect the like liberty of others.

Readers will rightly want to hear about problems thought to be rampant in the contemporary world, and alleged to stem from the institution of private property. The view advocated here does nothing to support the idea of an enforceable obligation to maintain a "safety net" of involuntarily supported social services. And there would be much else to discuss in regard to resources and their supposed scarcity, especially in respect of pollution and the like. All of these questions can, I think, be satisfactorily responded to, but not in a discussion of this size.[25] My argument has been concerned wholly with what has been regarded throughout the three or so centuries since Locke's work as a major problem for liberal theory. That problem is easily solved when we see that the Lockean Proviso as Locke framed it is a mistake. As a restriction on initial acquisition of the type it is all but universally regarded as being, it is baseless and must be jettisoned. But in the only form in which it is sustainable, our fifth option, it has no redistributive implications, requiring only that people not acquire by force or fraud.

Does the the property/liberty formula apply everywhere and always? In every society, there will be property: valued ornaments and differentiated useful implements have been private in every society. And all such tribes are anxious to claim hunting grounds or planted areas as tribal domains excluding all external competitors. But wherever the outputs of differing individuals is highly variable as a function of skill and knowledge, their products readily exchanged, and distinctive consumer profiles exist, individually private property comes to the fore. That efforts to countermand the institution in developed societies lead to poverty at best is the lesson of the twentieth-century large-scale experiments in communism, all of them dismal failures.

That property rights exclude, as it turns out, is their prime virtue. The exclusion involved is ultimately beneficial for the excluded, but in the first instance the basis for it is straightforward: first use underwrites ownership, with no restrictions other than the obligation to respect the similar right of others, because that protects the free exercise of human effort. The right to do that is really just the right to be us.

Notes

This chapter was published in *Public Affairs Quarterly* 13, no. 3 (July 1999), 205-27, and is reprinted with kind permission of its editors. Early versions go back to 1991, since which I have benefited from discussion at presentations to many audiences, notably at the Canadian Philosophical Association meetings in Calgary, Alberta, 1994. My thanks also to David Schmidtz, John T. (Jack) Sanders, and many others, including the editor of that journal, John Kekes, for helpful discussion.

1. Robert Nozick, *Anarchy, State, and Utopia* (New York: Basic Books, 1974), 174-82.

2. I am particularly unhappy to have to omit the extensive discussion deserved by Eric Mack's "The Self-Ownership Proviso: A New and Improved Lockean Proviso," *Social Philosophy and Policy* 12, no. 1 (Winter 1995), 186-218. In Mack's view, "the recognition that each person owes others as self-owners includes abstention from the disablement of their world-interactive faculties, talents, and energies" (201). We can disable these by making that world virtually unavailable to them as an object of interaction. My main excuse for not discussing Mack's important paper is lack of space; my secondary excuse is that I do not believe his thesis has a real-world divergence from my own, however much it would affect things in worlds very different from our own. But his paper richly deserves a careful reading by those pursing this topic. He and I also have benefited from papers by John T. Sanders, such as "Justice and the Initial Acquisition of Private Property," *Harvard Journal of Law and Public Policy* 10 (1987), 367-400.

3. Locke, *Second Treatise on Civil Government*, ch. 2, sect. 6. In P. Laslett, ed., *Two Treatises of Government* (Cambridge, U.K.: Cambridge University Press, 1960), 271.

4. Locke, section 27; in Laslett, *Two Treatises*, 287-88.

5. Nozick, *Anarchy, State, and Utopia*, 178.

6. See, for example, Matt Ridley, *The Origins of Virtue* (New York: Viking Penguin, 1997), 230-33.

7. To argue that specific preferences are *non*innocent precisely *because* not all could fulfill them is question-begging. It is also absurd, as the rest of the chapter will show.

8. See Allan Gibbard, "Natural Property Rights," *Nous* (1976, 77-86); reprinted in Robert M. Stewart, ed., *Readings in Social and Political Philosophy* (New York: Oxford University Press, 1985).

9. Locke, section 28: "If such a consent as that was necessary, man had starved, notwithstanding the plenty God had given him." Laslett, *Two Treatises*, 288.

10. Thomas Hobbes, *Leviathan* (New York: E. P. Dutton, Everyman Library, 1950), 107.

11. Hobbes, *Leviathan*, 149.

12. Hobbes, *Leviathan*, 107-8.

13. David Gauthier, *Morals by Agreement* (New York: Oxford University Press, 1986), 205. See also Mack, "The Self-Ownership Proviso."

14. For this reason, Randy Barnett has coined the term 'several property' to designate the notion. See his *The Structure of Liberty* (New York: Oxford University Press, 1998), 64-65.

15. James Grunebaum, *Private Ownership* (London: Routledge & Kegan Paul, 1987), 81.

16. Grunebaum, *Private Ownership*, 57-63.

17. Nozick, *Anarchy, State, and Utopia*, 176.

18. Nozick, *Anarchy, State, and Utopia*, 176.

19. In this system, "Only those who are laboring upon or using the land may claim title to it for the period of their use." Nobody would be allowed to *own* anything—that's how you or I would describe it, upon learning that this supposed ownership system didn't actually give anybody the right to buy or sell anything!

20. See chapter 9.

21. The point is delightfully as well as cogently made in P. J. O'Rourke's book, *Eat the Rich* (New York: Atlantic Monthly Press, 1998).

22. For the figures and original sources, see Ronald Bailey, ed., *The True State of the Planet* (New York: Free Press, 1995), specifically the chapters by Nicholas Eberstadt (7-48) and Dennis Avery (49-82).

23. The modern apostle in these matters is the late Julian Simon, to whom we are all in much debt. His last major work is *The Ultimate Resource II* (Princeton, N.J.: Princeton University Press, 1996), where the thesis is lavishly supported with facts and figures.

24. For an extremely instructive and admirably clear explication of the role of property rights for meeting any reasonable requirements intended by the Lockean Proviso, see David Schmidtz, "The Lockean Proviso," and the two subsequent sections in his *The Limits of Government* (Boulder, Colo.: Westview Press, 1991), 17-26.

25. See other relevant essays in Bailey, *The True State of the Planet*, for a quite comprehensive picture. And see chapter 16.

Chapter 9

Deserving Profits

The Challenge

"It is a peculiar smugness—and lack of theory—on the part of many of the well-off in advanced societies that leads them to suppose that they somehow deserve the luxury in which they live." So says Russell Hardin,[1] echoing a widely shared attitude. It is a matter of some interest, I would think, whether he is right about this, and we may take his remark as a suitable backdrop for the forthcoming deliberations on the desert or nondesert of profits in particular. Making a profit, as great a profit as possible, is at least one of the major objectives in business activity, and is often written up as the defining objective; to acquiesce in the disconcertingly popular view that profits are not deserved would be to undermine business quite fundamentally. And with it, as I would insist, our prosperity.

The thesis that profits are not deserved has been argued for, explicitly or implicitly, at different levels, of which I shall distinguish two. The more specific charge holds that desert is an important concept in social philosophy, perhaps that justice consists in giving people all and only what they deserve ('their due'); but that profits in particular, say because they are not worked for, are not properly deserved. Thus the "capitalist" economic system is unjust. But there is also a more general charge, stemming from Rawls, to the effect that desert can play no basic role in social philosophy, on the ground that the fundamental bases of desert would have to be "morally arbitrary." The upshot for the case of profits in particular is held to be that they also are not deserved.

And if they are not deserved, what would follow? The obvious suggestion is that it would then be O.K. to take them away from those who happen to have them, to "redistribute" them, deprive those who get them of the businesses which produce them, and the like. The resources in question would be regarded as available for public use, as it were. Plainly it is important to decide whether that is so.

In this chapter, I will respond to this charge, and uphold the thesis that profits can be deserved and often are so, though of course not always. And I shall try to correct, by setting in the appropriate perspective, the errors leading

131

to the opposite view. The inquiry will require us to think rather closely about three matters:

(1) the concept of desert, especially in relation to the neighboring but not identical notion of *entitlement*;

(2) an influential argument of Rawls that has been widely taken to undermine the notion of desert, or at least its applicability to most important issues about justice; and

(3) certain famous attacks on capitalists' roles in the productive system, to the effect that only those who do the "work" should be getting the rewards.

My strategy will then be twofold: one, to query how much it *matters* whether profits are "deserved"—to raise a question about just what is supposed to follow even if we were to grant that they are not so. On the other, I shall argue that in any case they (often) are, and are so in ways that are perfectly straightforward and not particularly problematic. Here I will complain that philosophical treatments of desert tend to leave out or soft-pedal the crucial role of the provider of the things deserved, the person from whom they are supposed to be deserved. Leaving out that person's interest in the matter turns out to be the root of the problem. When that is corrected, the case for the "capitalist" is, I think, complete.

A Central Distinction: Desert and Entitlement

No discussion of the present matter would pass muster without attention to a distinction made famous by Joel Feinberg,[2] and receiving well-deserved attention in a book-length study by George Sher[3]—the distinction between deserving something, on the one hand, and being entitled to it, on the other. We begin our investigation with it.

For individual A to be *entitled* to something, x, is for it to be the case that some structure of legitimate rules calls for A's getting or having x. It "calls for" it in the sense that x is *owed* to individual A; certain people are *required* to give x to A. One could eliminate the word 'legitimate' here, so that people could say, "I agree he's entitled to it: but entitlement has nothing to do with whether he should get it!" But it is more intuitive to use the term in such a way that one who speaks of entitlement presumptively thinks that the rules awarding the item in question are somehow justified, and would thus need to take back any claims to entitlement were the relevant structures shown to be invalid or shot through with injustice. What matters here is simply that nothing, so far, is implied about the *desert* of x by A. As Sher observes, "That desert and rights are distinct is suggested by the fact that persons often deserve such things as success, competitive victory, and wages, to which they have no rights, and equally often acquire rights to property and opportunities that they do not deserve."[4]

Sher goes on, following Feinberg, to observe that the concepts of desert and entitlement "belong to different parts of our ethical vocabulary": namely, to the parts concerning *value* and *obligation*, respectively. Most desert-claims, he notes, "are grounded not in anyone's obligations, but rather in the value of persons' coming to have what they deserve."[5] The most prominent and, for our purposes, nearly paradigmatic example of entitlement is where person *B*'s receiving of x from person *A* is called for by an agreement between *A* and *B*, where *A* previously had legitimate control over the disposition of x, as when *B* has bought something from *A*. Larger structures of agreement cover many further cases: various people have made arrangements, the terms of which are such that *A*, who is a party to that agreement, is required to transfer x to *B*, who is happy to accept it. Whether there are entitlements from nonvoluntary structures is another question. But where profit is in question, the agreement of the persons concerned is a sine qua non.

Deserving x, by contrast, is a considerably more difficult notion to pin down. When we argue for someone's desert of something, we point to such factors as the person's efforts to get it, or to other personal qualities which, we think, constitute relevant considerations that favor giving it to him. Indeed, desert needn't be attributed to persons at all: a starry night could deserve our taking time out from other activities to gaze at it. It is not greatly surprising that a philosopher such as Sher can devote a couple of hundred subtly argued pages to exploring this subtle and interesting concept.

Nevertheless—building in part on Sher's labors—I shall hazard an initial characterization (to be elaborated below), which will perhaps serve as an approximate definition:

> *To say that A deserves x is to say that some fact about A is such as to constitute a reason for A's getting or having x.*

Well, which facts about *A*? Either some action(s), or some relevant feature or quality; especially, in the case where *A* is a person, some other nonadventitious personal quality. Among prominent examples: having worked for x, exerted oneself toward the acquisition or bestowal of x in some relevant way, or displaying some appropriate quality of character bearing on x. It is natural to say, when desert is queried, "What has he done to deserve it?"; but also "Well, what's so great about him that he should get such treatment?" The treatment need not be good: for 'great', substitute 'awful' for the converse case. The general point is that those questions require answers when a case for desert is made. Desert needs a "case": that is, we must be able to point to features, qualities, or actions of A that call for the bestowal of x. These constitute the "merits" on the basis of which x is to be given. The more merit(s) of the relevant kind, the stronger the case for giving x to A.

Feinberg offers[6] the classic example illustrating the distinction of entitlement and desert: a (formally organized) footrace. Suppose that Jones crosses the finish line first. He is thus, by the rules of the competition, entitled to the prize. Jones may also have exerted himself mightily, trained countless hours, and in general gone all out to win. That would count toward making it true that he deserved to win. But the one who actually does win does not merely "deserve" the prize: the organizers actually *owe* it to him: it would be flying in the face of the constituting rules of the activity in question if he did not get it.

Suppose, on the other hand, that Jones wins by a fluke. It was, instead, Smith who went all out, trained assiduously, etc.; but alas, appendicitis strikes Smith at the halfway mark, or he stumbles on a stray stone. Fate or accident intervenes to prevent him from realizing his goal of winning. Sad. He *deserved* to win, but alas, he did not. So he does not get the prize. He is, unfortunately, not *entitled* to the prize. Everyone will sympathize at this unhappy outcome. But none will object that the prize should instead go to Smith.

The race example involves one of the most characteristic bases of desert: effort. Sher observes that "Of all the bases of desert, perhaps the most familiar and compelling is diligent, sustained effort. Whatever else we think, most of us agree that persons deserve things for sheer hard work."[7] But is it the *only* basis of desert? Can one, for instance, deserve something by virtue of what one *is*, rather than what one *does*? The example of the starry sky, I believe, shows that we can. What, after all, are the stars supposed to have done—come out and twinkle for us?

But we may dwell on an equally compelling example[8] involving persons: the beauty contest. Of two competitors, Ms. *H* and Ms. *K*, suppose that Ms. *H* is by nature irresistible, while Ms. *K*, not so well favored, works away at everything—her figure, her smile, the works. The judges nevertheless award the prize to Ms. *H*, despite her almost total lack of effort toward that end. Do we say that *H* deserves the prize, or not? If the judges declare *H* the winner, then of course she is *entitled* to it. But that's not all. Being, let us suppose, the clearly more attractive of the two, she also *deserves* it. The judges might, indeed, feel that Ms. *K* deserves a prize—an award for effort, say. But it is, after all, a beauty contest, they reflect, and if so, then the prize should go to Ms. *H*, who might reasonably feel hard done by were the clearly less attractive Ms. *K* to get it. It was, after all, a beauty contest, and not, say, a self-improvement competition. The one who is in truth more beautiful is the one who ought to be pronounced to be so, and to get the prize. Surely that's clear, even though effort and assiduity have little to do with it.

The specifics of the example should be set aside here. In a different contest, points may be reserved for talent, intelligence, moral character, or what have you. And whether there should even be contests for beauty at all is, of course, a debatable—certainly a much-debated—issue. But we aren't debating it here. Indeed, part of the point of using this example, which will undoubtedly be thought in bad taste by some, is to illustrate another important feature of the notion of desert: it doesn't just apply in contexts we approve of. We might be totally uninterested, or quite negatively interested, in bestowing any sort of favor or approval upon those who excel at certain things: the Mafia chieftain who gives an extra pat on the back to a favored assassin for a "job well done"; or Mr. Universe 1991. But that those who do figure in these cases recognizably employ the concept of desert rather than something else is perfectly clear.

That it is perfectly clear brings up an extremely important question about this matter: it seems that to say that someone deserves something is not only not to say that he or she will get it, but also, it is not even to say that he (morally) *should*; or at any rate, not just like that. "Meritorious" gangsters should *not* get rewards. But must we stick with this? Can we say in our hearts that *A* in truth deserves x, yet seriously deny that *A* should get x? Perhaps not. We can understand others' employment of desert-criteria without internalizing them ourselves. What the Mafia lieutenant *really* deserves, we might say, is not a pat on the back, but a long stay in the cooler.

Those who are inclined to down-rate beauty contests may feel that sex appeal, say, is not the sort of thing that should be publicly displayed, or that there is something morally criticizable about elevating individuals above others in that respect. But they may also feel, more germanely to the present discussion, that the way one is physically structured is essentially a matter of one's genetic endowment, something that one has no control over. And they may advance the view that to make the contest depend on what is beyond the control of the contestants is somehow *unfair*.

This leads us in the direction of the kind of issues brought up in a now-famous argument of John Rawls': can we justly base desert on qualities wholly beyond the control of the agent, qualities that are, as we may agree, morally arbitrary? We will devote specific attention to Rawls' argument later. But before doing so, we need to return to the distinction of desert and entitlement, and to ask: what really justifies these distinctions? Thus far I have only produced examples that, I suppose, most readers will find persuasive. But some may not, for they may think that the examples are tied to an ideology they reject. As arguments, they have the shortcomings that "intuitive" arguments always have: they persuade only those who are, or are nearly, already persuaded. Can we do better?

At this point, then, we have two jobs to do. The first is to defend the "entitlement" idea. What I have said above may in general be described as having been said from within an approach to our subject that includes recognition of entitlement as a proper basis for various goods; but what if someone wishes to reject the entire view? Have we anything to say to him? I think the answer is in the affirmative, and moreover that quite a lot of what there is to be said has been said. But not all. I hope that the further bit I add will also nail it down (knowing perfectly well, to be sure, that it won't do so for all). I pursue that in the next section.

The other matter is to try to get a good handle on the notion of desert, to develop a view of desert which will explain where it belongs in the theory of morals and what it is doing here. We will pursue that matter later in this chapter. Having done those two things, we will be in a position to address ourselves to the question whether profits are deserved, or better, when in general they are deserved and then whether it is reasonable to pronounce that they generally are or are not. And, perhaps more importantly, we will be in a position to say how much and why that matters.

Justifying Entitlement

Should we ever give things to people on the ground that they are entitled to them, as distinct from the ground that they deserve them? The answer will require an excursion into moral theory. My excuse for doing so here is that it seems to be essential; but my hope is that it can be done briefly enough to provide a reasonable glimpse at the answer, and yet keep the end of this chapter from disappearing over the horizon. The answers to both the question about entitlement and the question about desert on bases other than effort are, I believe, of a piece. We take up the first and more fundamental of them in this section.

The general answer I propose to give holds that a rational morality must be based on our interests, where 'our' refers, in particular, to us *agents*. The central, generating interests for morals are the interests of acting agents. Agents are the decision-makers; it is, to use a now familiar computer metaphor, they who have the central processors in this operation. We gather data from the outside, to be sure: how this is going to affect us is important, and something over which we have limited control. What we are going to *do* about it, on the other hand, is what we have control over. The control, of course, is in turn exercised, if we are rational, on behalf of our interests or, what is for this purpose the same, our values.

Among these interests will be some that it is reasonable to describe as "commitments" and others that it is not, such as breathing—crucial, but not something we deliberate about; still others are of varying degrees of importance, from trivial to overwhelming. Adjusting the mix of interest-pursuits is, generally speaking, what decision-making mainly consists in. That we have a certain interest is often obvious to us, but even when it is, how we are to pursue it when we must make trade-offs between that and various other interests will often be a perplexing issue. And it is by no means claimed that we will always or even usually settle such things by calculation or anything much resembling it. Reflection is often low level: we get a few more facts, we find ourselves deciding to do this rather than that, and it is only retrospectively that we conclude that our "maximum utility," say, lay in that direction.

What about the interests of other people? For us agents, that is, in principle and in general, a live issue. The interests of others, or at least others *in general*, do not come stamped with normative force. We can realize that another person's interest will be much affected by a certain action and we can react so as to promote it; but we might also decide to impede it, or we might remain indifferent: its effects on our practical life may be essentially nil. Are any general policies—policies for *all*, regardless of their particular concerns—to be recommended in this area, and if so, on what basis?

The word 'general' occurs several times in the preceding short paragraph, and is to be taken seriously. 'Others in general' are, simply, others regardless of their specific relation to us. We may love some few of them, perhaps dislike some others; but toward most we have neither attitude. They are miscellaneous people, people we don't know as particular people, but still, people, with many of whom we nevertheless interact. Not with all at once, of course, or indeed, in most cases, ever. There is, however, no telling whom we might cross paths with next among all these folks. What aspects of people in general, then, might concern one?

The answer to that question is, in form, obvious: we are concerned about their potential effect on our interests, our "projects," on what we value. To affect those interests is to affect them for better or worse. And to gauge this, we need to invoke a notion of our "status quo." A change for the better is an improvement on where we are; a change for the worse is a decline from there. When we act, we do so, we hope, for the better and in any case not for the worse. We each find ourselves with an assortment of resources, a major subset of which is our repertoire of personal assets and powers, and with a sizable and fairly amorphous set of interests, desires, goals. When we act, we utilize those powers, which can reasonably be regarded as really "us" if anything is—our bodies and minds; and we utilize such other resources as may be available. What makes a resource 'available' is that it responds to our commands, roughly speaking. The set of resources we command is what enables us to act. Accordingly, we are concerned that their availability be unproblematic.

Now consider the notion of desert. As noted, it is a value notion. Whether someone deserves something is a matter of how well that person meets certain relevant conditions; very often it is how well he meets them in relation to various other individuals. Whether we will measure up, in any particular case, is in general and in principle uncertain, to greater or lesser degree. If our ability to act in any particular way were always conditioned on our maximally meeting some normatively significant conditions, life for most of us would, in a word, be impossible. We would have no assurance of where we stand; we could scarcely get up in the morning with any confidence that we could do anything at all, for sure. We would continually be subservient to variable value-judgments, and not just our own.

When we are *entitled* to something, on the other hand, these questions of value are shoved to the rear. With an entitlement, we know where we stand, because where we stand doesn't depend on whether, on this particular day, we have got an 'A' instead of a 'B+' or even a 'C-'. An entitlement is comparable to a decision: when we have made up our minds, we are ready to act. The work of deliberation, whether it was done the best it could be done or not, is now done. The item in question is, simply, one's own, and whether it remains so depends only on things one decides oneself, or at least by oneself and certain definite other people. From the point of view of the rational agent, entitlement secures one against the unpredictable decisions, and thus the possible depredations, of others. These others, whom we don't know and have no particular personal interest in, are kept, so to say, at a safe operating distance by one's entitlements. Whether to become involved with them at some other level is then up to us.

It has become customary among moral theorists to distinguish between 'teleological' and 'deontological' theories, and to identify the former with systems in which values are regarded as *impersonal*, the paradigm example being utilitarianism. People then identify deontological theories as, for instance, 'right based' or 'duty based'. A right based system has it that morality suspends from fundamental rights, whereas a teleological system holds that morals issue from value-principles.

This seems effectively to saddle the deontological theorists with, in effect, either an intuitionist or a natural-law basis. Frankly, the two come to the same thing: a normative "natural law" is one which is supposed to be true just in the nature of things: fundamentally, one just "sees" that the principle in question is true—it's "self-evident." But then, that's exactly what an intuition is: a moral principle or judgment that presents itself without further reason.

I have long complained about proposing to found moral theory on intuition, and will merely reiterate the main objection here.[10] We need, most especially, to distinguish two senses of the term 'based'. In one of these, a moral system is "based" on its moral "axioms" or most fundamental ("first") principles. In this sense, whether a moral theory is teleological or deontological is a matter of what the normative principles look like on which, according to the theorist, all others depend. If an act of type F is right only because, given certain facts, such acts turn out also to be of type G, then the principles claiming the rightness of G are more fundamental than those about F. If what makes an act right is held always to be that it meets certain value criteria, e.g., maximization, then we have a "teleological" or "value-based" system in this sense; if not, then it is "deontological" (or mixed).

But that is not the only relevant sense of 'based'. For if we now turn our attention to the question what makes the fundamental principles *true*, then we have a different question: what is morality itself "based on"? And to claim that even the fundamental principles are "based on rights," for example, is to hold that rights are somehow just "there," metaphysical "facts" not capable of further explication.

To hold, as I do, that morality suspends from our interests is to deny that there are any such metaphysical facts. Yet it is not to commit oneself to utilitarianism, either. On the contrary: we need to realize that Utilitarianism is itself a "right-based" system in my second sense of the term. When Henry Sidgwick asks why we should regard the like utility of others as morally equal to our own, he cites a deontic constraint: it simply *is* thus equal, he in effect says. That is as much as to say that morality requires us to regard it so. And why does it thus require us? To this he has no further answer.[11] A more recent theorist, R. M. Hare, misleadingly talks as though we can prove this by the "logic of the moral concepts"—as though it were a purely conceptual truth that morality obliges us to accept Sidgwick's axiom.[12] He's wrong about this. A morality need not be utilitarian. Its principles can permit people to ignore the greater utility of others.[13] Whether and in what ways their utility should be taken into account is an open question.

What answers that question, then? Briefly, what answers it is the way they are likely to affect us, given considerations of interaction. Others impinge on us, bump into us. Some of them get, as the song says, "under our skin": our utility is directly affected by their utility. But most do not. With most of them, our interactions must be, in a sense, more superficial than that. Our main concern is that they not affect us adversely, that our interactions with them be on the whole for our good or at least not for our ill. And they, similarly, want this of us.

Some seem to suppose that it is rational for us to demand that those others not only refrain from making things worse for us, but also that they make some contribution, perhaps a substantial one, to our well-being. For instance, some even appear to think that what they owe us, or we them, is an equalization, along some dimension or other, of our respective levels of well-being. But it is evident that this is not a reasonable demand. If you are the party with the initially better situation, why should you accept such a requirement? Why *must* you do anything for me? If you have your choice to start with, and are given your choice between simply leaving me to my devices and working hard for me with no return on the investment, why wouldn't you leave and be done with me? What we do need with others, though, are general principles of *co-operation*: constraints from impinging on us to our ill, and provisions for enabling us to improve our lot from these interactions without doing so to others' (net) loss. These principles must be adopted in mutual interest, not out of a hunch about "general utility."

This specifically means that considering our general situations, it is not only in my interest that my entitlements be recognized and respected, but also that it is in my interest to recognize and respect yours. I benefit from your agreement to refrain from deciding whether to deprive me of my life exclusively on the basis of whether that happens to serve your interests at the time; but a necessary condition of your reasonably agreeing to this is that I likewise recognize your right to exist, agreeing not to contemplate the same practical issue regarding your life in that same myopic way.[14]

When we propose to insist to others, as a prerequisite for interaction, that they not feel free to injure us in respect of our bodies and any other resources we may have, this cannot rationally be based on notions of desert or value. I do not know how you value me, and I do not, in a sense, care. I do not claim to "deserve" to be who I happen to be; indeed, the whole idea of deserving such a thing makes no sense. Small wonder that I shall repudiate the general thesis that all rights must be based on desert.

Yet this is not because *rights* are metaphysically basic features of the world. It is because I'd have to be a fool to leave my prospects to the vagaries of desert-based notions, or for that matter of "general utility." Entitlements do not depend on such things. They are, instead, recognitions, agreements about who gets what: they draw lines and allot the desired things bounded by them to particular persons, not on the basis that those are the "best" persons to occupy those areas, but on the basis that they in fact, as it happens, do occupy them, have the strongest interest in continuing to do so, thank you very much, and will thus utilize their powers to prevent the rest from dislodging them. And we likewise will do so in relation to them.

That the "Social Contract," the general "agreement" to be made with all, has the general form of conserving and protecting what one has rather than supposed rights to the care and promotion of one's interests by others is likewise not due to metaphysics. It is, instead, because this is the best deal we can practically expect from everyone, given one's own typical lack of emotional concern for furthering others' projects. Drawing a moral line around one's own concerns, insisting on the noninterference of others, enables one to operate without the constant predatory and defensive activities that would be necessary in the absence of morals.

Note that it would be a mistake to depend on metaphysical claims about "natural" rights, or intuitions of same, for these purposes. If intuitions have any force, it has to be because they constitute a somewhat inchoate exercise of practical reason at work, a more or less dim hunch that this is the way to go, considering our respective situations. They are more or less educated guesses that this or that represents a reasonable *joint principle for interaction*. As such, it is subject to further explication and justification, but does not depend on an immediate ability to provide those.

Desert in Relation to Entitlement

The question will naturally arise what is the relation between desert and entitlement—or is there one? The answer, I suggest, is that we need such concepts as desert in order to arrive at decisions about what to do with whatever we are entitled to do anything with. Your entitlements do not answer the question whether I should cut you in or out of my will: you quite simply are not entitled to any of my estate, as things stand. If I happen to decide to do so and alter the terms of my will accordingly, or if I just decide to give you something, then, my having signed on the dotted line, they're yours. Whether the executors should hand over the money, or whether the bank should cash my check to you, are not matters for them to determine on the basis of your merits, your deserts: they are settled by considerations of entitlement. But my original decision to include you among my beneficiaries is clearly not settled, nor can it be settled, by entitlements alone. Entitlements frame the limits on our actions. I cannot decide to cut you out of my neighbor's will, for instance. But having command of some resources, my question what to do with them, once I have paid outstanding debts, can only be rationally addressed in such terms as whether you deserve a share. Once I have invested in a certain company, I am entitled to dividends, as decided by its board of directors. But should I invest in it in the first place, rather than some other? Plainly to decide that, I must turn to considerations of whether this is the best company for my purposes. And I may quite properly include the matter of whether it deserves my support among those considerations.

Philosophers have talked as though they must choose between "teleological" notions like desert and "deontological" ones like entitlement. But it simply isn't so. We really need both. Proceeding exclusively with entitlements would be irrational if it were even intelligible; but preceding exclusively with notions such as desert, as I have argued, is also impossible and therefore irrational. In the later sections of this chapter, I shall try to sort out the bearing of these notions on the question of profit. Whether we ever are *entitled* to profits, however, is surely part of what was intended by the broad question this chapter addressed. Suppose that many deserved them, but none were ever entitled to them? We should hardly have settled the broad question to anyone's satisfaction if that were our result.

Natural Desert?

Now let us turn to the second question: can we ever deserve things by virtue of natural qualities as distinct from achievements and efforts on the part of the deserving person? May we reasonably regard Harry as "deserving" his prize, or his reward, or his paycheck for that matter, on the basis of his native gifts? To do so goes somewhat against the natural grain, as it were, of the concept of desert. George Sher observes that "Of all the bases of desert, perhaps the most familiar and compelling is diligent, sustained effort. Whatever else we think, most of us agree that persons deserve things for sheer hard work."[15] And he goes on to note a "natural suggestion": that "the diligent deserve what they were striving to get by their efforts."[16]

Why should we attach so much weight to diligence, industry, persistence, and the like—to committed and directed activity? Sher offers the plausible observation that "Unlike other resources, our time and energy are not just means of augmenting the effects of our actions. They are, instead, the raw materials of those actions themselves . . . the very stuff of which we fashion our lives. . . . By single-mindedly pursuing the goal, he is weaving it into the fabric of his life."[17] And this, in the end, is "the correct explanation of why the diligent ought to succeed. . . . because their sustained efforts are substantial investments of themselves—the ultimate sources of value—in the outcomes they seek."[18] When such things are said, though, how are we to read the 'ought' in this last sentence—that the diligent "*ought*" to succeed? Not, Sher agrees, in such a way as to "imply either that the hard worker has any special right against anyone else or that anyone else has any special obligation toward him . . . In itself, diligent effort creates no entitlements."[19] And he quite properly also points out that diligence of itself is not normally enough in any case to constitute a case for deserving reward or even, in a sense, success. Thus take the cases of "the untalented poet, the mediocre tennis player, and the political hack." In their cases, he suggests, "the two sources of value conflict. If we focus on their diligent efforts, we are led to believe that these agents ought to succeed, while if we focus on the easy predictability of their failure, we are led to believe that they ought to fail."[20] That easy predictability is due, however, to lack of talent.

Return for a moment to our beauty contest of section two above. Ms. K deserves to win in that she worked hard; but Ms. H deserves to win because she simply, despite lack of significant effort to get that way, looked better. Similar cases readily crowd to mind: the prodigious violinist who plays better at seven than the normal symphonic violinist who has worked hard over a long life, the naturally talented writer to whom the felicitous phrase leaps effortlessly to mind, and so on. In all of these cases, the assigned criterion of merit is such that some will almost certainly have a natural advantage over others, one that no amount of hard work on the part of those others will ever overcome.

These cases are real. Natural beauty of person, talent, or intelligence, and indeed strength or, say, sweetness of character are all, I believe, *real* phenomena. Some people are born in such a way that given any chance, they will display these qualities in a degree far above the average. And the same goes for undesirable qualities. Those who think that this just isn't so are usually those who think that it *cannot* be so. They don't genuinely think that the evidence doesn't support the hypothesis that there are natural talents; rather, they think that it *cannot* support it, that the whole idea of natural differences of valuable qualities among people is a nonstarter. Though the evidence for such differences seems overwhelming, it does not matter very much for present purposes whether it is really so. What does matter is that it might well be so, that it is very, very widely thought to be so, and thus that our view of what to say if it is so matters, practically speaking.

It matters, I take it, whether there are appropriate responses to what we take to be natural inequalities, and whether the sort of responses we currently think to be appropriate are so. They might be inappropriate without this inappropriateness being a function of misperception of the facts: perhaps there is some *conceptual* inappropriateness, so that we are responding wrongly even if we are right in thinking the phenomena in question to be natural. Such is the view of those who hold that to employ such criteria of desert is always unfair. Are they right? Can someone be said to "deserve" anything by virtue of possession of a natural trait?

We should first point out that it is never absolutely the sheer possession of such a quality or talent that, just like that, does the "deserving." The possessors of the talents or other attributes that make things easy for them still have to have done *something*. It's just that what they may have to do can be relatively trifling, perhaps, as compared with those who hoped to succeed by diligence. Ms. H, in my beauty contest case, may, for example, have signed up at the last minute, upon the suggestion of a friend who shoves the entry form and pencil before her, and she may have agreed to enter just for a lark rather than with serious hope of, or even interest in, achieving victory. Then her natural assets, to her surprise, prevail. Still, she would not have won if she hadn't even applied or showed so little interest in it as not even to have walked attractively across the stage at the appropriate moments. We can also note that there are, after all, no qualities whose display by humans is totally passive. No matter what one's natural endowment, there are things one could do to wreck things: pour acid over oneself to extinguish natural good looks, take mind-destroying potions to reduce natural intelligence to a residual level, and so on. People who do not do such things thereby have, after all, "done" something, even if all they have done is to refrain from doing something. And recognitions of possession of such qualities does, in a minor way, serve to motivate people not to destroy or hide them; and also, as in the beauty contest, to put one's qualities on public display, benefiting many more than would otherwise be the case.

In these rather marginal ways, then, we can say that all desert is conditional upon effort of *some* kind. But it is indeed marginal: what really turns the trick, given the perhaps tiny input of effort, may be the natural talents or qualities display of which earns the prize. Is this morally acceptable? Does the naturally beautiful or naturally talented competitor then "deserve" the prize? Certainly! The criterion is beauty, or whatever, and however she or he came by it, there they are, displaying that quality or talent in sufficient abundance to beat out all comers.

What do those who object have in mind against this seemingly obvious point? Some, as we noted above, may be questioning the purpose of the whole exercise: who cares about "beauty" anyway, they may ask. It's just "in the eye of the beholder," after all, and carries little weight against more important qualities like character or intelligence. Why, they may ask, are we wasting our time in this trivial pursuit? The replies to such objections are, I think, conclusive. The answer to the question, 'Who cares, anyway?' is: those who went to the trouble of organizing the contest, attending it, putting up the prize money, and so on—that's who. And to the second, those concerned may simply say that it's not trivial to *them*, or that even if it is, it's amusing, interesting, or whatever. And that will be answer enough.

In point of fact, most people taken off the street, of whichever sex and of whatever age above childhood, are likely to have an interest in beauty of person, and there is in fact likely to be a fair amount of agreement among them as to who has more of it than whom. There is, in short, a general human interest on which such contests may have a rational bearing. Beauty of person is in its modest way a good, and why shouldn't we recognize it in public contests? But this is overkill. It is not necessary for the concept of desert to be wielded that the deserving qualities be of wide and general interest. For all we need is that it matters to *those concerned*. From their point of view, there is no good reason to exclude, and every reason to include, the naturally advantaged. The possession of certain qualities is what they are interested in, and their interests are what make the whole thing go round.

The point, then, is this: desert must not be thought of as a fundamentally two-place predicate, '*A* deserves x'. That is suggested by our opening characterization ("To say that *A* *deserves* x is to say that something about *A* is such as to constitute a reason for *A*'s getting or having x"). It's right, so far as it goes, but it doesn't go far enough. We need to give explicit recognition to the fact that desert is fundamentally a *three*-placed affair, at a minimum. The "something about A" that constitutes the reason in question does so *for* those whose possible bestowal of what is deserved is in question. The proper formula, then, is '*A* deserves x from *B*', where *B* is the bestower of the benefit in question. And our opening formula needs to be fleshed out thus:

> To say that A deserves x is to say that something about A is such as to *constitute* a reason for A's getting or having x from B—in other words, it constitutes a reason for B to see to it that A has or *gets x*.

And that person, B, bestows this benefit on the basis of B's own interests. B singles out the "more deserving" on the basis of criteria of importance to B. For talk of desert to make sense, then, we need a point of view and an agent who can act to forward the interests recognized in that point of view, an agent who discerns aspects of the environment, e.g., of various other humans in her environment, whose qualities and doings can or do make a contribution to things that matter to her.

This is not to say that the concept of desert applies every time any rational person decides, for whatever reason or for none, to bestow some benefit on some person. To say that someone deserves something is to say that someone meets the criteria laid down by the rewarder. What the sponsors, the providers, of the reward say is, "We are looking for persons with such-and-such qualities; we will count this list of talents, accomplishments, or features as the basis upon which we will bestow the reward." Absent an understanding of that kind, nobody would be able to recognize the case as one of meriting or deserving in any sense. The reward would be a sheer windfall, indicating no merit of any sort, but just good luck. Though one could stretch things and regard "luckiness" as itself a rewardable attribute.

Now, of the qualities in persons that interest people, some are more improvable by effort than others. Our interest in recognizing them, by expressions of approval, formal public recognizances of merit, or more substantial benefits, consists considerably in encouraging people to make efforts in the appropriate directions. That's a major part of it, certainly. But not all. Just as we may admire the sunset, going so far as to exclaim enthusiastically, but to no one in particular, at its beauties, so we may admire human qualities even if they are not ones that can readily or even, perhaps, at all, respond to deliberate cultivation.

And that, in a nutshell, is why desert is not confined to achievement requiring substantial and directed effort. From the point of view of those who do invest effort in this or that object, such as the worker in some business, it may seem that all that matters, the only relevant desert base, is effort. But the rewardee is not the only one who matters. On the contrary: it is the *rewarder* whose interests crucially determine the nature of the competition or other social undertaking that creates the context in which the notion of desert is applied. Sometimes this is the same person. One can have a sense of achievement, a sense of desert via accomplishment, or the reverse: one gives oneself a pat on the back, or a kick in the backside. But we are not the only ones who matter—and if we are, we have no reasonable complaint to the others who do not share in our self-recognitions.

A cautionary note should perhaps be added on the subject of "Meritocracy." Nothing that has been said has any tendency whatever to support the idea that we, either collectively or individually, should bestow political power, or any power, on individuals of natural ability, energy, beauty, or the like. One reason for this is that nobody deserves anything for just absolutely being whatever she or he happens to be: we must, as we have seen, do *something*. And in the case of political or any sort of power, what we do has to serve the interests of those bestowing it. All must earn their way, though that will be far easier for some than others. To take a major kind of case in point, the rich do not deserve anything just for being rich. But, having money, they are in a position to make offers for things they want that somebody out there is unlikely to refuse; and they are in a position to fund this or that venture. But they must actually *do* so. Meritocracies, like aristocracies, would require the rest of us to bestow benefits—praise, social position, whatever—on persons *for free*, that is, irrespective of what they do for us. That is an absurdity which the point of view developed here should help to expose, rather than be thought to invite as a supposed implication.

Rawls on Desert

Rawls' famed argument against desert starts from the indisputable premise that nobody can conceivably be said to "deserve" her genetic endowment, parentage, or existing social and natural environment, since prior to being "given" those things, there was no individual to give them to, they being what make that person the individual she is; and of course afterwards, it's too late to do anything about them. Then the argument proceeds to point out that whatever we may do to deserve anything, the possibility of doing it is contingent upon our having a natural endowment of a relevant type. So much is uncontroversial. But it then goes on to argue that if one's desert basis for benefit x, say D, is one whose very existence, or one's very capacity to display it, is in turn contingent on some undeserved attribute F, then one doesn't deserve D; and since one doesn't deserve D, then one doesn't deserve x either. "The assertion that a man deserves the superior character that enables him to make the effort to cultivate his abilities is equally problematic; for his character depends in large part upon fortunate family and social circumstances for which he can claim no credit. The notion of desert seems not to apply to these cases." And if not, then "the more advantaged representative man cannot say that he deserves and therefore has a right to a scheme of cooperation in which he is permitted to acquire benefits in ways that do not contribute to the welfare of others. There is no basis for his making this claim."[21]

Many criticisms have been launched against this remarkable argument. Sher, for instance, suggests that the claim that if F is necessary for D, then we can deny desert of x, is too strong, for two reasons. One is that if we interpret Rawls' argument as essentially one of fairness, then, he thinks, it can at most apply to desert-bases in respect of which we *differ*, and applies only to the marginal benefits of our differential endowments[22] rather than all benefits of all endowments whatever. The other is the claim that D's being conditioned by F is not enough; F should be not only a necessary but a sufficient condition for D before D gets ruled out of court. Thus of two persons with equal intelligence, say, one might apply it while the other idles. So the undeserved condition doesn't actually cause the desert of the deserver; additional effort makes the difference, and this is a real merit of the deserving person.[23]

But these counters, I think, do not get to the heart of the matter. For one thing, the second really gets us into the Free Will problem in a major way, and that is one we should stay out of: the idea that people come in for desert by volitions of their own that are totally uncaused by any factors they can't control is surely too obscure, too "far out" to be relied on in serious ethical applications. It belongs very strictly to metaphysics rather than to ethics.

But more importantly, Sher's first objection involves a basic misunderstanding, with which we must now come to grips. The problem is this: if Rawls' argument is right at all, then it undermines *all* arguments for desert, not just those involving marginal differences. It is true that Rawls is especially concerned with fairness, and this will make him sensitive to proposals which would distinguish one person from another. But that's only what Rawls is interested in. His actual argument, however—whatever he may have intended—is not sensitive to such distinctions. If we do not deserve anything for which we do not, in turn, deserve the basis on which we allegedly deserve it, then we do not deserve *anything*, regardless of how many other people are similarly or differently situated. That I deserve x neither more nor less than you do doesn't show that all of us do deserve it, and this argument of Rawls cuts to the bone: if it is right, then none of us deserves anything at all. If justice is regarded as a matter of giving people what they deserve, and Rawls' argument is sound, then the correct inference is that we shouldn't give anything to anyone.

An interesting further question to pose for the enthusiast who rushes to embrace this position about justice then arises: ought we, in addition to giving them nothing new, also to take away that which the undeserving—that's all of us, remember—already have? If so, then to be consistent we should commit universal suicide (or perhaps murder, should some be reluctant). We do not, after all, deserve life.

If the proponent shies away from that conclusion, holding only that we should not give people *further* things just because they "deserve" them, though they may—lucky blokes!—keep the unmerited things they already have, then we might further ask how we are to make a principled use of that idea. If we may properly give some nice things to ourselves despite our total lack of desert, why couldn't we also give them to others whom it happens to serve our purposes to give them to? Indeed, couldn't we just do whatever we liked with them? There would, I think, be no reasonable reply to that query.

But if so, then nothing really stops us from being allowed to give anything we want to anyone we want to, and to retain what we have (viz., our very selves) together with whatever we can get by utilizing those selves. We are home free, so to speak. And what will we do with our freedom? Surely, we will reestablish notions of desert *without* the Rawlsian rider, feeling free to reward those who do things useful or interesting to ourselves, regardless of the metaphysical underpinnings of those actions or displays.

If we are to use notions of desert at all, then, Rawls' argument must be rejected entirely. We must admit that persons may indeed deserve things without having also "deserved" all, or for that matter *any*, of the various personal qualities by virtue of which they come to have done or exemplified whatever we think makes them deserve the item we propose to award them on that basis. The proper way to look at desert is from the point of view of the holder of the assets or benefits to be distributed. Why should we reward individuals who do x, or who have property G? The answer, fundamentally, is that it *serves our purposes to do so*. Desert is not a one-way street. That is the view which stems from forgetting that it is a three-place and not a two-place predicate. That third place is vital, for it is what makes sense of the whole thing. It is we agents who bestow praise and blame, rewards and punishments, and if we are rational, then we will do so on the basis of the contributions such activities make to what *we value*. "Desert bases" do not operate all by themselves: people do not deserve things of nobody, or of abstract entities or "brooding omnipresences in the sky." If they deserve things, they deserve them from *us*—the people who have them to give, and the motivation to give them.

Being Entitled to Profits

So far, I have attempted to explain why we have major use for (1) the general notion of entitlement as distinct from desert, and (2) for the coherence and rationality of awarding things on the basis of the possession of properties or the exercise of capacities which may not themselves have been deserved. What does all this have to do with our present subject, the desert of profits?

I take this present subject to concern not only desert in any narrow sense, but also more generally with the moral grounds, whatever they may be, for recognizing the legitimacy of profits. Those denying the desert of profits do so, surely, in a spirit of denying their legitimacy, denying that we should let people "get away" with them. Property is Theft, says Proudhon; so are profits, says Marx. The implication is that we shouldn't permit them. The question is whether they are right about that, and not just whether they or others are right about a much narrower thesis that profits are not, technically, 'deserved'.

The outlines of my answer to this important question are as follows. First, if people are ever *entitled* to profits, then it may not matter whether they also deserve them. If the entitlement system by which they are so entitled is defensible, then profit will be defensible as a corollary. And second, when they do deserve them, if they ever do, then it need not be by virtue of exerting great effort or of applying skills or qualities acquired only as the result of earlier effort or even of any intentional, directed activity at all. We may have perfectly good reason to bestow "rewards" of the specific type that profits are, on the particular agents who serve us in the ways in which their profitable activities do. In this section, I consider Entitlement.

Let's first remind ourselves of the general idea of ownership. It is, to begin with, clearly in the Entitlement rather than the Desert category. To *own* something is to be *entitled* to do as we wish with it, of course within whatever restrictions are imposed by others' rights. Some[24] have pointed out that that we can disassemble the set of possible things that might be done with anything into various different subsets: e.g., specific use, disposal, transfer, rental, and whatnot. This truth has led them into a falsehood: that the notion of ownership is wholly synthetic—actually, so to speak, composed of a set of wholly distinct rights, the uniting of which is (a) logically unnecessary, and (b) wholly conventional, in particular, legal. That inference is wrong. The fact that A can be broken down into B, C, and D does not prove that A is essentially nothing but the adventitious sum of B, C, and D, and especially does not prove that A has to be put together by convention. Nature does it all the time; and while it is not exactly "nature" that puts together the various separable powers of ownership, neither is it simply convention.

In the case of property ownership, the unifying property of these diverse possible acts is easy to identify. No matter what we do with items, what unites them all is simply that we (can) *do* them. And if a moral case can be made for allowing people, in general, to do things that they want to do, then we have a moral case, prima facie, for property. For me to have the right to x, where x is an object of some sort, is simply for me, in general, to have the say-so on what happens to x. Whatever use can be made of x, the person wanting to do this, if not myself, has to "clear" it with me. If it's mine, then if I want to go fishing with it, my own "permission" is automatic; but if someone else wants to, it is not, and the permission must be obtained or reasonably inferred. Such is the nature of entitlements.

Why should we accept a general right of liberty, anyway? And even if we did, does it indeed lead to a right of private property? These are much disputed matters, and I have elsewhere entered my argument at length. But the case can be quickly sketched here. The answer to the first question is simply that liberty is being permitted to do what we like or want. But "what we like or want" is us, really—our lives being lived. To ask the question why one has an interest in being allowed to do what one wants is to ask a self-answering question: that one has an interest in doing something is precisely that one wants to *do* it, and not to be allowed to do it is to be disenabled from doing it. Accepting a general right of liberty will, of course, not allow one to do certain things that one might have wanted: namely, to interfere with others' liberty. To say that there is a general right of liberty is to say that everybody has it, not just certain people or oneself. So acceptance of this general right is rational only if one gains more than one loses by embracing it. And why think that? A large question, to which, again, I think there is a good answer. For to say that we may interfere whenever it pleases us is to license and, given people with conflicting interests, in effect to invite war, conflict, aggression and defense. But these are inefficient activities. We will do better if we mutually refrain, instead permitting each other to get on with all those activities that can be pursued by peaceable methods, namely by agreement with those affected.

But we can make sense of this, indeed make it possible, only with property rights. You and I cannot bargain about anything if we have nothing that is ours to bargain with. If I have nothing to offer, I can make no offers, and so the question whether the offer is good enough for you to accept cannot arise. A general right of liberty, however, does give each and everyone the right to himself or herself, at a minimum: to use our own persons as we think best, free from arbitrary depredations.

Does it also lead to property rights in external things, things other than selves? Here what people have insufficiently appreciated is that a "right to an external thing" *is* a further right to one's own actions. We have property when we are allowed to do things *with* particular external things. The doings are ours, and they are what count.

But if we are disposed to allow others to do what they want, to pursue their lives as they see fit, then this means that we are disposed not to interfere with their activities, unless and until those activities in their turn interfere with others. To make sense of this, however, is to recognize the classic principle of First Occupancy—First Come, First Serve, as it were. Those who begin performing activities that involve the use of things that are not previously used are not, thereby, interfering with anyone else. They are, of course, preventing others from utilizing that very thing. But we *cannot* both utilize that very thing, so that's not an objection unless one objects to anybody doing anything with anything. Others, who come later, will just have to confine their actions to the use of *other* things, either things which they can arrange for the use of with their current owners, or else other unowned things. A property rights scheme based on first acquisition, i.e., on first use, is the only scheme that can coherently claim to defend liberty. Once we have something that we may do as we please with, it may please us to trade it with someone else who would be more pleased with what we have, while we are more pleased with what he has. The right to do that is a simple entailment from full ownership, as defined above. If I may do what I please with x, and you may do what you please with y, then obviously we may exchange it, again with the usual restriction that in the process we may not violate the rights of those not party to the transaction. Our entitlement rights to what is ours include, then, the right to lend or otherwise conditionally transfer what we own to others on whatever conditions we mutually accept by trading them to others in return for what we find more suitable. So long as certain fundamental restrictions are observed—namely, that no fraud or force is employed in the exchange process, both parties acting (sufficiently) voluntarily, and provided that no negative side effects on third parties are involved, such as to amount to an imposed and unaccepted use of what those other parties legitimately have—then the parties come as a result to be *entitled* to their respective new bundles of goods or services.

What about profit, then? Profit, I take it, is the difference between what it cost me to acquire item x and what I get from transferring x to someone else, call it y. In the special but familiar case where the costs are monetary and where y is money, then the monetary value of y, minus the cost of x, is the profit to the original owner of x. Of course the customer supposes that his newly acquired x is better than y, the money he paid for it, from his point of view. He too profits, though not, of course, monetarily—unless, as is often the case, he in turn purchases x for investment purposes which turn out to be successful. If we grant the case for a general right of liberty and that this makes for a general right of property, then the in-principle legitimacy of profit, in this generalized sense, automatically falls out.

But I have thus far used the term 'profit' in a broad sense, and it will be objected by some that it is too broad. What, they will want to know, about profit in the special sense in which profit is not just "return," but that very special return which is neither interest nor wages nor rents (at going rates)? Here I wish to endorse the general view of Professor Kirzner.[25] The entrepreneur should be regarded as "finding" something, "discovering" it. What he finds, and takes advantage of, is an opportunity to provide people with services that no one else has thought to provide (or if they have "thought" to, have not actually done anything about). So viewed, then our account makes clear why these too are things to which people can be entitled. Those the entrepreneur sells his newly created items to someone who judges them to be worth the agreed price, a price which, let us suppose, yields the entrepreneur a greater return than would such familiar investments as lending out his capital, if he has any, at specified rates, or performing familiar services for others at "going" rates of pay. And why not? The customer is under no obligation to buy, after all. If he buys nevertheless, it is because at the time, he judges the newly available item to be worth what is asked for it in comparison with any other purchase or other use of his money that he could have made instead. He thus agreed to the exchange. No more is needed. The entrepreneur has made a profit to which he is entitled, for the same reason as he is entitled to a newly discovered mineral or piece of land which he occupied and put to use prior to anyone else's putting it to that or to some other use.

We are, then, often entitled to profits. Profits can be legitimate. But entitlement, as we have seen, does not entail desert. Do we ever *deserve* profits? The stage is now set for a clear answer—in the affirmative.

Deserving Profits

In some cases of legitimately owned goods, we might do nothing with them, but in most we will do something, either using them as they are or using them to better our situations. So far as miscellaneous other people are concerned, we ordinarily do not see any direct point in simply giving them useful things of our own. That comes under the heading of gift or charity, not business or investment. On the other hand, in the absence of charity we may nevertheless do well to share the use of our worldly goods with others, on favorable terms. The things available for profitable use are diverse. "What profiteth a man if he gain the whole world but lose his own soul?" asks the New Testament.[26] The implication is that he would profit more were he to take the option that leaves him with his soul, minus the whole world, rather than vice versa. Here the profit is spiritual. And the passage makes no bones about it: in spiritual matters, we are to maximize our returns on investment, whatever the implications for more mundane concerns. Again, one can have a profitable afternoon discussing the theory of universals with a colleague: the profit is intellectual. Another can have a profitable session with a famous ski instructor. The profit is athletic. All of these are reasonable uses of the term 'profit': all imply that a certain disposition of one's resources, including one's time and energy, has had the result that you are now, as a result of your investment, better off in some valuable respect than in the situation ex ante, and all suggest that this is a good thing to do.

If we turn now to the possible desert of more mundane, monetary type profits, we will note, firstly, that some who do very, very well might quite possibly have been, in the main, simply very, very lucky. But then, if we can point to those, we can also point to others who have done well because they have been very, very acute, shrewd, persistent, imaginative, enterprising, even rather courageous, and so on. The ones who succeed for these reasons are the ones of whom we are inclined to say that they "deserved" their success. Are we ever right to so conclude? Russell Hardin, as we saw at the outset, apparently thinks not, and his skepticism is widely echoed.

Now, one might suggest that the facts adduced above *show*, all by themselves, that we are correct about this. After all, we might say, what I have noted are paradigm cases of the use of the word 'deserves'. If I am right about what people would likely say in such cases, so this argument would go, then there is no more to be said. But as is clear from the foregoing, I reject this easy way with the subject. I do want to allow for the possibility that somehow we are all making some kind of mistake. I don't think that what we have is essentially, let alone exclusively, a matter to be settled just by noting what we say, and I do think that it is appropriate to ask why. But still, I do think that we have good answers, that the answers have been given, in general outline, and that they do support such ordinary cases as the one I have described.

Of course, they will support them only if the activities which make profit possible meet the conditions of legitimacy imposed earlier. Profits may not be made at others' expense. More precisely, they may not be made by fleecing, defrauding, and so on. The earlier conditions are often enough met, we think. But what about the 'and so on'?

There are, I think, two major candidates for plausible objection. The first is that profits are always made in some way *at the expense* of others, and thus never meet the legitimacy conditions: profits are a form of theft. The second is that there is only one legitimate kind of desert-basis for material goods, namely Labor; and profiteers, necessarily, do not exemplify it. Profits, as such, *cannot* be deserved. Both are familiar charges from assorted quarters on the Left. Both, I think, can readily be shown to be either baseless or to require extraordinary assumptions or attitudes unmotivated from the point of view of ordinary folks.

What about the first charge? The idea that profits are typically earned through violence or fraud is too obviously contrary to the available evidence to take seriously at this level. What is needed is some kind of side effect of profit-making, reasonably enough construed to be a necessary one, that undermines the legitimacy of such activity. On the face of it, all parties to profit-making act voluntarily enough—customers aren't forced to buy, entrepreneurs to invest, or employees to work. Some will object that even this isn't so. But it is difficult to see how any sense in which it is not so can be relevant. In the Sweat of Thy Brow, as it says in a familiar and much-admired source, Shalt Thou Eat Bread. But though everyone must, in some way, sweat, thou doesn't have to sweat for any *particular* employer in a market system; and in a nonmarket system, everyone sweats for the same employer—the State. On the whole, we must look elsewhere.

Most who do so quickly turn to notions of fairness and equality. Exchange systems of course permit that goods are "distributed" in ways that many onlookers will regard as "unequal." Somehow, they think, exchanges between A and B are such that A winds up with "more" than B—even though what A has more of isn't the same as what B has "less of," so that a question arises how this estimate of inequality is to be got off the ground in the first place, and even though both parties are satisfied that they have made the best exchange possible in the circumstances. Still, the theorists we have in mind don't like this. They suppose it to be "unfair." Very well: but for all that, we reply, it is nevertheless just. The justice of assorted holdings is no particular function of their relative "sizes," as such. If all relevant parties are agreed, and none act with their eyes closed or with wool drawn over them by the other, then charges of unfairness, we may reasonably argue, are irrelevant.

Those who think otherwise may have one of two sorts of reasons for thinking as they do. One is that there is some sort of Natural Right to an equal share of valuable things. But resorting to natural rights is not helpful if we seek a basis of rules for interaction among diverse people, many of whom do not recognize the allegedly natural right in question. Can it be defended, as distinct from merely asserted? I think not. Indeed, it can instead be attacked, and fatally. Of course one defense would be that we all deserve equally, that our desert-base, our relevant merits, are in all cases identical. We have dismissed one special form of this argument, the one that has it that they are identical because they are all nil. We will consider below a variant, in the view that there is just one relevant desert basis, labor, which implies that we should all get, if not straightforwardly an equal share, at least a share proportional to our labors.

No matter who has what and no matter how they came by it (saving the one special case of having got it by force or fraud), one can relate to the de facto possessors of resources one would like to have in only two ways: by using force, or by voluntary methods. And of the latter, again, there are two: persuade them that there is some good reason for yielding up, say, the excess of their resources over one's own to oneself, simply because they are such "excesses"; or else make them an offer, one that makes it worthwhile for them to trade. The trouble with the first of the voluntary methods is that there are no good arguments for equality. Those who would need to be persuaded of its merits will not be rationally persuaded. But that's what counts for our purposes. If there are no good reasons for insisting that you and I must have the same, then we have no moral basis for requiring equalization.

As to force, we should first point out that anyone who agrees that x may not morally be *required* has already agreed, in effect, that force may not be employed to bring x about. And most will be disposed to agree that the use of force to pursue our various private purposes is immoral. But a deeper inquiry might be sought. Why morally proscribe the use of force for whatever there is no moral warrant for requiring people to do?

I have in effect addressed this in making the case for a general principle of liberty, which of course implies precisely such a proscription. But I want to add that that case for liberty consists, in considerable part, in showing that in using force there are problems, of which the most fundamental and far reaching is that it doesn't pay. The victims of force will, for one thing, resist, and if they are the possessors of greater resources (which by hypothesis they are, in the present case), then there is the little problem that they are more likely to win anyway.

But otherwise, the problem is that force is *suboptimal*: the two parties waste resources fighting, which cuts into the supply of resources that might otherwise be distributed to mutual advantage. There is the most excellent reason for ruling it out.

And that leaves us with voluntary exchange, which is justified by considerations of advantage. No fancier reason is needed. For it to make sense for me to want to trade with you, all we need is that I suppose I would be better off as a result, if you will agree; and the same for you vis-à-vis me. So both you and I reasonably think that we would, respectively, be better off with what we would have afterward than we are with what we have now. What better reason could there be?

By contrast, considerations of the ratio of your to my goods, ex post, is on the face of it irrelevant. Obviously I think I have more than you after the exchange, since, after all, I value what I have, by hypothesis, more than what you have, which is what I had before, and my lesser valuation of which is precisely what occasioned the exchange from my end. But the same with you. And we are both right! The relevant values to bring to bear here are, surely, yours and mine. And if we both think we have come out ahead, how could any other consideration be relevant?

Once we regard people's resources as properly *theirs*, then the case for claiming that they are "harmed," damaged, or injured by free exchange falls to the ground. By definition, free exchange does not deprive people of what is theirs. The worst that can be said of it is that (1) it might not give you as much as you'd have liked, and (2) if you had nothing to start with, then no benefits from exchange are possible for you. In those cases a system insisting that all transfers of goods be by agreement leaves you only with the option of asking for charity. Which is unfortunate for you, but first, we should note, not necessarily a state that any others have *put* you in, and second, not as bad as some states they could put you in even so, given sufficient ill will. Now, not giving B as much as B would like hardly counts as a "harm" or "deprivation," so long as we don't beg questions. Neither does giving him nothing when he has nothing. In order to so count it, we must presuppose that B had a right to more, e.g., to "enough," or to an "equal amount." But that is the view which, as I have argued, lacks general rational support. The "support" we see for it always consists in sheer assertion, in the end.[27]

Labor, Desert, and Value

What about the other thesis, then? Do we not think that it is just that a person get what she deserves, and unjust that she get anything else—viz., either more or less (or something qualitatively different) than her deserts? That the expression 'just deserts' is essentially pleonastic? As we have seen, the short answer is no: "we" do not, indeed, think this. The race goes to whoever crosses the finish line first, whether or not that person is a distinctive case of The Swift, who may have had a bad day. Nor do the organizers of the race necessarily care whether the winner worked harder than the others to become so. And in any case, we are not always—for most of us, not even usually—engaged in a race. We are, instead, just getting on, and what we have in the way of resources are considerably assets which we have done no racing for, but simply found ourselves with. In this, there may or may not be anything "unfair"; but there is nothing unjust. If we turn to the subject of holdings gained from operations on a free market, then, we can take a similar line. We can insist that what people are entitled to is one thing, what they deserve another, and that sometimes, or perhaps often, the twain do not particularly meet, or have at best a nodding acquaintance. When they don't, the relevant "prizes" nevertheless rightly go to those entitled to them—even though we may often add, as a further thought, that it would be nice if those who get them would do something for the deserving but unrewarded persons who lost out. But then, it would also be nice, if niceness is in question, to do something for the *un*deserving and unrewarded who likewise "lose out."

But this is not an adequately satisfying answer. For one thing, we will surely feel that if desert and entitlement run too independently of each other, then perhaps something is wrong. And for another, entitlement can't be self-justifying. There have to be good reasons why we should have such a system. Of course, I have attempted to provide some of those good reasons in the preceding sections. One might even translate those reasons into the vocabulary of desert by suggesting that we *deserve* to have an entitlement system. Nevertheless, the first point is important.

Let us turn, then, to the special case of workers versus profit-makers, by considering the classic thesis known as the Labor Theory of Value, a theory that has been much discussed even in recent years[28] as well as in the last century. That all such theories fail if intended as explanatory theses about exchange values in market societies is, I trust, something that can be taken as simply established by now (though you never know—indeed, that is much too optimistic: we may be sure that somewhere, some theorist, probably of Marxian persuasion, will nevertheless trot it out again). But one can put the criticisms in a nutshell, helped by our discussion of the notion of desert: the trouble with the Labor Theory is that it focuses, myopically, on what we may call the "input" side, the production side of the value-transaction. Indeed, it does its best to forget that it is a transaction we are talking about here. And for that reason, it actually fails to give anything like a proper account of the deserts of labor itself.

The idea that labor of itself "creates value," when one takes into account the two-sidedness of exchange, is a sheer fallacy. Labor is indeed normally *intended* to create value (or rather, to create valuable things[29]), true. But it can *fail*. We can spend years in fruitless effort—spend twenty solid years, eight hours a day, twiddling one's thumbs or, like Hobbes, trying to square the circle—effort that creates no value at all unless we wish to count passing the time of day as a "value," or perhaps that attempting to do the impossible at least adds to our knowledge of what is possible. But otherwise, as Sher observes, no prizes are given to "someone who excels at balancing a telephone on his nose."[30] And even if we do, it is not a value *for* anyone except the twiddler or the phone-balancer. It doesn't matter how much effort and ingenuity or indeed "autonomy" goes into this absurd activity. Suppose, for example, that it is devoted to making a Rube Goldberg machine of surpassing ingenuity, though utterly useless. Doubtless this will have curiosity value, after all; and if we count such species of value, then no doubt it will be exceedingly difficult to come up with an example of an activity that is of no conceivable value to anyone. Yet if our Rube Goldberg inventor asks us to buy his product, indeed insists that we do so and moreover that we pay him at the going union-scale rate for the kind of labor he put into it, then if *we* have anything to say about it, he will find no buyers.

It is futile to point out, as Jeffrey Reiman does in a recent contribution, that a person's labor is "his very life. . . . In capitalism," says Reiman, "Marx held that workers work without pay because they give their bosses more labor-time than the amount of labor-time they get back in the form of their wage. . . . The worker gives a surplus of labor over the amount he receives in return, and this surplus labor is held to be unpaid."[31] As Reiman goes on to recognize, it only follows that the surplus given is "unpaid" if labor is "the proper measure of what my boss and I have exchanged."[32] To this end, Reiman seeks "a neutral way of characterizing what it is that people give one another," where "By neutral, I mean a way of characterizing that does not presuppose the validity of any of the systems of ownership that are under inspection." He comes up with the suggestion that "all that remains that workers give in production is their time and energy, in a word, their labor."[33] And, he suggests, "this labor-time is really given in the sense that it is 'used up' . . . workers have only finite time and energy, and thus less left over when they have given some up." This contrasts, he thinks, with their talents, which

> First of all . . . are the result of their natural gifts plus the time and energy they devoted to developing those gifts. . . . But the "natural gifts" themselves are . . . given to the worker and thus merely passed on by him. What's more, talents are not used up in exercising them . . . Outside of ownership, labor and talent, all that is left in any part of the social product are the natural materials that went into it.[34]

Let us grant all this. But what does it prove? Even if we suppose that labor is somehow what we ultimately exchange—and only a very stretched use of the term would support that—what Reiman forgets is that he's asking us to *buy* it; and from our point of view the sheer fact that the worker's labor is his, and even the very stuff of his life, may be of no particular interest to us, the other person involved. We have our own lives to live. We are interested in a range of things having no necessary relation to degrees of effort, ingenuity, persistence, or whatever, either in the abstract, or on the part of whoever might produce anything. What interests us is *results*, not effort. And not just any results, but only those pertaining to our own lives—our own goals, purposes, ends. What we want is a better mousetrap. We have no independent interest in the amount of work someone may have expended in trying to come up with one, or in making the inferior ones that won't do.

And if we now ask, "Who *contributes* to the end of bringing into existence these various goods?" then the capitalist can hardly be left out of account. In providing capital, he enables various people to produce what would not otherwise be produced. Thinkers who sympathize with Marx on this matter are quick to point out that this function of providing the capital could conceivably have been provided instead by some other means than the voluntary enlistment of individuals who own the funds or other forms of capital required.[35] And no doubt it could. For instance, it could instead by provided by slave labor and managed by the Party hacks—that is, by taxing all, whatever their interest in the matter, to supply capital out of the "public" treasury instead of from the private treasuries of persons interested in making money therefrom, and having it managed by public "servants" rather than persons who have a direct personal stake in how it does. But whoever supplies it and however it is supplied, what is supplied is, in the circumstances, necessary for enabling people to engage in the direct acts of production that yield the desired products. Supplying that capital is thus a function that merits the consumer's favor—that is, his voluntary purchase of the goods it enables to be produced at the price which earns that favor.

Once we look at it from the point of view of the consumer, then—especially, the consumer without any ideological axes to grind—it is perfectly apparent why it is rational to "reward" the supplier of capital: for what he supplies is, unquestionably, of value to us. It's what we want. For twice the price, say, we can get a similar product from workers in a commune, collectively but laboriously constructing their own machinery and "organizing the means of production" with no outside capital. Very well: perhaps I might be persuaded of the superior virtue of doing things that way: but what if I'm not? Why must I, a mere consumer, be interested in such things? What if virtue isn't what I'm in the market for? (My New Testament apophthegm implies that I'm a fool not to be, and it may be right; but it may also be wrong in implying that material wealth is incompatible with spiritual accomplishment or virtue. In any case, I may well say, it's not the business of the people who make my shoes, or whatever, to go on about my spiritual welfare.)

Marx, of course, confined his version of the theory to the production of useful goods, and moreover, to their production by currently competitive technologies. Those two restrictions, indeed, are all that could have kept the theory in the field for so long. Without them, as Marx was aware, the theory would be a nonstarter.[36] Obviously the incompetent who produce one item per hour should not get paid the same as the supercompetent who turns out a dozen in the same time. But those restrictions also enable him to obscure the real issues. For Marx is thus able to keep the consumer on the shelf, as it were, looking only at producers, that is, workers and capitalists. And then, of course, the Marxist has an easy time of showing that the capitalist doesn't "do" anything, in the sense in which workers do things. Only workers produce, say the Marxists; capitalists don't really produce, they just collect the spoils.

Yet Marx, one should note, seemed to think that workers who do more should get more. But *who* "does more," in the sense relevant to this theory? The problem is that there is a sharp divide between two ways of answering:

(a) On the one hand, we have pure "input side" measures—the ways that are clearly more appropriate for a labor theory of value in the narrower sense. More labor is more hours spent, more calories expended, more sweat dripped.

(b) On the other hand, we can focus on *output*, and just say that by definition he who produces more has "worked" more, has "done" more—regardless of how much sweat emerges, how many hours he works, how many calories he burns up.

Once we have made this distinction, however, we can see that Marx's two restrictions preclude criterion (a) from being meaningfully deployed. We are only *allowed* to look at those workers who not only (a) produce something useful, as determined by the fact that somebody, given his choice, will buy it, but (b) who produce it comparatively efficiently. This comparative efficiency, of course, comes about as a result of the fact that those who buy the product do so more or less rationally—preferring it, for example, to similar items that cost more. Of course this criterion for assessing efficiency[37] smuggles what was supposed to be the rival theory in by the back door: Method X is more efficient than Method Y if X-produced goods survive on the market and Y-produced ones don't; product P has utility only if someone will actually buy P when it is offered for sale.

The conclusion remains, then, that (a) and (b), no matter how you slice them, will give you differing results. I have read of a factory that employs no workers on its assembly line—that sort of work is all done by alert, competent, tireless, reliable, nonunionized robots. The engineers who look after the robots emit little sweat (though, contemplating this author's modest experience with digital-controlled equipment, probably plenty of tears!); but if we identify *them* as the only available candidates for Marx's "workers," then we shall have to say that they do vastly more work than their production-line human counterparts in less advanced factories, for one hour of their time doubtless accounts for many times the output of one hour of Detroit assembly-line worker time.

If we go in this direction for long, however, we may well point our finger at the supplier of capital for this operation as also having contributed mightily to production, and in that sense done "work." If the Marxist's reply is (as it is) that the "work" done by the capitalist could have been done by "society," he becomes susceptible, courtesy of the Honda factory, to the response that the work done by Marx's proletarian can instead be done by robots, and so what? No one is indispensable; everything *can* be done in some other way; and the only question is, which way is the best, under the circumstances? It is the judgment by the relevant parties, *namely the consumers*, that matters.

It is, in fact, quite easy to compare the performance of private-sector and public-sector investors, come to that. And when we do, both experience and theoretical reflection strongly argue that from the social point of view, the capitalist way is better. Private capital tends to be more productive because more efficiently deployed and allocated than "public" capital—in addition to having the not insignificant advantage of being compatible with respect for the freedom of the participants. But the point of all this is not that in order to justify utilizing the concept of desert at all we are forced to make this case. All we have to do is to point out that the people who most relevantly apply the concept, namely consumers, could reasonably make such judgments. It is their point of view that is the *source* of "desert" in these contexts. And it is a point of view which clearly makes sense of regarding the profits from good investments as (often) deserved by those who make them. That the capitalist deserves his profits, when he does, stems from the fact that his investment activity causes desirable services to be performed—services that would not otherwise have been done, either at all or as well.

The general effect of this argument is to show that profitable investment is a genuine case of merit. The person who invests does something with his resources that he or she needn't have done, and what he does is useful to those whose enterprises are supported by the investment in question. Were it not so, of course, they would not pay him for it. People have pointed out that and how entrepreneurs perform useful functions, notably the function of organizing production, and especially of organizing it more efficiently than it would otherwise have been, thus enabling more to be produced with the same inputs, and thus more profit to be made.[38] All this is right. But we should not suppose that we could come up with a metric of merit over entrepreneurship in the abstract. Other things being equal, we might agree, he who is more entrepreneurial—more innovative, more exploitative of market opportunities, and so on—will deserve more. But a less entrepreneurial person who makes a greater though more conservative investment may nevertheless properly make more money, just as the beauty queen who had more to invest, though she had to do much less by way of getting the investment made, may nevertheless deserve the greater prize.

To repeat: we only go up blind alleys if we myopically fix our gaze only on desert-factors in abstraction from what causes them to *be* desert-factors, namely, the interests of the agents—in this case, ultimately, the consumers—who hold the purse strings, loosening of which is the source of the relevant rewards in this area. What is done that deserves reward is the marshaling of resources in the direction that elicits the purchasing-response from consumers. No further justification on grounds of high moral character, etc., are required here.

At the risk of overworking an example, let's return just one last time to our beauty contest. There have been controversies about these events in recent years, the question being whether their purposes are such as to deserve public attention. Now, these questions are relevant. We can apply desert-concepts in the absence of a verdict on the ultimate significance of the activities that form their background, but if the verdict is negative, they do not stick very well. When people insist that the pursuit of profit is not a meritorious activity, they deserve answers. The point of this chapter is that we must look in the right place for those answers: namely, to the purposes of those who supply the rewards and recognizances in question. To hold that profits do not matter is, I suggest, really to hold that the goods and services whose production and distribution make profits possible do not matter. To those who say that it's "too easy," there is a similarly easy reply: "Fine—then why don't you go out and make some yourself?" While it is, no doubt, easier if one begins with an inherited fortune or the like, that is by no means necessary: people have very often made fortunes from trivial or no initial capitals. Beauty crowns, as a matter of fact, are rarely won by the "natural" beauties who invest no further effort in the competition (indeed, 'never' might be closer to the truth, I understand, in regard to the major ones), and the number of shirts lost in the pursuit of profits is enough to deter many from seriously engaging in such activities. The idea that profits are made by people who "do nothing" is not only false in conception, as we have seen, but also false to real fact. The truth is that many of us don't embark on investment programs and the like because it is too time-consuming and too demanding. There's a folk saying on this subject which we do well to bear in mind: "If you're so smart, why aren't you rich?" The point, I take it, is that 'being smart' isn't enough. To those who supply the further qualities required, we consumers—and that's all of us, remember—have reason to be grateful. Luckily, those who get the profits in question don't need our gratitude on top of it; but if the institutions making profits possible are under ideological threat, then a sober recognition of their foundations is not without point.

Summary

We began by formulating the familiar distinction between entitlement and desert. Entitlement is the "deontic" member of this pair: its domain is the right, the required, when we *owe* someone something, and so on. Desert, by comparison, is a value concept. Its implications for action are less clear and more disputable. Those very facts about it are among the main reasons we want to have entitlement notions as well. Were they to drift too far apart, however, entitlement would certainly be threatened. Rules of entitlement need justification, and desert notions will figure somewhere in that justification.

The questions about desert concern when such considerations are in order, who applies them, and why. And here our answer is that when someone deserves something, she or he deserves it *from* someone. No sense can attach to simply "deserving" something, all by itself. It takes a minimum of two parties (saving the odd case where the same person occupies both roles). And those who bestow the prizes, who hold the goods in which the rewards consists, and so on, are the fundamental wielders of these notions. They apply them on the basis of the interests and values they bring to the context. This explains why desert is not exclusively reserved for such things as effort, diligence, and the application of ingenuity. It is also available for the exercise of native intelligence, talent, and skill, or the display of natural charm, which are not producible merely by effort alone. Nevertheless, those who have the relevant interests in these displays or exercises may see fit to reward them.

Thus we can rule out one-sided theories such as the Labor Theory of Value, theories which would look exclusively at the deserving individual without reference to why he deserves what he does or from whom. To understand profit and its role, we need to look at it from the point of view of the purchaser, the consumer, and not that of the producer in independence of the rest. The relevant interests of those who supply the prizes and rewards will, in turn, be such as to give rise to criteria of relevant performance, achievement, and exemplification of appropriate qualities. We must be able to grade items on the basis of the degree to which they satisfy the relevant criteria. In the case of profit, the relevant criterion is that the profiter has put his money in the right venture at the right time, thus bringing the customer the wanted products before anyone else did, or at a lower price, and so on. Our purchase of those products is likewise the supplying of the appropriate reward.

When all this is appreciated, then the case becomes clear that profit-making, like any number of other activities, is reasonably eligible as an area for the application of desert concepts. Those who make profits by the normal, legitimate means are not only entitled to them but can deserve them, and often do—happily for us!

Notes

This chapter was originally written at the Social Philosophy and Policy Center, Bowling Green State University, September 1990 for the Liberty Fund Symposium on Morality and Profits, Montreal, December 1-3, 1990. I wish to thank both the Social Philosophy and Policy Center, where I was a Visiting Research Scholar at the time, and the Liberty Fund for enabling me to pursue this subject at those times; also, my fellow participants for many helpful comments and questions. The essay was published in Mario Rizzo and Robin Cowan, eds., *Profits and Morality*, (Chicago: University of Chicago Press, 1995). © 1995 by The University of Chicago. All rights reserved.

1. Russell Hardin, *Morality within the Limits of Reason* (Chicago: University of Chicago Press, 1988), 132.

2. Joel Feinberg, "Justice and Personal Desert," in his *Doing and Deserving* (Princeton, N.J.: Princeton University Press, 1970), 55-94.

3. George Sher, *Desert* (Princeton, N.J.: Princeton University Press, 1987).

4. Sher, *Desert*, 194.

5. Sher, *Desert*, 195.

6. Feinberg, "Justice," 64.

7. Sher, *Desert*, 53.

8. Which also figures in Feinberg, but offered here with my twists.

9. John Rawls, *A Theory of Justice* (Cambridge, Mass.: Harvard University Press, 1971), 102. See also chapter 4.

10. Jan Narveson, *The Libertarian Idea* (Philadelphia: Temple, 1989; now Broadview Press, 2001), ch. 10, 110-21.

11. Henry Sidgwick, *The Methods of Ethics* (London: Macmillan, 1961), 274.

12. See, for example, R. M. Hare, *Moral Thinking* (Oxford, U.K.: Clarendon Press, 1981), 5-24.

13. An argument to that effect is in my "The How and Why of Universalizability," Nelson Potter and Mark Timmons, eds., *Morality and Universality* (Dordrecht, Netherlands: Reidel, 1981), 3-46, and more briefly in Narveson, *The Libertarian Idea*, especially 153.

14. Much of my inspiration for accepting this "social contract" view stems

from the work of David Gauthier, such as his *Morals by Agreement* (New York: Oxford University Press, 1986). This author's seminal work has been the subject of much discussion, and I do not concur with all of his views. An immensely valuable compilation of recent reflections on his work is to be found in Peter Vallentyne, ed., *Contractarianism and Rational Choice* (New York: Cambridge University Press, 1991). One particularly important point of dissent relevant to our present subject concerns Gauthier's views about "economic rent." While I have expressed criticisms of it (Narveson, *Libertarian Idea*, 203-6), a far more trenchant critique is in Eric Mack, "Gauthier on Rights and Economic Rent," *Social Philosophy and Policy* 9, no. 1 (Fall 1991).

15. Sher, *Desert,* 53.

16. Sher, *Desert,* 54.

17. Sher, *Desert,* 61.

18. Sher, *Desert,* 62.

19. Sher, *Desert,* 54.

20. Sher, *Desert,* 67.

21. Rawls, *A Theory of Justice*, 104.

22. Sher, *Desert,* 26.

23. Sher, *Desert,* 30.

24. See Jeremy Waldron, *The Right to Private Property* (Oxford, U.K.: Oxford University Press, 1988), 49, for the classic list, which in turn is due to A. M. Honoré, "Ownership," in A. G. Guest, ed., *Oxford Essays in Jurisprudence* (Oxford, U.K.: Oxford University Press, 1961). Waldron does not make the mistake I mention, but see Allan Gibbard, "Natural Property Rights," *Nous* 10 (1976).

25. Israel M. Kirzner, "The Nature of Profits: Some Economic Insights and Their Ethical Implications," advanced elsewhere in the volume in which this chapter was originally published: Mario Rizzo and Robin Cowan, eds., *Profits and Morality* (Chicago: University of Chicago Press, 1995), 22-47.

26. Matt. 16:36.

27. See chapter 4.

28. For a few (of many) examples from the mainline journals: G. A. Cohen, "The Labor Theory of Value and the Concept of Exploitation," *Philosophy and Public Affairs* 8, no. 4 (Summer 1979), 338-60; Jeffrey Reiman, "Exploitation, Force, and the Moral Assessment of Capitalism," *Philosophy and Public Affairs* 16, no. 1 (Winter 1987), 3-41; Ian Hunt, "A Critique of Roemer, Hodgson, and Cohen on Marxian Exploitation," *Social Theory and Practice* 12, no. 2 (Summer 1986), 121-71.

29. As G. A. Cohen, himself a Marxist, established so decisively in "The Labor Theory of Value and the Concept of Exploitation."

30. Sher, 119.

31. Reiman, "Exploitation, Force, and the Moral Assessment of Capitalism," 6.

32. Reiman, "Exploitation, Force, and the Moral Assessment of Capitalism," 9-10.

33. Reiman, "Exploitation, Force, and the Moral Assessment of Capitalism," 9.

34. Reiman, "Exploitation, Force, and the Moral Assessment of Capitalism," 9-10.

35. Cohen, "The Labor Theory of Value and the Concept of Exploitation."

36. See chapter 3.

37. This is effectively pointed out by Robert Nozick, *Anarchy, State and Utopia* (New York: Basic Books, 1974), 256-62.

38. Scott Arnold, "Why Profits Are Deserved," *Ethics* 97 (January 1987), 387-402, with discussion by Edward Nell and a response by Arnold.

Chapter 10

Fixing Democracy

Introduction

Why should anyone think that democracy needs fixing? In a sense, many thinking people agree that it does. This or that deviation from what is thought to be democracy is proposed often enough. But such suggestions are not based on any very profound consideration of the subject. That is not necessarily a bad thing; patches are sometimes recognizably beneficial without knowing medicine. But the present effort is a bit more radical than that. I shall argue that what is wrong with democracy is wrong in principle, rather than a more or less accidental or incidental problem. What is wrong with democracy is, virtually, that it is democratic. No doubt that sounds slightly daft, for democracy is one of today's entrenched sacred cows. It is not difficult to see why it is so, but its popularity doesn't necessarily attest to virtue. At any rate, my problems with it will here be explained at some length (though not softened). Perhaps it will still sound daft afterward to many, but I hope to persuade the reader that it is nothing of the sort. My criticisms, moreover, do not stem from some wild idea of democracy, nor of what it is all about; they are, indeed, based essentially on common sense. But to get there, we must first say quite a bit about what democracy is.

Democracy

Of course—and this is my first heresy, I daresay—we all do know what it is. Democracy is easily defined: it is "rule by the people," a hoary but perfectly legitimate phrase, derived, after all, from the Greek roots, roughly 'demos' ('people') and 'cracy' ('rule'). But a more precise explication is possible, and useful: democracy is the *equal division of fundamental political power among the governed*. At bottom, each (adult, or "capable") person subject to rule is to have equal power to effect that rule. That is a conceptually more precise characterization, and its claim to be an explication must be defended. But the derivation is easy. Rule by "the people" is opposed to rule by "the few" or "the one": democracy is, by contrast, rule by "the many."

163

But whatever motivation could there be for that? The answer is simple, and compelling: the problem is that those who rule are different, and therefore more or less different in interests, from those who are ruled. Thus the ruled not only can't rely on the rulers to do them much good, but can virtually rely on them to do the reverse. After all, the rulers have power over the ruled. What is to prevent them from using it to line their own pockets instead of promoting the well-being of the citizens? The solution—that's the idea, anyway—is for *everybody* to do the ruling, thus making the class of the ruled identical with the class of those ruling. The same reasoning tells us, further, that the rule by all must be equal; for if a few have 99 percent of the power, and the rest 1 percent, what's the point? Even if some merely have *more*, for what possible reason could that be? Ask the ones with less, and they will reasonably complain, seeing that the consequence for them is that they are, again, under the thumb of someone over whom they have no control, the whole point of the move in the first place having been to get out from under such thumbs. Plainly, equal division is wanted.

We have to include the word 'fundamental' in our characterization, because once you get above a modest size, the day-to-day ruling must inevitably be done by relatively few; so if the idea of democracy is to have any purchase, the power of the many will have to be used to select and, by their votes, more or less control the doings of the few who do rule. One of the ways in which it is popular to propose to fix democracy, indeed, is to make more, rather than less, of the day-to-day ruling subject to the decision-making of the entire populace—to eliminate the middleman, as it were. That that is hardly a way to improve things will be part of the burden of our deliberations here, as will be seen.

Meanwhile, the democratic root idea, we may argue next, entails voting as its fundamental procedure. There are two reasons for this. The vote embodies political power: voting is a procedure that has effect, the effect, namely, of enforceably requiring everyone to do whatever was being voted on. The second is that a vote is a *unit* of such power. If power is to be equally distributed, we must have some metric for this. The vote achieves this admirably: if each person gets exactly one, we have distributed power as equally and widely as humanly possible. To see why, consider that requiring more than a majority for passage would give more power to the "nays" than the "yeas" and is thus prima facie antidemocratic (though a majority could vote to require more than a bare majority on some matters, to be sure). Majority rule is the outcome: 50 percent + 1, in principle, as the minimum sufficient for decision, at least in two-value cases where all vote. That such cases are actually very rare is important, and will be discussed in the following section.

One of the most widely touted complaints among today's political thinkers is that despite the formal equality of the vote, some nevertheless have more power than others, because they are able to manipulate or otherwise exert influence on voters that is quite disproportionate. But this complaint confuses power with influence. If I can persuade you to use your power in one way rather than another, then I have influence over you, yes: but it is you who uses your vote, and the decision to use it that way is yours, not mine. Unless I am in a position to threaten you with some evil, my influence is not power. And if I am in such a position, something is indeed wrong: then, indeed, I have power and not just influence. The point about the vote is that it is a formally certified unit of power, and what influences the voter to vote is left wide open. It has to be left open, of course, for otherwise we are dictating to the citizen and not vice versa.

Democratic governments are *governments*, though: the power is distributed equally, but there *is* some. Democracy is not to be confused with anarchy, the situation in which no one at all has any strictly political power. Political power consists in being able to coerce people into conforming with the desires of the person or persons who wield it. The *idea* of democracy says nothing about rights, as such: it is, in essence, pure procedure. Its agenda is wide open: anything whatever can, in principle, be decided by voting. The enthusiast for democracy thinks that not only *can* it be so used, but also that it actually *should* be. We will see reason why such enthusiasm should be tempered.

Voluntary Association Democracy

Why is majority rule ever thought to be sensible? There is a brief and very instructive answer. Theorists in the classic strain tend to treat societies and states as if they were actually, literally, *associations*. The members of an association form the group by associating with each other. They come together in pursuit of some common purpose, which they expect to be able to pursue better in association with like-minded others. Often they could not pursue at all except thus, as when the purpose is to execute group dances or football games, and so on. At any rate, this gives the group a unanimity of purpose that is available for motivating the formation of committees and subcommittees, the selection of executives, and such things. That sort of organization makes lots of sense in an association, for after all, everyone has the same general goal or goals. Whatever executive is elected, he or she will, it is certain, be promoting the goals of the association, and if Jones thinks that Ms. Robinson would do it better than Ms. Smith, still, he'd rather have Ms. Robinson do it than no one at all.

But in a *society*, as distinct from an association, things are different. The members did not, for the most part, "come together"; they did not "associate" in order to create the society. Instead, there are just all these people around, and typical members were born into their midst, willy-nilly. Whether all these people have similar goals is a matter of psychology—and often enough made by theorists into a matter of metaphysics. There is no necessary agreement on much of anything, and therefore no presumption that anybody who gets elected is better than nobody even if one might prefer someone else. There is no a priori reason to think that the rules generated by a legislature, however true that it was elected, will leave one better off than no rules at all, and especially, better than no rules on the particular subject that the legislators rule on.

So the most compelling possible justification of democracy simply doesn't apply when we get to the case at hand, that is, the case of general politics—of the State. The difference this makes is profound.

But we will suppose that some sort of case can be made for political democracy. Let us, then, consider what a pure democracy would be like—and what we would have to do about it if we had one.

Constraining Democracy in the Interests of Democracy

But a system of pure majoritarian rule could be unstable. Suppose we vote on whether some may vote. For example, suppose that a majority votes to disenfranchise the correlative minority in the community (easily imaginable to the modern citizen, aware of the electoral victory of the Nazis in the 1930s). Then the newly narrowed down electorate repeats the process, voting to disenfranchise the new minority. With iteration, democracy could lead to dictatorship. Something has gone wrong!

Therefore, we must make a distinction between what we may call the "pure idea" of democracy, on the one hand, and a modified system that can be expected to remain democratic over time—stable democracy, democracy as an ongoing system. A system concerned to preserve democracy against budding Hitlers must modify the democratic idea by imposing *restrictions on the operation of the democratic procedure*. It does this by giving citizens certain rights, which we may call "democratic rights." These are rights in the straightforward sense of being rights *against* democracy: the right to vote, for example, will be your right no matter how many other people would like to deprive you of it. Since democracy just is rule by the people, constitutional provisions preventing the operation of such rule in certain cases is, on the face of it, antidemocratic. But perhaps only "on the face of it," for perhaps there is a further component of the idea that may motivate this, upon analysis.

The Democratic Constitution

We can expand this idea a bit without departing from the root idea—indeed, arguably, the expansion is motivated precisely by the root idea. Thus we arrive at what we may call the *Democratic Constitution*. A constitution is a set of basic provisions regarding the political system that constrains the actions of political figures, including, in the case of democracy, the electorate itself. But what makes it a "democratic" constitution is that its provisions are aimed at keeping the democracy democratic. Briefly, it will include some such provisions as the following:

(1) The Right to Vote

As already noted, we must make voting a right, which is to say, not itself subject to voting. Whether you have the vote or not is determined solely by whether you are a (competent?) member of the community. The question of just when a human being is qualified to be a citizen as well is, of course, a tricky and interesting one. But the idea of democracy surely limits what we can do here. The claims of ancient Athens to be such, with its extreme restrictions, is problematic, as would be the move to impose substantial knowledge tests. If we are to have rule by *the* people instead of rule by *some* people, requirements other than those needed in order to be able to understand and fill out a ballot at all are inevitably problematic.

(2) The Right to Periodic Elections

A government elected for life has no controls by the people after election; a government elected for a day could get nothing done. If democracy is to be realized, elections must be frequent enough so that if the people don't like what's going on, they can change it, yet infrequently enough so that governing can be accomplished during the time those elected are in power.

How often, then? That is, of course, a difficult question of detail, and it is hard to say where detail starts and principle leaves off; but a year or so for general political communities seems minimal, while seven is probably too long. This restriction can be hitched to the basic idea of equality-of-power as follows: in an excessive period, government comes increasingly to exert unwanted power over citizens who can do nothing about it until the next election; in a deficient period, government gets nothing done between elections, and thus citizens seeking to use political power are frustrated. A happy medium enables government to do something, yet not get far out of hand. After two weeks, in a modern society, it would be too early to say whether things were working out as people hoped. After two years, though, the chances that things aren't going right, or that they are, are quite good. After five, they are excellent. Of course, this "medium" is only "happy" if government is, but for the moment we are assuming that happiness through government is not impossible.

(3) The Right to Run for Office

If some people are not allowed to run for office—say, only those appointed as candidates by the preceding government—then those with the appointive power have more power, contrary to the democratic idea. The cure is to give *all*, in principle, the right to run. Thus we must look askance at laws requiring proposed candidates to meet various restrictions, though in the name of practicality we may perhaps concede that a multiplicity of candidates with no real chance of election is not really essential to democratic principle.

(4) Freedom of Political Speech

Suppose we are not all allowed to communicate with each other: some candidates have, by statutory right, the ear of the people, while others do not. Those who do would then have more power, prima facie, than those who don't. This is not meant to obscure the line between influence and power: the point here is that power is exercised in order to see to it that the people do not hear certain things: it is power used to alter the influences that people are able to expose themselves to. That those who say some things will have more influence than those who say others or who say nothing is, of course, only to be expected. But intervening forcibly to distort the voter's information is another matter. To prevent such distortions of power, freedom of political speech is the only answer.

Voters, of course, need, or presumably would like to have, not only information, but good information, if they are to effect their wills. This is hard to get—how do we know which information is good? There is no guarantee. A longer answer would envisage procedures or various kinds—say, certification by experts. And who decides who is an expert? Things get complicated, but, fortunately, not quite impossible. Freedom of (political) speech, for all, is the best we can do. If some don't have it, equality of power is again compromised.

(5) The Right to Fair Criminal Procedures
    Governments can quell the opposition by putting them in jail, or being able to credibly threaten opponents with jail and other forcible restrictions of their freedom. Rights to good procedures for conviction and punishment are necessary to minimize this. It is symbolic, perhaps, that jury trial in criminal proceedings require unanimity for conviction—not just majority rule.

6) The Right to Non-Coercion
    Aspiring power-seekers can win by beating up or threatening opponents. The secret ballot helps, of course; but killing off the opposition is sure to keep them from voting the wrong way, or getting elected. Violence, in short, is another way to stay in power. Something like a general right of personal security in respect of political views, or perhaps a right against arbitrary coercion by or against aspiring politicians (if that's different), is needed.
    But what about rights to personal property? Again, if the government can deprive people of their houses, businesses, or incomes, then it obviously has a very large repertoire of coercive means available to it for controlling the public. Interestingly, it is this that is the sticking point for all proponents of democracy. A government that cannot tax cannot govern—indeed, we might say, is not a government at all. The ensuing discussion will contemplate this matter at greater length.

Democracy versus Liberalism

The provisions suggested above are familiar items of liberalism. It might even be suggested that 'democracy' and 'liberal democracy' are synonyms. Are we on the high road to liberalism, then? We are not. Note carefully that the preceding constitutional provisions are (or at least, I'm trying to make them) specific to the maintenance of democracy only.
    But liberalism is another matter. Which other matter is it? There is a good deal of ink spilled on things like this, and the claim is often made that this, and democracy too, is an "essentially contested concept" or something of the sort. But contesting concepts is a lifetime-consuming business—one for which we do not have time, thanks! And anyway, it, again, is really not so very difficult to see a basic idea here. Liberalism has, again, a clearly definable root notion that, I think, underlies all of these. We may spell that out in two succinct theses:
    First: the proper purpose of government and of morals is to promote the common good of all who are subject to it, rather than of those who rule.
    Second: for these purposes, the "good" in question is determined by the

values *of the ruled* themselves, rather than by those of any outsiders. This last is what's special. Conservative theories, by contrast, impose some concept of what is good for people on those people, whether they share it or not. In sum, liberalism holds that government is *to promote the good lives of its subjects as they themselves see that good.*[1]

Closer examination will show strains of a serious kind between the basic idea of liberalism and that of democracy. Interest in democracy has certainly been motivated by the same kind of concerns as are basic to liberalism. But when push comes to shove, as it often enough does in a democratic system, democracy is incompatible with liberalism. And insofar as they are incompatible, liberalism, I think, is much preferable.

Liberalism and the Common Good

Can there be a good of liberalism that is nevertheless, à la Aquinas, the *common* good? It is easy to see why one would be tempted to answer in the negative; after all, each person's utility profile is different from each other's, and yet we are saying, are we not, that utility is the good and must be.

But in fact we are not saying that, as it would usually be understood, namely, as an assertion of Utilitarianism. Nevertheless, there is a common good of liberalism, and the reason for thinking so reaches to the foundations of morals and politics, and is fundamental to liberalism. Liberalism recognizes that individuals have their own values, their own agendas, their own interests, and that these differ greatly from one person to another. Government is a creature of human making: we the people, collectively, are in charge. This being so, we will rationally desire a government so long as, and only so long as, it serves our interests. But this is true for *each* person. It is definitely not true in the usual understanding of collective goods—in particular, of aggregates, where the interest of the whole is reckoned to be the sum of its parts, positive and negative. Individual A will favor a certain good only so long as it serves A's interests—which need not be egoistic, as it should be unnecessary to add, by now. In order for the impositions of government to be acceptable to any person, they must be so to every person. Otherwise, we are back to some people imposing on the others—the very thing liberalism is out to avoid.

"Is it justified?" is a question that can only be raised by individual minds; the only sense to a "social" version of it is one that makes the social answer some function of the individual answers. But as I say, that function can't be sheer aggregation, which, notoriously, can be at the expense of individuals. Therefore, it must be a Common Good that we aim at. Only such will serve your interests, no matter who *you* may be. Since values differ, finding a "common interest" may seem to be difficult, and in one sense it is: the common good can't be ice cream for all. But in fact, it's not quite so difficult after all, at least in general outline. For we have a common interest in whatever sort of rules and procedures, if any, would enable each of us to do the best we can in our different ways, given the presence and the natures of the others. This virtually means that the common good is freedom or liberty—that is, the absence of aggression, of imposing one person by another. Liberalism thus attempts to bring about this freedom by prohibiting the aggression that is its antithesis.

In view of this, Pareto must be our guide. Individual actions and social programs are acceptable if they are good for at least some, even if only the agent himself and no one else, and bad for none, where these valuations are those of the individuals in question, as applied to their own cases. The good in question will often be a "net" good, of course: the costs to the individual in question are to be exceeded by its benefits to the individual concerned. And the pursuit of many goods involves risk—expected payoffs governed by probabilities well below unity.

Now it is scarcely possible, even in tiny communities, to have public actions literally promoting every single person's good at once, advancing it beyond some relevant baseline in lockstep. But it *is* possible for such an action to do some people some good without doing anybody else any net harm—without imposing, as Jan Lester[2] puts it, net (uncompensated) costs on anyone.[3] For this reason, liberalism must concentrate on individuals' rights. It will be spelled out as a program of such, imperfectly modeled in the American Bill of Rights, the Canadian Charter of Rights and Freedoms, and other documents of the kind.

At the top of this list, certainly, will be a general right to freedom of action: to nonviolence against one's persons, and noninterference, so far as possible, with one's plans and projects. What will be generally forbidden is some people attempting to gain at the (net) expense of others who do not agree to the imposition in question.[4] The general desideratum will be to make society, as nearly as possible, an organization for the mutual benefit of all concerned. But remember: these benefits are spelled out by each individual in ways that differ. The rule, then, is not to subordinate some people to others, by forcing some to do what is for the benefit of others. We must do better: by allowing all actions that do not impose on others, and thus all that are consensual to all concerned. That is what liberal bills of rights fairly generally do, when they guarantee the integrity of the person, given nonviolent behavior, and freedom of thought, speech, religion, association, and voluntarily arranged employment. This, if effective, enables us all to pursue our goods within the confines of others' free pursuit of theirs.

Liberalism versus Democracy

The short list we previously ran through, of what we may call democratic restrictions on democracy, concerns provisions for the preservation of democracy. But it does not concern provisions for anything else. Should it? Or are there connections between other freedoms and democratic ones? Such has been the expressed hope of influential writers. Consider, for instance, this, from one of the most eminent students of democracy:

Democracy guarantees its citizens a number of fundamental rights that nondemocratic systems do not, and cannot, grant.

Democracy is not only a process of governing. Because rights are necessary elements in democratic political institutions, democracy is inherently also a system of rights. Rights are among the essential building blocks of a democratic process of government . . .

Citizens must have a *right* to vote and have their vote counted fairly. So with other democratic standards: clearly citizens must have a *right* to investigate alternatives, a *right* to participate in deciding how and what should go on the agenda, and so on.[5]

But it is not obvious that democracy, as such, requires the panoply of rights guaranteed by typical contemporary constitutions. A democracy, even with the above constraints, could dictate religions, outlaw marijuana, homosexuality, Catholicism, certain hairstyles, and any number of other things; and it can confiscate personal property and income—in fact, democracies have actually done, and continue to do, many of those things and more.

Liberal rights and freedoms have some bearing on democracy, as we have seen. But not much. The possibility of democracy itself being threatened by such arbitrary invasions is, in the frontline democracies of today, remote. In any case, it is absurd to think that rights against arbitrary usage are needed *only* in the interests of *preserving democracy*. No matter what kind of government we have, the citizen has an interest in personal security. We do not seek security in order to shore up democracy; it is, at best, the other way around.

As we saw, Professor Dahl himself agrees that a democracy will require genuine rights to the various things I have suggested. How does it manage that? An interesting question, to be sure, and not easy to answer; but apparently some degree of security of the citizen has somehow been achieved in these favored countries. That brings up a question: if it is really possible to have *any* effective constitutional-level restrictions on *anything*, then why not have a constitutional restriction on interpersonal violence itself? To be sure, there are gestures in this direction. The Canadian Charter, for example, asserts this:

Everyone has the right to life, liberty and security of the person and the right not to be deprived thereof except in accordance with the principles of fundamental justice.[6]

The same document, however, goes on to restrict this:

The Canadian Charter of Rights and Freedoms guarantees the rights and freedoms set out in it subject only to such reasonable limits prescribed by law as can be demonstrably justified in a free and democratic society.[7]

So rights, which are supposed to constrain the operation of the majority principle, are extended to the citizen only consistently with democracy. What does this mean? It plainly means, both in theory and in practice, that a legislature will decide what your rights are.

But why should we go the roundabout route of ensuring *democratic* rights, in hopes that the majority will be nice guys and not vote to beat up on the minority?

Conspicuously absent from the theory of democracy are the strictly liberal rights in the classic understanding of liberalism. Freedoms—of religion, of association, of expression, of nonpolitical speech, and above all, of economic activity, not only have no fundamental place in democracy, but are generally and constantly threatened, ignored, or simply obliterated in it. The majority's natural instinct is to suppress the minority in any and all these respects. In fact, democracy is basically incompatible with the serious recognition of fully liberal rights: rights to do, think, and carry on life activities as determined by one's own lights rather than those of the majority's. For the root idea of democracy, as a system of government in good standing, says basically that majorities can do anything they like (the "sovereignty of parliament"). And so we arrive at H. L. Mencken's classic characterization:

> Democracy is two foxes and a chicken sitting down to decide, by majority vote, what they shall have for lunch.'

Government, it seems, is still a gang of thieves, only it's a much bigger gang.

Consider, in particular, the economic side of this. If a person's income isn't his own, then effectively almost nothing else is, either. John Locke, it will be recalled, proclaimed that

> The *Supreme Power cannot take* from any Man any part of his Property without his own consent. For the preservation of Property being the end of Government . . . it necessarily supposes and requires, that the People should *have Property*, without which they must be supposed to lose that . . . which was the end for which they entered into [Society], too gross an absurdity for any Man to own.'

Locke seems not to have realized that this provision, if taken seriously, spells doom to *all* government, not just nondemocratic government. The "gross absurdity" is not only "owned" by some few, but appears to be accepted by almost everyone in contemporary democracies. Still, these are the same people who accepted the grossest tyrannies of the most evil dictators and central committees that ever occupied the halls of power. It is not clear what we can infer from common acquiescence to the income tax and other indignities. It is rather clearer, however, what we can infer from the tendency of contemporary academics, among whom democracy has the status of a sacred creed which we are scarcely allowed, let alone invited, to question.

But it is by no means only a matter of income. Democratically elected governments can visit severe penalties on people for taking drugs, failing to hire certain people, driving swiftly no matter how safely, and innumerable other acts beneficial to those concerned but harmful to no one. Powers to do that are incompatible with that universal freedom that Kant holds up as the defining feature of justice.

Liberalism is incompatible with dictatorship. But democratic government is really, in principle, the dictatorship of the majority. It exemplifies government à la Thrasymachus: intelligent rulers, said he, will exploit the ruled to their own maximum benefit. It is a device for enabling the majority to extract benefits from the rest. Those majorities do this by proclaiming that they are benefiting "society"—in the view of everyone who agrees with them, anyway—that is, themselves.

Modern experience and analytical hindsight, we should add, has made it obvious that democracy decidedly doesn't do what people thought it would. Democratically made laws, democratically constructed institutions, not only fail to serve the common good, but can be expected not to serve the majority either. This result, surprising to many people, is due to the fact that democracy is inherently liable to rule on behalf of special interests. That is because the costs of catering to them are widely diffused among, and generally scarcely even noticed by, the voters, while the benefits go disproportionately to groups who can make significant differences to the legislators' probability of being elected. In practice, democracy is government in the interests of an indefinite number of organized pressure groups, redounding to the greater power of those who rule—hardly what the theorists of democracy thought they were advocating.

It may be thought that democracy could cure that problem, at least, with an increase in *knowledge* by the electorate. This is an illusion. Democracy is necessarily rule by the (relevantly) ignorant; the knowledge needed for wise rule is possessed by no one, let alone by all or most. Notoriously, democracy fares no better, and usually worse, among highly intelligent electorates (faculty meetings in universities will do for an example) than it does among hoi polloi. Nor is there anything the least bit surprising about this. Ruling over others is extremely difficult, once it is accepted that the rule is supposed to be in the interests of those ruled. One is tempted to say that, given the latter provision, it is essentially impossible. How can A rule over B if it is up to B to decide whether A's rule is for B's good? If A is B's doctor, we can see why B might want to accept a regimen proposed by A. But it is another matter for B to turn his life over to A. For all practical purposes, though, that is what democracy does.

Interest-Group Influence in Democracies

In biggish societies, democracy must, of course, be representative. The representatives are pretty free to vote for such laws as they please. Their only constraint is in getting elected and reelected. Those facts make a huge difference.

In the first place, democratic agendas on ballots must be short. The voter cannot rationally choose among 55 candidates or 7,542 alternative wordings of a law. Inevitably, we end up with political parties. And those parties are concerned with corporate reelection. Individual legislators will have to toe party lines on most issues.

More importantly, though, is a second point that follows from the first. In an n-party system where n = 2 or a few more, the n parties which manage to continue to exist do so because none of them differs strikingly from the others. For most voters, for the major parties, choice is a matter of Tweedledum and Tweedledee. Voters will choose one party over another, not on the basis of minute or vague differences in proposed policies, but of the "cut of the candidate's jib." Candidates from major parties can expect to get somewhere near 50 percent of the vote (if there are two), without doing anything in particular to deserve it. However, if a group forms, with a special interest which it would like to promote via legislation, things change. If it can offer a candidate nearly 100 percent of its members' votes in exchange for the candidate's voting for legislation favoring this group, it is very likely to succeed, for the public is none the wiser, generally speaking: it knows too little to discern what's going on, and though it pays the costs, it can hardly even assess them—indeed often can scarcely discern them. Small wonder that rational candidates will listen with avid ears to the "lobbyist." This phenomenon is so important that the study of modern politics is largely the study of pressure groups—special-interest politics. What we can expect is an avalanche of laws favoring special interests at the expense of the rest of the people. If there are enough of such groups—and there are thousands nowadays, in any large modern democracy—then we can expect that everyone will be worse off: the benefits the special-interest beneficiaries receive from those laws favoring special interests are more than offset by the costs imposed by the other laws favoring all the other special interests. Yet nobody will be motivated to change the situation. It is, in fact, classic prisoner's dilemma. If you go for the special interest, you get an advantage over those who don't; if you don't go for it, you lose out to those who do.[10]

The Muddle of Contemporary "Liberalism"

Contemporary use of the word 'liberal' muddies the conceptual waters. Contemporary politicians, and most political philosophers, pundits, and journalists who allege that they are liberals, mean by it, in general, virtually the reverse of the classical variety, even while accepting its fundamental premise, that government is supposed to be in the self-assessed interests of the governed. In their view, governments have a mandate to spread wealth in various ways contrary to the wishes of those who generate it: by supporting the otherwise-poor, as they suppose, by looking after our health, as they suppose it to be, by underwriting what they claim to be education, by restricting or prohibiting various dealings with foreigners, and so on. That many or, likely, most of those who are supposedly benefited by these laws do not see them to be such is brushed aside—after all, the majority has spoken! (Or rather, of course, that a rather small set of individuals who managed to get pluralities in elections participated in only by a modest majority of the populace, have spoken). The question whether liberalism in the classical, and clearer, understanding of that idea is compatible with any government at all is still, to be sure, under investigation; but that it is incompatible with virtually all contemporary government activities is quite clear. And those activities are certainly carried on under the auspices of democracy.

Contemporary so-called liberalism lives up fairly nicely to Mencken's specifications, except that it is not even the majority who get the chickens. Under the guise of vague-to-meaningless slogans such as "equality of opportunity," "level playing fields," "access to the means of production," and many more such, citizens of modern democracies are deprived of substantial fractions of their incomes for the benefit of any number of special interest groups and, always, the politicians and bureaucrats required for the administration of the laws by which they are promoted.

I conclude that democracy is incompatible, or at least uncomfortable bedfellows with, liberalism. Liberalism depends crucially on the Paretian, individual-benefit basis of the liberal view. If we adopt Pareto and the general liberty principle, then the freedom of maneuver of government is reduced to nothing, or next to it, given the latter. This does not sit well with those who have tasted power.

It also seems clear that, given the choice between the two, democracy has virtually nothing to be said for it. Given the choice between doing what *you* want, on condition that it harm no one else, and being forced to do what a lot of your fellows want, what argument can be adduced for generally preferring the latter?

Meanwhile, democracy's popularity may seem paradoxical. If an outrightly liberal constitution would be best for everyone, then why is it remarkably unpopular? But the paradox is not so hard to resolve. Just as bread and circuses diverted the Roman populace, so in democracy people are offered what look like advantages, because the costs are—or rather, seem to be—borne by others. A modest amount of myopia and a large amount of obscuration concerning the real costs of supposed benefits are quite sufficient to keep the public voting for non-liberal measures.

To be sure, there is also the point that democracy, like monarchy, war, and natural disasters, is *fun*. It offers drama, of a sort, and keeps the newspapers full. In any case, democracy, like government, is an entrenched system. How, then, is one to get the liberal solution adopted? Probably not by democratic means. But those are the only means we have, for quite some time to come. Meanwhile, however, we ought to keep in mind democracy's seamy side. The question is, what, more or less realistically, can be done about its more conspicuous evils?

Fixes (1) by Increasing Democracy

The most popular proposals for fixing democracy go in the direction of improving participation. That's the idea, anyway. But those who propose this do not, I think, realize what they are getting into. Take a hundred people—never mind a million or a hundred million—and say that everyone has the right to be heard by all the others, including comments on some or all of the others' expressed views. Then ask what your time budget is. If those hundred are as opinionated as typical people I know, the job of "participation" will be impossible to complete even given so small a group. (How many *couples* manage it?) That the whole idea is crazy should at least be suggested by this.

However, what's really wrong about the idea is that it assumes that, somehow, democracy is in principle right. This, I think, is what is not plausible. The familiar defense of democracy is that, while it's a bad system, it is at any rate better than any other system. But insofar as this is plausible, what makes it so? If it is agreed that the moral authority of democracy is hardly self-evident, then we must ask what criterion we are to use. The correct defense of democracy is clear: that the more or less successful ones have managed to incorporate at least a considerable modicum of liberal freedoms into their constitutions, or at least an appreciable amount of respect for them into their publics. As a result, a tolerable measure of widespread prosperity, and a tolerable degree of real capability of enjoying the sorts of lives its various citizens prefer to lead, has been achieved in many democratic countries, reliably enough to have kept it popular. And in countries allegedly democratic but in which not even rudimentary liberal freedoms are respected, democracy itself tends to go down the tubes along with everything else. That's something, indeed, but it certainly isn't what defenders of democracy promised.

I think, in fact, that these defenders generally speaking have not seen that what they're defending is not democracy, but liberal freedoms in greater or less measure, together with the supposition that democracy will continue more or less to uphold them. But 'more or less' is too generous: 'less' is certainly what the public will get.

Indeed, I think the supposition that democracy is the prerequisite for and basic upholder of liberties can only be founded on one or the other of two unwelcome factors: muddle and political interest. The former is what I shall try to explain here. The latter, however, is obvious and increasingly rampant. It is obvious why politicians want to convince people that "they" are the authors of all these impositions that the politician plans for them: that's how you get, and remain, in power. The question is whether that is anything but hoodwinkery. Abraham Lincoln famously said that you can fool all of the people some of the time, and some of the people all of the time, but you can't fool all of the people all of the time. I'm not so sure about that; but in any case, democracy involves fooling nearly all of them nearly all the time, and in that it has been eminently successful.

Democratic Voting

As to muddle, let us turn for a moment to the subject of the basis of voting. When you vote, what should your vote be based on? There are two more or less plausible, but mutually uncomfortable, answers: self-interest, and "principle," or what amounts to the individual's political philosophy. This distinction, between voting on the basis of self-interest and voting on the basis of political outlook, is fundamental; I suspect its blurring is the main reason for the continued popularity of democracy in the philosophical community—apart from a certain regard for the side with the butter. A few comments on each are in order.

(1) Self-interest

Life would be simpler, indeed, if people merely voted on the basis of self-interest, did so because they thought that was just what they ought to be doing, and everybody knew it. The trouble is, of course, that when we ask whether it would be rational to favor democracy if indeed a vote is merely an expression of self-interest, the most obvious answer would be no. For after all, what democracy will do is to run *your* self-interest under a steamroller, virtually no matter what it is. True, most people only look at the issue at the time, and hope to be with the majority on it. But if there are N issues, the chances that the majority will be on your side in even a modest majority of those issues is practically nil. No two people have identical utility functions, and overlaps among our utilities are extremely thin. The idea that there are political policies that will cater to the majority, in the sense of promoting the interests of each and every person in that majority, and doing so better than we could do by just making arrangements with particular people, is too absurd to be worth more than a moment's consideration.[11]   This is the version that encourages Mencken's assessment (another specimen: "An election is a futures market in stolen property").

2) To Each His Pet Theory

On this alternative view of the matter, a majority decision is a sort of partial consensus on what the public rules should be. We are asking each person for his account of what the public should be like—what the city should look like, what the country as a whole should be doing, and so on; and then the electoral result will go with the view of that kind which gets the most support.

Now, this idea sounds tonier, but it has the same fundamental problem, and in a way a worse one: why on earth would any rational person want such a thing? Why should I *care* what your political philosophy is, or you mine? Especially, why would I care about it to the point of actually choosing to be subjected to it, should it happen to have the support of 51 percent of my fellows—to be, then, the average political outlook among my fellow ignoramuses?

Friends of democracy, and assorted pie-in-sky theorists, may at this point wax rhapsodical or insist that by a process of sufficient communication we can gradually improve the political views of each person to the point that the view of the majority will somehow coincide with the truth. But that suggests that there *is* a right view, and that it is right whether or not a majority would or does vote for it; and if so, then what does majority endorsement have to do with it?

In any case, that process of communication is essentially impossible. What is possible, as the melancholy history of Communist experiments in the twentieth century illustrate well enough, is an enormous barrage of propaganda, possibly resulting in consensus of a sort. That those barrages have taken place in countries that were hardly democratic on any tolerable notion of the subject—for instance, they didn't get to vote for candidates other than those put forward by the government in being—should help lend insight into the essential futility of this whole idea. One should also note that on this version of the matter, it would be all too easy for a majority of the voters to vote out democracy (and one could be forgiven for suggesting that is exactly what they've largely done—turning power, gradually, over to regulators, bureaucratic fiefdoms, parliamentary secretaries, and assorted pressure groups).

The fact is that democracy is an amalgam of two ideas, each of them pretty close to ridiculous taken by itself; but if you leave them confused, they seem to be able to befuddle intelligent people into acquiescence. Either we are all being forced to serve the private desires of others, or we are all being forced to adhere to the probably hysterical moral and political predilections of those others. Neither is an obviously appealing prospect.

"Well," you may say, "what's the alternative, after all? Nobody wants a return to dictatorship." In a sense, that is true, although it is also true, I think, that everyone wants a return to dictatorship, only on his own terms. But never mind: the point is that a return to what is usually called 'dictatorship' is obviously not the solution. To be sure, it is not clear that there is a "solution" either, but we should, after all, try.

Step one is to recall what government is all about, on the liberal view (which is the right view, as I assume and believe, or at least hope, that readers agree about). There is a short and crisp answer to this: government is a device hopefully enabling us each to get on with his or her life, as best we can. It is not a device for telling us how to live, and it certainly isn't a device for transmitting the views on that subject held by a small number of alleged rulers or their elite friends to the unwitting masses.

The people who will see this paper or hear this talk are mostly intellectuals, and people like that have a special problem, because, being intellectuals, we of course think that we *do* know what's good for people. And it's even possible, though not likely, that some few of them do. Of course, any two of us will have differing views about what's good for people, and if the two happen to share the seat of power, then if history tells us anything it is that they will probably end up killing each other off in their efforts to get their own particular view written into the law, rather than the other erstwhile partner's. Meanwhile, the point is, it is extremely difficult to get people like us to just shut up and let people do their things. Playing the role of supernanny is just what we smart people were cut out for, isn't it? But the answer to that is frankly pretty obvious: no, it isn't. That role is just wrong, as well as bound to lead to whacky or unworkable or, most likely, horrible results.

If the correctly understood purpose of government means anything, it certainly means this: anything done by a group of voluntarily acting people, whose actions do not significantly affect people outside the group, is legitimate. That is the principle of Freedom of Association, really.

A point about 'significantly affect': I hope that the preceding deliberations will have persuaded the reader that some effects count and some don't. No matter what we do about anything, politically or otherwise, it will certainly "affect" someone else significantly in the respect that that person will have some views about what you, whoever you may be, ought to be doing, that your actions don't conform to (or do). But these are effects that *don't* count, for political purposes. That is to say: the fact that some or a whole lot of other people dislike what a particular person is doing is a fact that should have no political weight. It is, in brief, none of their business. If we think that it is, then we are on our way toward bad government.

In order to talk sensibly about affecting other people's welfare, understood along liberal lines, we do, indeed, need to be able to detach people's interests from each other sufficiently so that we can assess individual welfare independently. Now, people are not, generally speaking, independent: they have friends, lovers, family, associates. That is true, but it is the beginning of wisdom on political matters to appreciate that that fact has absolutely no bearing on the point being made here. You can have any relations you want, in any degree of intensity, with anybody you want to have them with, *provided* that the others agree to have them with you. Liberalism does not presuppose atomism, and indeed, the whole idea of atomism, that ancient tired charge against liberalism, is strictly incoherent, since there would be no occasion for political theory of any type whatsoever if people were indeed atoms. But liberalism is, certainly, a moral and political theory. It should be thought rather strange that unless people have the right to compel each other to do this or that, they are "atoms"!

On the Edge of Anarchy

That is the title of a good book by John Simmons,[12] but the point of borrowing it here is to call our attention to the fact that liberal theory has a strong internal bias toward anarchism—a point made a bit more difficult to appreciate by the fact that liberalism's original inventors, Hobbes and Locke, introduced their theory in support of government, monarchical if need be in the first case, and democratic in the second. However, as already noted above, Locke lets the cat out of the bag when he insists that democracy can't be allowed to override the rights of property. If it can't, of course, government is not really in the cards. And one option, becoming more theoretically live in rough proportion to the rise of big government in our day, is indeed to go for anarchism as such. But the present effort is designed to explore the possibilities for putting the brakes on government without necessarily committing ourselves to anarchy.

With that in mind, let's review the liberal argument, such as it is, for government. Government is a coercive agency; yet if there's anything liberals don't like it's coercion. So when is coercion justified on a view that coercion is basically wrong? The obvious answer is that it is justified if it is needed to counter someone else's coercion (assuming, as we will for the present, that coercion against those who have not in turn coerced, or are not in the way of coercing, any others is aggression). But anarchists are, or should be, quick to point out that the aggression that is wielded, however justly, to counteract initial aggression by others, need not, logically, be wielded by a government.[13] They can also argue, plausibly, that it not only need not be but ought not to be. The weaker point is surely correct and enormously important. If there is an effective counter to it, it must be of a certain very narrowly constrained type. Namely, it would have to meet the following conditions:

(a) Wielding the coercive apparatus in question is literally to everyone's advantage, or at least, to no one's disadvantage (other than aggressors themselves), and

(b) It is impossible (or uneconomic) for it to be wielded by anything short of a government.

It is extremely difficult to meet these two conditions. At the least, (b) has to be modified to read "for it to be wielded sufficiently" or some such qualifier, for otherwise it would be false in all cases, since there does not seem to be anything at all that literally cannot be done without government—except govern, of course.

There is a way of putting this which may help to focus the argument. The idea of justifying government is that there are collective decisions that "need to be made." But the truth is that most decisions made by almost all legislators almost always do *not* "need to be made." What is true in almost all cases is that it is possible for different people to do different things, yet harmoniously. The case isn't one of necessity, then, but of opportunism on the part of the legislature, whose members, of course, like to do things and to be seen to be doing them. So much do they like this that they also like depriving individuals of the power or opportunity to do them on their own. But this should be regarded as outrageous, rather than a sign of civic concern and virtue.

What we (theorists and concerned citizens) really need is an effective device for sorting out things which, in the relevant sense, "need to be done" from those that do not. So when is it true that something "needs to be done" in the government way—that is, by coercion?

Example: this man has cancer and will die if he does not get exotic medical treatment. That is also true of several million people who are not citizens of the same country, and no government will accept a responsibility to spend its taxpayers' money in getting all those people's needs filled, even if they have no government standing by ready to help, nor even any private means of doing so. In what sense, then, does this man's "needs" constitute a case for public action? The short answer is none. Those who think so perhaps do not understand that they are arguing that if x is a good thing for A, then B may properly be coerced into providing the assistance in question. Nevertheless, that is, precisely, what they are arguing, and when you put it in black and white like that, we see a certain paucity of argument about the matter among the politically concerned.

The correct general criterion for our purpose is this: we need collective action when if it is the case that, if it does not obtain, then everyone is worse off, in identifiable ways. That is a daunting criterion. Yet, after all, it merely says that nothing should be done by the public, by coercive central agencies, unless it is of benefit to everyone that those agencies be doing those things, and being able to do so. That leaves a great deal being done by the rest of us—namely, practically everything.

We may accept one, possibly important, modification, if such it be. Suppose that only 90 percent would directly benefit, in the sense of each getting what she judges to be her money's worth, while the remaining 10 percent would be subsidized by the others. Suppose, further, that a mechanism for actually ministering to those others is at hand. Finally, let us suppose that ministering to those others costs less than what is saved by making the whole scheme mandatory, thus saving on many administrative and collection costs. This, it seems, could be a good deal.

I previously argued, though I now think wrongly, that the Ontario Health Insurance Plan met this criterion;[14] it is presumably possible that some legislation does meet it. But clearly very little if any does so. The farmers who are subsidized heavily by governments, doubling or trebling the cost of most people's food, the enormous range of other producers of this and that who are maintained by governments at the expense of the public, and so on, are certainly unlikely to be able to make good on a claim that their services are worth that kind of imposition—if the public in question had anything directly to say about it. But what they have to say about it, when filtered through the obfuscative machinery of modern legislation and administration, amounts essentially to nothing, for any given individual.

Radical Fixes

In principle, we might suggest, nothing would come before the public, nothing be doable by political procedures, that was not doable otherwise. That might, as the anarchist claims, leave nothing at all. But if it did leave anything, those things would be matters about which nobody could reasonably complain.

There may be an issue of principle here, to be sure, as many contemporary libertarians suppose. Consider hardworking Molly, who bears no love toward her fellows and does not want any of her money spent on fixing the physical problems of the ne'er-do-wells, as she sees them. Would it not be wrong, then, for the government to take some of her money and spend it on them? However, there might be a decent reply to Molly. First, the administrators of the system could plausibly point out that they are not in fact spending any of her money that way, really. For, they would point out, if she were strictly on private insurance, it would cost her more than the fraction of her taxed payments that now do in fact go to the indigent. And secondly, they could argue, given the first point, that for her to insist on withholding it from the poor, even though it cost her more to do so, would seem to violate the Pareto Principle.

Molly has a further counter to this, however. She could insist that coddling the poor has bad side effects on them, motivating them to refrain from working, as hardworking Molly has chosen to do all her life. It is possible that she is right about that, too—though it is also possible that she is wrong, and even more likely that she is right for some cases and wrong for others.

But the premises of the first response to Molly are extremely strong, and thus most unlikely to be confirmed. Since it is very difficult (impossible?) to arrange a system having the above feature, another remedy suggests itself:

abolish taxes, replace them with user fees, and require that competitors be allowed for all services. This is a large subject, of course, and it is radical in that governments aren't interested in allowing competition, and they certainly aren't interested in replacing taxes with something that might require a more direct showing of value for money.

I recently heard a serious paper—that is, it wasn't intended as a joke—in which government was defended on the ground that it was necessary for various services, among which the author mentioned garbage disposal, provision of clean drinking water, education, and military defense. In a subsequent e-mail exchange, the fact that the first three of these have not only been frequently provided independently of government, but were always so until recently, didn't seem to phase this writer.[15] Military defense is of course rather special. What's most interesting about it is that what makes it necessary is the existence of other states which are aggressive; absent those, there would be no need of military "defense," though of course the temptation to become aggressive might be there. But at any rate, the general point is that it is very difficult to name any service provided by the state that could not be provided alternatively by a voluntary institution. Requiring the service to be supported by fees rather than taxes and requiring that competition be permitted would go far to reduce the enormous ravages of the modern state. After all, if the claim is true that some things can only be done efficiently by government, then allowing competition from private providers ought to have no effect: the government would continue to be a monopoly provider, but the monopoly would be a result of its superior efficiency rather than of making competition illegal. Few of us would sit on the edges of our chairs awaiting the day when such superior efficiency on the part of the State comes into clear view.

Many, of course, do not see those as "ravages" anyway. For them, evidently, a rather different sort of argument is required. Democracy is then being defended on *non*liberal grounds—quite a different proposition from what classic defenders of democracy had in mind. After all, if we want government to promote the True Faith, or turn everyone into tennis players, or impose some other vision of the good life, why on earth would we want democracy?

There is a possible answer to the last question. Perhaps we know that with democracy there is some chance of imposing that vision, whereas in a nondemocracy the likelihood of success is too small. You can talk the public into allowing the government to set up an Environmental Protection Agency, for example, when it would be much harder to talk a dictator into doing so—unless, of course, the theorist who wants to do this is the dictator. But democracy is the best bet for aspiring dictators in the present era. The legislators in democracies are keen to do things to justify the expenditure of a great deal or your and my money, and the way to do that is, of course, to convey the message that experts have assured them that this is a good thing.[16]

The challenge for critics of democracy sympathetic to the foregoing is to find a constitutional amendment which both has some chance of keeping most bad legislation—which is to say, most legislation—from happening, but yet which has some chance of actual passage through the political procedures available for such things. I do not pretend to have a proposal that would meet both of these requirements, but it seems like the way to go. Until then, we may rest assured that the public will continue to be both fleeced of their money, and probably also constricted in their other liberties, more effectively and thoroughly than they ever were in the days of kings and emperors of old.

Notes

This previously unpublished paper was presented, in different versions, first at a conference at the University of Montreal, 1991; at the Mershon Center Institute Conference on The Philosophic Foundations of Democracy, at Ohio State University, 1995, at meetings of the Ontario Philosophical Society in Toronto, 1997, and at various other places, notably a Jowett Society meeting in Oxford, 2000. I owe thanks for the ensuing discussion to many members of those audiences.

1. I have developed that idea in "Liberal/Conservative: The Real Controversy," *Journal of Value Inquiry* 34, nos. 2-3 (September 2000), 167-88. Also in Jan Narveson and Susan Dimock, eds., *Liberalism: New Essays on Liberal Themes* (Dordrecht, Netherlands: Kluwer Academic Publishers, 2000), 19-40.

2. Jan Lester, *Escape from Leviathan* (New York: St. Martin's Press, 2000), 58-61.

3. There are caveats about probabilistically assessed gains. The short version of what to say about these is that for each the program in question must be a good bargain when taken together with whatever else needs to be part of the deal.

4. I take David Gauthier's "Lockean Proviso," which forbids pursuing one's own utility by imposing disutility on others except in cases of self-defense, as my model. See David Gauthier, *Morals by Agreement* (New York: Oxford University Press, 1986), chapter 7, 190-232.

5. Robert A. Dahl, *On Democracy* (New Haven, Conn.: Yale University Press, 1998), 48-49.

6. *Canadian Charter of Rights and Freedoms*—Part I of the Constitution Act, 1982 (Ottawa, Canada: Government of Canada, Publications Canada, 1982), Section 7.

7. Canadian Charter, Section 1.

8. I have not been able to track down the precise source of this delightful quip in the voluminous writings of Mr. Mencken; some Mencken scholars are uncertain that it was he who said it at all; all agree, though, that it is the sort of thing he *would* say!

9. John Locke, *Second Treatise of Civil Government*, in Peter Laslett, ed., *Two Treatises of Government* (Cambridge, U.K.: Cambridge University Press, 1960), 361.

10. For a brief and very lucid explanation of how this works, see James D. Gwartney and Richard L. Stroup, *What Everyone Should Know about Economics and Prosperity* (Vancouver: Fraser Institute, 1993), 86-89.

11. An early contributor to this topic was Elizabeth Anscombe. See her "On Frustration of the Majority by Fulfilment of the Majority's Will," *Analysis* 36, No. 4 (1976)—reprinted in *Ethics, Religion and Politics (Collected Philosophical Papers*, Vol. III, University of Minnesota Press, 1981), 123-29.

12. A. John Simmons, *On the Edge of Anarchy* (Princeton, N.J.: Princeton University Press, 1993).

13. See chapter 11.

14. Jan Narveson, *The Libertarian Idea* (Peterborough, Ont.: Broadview

Press, 2001), 251-57.

15. George Klosko. The article, considerably revised from its original version, has since been published as "The Natural Basis of Political Obligation," *Social Philosophy and Policy* 18 no. 1 (winter 2001), 93-114.

16. See, of course, chapter 7.

Chapter 11

The Anarchist's Case

Introduction

The anarchist is all but universally regarded as a wild-eyed, dangerous character. Wildness of eye is imputed on the basis of conceptual confusion and impractical utopianism: anarchism is thought to be virtually self-refuting, impossible to expound clearly, and dependent on obviously false estimates of the capabilities of human nature. The ascription of danger has two sources: first, a perception that the anarchist is out to destroy something of great value, something on which the stability of society rests, which of course is assumed to be or be due to the state; second, that some who have called themselves anarchists did actually throw bombs and the like. These are not just frivolous charges: certainly some purported anarchists are guilty on both counts. Both must be refuted, at least in principle, if anarchism is to be regarded as a legitimate option in social theory.

At the same time, however, the charges against the state that motivate anarchism have a tendency to be swept under one or another of several available carpets. We move the theory of anarchism out of the dustbins of political theory if we can give decent replies to the familiar claims against it, while at the same time pressing our complaints against the state in a clear-eyed way, both as regards its theoretical claims and in the cold light of the empirical facts. And we move it to the front of the desk if, in addition, we can supply positive motivation for the anarchistic outlook.

The present chapter undertakes sketchy, outline-level responses on all of these fronts. The task is rendered more manageable by the perception that the critique of the state is largely coordinate with the positive construction required. What's wrong with the state is what's right with anarchy. More than that, it's also what's *good* about anarchy. However, the new case for anarchism requires complete repudiation of the older, utopian-socialist type of theory. No one in the history of social theory has been wronger about anything than Marxists about the nonnecessity of telling us quite a bit about what their system would be like if the Revolution succeeds.

To see this, of course, we must expound the moral outlook underlying anarchism. To do this, we must first make an important distinction between two general options in anarchistic theory, one of which fully deserves anarchism's disdainful view in the public eye, but the other of which is not only enormously plausible on the face of it, but apparently feasible as well. The two are what we may call, respectively, the socialist versus the free-market, or capitalist, versions.

Anarchism 1: The Socialist Version

Anarchism is the view that the best state of society is the stateless state: society lacking centralized, authoritative decision-making and decision-enforcing agencies. Is this compatible with any sort of socialism? By the latter we understand what Marx understood by it: rejection of private ownership of the "means of production." It is useful to open our discussion by considering whether socialist anarchism—by long odds the historically most popular version—makes any sense. We begin by seeing why it does not.

States tell people what to do. They don't just *tell* them that, of course: they do so with "authority," meaning, in effect, that they make their directives stick by backing them with highly credible threats to use force against those who do not comply. States enforce uniformities across society: all are required to do things one way rather than any of an indefinite number of possible other ways. In a free-market or private-enterprise economy, productive resources are under the direction of individuals or voluntarily acting groups, acting on their own. If it is claimed that this is somehow morally wrong, because we do not approve of what those individuals do or fail to do with the products resulting from this uncontrolled activity, or to the manner in which they are produced, then there is a problem. For socialism imposes requirements on at least the disbursement and/or production of those products that are typically at odds with the interests of the producers. The socialist's proposed cure for the alleged deficiencies is to scuttle private control, thereby opting for an enormous range of what he takes to be "corrections" of voluntary activity. Since those activities are voluntary, the "corrections" in question must be markedly at odds with the intentions of the producers. A uniform system is imposed where what would happen otherwise can be expected to be quite nonuniform. Could this possibly be done in the absence of central authority? The short answer is that it cannot.

At this point, to be sure, the socialist will opt for democracy—in the workplace, in the committee rooms, and in society at large—but democracy cannot bring about society-wide changes of heart; it merely settles things by voting. Any expectation of unanimity regarding such things as what to produce and for whom deserves the name "utopian"—assuming, what we should not accept anyway, that a society in which uniformity of production and consumption prevails is such a good thing that an extreme state of it deserves the adjective "utopian" rather than the reverse. The majority, then, will simply overrule the minority, just as it does at present. There is, then, no possibility of achieving socialist goals without a state or what amounts to one. Those who hope for it without the state are starry eyed; those who prefer the state to the nonattainment of those goals are not anarchists; and those who suppose that decision-making methods coercively enforceable over all does not amount to a state are confused.

It is regrettable that so much and so interesting a stretch of intellectual history should have to be dismissed so briefly, but there is no way around this result, and nonmarket anarchism will accordingly be ignored hereinafter.

Anarchism 2: Market Anarchism

The alternative version is what is now called "market" or sometimes, if misleadingly, "capitalist" anarchism. The moral of my story so far is that if anarchism is possible at all, it must be in the market version. There, production is always under the control of individuals or groups acting on their own, and distribution likewise is effected only by voluntary exchange, which may be assumed to consist typically of commercial exchange. In short, it consists precisely of that very "anarchy in the system of production and exchange" that Marx deplored. On the face of it, then, the market system is such that everything that is done is done because somebody wants to do just that, rather than because someone has threatened the doer with evil if he does not.

So, at first sight, it looks as though, at one stroke, we have the reason both why the market system should be feasible, and at the same time why it should be desirable. But that would be too quick. Some theorists, of course, will insist that people getting what they want has nothing to do with whether it is a good society anyway. In the present discussion, we will ignore such complaints. But even granting liberal premises, it is still too quick. For perhaps a society in which people *do* what they want is not necessarily a society in which people *get* what they want. Some will be inclined to get what they want by doing what others do *not* want: by using force, in short. And many will no doubt complain that a society in which everyone does only what he wants will fail to bring it about that many get what they not only want but need. To say that a market-anarchic society is one in which people "do what they want" is thus cheating. The *idea* of a market society is that people do what they want, yes; but what do we do about all the people who won't *let* some of them do what they want? Anarchism in the sense in which they do what they want would seem to have to be the result of the operation of a normative system in which people *may* not use force: interferences with voluntary activity are forbidden. But surely, it will reasonably be said, at least some of those people, in turn, will not be put off from using that force except by the prospect of force being used against them. Does this not bring us back to the state? And if the case is accepted that the needy must be helped regardless, then similarly a role for the state may seem to be assured.

It would take more space than is available here to respond to the latter group. If it is accepted that one may permissibly help the needy by coercing one's neighbors to do so, then lessons in both economics and morals are required before the discussion can resume on a reasonable plane. However, the anarchist's case that the needy will almost certainly do better without the State would at least have to be regarded as plainly relevant by all concerned, if it can be made out. But if the answer to the former question, about private violence were to prove to be, as Hobbes and his successors all insisted, in the affirmative, then it would be game over for anarchism.

Fortunately, that answer is by no means certain. It turns out that there are very good reasons for thinking that the private allocation of force, without central control, is indeed possible, both in principle and, on the basis of ample evidence, in practice as well.[1] Careful attention to both evidence and analysis will make this clear beyond peradventure; yet it is quite understandable why people should believe the contrary. Their governments, after all, have been telling them for several millennia that it is not. And should we not believe everything our governments tell us?[2]

In a real society, some people will resort to force. For that matter, to speak of "resorting" to force may be to understate the case: some people may positively relish the idea of using force. Whatever their motive, the use of interpersonal force inherently conflicts with market liberty. More precisely, it is the use of coercive force that does so: the ballet dancer who lifts his partner in a graceful maneuver uses force, but does not coerce. The coercer, on the other hand, uses power, which often enough is force, in order to get his victim to do what the victim would have preferred not to do. Let us understand this to be the sort of force we intend in present contexts. We may thus say that a libertarian society is one in which force may not be used against those who, in their turn, do not use it against others. The word 'may' is a moral one: the sentence containing it says that the use of force against the innocent is wrong. The status of this prohibition as a moral claim raises several questions. I shall address two in particular, one essential for present purposes, the other important for wider purposes of social theory.

Defining Libertarian Rights

The first question is, just what is meant by 'may'? Fortunately, it is also fairly easy to answer: to say that someone "may not" do something is to say that he is prohibited from doing it. But doesn't that just mean, in turn, that he *may be prevented* from doing it? There, however, is that word 'may' again. Have we made any progress, then? Indeed we have, as I shall now explain.

Someone, S, who believes that a person, A, "may" be prevented from doing something, x, envisages that some person(s) B (who may or may not be identical with S) are such that if B acts to prevent A from doing x, then S will be inclined, in turn, not to intervene to prevent B from so intervening. If, on the other hand, S believes that A may not be so prevented, then S will incline to disapprove of B's intervention and will be inclined to do, or at least to support the doing of something to see to it that B does not do that. Moral attitudes,

attitudes of approval and disapproval, are directed at two sorts of activities, not just one. First, they are directed at the actions of people in general, people having no particular relation to the activities of further people. But second, they are directed at activities that, in their turn, are intended to control or influence people's actions, not necessarily consensually. In other words, we may distinguish between simple approval and disapproval, on the one hand, and approval or disapproval of reinforcing activity on the other. A theory of right and wrong, insofar as it is relevant to political theory, is a theory about the latter: about the use of methods of social control or influence, including force. Qua political theory, it is essentially about the use of force in particular, for a state is just a monopoly of control over the use of force.

A libertarian morality, then, holds that force may be used only to counter[3] force. Many put this in terms of "initiating" or refraining from initiating force, and we will accept that terminology as broadly appropriate. The innocent do not initiate force against anyone; the guilty initiate force against the innocent; and a libertarian morality says that we are not to use force against any except the guilty. Market anarchism is really just the instantiation of the libertarian moral theory.[4]

It is of fundamental importance to note that force may be used only to counter aggressive force, but it does not follow that we must use it. The misconception that libertarianism says the latter is perhaps the major source of supposed support for statism from within what is claimed to be libertarian theory. Some will think this nonobligatoriness of using force even when justified the Achilles' heel of anarchism; others will think it liberating and right. Whichever, only the weaker view is really consistent with the libertarian idea.[5]

The idea of a market is the idea of people who are free to make exchanges and, in practice, often do so. No one is to intervene to prevent initiation or completion of an exchange, so long as it is a free exchange in the sense that both parties to it voluntarily agree to that exchange. (How much information they must supply each other in order for it to be accounted 'voluntary' is, of course, an important question; but the information supplied must be, literally, information, not *mis*information. Fraud, in other words, is ruled out.[6]) Importantly, there is no assumption or presumption that the parties to exchanges are antecedently equal in any respect other than that each is under no coercive pressure from other persons to choose one way or another: no one acts under threat of force by another. They may act under self-imposed compulsions, of course—that is quite another matter. They may well act under threats of withdrawal of love, companionship, or other services previously voluntarily supplied by spouses, friends, or associates. But they do not act under threats of force, unless there is a previously accepted arrangement calling for such means in the case in question. (Boxers in the ring have agreed to attempt to hit each other. Plenty of force is employed, but no coercion.)

Moral Reinforcement

The second question to address, then, is: what resources for enforcing market arrangements could there be in an anarchic society? May we expect such arrangements actually to be made when needed and to be effective? Putting the matter this way might suggest the need to alter our definition of 'market society' as one in which people do not initiate force. But if we are to have a useful definition, applicable to real-world society, we shall have to say instead that a market society is one in which the rule is not to initiate force. In what sense, though, may a society be said to "have" a rule? The answer lies in the prevailing pattern of attitudes among its people. If virtually everyone in the society has the appropriate attitudes and generally acts on them, then we have a market society in about as full a sense as could be realistically hoped.

The societies that we live in are not fully market societies. There is a good deal of the market attitude in many people, and yet most people are not anarchists. They think, or at least think they think,[7] that it is just fine to have a centralized authority with the power to enforce rules. And most of them perhaps think that that authority may do much *more* than that. It is, to be sure, unsafe to speculate about what people "really think." Much of what they think, after all, is heavily influenced by information, much of which may well be misinformation. It is the job of a theorist who thinks that what appear to be the prevailing attitudes on some matter are wrong to identify the errors that lead people to make the professions they do, in hopes that recognition of those errors will revise those professions. And when this is done, the market theorist supposes that every reasonable person will wind up accepting the market idea rather than some other. His claim, in short, must be that anarchism is *reasonable.*

The informal enforcement of morals consists in the main of two things. One is that expressions of approval and disapproval are marshaled on behalf of the type of behavior called for by the principles under consideration. Strongly supplementing these are a range of more robust responses to behavior, including such things as "admission to the society" of the persons in question. Our dealings with those who adhere to those principles are likely to be more extensive and more profitable than with those who do not; withdrawal of opportunity for such dealings is a considerable inducement to deal honestly if one deals at all.

The other sort of enforcement, of course, is by outright employment of coercive force. Precisely what it may be used for is an important question, to which the market anarchist answers, broadly, that it may be used when necessary for the defense of oneself or legitimately acquired property, or of anyone else or their property, provided the others are willing to be defended in that way by you. And for nothing else. The question of the viability of anarchism is open precisely because such force, which we may assume would sometimes be necessary, is not and need not be wielded exclusively by governments. Is there anything about power that inherently drives us to statist control over its use? The tendency has been to assume this, but that assumption is in question here.

Forcible Enforcement

Many agreements among individuals are not enforced, or at least not overtly so, and yet these agreements are effective. Friends and acquaintances, colleagues, relatives, and even random strangers often enough make agreements that the parties to them keep, feel obliged to keep, and moreover, keep because they feel thus obliged. How is this possible? Hobbes argues that agreements in the "state of nature," the stateless state, would not be valid, citing the frailty of "mere words." But he overlooks the fact that much "enforcement" of agreements is internally monitored by the parties to them. The costs of reinforcement in such cases are very low—or at least those costs are psychical rather than physical. Many other agreements, to be sure, are enforced, or at least are agreed to be enforceable. This brings up the question, which are which? How do we decide whether an agreement is enforceable or not?

The terminology in which this last question is formulated is, however, insufficiently discriminating. For there are many means of enforcement. If a loved one will receive you coldly unless you do x, that is likely to induce your performance of x; but between persons who scarcely know each other or who do but do not particularly care about each other, that is unlikely to be effective. We must distinguish, at least, between, on the one hand, enforcement that consists in effective threats to punish or to forcibly restrict the party's freedom and, on the other, enforcement confined to withdrawal of previously supplied services or alteration for the worse of previously held attitudes. Since we are talking about social arrangements, arrangements to prevail in a sizable society with many members who are unfamiliar or not particularly friendly with each other, it is the former that requires special attention in the present context. Politics is about the use of force. The market anarchist's thesis is that force may be used only to counter force and not for any wider purpose. We assume that force against people's property is included in the proscribed uses of force.[8] Clearly, the libertarian view entails the market anarchist's: we may make whatever agreements we wish, such as that if I don't do x, you may hit me, or I shall pay a fine of $n to your lawyer, and so on.

A market society, then, may now be described as one in which the accepted rule is that one refrains from using force just to get one's way, confining the use of force instead to defensive activity or to any employments agreed to by the parties against whom it is used. There are then two questions to ask. One is whether we can expect a society so organized to work—granting that it is very unclear just what "working," in the relevant sense, consists of. One aspect that seems clearly relevant is stability. Would any such society be able to achieve stability? That is, would such a society persist in that form, or would it be crucially susceptible to takeover by a state-type agency? Would an anarchy inevitably turn into an "archy" of some kind? Why should or would everyone accept that rule—the rule of liberty, as we might call it—and not some other? Why should we accept a principle that restricts use of coercion so narrowly?

The first question sounds like one for or against which it should be possible to assemble empirical evidence. If that is so, then the evidence certainly looks to be entirely against the anarchist. There appear not to be or to have been any anarchies amongst sizable and enduring societies on earth. But that is much too quick; a distinction must be made here. A state assumes power over all, and in principle it assumes unlimited power—power in all respects; yet, the extent of power actually wielded or even merely claimed by states, though it has varied a great deal, has never been totally unlimited. Within the boundaries of political states, there are and have been many areas of life within which anarchy is the order of the day. People frequently interact in various ways without evident leaders and in the absence of acknowledged central rule makers among the group of participants. This, indeed, is what makes sociology and economics possible. People relate to each other on their own various terms, and structures and patterns result that are of interest to the social scientist. The question is whether these innumerable constellations of independent actors are dependent for their existence on an overarching state, as some appear to think, or at any rate whether an anarchic condition would inevitably be such as to evolve into statelike arrangements.

Market Enforcement

At the level of logic, at least, the anarchist seems to be on solid ground. Market interaction requires that people predominantly respect the property rights of those with whom they interact. The occasional violator either gets away with his violation and is subsequently ignored, or something is done about him and he gets punished or his victims suitably compensated. Those who administer the punishment or compensation can be acting on behalf of the victim exclusively and need not have assumed a general duty to rectify all situations in which violations of rights have taken place. There is certainly no strictly logical necessity that any centralized agency possessed of statelike powers perform such functions.

It seems to be true, nevertheless, that constellations of independent actors readily succumb to statelike arrangements. We may describe this either (1) as a matter of participants seeing advantages in, or a "need" for, such an agency, or (2) of their falling prey to the wiles of the power hungry. Which of the two it is, though, is an important question. People will likely see the need for such an agency if there really is a need for it, but it does *not* follow that if they profess to see such a need, then there also *is* one. Whether there is would seem to be a matter of logic, conceptual analysis. Either there is something about human interaction that inherently requires states, or else those who profess to see such a need are mistaken.

They may be not only mistaken, however, but biased as well. We can expect the holders of power to be disposed to spread the doctrine that states are necessary even if they are not. Government may rest on error, and the error may even be deliberately fostered by those in power. Government may, in short, rest essentially on what amounts to fraud.[9]

If government is unnecessary, though, something else is: a basis of interpersonal agreement regarding the underlying rules to be followed, and moreover, that those rules include essential prohibitions of force and fraud. That is, the fact that someone got something by force or fraud must be accepted by essentially all as constituting a basis for grievance, compensation, and perhaps retribution. Thus it sounds as though there must be what has been called a "natural law" of human association. Especially in view of its historical associations with our project, a few words about it are in order.

Natural Law

Most ways of expounding the idea that some moral rules are "natural" have the notable disadvantage that what they claim appears to be empirically refuted. Obviously it is untrue that people *do* behave strictly in accordance with the tenets of any recognizable version of "natural law." And apparently it is untrue that all human infants emerge into articulate consciousness espousing those rules. Most of them do manage something of the sort, to be sure; but (a) by then they've been exposed to a good deal of social teaching and reinforcement; and (b) unfortunately for the natural law hypothesis, it seems that there is a good deal of variability in what particular individuals end up accepting in the way of general rules of conduct, especially insofar as they are members of differing groups. St. Thomas's dictum that the natural law is "written on our hearts" evidently needs to be taken with quite a few grains of salt. What, then, are we to replace it with?

There is, I think, a fairly short and quite reasonable answer to this, supplied in essentials by Thomas Hobbes, whose Laws of Nature are claimed by him to be "theorems" of prudence. People concerned about their own well-being, he thinks, will have to accept these rules as being rationally called for by a combination of four things: (1) their interests; (2) their powers; (3) the proclivities and capabilities of their fellows; and, of course, (4) the characteristics of the nonhuman environment. People wishing to do well will see the benefits of association with their fellows, and will see the need for such association to be along peaceful and cooperative lines rather than the reverse. The need in question will be perceived, in Hobbes's account, as arising from the evident rough equality of the human capacity for destruction and violence and the evident impossibility of getting on if others are free to use those destructive capacities. In short, Hobbes argues that the general shape of the rules of human interaction are not self-evident and certainly not matters of some special sort of "intuition," but are instead pretty straightforward inferences of common sense about the four factors mentioned.

Yet Hobbes, as we know, was also the champion of the state, of "Sovereignty" as an essential device for securing the actual benefits of the rule of natural law. Natural law, he thinks, will rule only if *somebody* rules. But—fortunately for the would-be anarchist—Hobbes's argument is flawed, and fatally. It is important to see where he went wrong in order to understand which way is right.

Hobbes's argument makes use of an idea that is still regarded as virtually a theorem of decision theory. A familiar type of human interaction exemplifies the general structure known as Prisoners' Dilemma. In such a structure, each participant chooses freely between two alternatives whose payoffs are a function of what others choose as well. If all choose x, then everybody is better off than if all choose y; yet each individual is best off if he chooses y while the others choose x. Since he will then be better off than in any alternative outcome, that is the one he will prefer. So Hobbes held, and most modern decision theorists join him in holding, that the rational actor will indeed choose y in such situations. All making this individually best choice in a condition in which there are absolutely no rules about *anything* leads to the famous "war of all against all," in which everybody is enormously worse off.

In order to head off this unfortunate result, thinks Hobbes, situations with such structures need to be fundamentally altered. Those who choose y must not be *able* to do so without entailing some further disutility not included in the original picture. This disutility is a penalty. In the Hobbesian scenario, it is to be wielded by a state. Why a state? Because, Hobbes reasoned, only a state has the necessary power to force any and all miscreants into line.

There are several questions to ask. First, is the "state of nature"—the situation we would have in the absence of government—indeed of broadly Prisoners' Dilemma type? Second, is the proposed inference to the individual superiority of the noncooperative strategy sound? And third, even if it is, would there be means of dealing with it other than Hobbes's proposed Sovereign?

Regarding the first question, most theorists who have considered the question at all have, in effect if not on the verbal face of it, accepted Hobbes's characterization. We should perhaps take note of a possible description of society according to which the situation facing humans is not even a Prisoners' Dilemma, but instead a *zero-sum* game—a situation in which one person's gain is another's loss. Of course, if nobody can improve his own situation without worsening that of someone else, there is no hope of cooperation, and the general advancement of society is simply out of the question. Fortunately, the zero-sum thesis is simply wrong.[10] (The modern version of it invokes claims about limited resources and the like. Those versions are also wrong, but the point cannot be argued here.[11])

A situation in which all are free to resort to violence at will is dominated by one in which no one is: every single individual will do better than that very individual will have done if everyone, including himself, takes on a reliable commitment to refrain from violence (and the other vices detailed in Hobbes's list—all of which, of course, Hobbes claims, I think correctly, to follow from the fundamental vice,[12] which is the disposition to resort to violence in the promotion of one's various ends). Is there any real reason to doubt this thesis?

This, it turns out, is a rather tricky question. The short answer is "No": of course everyone will do better to take that alternative than to take the single alternative of having no commitments *at all*. But is that really the only other option? It seems not. In real life, people are often reliable but sometimes not. A selective mix of cooperation and defection will at least seem to pay, and is certainly what almost all individuals actually do exemplify in any considerable stretch of social life.[13]

Matters get considerably more complicated when we consider the possibility that human interactions might have the structure known as "Chicken" rather than Prisoners' Dilemma (henceforth PD, for short). In both games the participants have a common second-best; but in the Chicken game they have a common worst outcome, in contrast to the PD, in which both parties have a common third-best outcome. In PD, therefore, one player's best is the others' worst: A's best response to B's threat of aggression is defense—A can't do better by knuckling under. But in Chicken, unfortunately, he *can*. If he insists on resisting, and the other does not back down, then both will lose; if, instead, A knuckles under, then A may be enslaved, but at least he is still alive. Faced with the choice between being the chicken and being the hawk, A may prefer being the chicken, nor is A clearly irrational in so choosing, as Peter Danielson[14] so cogently points out.

This problem is clearly not an easy one, but certain general comments are in order. One is that if it is possible to prevent social Chicken games from developing, then it is plausible to say that we should do so, and plausible for the same reasons that recommend cooperation in PD. It is not at all surprising that it is a theorem of commonsense morality that we ought not to employ coercion, just as we ought to refrain from violence. This response may be lame, for the question then is whether social rules of that kind have the clout necessary to achieve their purpose. But then, the very same question can be asked about PD; and certainly the answer, in a vast range of real-life cases, is that it certainly does. Social life is generally not a fracas, despite the many temptations for the unscrupulous or the sociopathic. That we have much to gain by cooperation and much to lose without it, as a general observation about our situations vis-à-vis our natural environment and each other, seems too obvious to need more than a mere mention.

Nevertheless, Danielson's challenge does seem to me to be right in one very important respect: it probably accounts for the existence and survival of the state. We shall return to that later.

The second of our three questions is whether the Hobbesian deduction from the premise of individual rationality is correct. Now on this, it seems to me, there is room for another view. That other view has been interestingly expounded by David Gauthier in recent times. Gauthier holds that the disposition to choose the "defect" option in PD is a mistake. We should instead adopt a disposition to cooperate, provided that the person with whom we are dealing is also disposed to do so, and to defect only if it looks as though that's how he is disposed. This Gauthier calls "constrained maximization," in contrast to the strategy of "straight maximization," which calls for defection no matter what the other person does.

Gauthier's solution has seemed to many to smack of moralism. And it is undoubtedly more complicated than the game theorist's response. Instead of adopting a simple, unconditional "nasty" strategy, the rational individual, according to Gauthier, sees the need in such situations to operate on a more complex strategy. Now, the complexity of this strategy is seen to be especially deep when we ask how we could know that the other person has the similar disposition—and above all when we reflect that that disposition is a disposition to cooperate if I am disposed to cooperate, so that part of my solving my problem about him is that he has to have solved the same problem about me.[15]

Even so, though, it looks as though there must be some kind of empirical solution to this problem, for we in fact do successfully cooperate, without depending on coercive enforcement agencies, in countless cases; and we all think that people should keep their agreements and that people who do not are on that account to be criticized. Is this last fact to be shrugged off as irrelevant? In accepting it, after all, I move from the rationality of actually doing the cooperative thing to the rationality of certain types of reactions to those who do not.

But this, I insist, is actually sufficient for our purposes. It is rational for me to insist on your keeping your agreements with me and for you to insist on my keeping my agreements with you. The perception that this is so, as well as lively awareness of the likelihood of follow-up reinforcement, seems to be extensively motivating in human affairs, and for good reason. Other theorists have pointed out that if we turn from the *one-shot* PD to the *iterated* dilemma, in which we face, time and again, the same general structure with the same people, then the rationality of a rule to treat the other this time as he has treated you previously is very plausible indeed.[16] People with a continuing tendency to defect will certainly do worse than people with the tendency to cooperate as long as the other person has done so. It is obvious that they will, and easy to demonstrate to them. Iteration, indeed, seems to be a context in which we have the kind of evidence regarding dispositions that the Gauthieran cooperator requires.

I shall therefore propose that we settle for something very close to the Gauthieran conclusion. It *is* rational to be disposed to cooperate where cooperation looks to be likely; it is rational to insist on cooperation wherever cooperation is possible—as it generally is; and it is irrational, in real life, to behave the way a Hobbesian state-of-nature maximizer is alleged to behave.

This brings us to the third question: even if we were to accept the miserable view of the standard game theorist, would there be means of dealing with it other than Hobbes's proposed Sovereign? It is here that the anarchist's case is the strongest, since the answer is so obviously in the affirmative. The topic, we should be careful to recognize, takes in a great deal of terrain. Hobbes's Sovereign is intentionally totalitarian, the scope of his power essentially unlimited. No one should want to defend such an institution. Those who think that the state is justified insist that a state must be very much less nearly omnipotent than Hobbes's argument would have it. In particular, virtually all theorists ever since, including his successor John Locke, insist that a state must be, broadly speaking, democratic *and* must operate in an environment of constitutional restrictions. The point is, then, that there seem to be many alternative sorts of Sovereigns alongside the anarchist's alternative of no Sovereign at all and that none of them accepts the fundamental argument of Hobbes. It is an important question whether this is somehow a pipe dream, but facts must be faced. Contemporary states do frequently refrain from various policies because it would be evidently in violation of their constitutions, and governments are, every now and then, chucked out of office by electoral processes.

What should we do in the face of this apparent plethora of possibilities? The anarchist's answer is that we must find out what is wrong with the state *as such*, so that even as minimal a state as we can imagine will still suffer from that defect. In addition, the would-be anarchist must show that no state has compensating advantages such that it is nevertheless preferable to anarchy. Even if we can do that, there remains the daunting question of whether anarchy is really feasible in the world we live in. It may be that for some reason it is not—some reason other than any having to do with the virtues of states, if there are any. That would be a dismal result, indeed; even so, one might learn something from it.

The Case against the State

Why think that there is anything inherently and necessarily wrong with the state? To see the answer to this, we need to attend carefully to the distinction between states and associations. The bridge club, the gardening society, even the philosophical association can decide to set up a governing board, hold elections, subject themselves to the resulting rules, and so on. The individual may join some organization ruled, for all practical purposes, by an absolute monarch. What distinguishes the state from all these is that those subject to it don't *join*, and that its authority extends to all, in respects that have nothing to do with any reasons why those, if any, who do join did so. Given that many are certain not to share the purposes proposed as justifying what the state imposes, it is highly probable that they will be badly done by.

Is it certain, though? Let's think about that one. We may here propose a general formula for acceptable law. What is needed is that *each individual* subject to it is better off, *in his own terms*, from being so subjected than he would be if not so subjected to it. Bear in mind that this recipe applies not only to the general idea of law. It applies also to its *application* and does so in *each individual case*. Officer O'Malley rightly applies the law to Jones at time t only if subjecting Jones to this penalty at this time is such as to bring it about that Jones is better off on the whole, in his own view, than he would have been had he not been subject to the law in such a way that this penalty is called for by persons doing just what Jones does at t in the circumstances prevailing then.

It is logically possible that this criterion could be met. But it is incredibly unlikely. State officials are paid to administer some or other laws. Making their pay contingent on the right administration of those laws is exceedingly difficult—to the point of being humanly impossible. This probability is enormously increased if the people who administer the rules are hired by Jones to do so, and moreover to administer precisely the rule now being administered. (Enthusiasts for the state sometimes argue that that is the situation with the state. In order to make that stick, they must stretch the sense of 'hired' beyond recognition.) From the point of view of institutional design, an institution that incorporated the distinctive feature of the market, that the consumer is boss—"consumer sovereignty"—has a far better chance of success than any recognizable state.

Democracy, to be sure, is widely advertised as incorporating this feature. If you find that idea compelling, just imagine a supermarket that advertised that you would, upon entering the store, enter a vote for a "buyer" who would buy whatever he thought was likely to get him more votes from all the customers than either of two other "candidates" for this position, and he would then give you whatever share of the goods he felt like, and there was nothing you could do about this until the next such election, four years hence. Only someone with remarkably dim perceptions of the functioning of the state, or with a bizarre sense of humor, could regard democracy as providing anything much resembling market services. For the rest, the track record of actual democracies in providing genuine services to their citizens is sufficiently dismal that what little theoretical support there is for this form of government at the conceptual level is reduced to nil at the empirical level.[17] Lord Acton is too often quoted to the effect that "All power corrupts, and absolute power corrupts absolutely." But those who blithely quote him concentrate only on the evils of the spectacular tyrants of history—the Stalins, the Napoleons, and so on. But the anarchist's real case concerns the little guys—the ones elected by the people in hopes that they will actually do some good. Political power is inherently likely—"certain" is close enough to the truth—to cause more evil than good, and the good that it occasionally does can be better brought about by people who, either because it pays or because they are interested in it, are motivated to do it rather than to bring about the side payments of politics.

Prospects for Anarchism: Not Good

There remains the question of why anarchy is not more popular than it is. With proper perspective, of course, it is in fact enormously popular, in the sense that the functionally anarchic parts of our societies, such as the markets for most consumer goods (despite the limits imposed by taxes and the welter of regulations hovering over everything), not only work superbly, but are perceived by all concerned to do so in practice. Nevertheless, anarchy in the sense of the total absence of government is so far from popular as to be almost entirely ignored, and treated with derision insofar as not ignored. Why should this be so, one wonders?

There are, I think, three kinds of answers, not entirely unrelated.

(1) Throughout this chapter I have ignored the nonrational aspects of government. Six million Britons volunteered to fight for their country in the First World War, even those who knew what was in store for them at the front. The first Canada-Russia hockey series culminated in a closely fought game that was televised around the world; in Canada itself, the country essentially came to a halt during that game. This author recalls being at Stratford at a production of Shakespeare when, during the third act, suddenly the action on stage came to a temporary halt, and one actor stepped to center stage to inform the audience that Canada had just won the series by virtue of a heart-stopping goal in the last

seconds of the final game. The audience broke into a five-minute ovation before Shakespeare could be resumed. It is fair to say that things like this cannot be readily factored into my arguments above. Is the state justified because otherwise we would not have Canada-Russia games? Because the Olympics would never be the same? Because if the state goes, so does its pomp and majesty and suchlike? And a lot of what has been most interesting about history along with it? We'll leave the reader to ponder that one, but I do not want to underrate that factor. The question is whether the entertainment value of the state is really worth the costs. Frankly, I doubt it, and I doubt that most ordinary people would think so either.

(2) There is no such thing as a free lunch—but there is such a thing as a boondoggle. Modern government encourages 90 percent of the populace to think it's getting something for nothing. The great majority of citizens belong to at least one group or other that has managed to induce legislators to do something for its own particular special interest. What it does is to provide a service that is virtually free to many people in its constituency—free in the sense that its (highly inflated) price is paid for by *others*. Each beneficiary group throws a cost onto the rest. This would not matter if everyone was a member of enough beneficiary groups and the service provided was sufficiently efficient that it would be worth it, from the point of view of each person, to pay as much as he is in fact paying in taxes for what he gets. But this is very far from being the case—a fact that much too rarely comes home to the clueless or bemused taxpayer.

(3) Why is the taxpayer so clueless and bemused? Here we come to the most important reason of all: the self-interest of the governing class, which with big government is very large. The bureaucrats, policemen, secretaries, parliamentarians, and so on are interested in jobs: in keeping them and in their being secure. The power of government enables them to be fairly secure—in many cases *very* secure. It is also attractive on its own, enabling the officeholder to wield authority over underlings and power over ordinary citizens.

To this, unfortunately, we can add the interests of considerable segments of modern populations who perceive that their careers or other interests are forwarded by the continued power of government. Not only popular media, but most of what we might call the intellectual upper middle class, support the welfare state, the art-subsidizing state, the medical state, and the rest. All this effectively acts, in the end, to keep the lower orders down rather than to provide the help that well-meaning and intelligent people supposed they could provide by all these means. But that is not a message that easily gets through to such people—who, after all, forearmed with the meaningless but effective epithets of today's politics, stand ready to dismiss analysis as "right wing," after which who needs to read further?

Good government is government in the interest of the governed, not of the governors. But, as we are coming more and more to appreciate, under the impetus of Public Choice analysts as well as common sense, the law is predominantly driven by the interests of the *governors*, not of the *governed*. And part of the package is that government has the power to induce people to believe that what it does for people is both necessary and useful.

Why does government remain in power? Why, in fact, are there still governments? The short answer is that governments command powers to which the ordinary citizen is utterly unequal. When an individual tries to defy the authorities—to "fight city hall"—he will be met by resistance. The ordinary citizen invariably pays his speeding fines instead of fighting them in court: the probability of losing is high, and even if he wins he has paid so much in time, trouble, and money that the gain is scarcely worth it to him. Multiply this by virtually the entire population, and the point becomes clear.

It is true that most laws are evaded or ignored much of the time and indeed, in a great many significant cases, most of the time. One may speculate that if the population suddenly were to "work to rule" and obey all the laws, society would come fairly close to grinding to a halt. The cost of this would likewise be terrific. How does all this happen? The secret lies in the Chicken game. When both parties resist, they both come out worse than if one or the other had knuckled under—but the cost to the individual of knuckling under is characteristically lower than the cost to the state. It's an unequal competition, and the individual generally loses.

Only at the polls does the citizen exercise real power—but that power is also minuscule, as we know. Moreover, the differences among candidates are generally trivial, so far as the citizen is concerned. None of the candidates is about to run on a platform of disbanding the government, nor would they get many votes if they did. Citizens are firmly, though not rationally, convinced that their government is a good and necessary thing, however poor its track record in detail. All candidates continue the time-honored tradition of promising what they know perfectly well cannot be delivered, and what they do deliver is at costs the citizen either doesn't understand, or believes will be largely paid by others.

Despite its brilliant track record and the abysmal track record of governments, the market has, therefore, little chance of expanding into domains taken over by the public. Superior force has a way of winning the battles. Government, indeed, depends on the market: if there is no income and wealth to tax, government goes out of business. This imposes a limit on the destructiveness of government activity, indeed, but that limit is very high, and government's capacity to keep us near that limit is immense. Prospects for anarchy, then, are not good. We will not soon see the end of government.

It is, however, unnecessary to talk, globally, of "the end of government." Privatization in this, that, or the other domain is in principle possible and occasionally even happens. Many governments are about at the limit of their capacity to increase borrowing, after years of irresponsibly promising voters what others will pay for. They must, perforce, reduce spending at last. Here and there government programs will be virtually or completely suspended, and the beneficent influence of anarchy will be reinstated. The most that the anarchist can realistically hope for is an occasional small victory of that kind. At the practical level, his best hope is to chip away at small things. For the rest, patient labors expended in demonstrating, to the few who will read, that government provision of services is a bad idea in domain after domain are about the best anarchists can do for the foreseeable future. A certain amount of intellectual satisfaction is the reward for that, no doubt, even if its immediate gain for the typical citizen is small.

But as for a general dismantling of Leviathan—don't hold your breath.

Notes

This essay was included in the collection edited by John T. Sanders and Jan Narveson, *For and Against the State* (Lanham, Md.: Rowman & Littlefield, 1996). It was also presented at the international meeting of the Society for Value Inquiry in Helsinki, Finland, 1994, among others. My thanks to Rowman & Littlefield for permission to reprint it here.

1. See David Friedman, "Anarchy and Efficient Law," *For and Against the State* (Lanham, Md.: Rowman & Littlefield, 1996), 235-54.

2. See A. John Simmons, "Philosophical Anarchism," *For and Against the State*, 19-41, and Leslie Green, "Who Believes in Political Obligation?" *For and Against the State*, 1-18.

3. We cannot here go into the important distinctions between preemption, punishment, and exacted compensation.

4. See Jan Clifford Lester, "Market-Anarchy, Liberty, and Pluralism," *For and Against the State*, 63-80.

5. See Peter Danielson, "The Rights of Chickens," *For and Against the State*, 171-94.

6. It might be wondered why fraud is ruled out. The answer is straightforward. To communicate successfully, parties A and B require a common system of language sufficient to get the message in question across. These messages concern the way things are around them. If A intentionally misleads B, A utilizes this common system effectively to bring about that B believes Q rather than P, where P is, so far as A knows, true. Now, when B acts on Q rather than P, B expects to bring about a result, R, which B supposes will occur if and only if Q. Since P is what is true, however, B's action will not result in the intended R. A has thus effectively brought it about, by action for which A is responsible, that B does not do what B wants. This, by definition, infringes B's freedom.

7. See Green, "Who Believes in Political Obligation?" *For and Against the State*, 1-18.

8. Again, it is too large a subject to go into here how a rule of property flows from the general rule against violating liberty. See *The Libertarian Idea* (Peterborough, Ont: Broadview Press, 2001), chaps. 6–8. An unpublished paper by the author, "The Justification of Private Property by First-Comers," is available on request. See also "Libertarianism vs. Marxism: Reflections on G. A. Cohen's *Self-Ownership, Freedom, and Equality*," *Journal of Ethics* 2, no. 1 (1998), 1-26

9. This thought is developed in chapter 7.

10. I am assuming that the zero-sum claim is a general claim about humans. There perhaps are some few who get their kicks from seeing other people suffer, but to suppose that this is the dominant motive of typical human beings is to suppose what flies in the face of the evidence.

11. Among many valuable books and articles rejecting the current versions, the most amusing is P. J. O'Rourke's light-hearted but incisive *All the Trouble in the World* (New York: Atlantic Monthly Press, 1994). See also chapter 16 of this book.

12. R. E. Ewin, in *Virtues and Rights* (San Francisco: Westview Press, 1991),

argues that the Hobbesian moral rules are, as Hobbes at some places says, virtues and not "laws," despite their title of "Laws of Nature." In one sense, he is certainly right: morality has to be a matter of the internal disposition of the soul. But in another sense, the claim is wrong, or at least very misleading, for these laws may certainly be appealed to as the basis for settling claims and even, if need be, settling them by force.

13. A fascinating study by Jeffrey Olen, *Moral Freedom* (Philadelphia: Temple University Press, 1988), makes this point very effectively.

14. Peter Danielson, "The Rights of Chickens," *For and Against the State*, 171-94.

15. Peter Vallentyne, ed., *Contractarianism and Rational Choice* (New York: Cambridge University Press, 1991), has a number of critical essays on the work of Gauthier and a response by him that readers somewhat versed in game theory will find extremely interesting and helpful.

16. See John T. Sanders, "The State of Statelessness," *For and Against the State*, 255-88.

17. A footnote referring the reader to detailed support would run to several volumes, but a good start is provided by William C. Mitchell and Randy T. Simmons, *Beyond Politics* (Boulder, Colo.: Westview Press, 1994). For another, see Anthony de Jasay, *Before Resorting to Politics* (Cheltenham, U.K.: Edward Elgar, The Shafetesbury Papers 5, 1996).

Chapter 12

Have We a Right to Nondiscrimination?

Prefatory

Discrimination stands very high on the list of what is currently accounted injustice. Indeed, the pages of North American journals, at least, tend to be filled with articles addressing the issue of whether *reverse* discrimination is justified or not; but that discrimination itself is unjust is scarcely ever questioned. The point of the present chapter is to question it anyway. I largely share the tendency to regard much of what is currently regarded as discriminatory as a bad thing, something to condemn and certainly to avoid. I am much less certain, though, that it is in addition something to prohibit by the machinery of the law. At a minimum—and this is the motivation for the chapter–I am puzzled. So the reader may construe the following investigation as an invitation to come forth with a clear account of the matter, at any rate, for I am quite sure that none has as yet been given. And that seems to me to be a very bad thing. When we prohibit the activities of voluntary and rational human beings, we ought, one would think, to have a clear and compelling reason for it. The current tendency seems to be to assume that the wrongness of discrimination is self-evident. That attitude, I am sure we all agree, will not do.

Initial Definitions

Discrimination requires three persons at a minimum: (1) the discriminator, (2) the discriminatee, that is, the person discriminated against, and (3) the parties who have been favored in comparison with the discriminatees; perhaps we can call this class the beneficiaries. Further, there has to be some characteristic possessed by the second class of persons on account of which they are treated less well than the third; being black, or a woman, or a foreigner, or non-Christian, for instance. This property we might call the Discriminandum. Finally, note the expression 'discriminated *against*.' It is essential to the idea of discrimination, I take it, that the discriminatee is treated badly, adversely, or at any rate less well than the beneficiaries.

All these are necessary conditions. I believe we have a sufficient condition if we add that to discriminate against someone is to treat that person in the undesirable way in question *because* the person has the property in question. But we should perhaps make room for a notion, presumably lower on the scale of moral culpability, of inadvertent discrimination. Here, the persons badly treated are not intentionally singled out for their possession of the Discriminandum in question; but it turns out that the class distinguished by possession of it is, nevertheless, coming out on the short end of the stick just as if they were intentionally thus singled out.

As with so many of the expressions we employ in day-to-day moral activity, it would be possible to expend time and energy deliberating about whether the word 'discriminate' is logically condemnatory or not. I don't think this time would be well spent. Smith may be complimented for being a discriminating judge of wine, or of music; Jones may be condemned for his discriminatory practices in business. I believe we can readily enough identify a sense of 'discrimination' which is logically neutral on the moral issue, and indeed, the proposed definition assembled above really is so. Confining ourselves to the more dominant intentional sense of the term, let us begin as follows:

D1: A *discriminates against B* in relation to C by doing x = (def). There is a property, K, such that B has K, C does not have K, A treats B worse than C by doing x, and does so *because* B [has] K.

That A treats B worse than C is not, itself, a morally significant fact—a point I shall expand on below.[1] And—as I shall also be at pains to point out—there are obvious cases of treatment fitting the above which no one would take to be unjust. There are two suggestions to consider for expanding the above in such a way as to bring it more nearly into line with the use of the term in which the current controversies are couched. Each deserves some further treatment of its own. Meanwhile, the partial definition given so far may serve as the basis for raising the important questions. What we want to know is: what values of K and x are such that to do x to a K *rather* than a non-K and *because* the person in question is a K rather than a non-K make the doing of x unjust?

Incidentally, I will tend to favor the term 'unjust' for these purposes because my main interest is in the moral status which would ground restrictive legislation. Whether some lesser charge than injustice might be brought against one who discriminates is not a matter I shall be much concerned to explore.

Nonbasic Discrimination

One way in which D1 can be expanded would be by restricting the value of our act-variable, x, in such a way as to guarantee that discrimination is unjust. There are two ways to do this (at least). One would go like this:

> D2: *A* discriminates against *B* in relation to *C* by doing x = (def). *B* is a K, *C* a non-K, and *A* does x to *B* because *B* is a K *and x is unjust.*

This makes discrimination unjust by definition, but also trivializes the matter. What we want to know is whether there are acts, x, such that x is unjust *because* x is discriminatory. We do not wish to know whether there are acts, x, such that x is unjust because x is unjust.

A more interesting way might go like this:

> D3: *A* discriminates against *B* in relation to *C* by doing x = (def.) *A* does x to *B* and not to *C because B* is a K and *C* isn't a K, and x consists in harming *B*, e.g., by killing, torturing, maiming, or depriving *B* of rightful property, etc.

I leave an 'etc.' in this definition because my intention is to incorporate into the definition of discrimination a restriction on x to certain kinds of acts which are generally recognized to be morally wrong (and, indeed, are morally wrong, in my view). But I don't wish to incorporate a use of the term 'unjust' in the definition. The idea is to identify discrimination with the doing of evil acts, even though the evilness of those acts is not logically part of the description of those acts. (I have failed even so, in view of the reference to "depriving of rightful property"; finding a nontendentious description of violations of property rights is not easy, and I request that this failing be overlooked for present purposes.) D3 makes discrimination wrong, all right, and it is not trivial either. But it has a different and crucial defect. For the restriction on the range of acts to be considered discriminatory acts are wrong, all right, but not wrong *because* they are discriminatory. For they would be wrong even if they *weren't* discriminatory, except in the special case when they were justified punishments of person B. But this special case is special; usually when hiring is done, the applicants are not guilty of any crimes or other wrongful acts.

Let us call those acts, possibly motivated by discrimination but wrong even if they are not, acts of *nonbasic* discrimination. Now, there are plenty of examples of nonbasic discrimination, and indeed, I think that most examples of discrimination which one might be inclined to go to as paradigm cases of it would be nonbasic discriminations. Think of black people being lynched, or Jews sent to the gas chambers at Auschwitz, for instance. It is quite true that the reason why these people were so treated is that they were black or Jews, and quite true that they were discriminatory. But surely what makes it wrong to lynch an innocent person is not that that's no way to treat a *black* person, or a *Jewish* person, but rather that it's no way to treat *any* innocent person. A good deal of the progress which, I think we'd all agree, has been made in the treatment of other races in North America (at least) in the last few decades has taken the form of getting people to appreciate that the basic principles of morality are color-blind. We think there are basic human rights, held by everybody of whatever race, color, etc., and we are at the point where even sheriffs in small towns in Alabama could probably be got to subscribe to that thesis, at least in point of lip service and maybe to some degree in action as well. All this is very real progress, and insofar as the hubbub about discrimination is about this sort of thing, the hubbub is justified. The trouble is, it seems clear that what I have called nonbasic discrimination is not the sort of thing which we can use to show that discrimination *as such* is wrong—that there is anything that is wrong just *because* it is discriminatory. 'Discrimination', given our new definition, D3, has yet to signify a basic wrong, something which we have a right that others not do to us, which we wouldn't have had anyway.

There is, no doubt, an interesting question on the matter of whether nonbasic acts of discrimination are *worse* because they are discriminatory. It has been suggested to me,[2] for instance, that if the Nazis had gassed people at random, or by lot, rather than picking on the Jews in particular, then that would strike us as being hideous and awful, but not *unjust,* or at least not as unjust as what actually happened. It is unclear to me whether this is so or not. Perhaps one reason why one might think so is that we tend to connect injustice with *unfairness,* and it may be agreed that it is unfair to gas people for being Jews, leaving non-Jews intact. And that defect could be rectified by establishing a lottery. But on the other hand, a just community will surely be just as concerned to prevent random gassing of innocent people as it will to prevent selective gassing of them, will it not?

Suppose that instead of gassing you because you are a Jew, I gas you because I dislike your taste in ties. Is this in the same boat, or not? Or suppose I gas you because I have embezzled your money and don't want you to tell the authorities I have done so. Gassing people at random is in one sense more terrible than any of these, in the same way that terrorism in general is terrible: it might befall anyone at any time. But all of these things are terrible, and I doubt that there's any point in trying to say in the abstract which is worse. In general, I suspect that the reason we are so impressed with the case of the Jews is twofold. First, anti-Semitism is popular, for some reason, whereas anti-tie-wearing (to the point of gassing) is virtually unheard of, and random gassing is exceedingly rare, though random violence is not. And second, anti-Semitism is *divisive.* It sets people against each other. Policies of anti-Semitism will tend to produce in many people the attitude that there is actually something wrong with being Jewish, that Jewishness is a property which literally deserves extermination, or whatever. There is therefore a public interest reason for worrying about anti-Semitism that isn't there in regard to the other two practices.

Moral Irrelevance

The most popular candidate for a principle of nondiscrimination, no doubt, would be one which makes use of the notion of "moral irrelevance." On this view, discrimination would be defined in some such way as the following:

D4: *A* discriminates against *B* in relation to *C* by doing x = (def.) *A* does X to *B* and not to *C* because *B* is a K and *C* is not, and K-ness is *morally irrelevant* to treating people in the way that x treats them.

What is meant by 'moral irrelevance' here? I suppose that a property of a person is morally relevant to a manner of treatment if it is the case that by virtue of having that property, one is morally entitled to a certain sort of treatment. And indeed, we do frame some exceedingly high-level, abstract-sounding moral principles in some such manner as that. To use the words of Sidgwick, for instance: "If a kind of conduct that is right (or wrong) for me is not right (or wrong) for *someone else,* it must be on the ground of some difference between the two cases, other than the fact that I and he are different persons."[3] This suitably self-evident-seeming idea readily lends itself to evolution into a principle about the treatment of others: if I am to treat *B* differently from *C*, then there has to be some difference, other than the fact that *B* is *B* and *C* is *C*, which justified this difference of treatment.

Principles as abstract as this have some well-known problems. Those, for instance, who practice racial discrimination are certainly not treating *B* differently from *C* just because *C* is a different person from *B*. They are treating *B* differently from *C* because (for instance) *B* is black and *C* isn't. Obviously a thicker theory about which properties are relevant to which sorts of treatment is required. But I think the plot can be thickened before we get into detail on that matter. We need at a minimum to distinguish two different levels of moral relevance.

(1) A property might be morally relevant in the sense that we are morally required to treat people who have it differently from people who don't.
(2) A property might be morally relevant only in the sense that it is morally permissible to treat *people* who have it differently from people who don't.

Now, we may agree straight off that there must be morally relevant proper*ties* grounding any differences of treatment in the second sense. For after all, if it is not morally permissible to treat *B* differently from *C*, then no doubt it is wrong to treat them differently; and if we confine ourselves to the sorts of wrongnesses which ground restrictive laws, unjust-making wrongnesses, then it is obvious that moral relevance in sense (2) is a necessary condition for treating people justly. But it is also trivial to say that. What, however, about sense (1)?

Discrimination and Employee Equity

It does, I must say, seem perfectly obvious that in order to justify difference of treatment of two persons, *B* and *C*, there does not need to be a morally relevant difference between them in sense (1). I do not mean merely that we might find different ways of treating *B* and *C* which treat them equally well, so that neither has any complaint coming on the score of having been less well treated. I mean, more interestingly, that we may very well treat one person less well than another without a hint of injustice, and without appealing to any differences between them which are morally relevant in the stronger sense. Moreover, I think we can find examples of this type which are also frankly discriminatory in the sense not only of D4, but also relative to current thinking, in that they discriminate along the very lines which figure in many of our laws as well as private judgments.

Such, for instance, seems to me to be the case with marrying and offering to marry. It seems that there are virtually no morally relevant characteristics in this whole area. Suppose I decide to marry Jane on the ground that she has lovely blue eyes, whereas Nell has to make do with plain old brown ones. Well, where is the duty to marry blue-eyeds rather than brown-eyeds? Obviously nowhere: so do I perform an injustice to Nell in thus behaving? I think not. Nor is the situation any different if we think of the standard discriminanda currently in the public eye. If I marry Amanda because she is black, I do not behave unjustly to Sue who is white; or if I marry Cathy because she is of the same religious persuasion as I—or because she is of a different persuasion, for that matter—I do not thereby wrong the unfortunate (or fortunate?) candidates who are thus rejected.

Similarly with friendship. If I like *A* because he is intelligent and charming, while refraining from befriending *B* because he is uninteresting, I do not thereby wrong *B*, despite the total lack of any moral duty to befriend all and sundry, or to befriend the intelligent, or the charming. In short, I think it clear that the general claim that we can justify treating one person less well than another only by invoking "morally relevant" characteristics in the interesting sense distinguished above simply will not wash.

It is manifestly clear that we can act well or badly, and in particular, intelligently or unintelligently, in these contexts. You may certainly criticize my taste if I marry someone because of the color of her eyes, or her skin, or even her choice of religion, perhaps. These decisions may be personally justified or not. But morally? It would take a special background to bring morality into it. Perhaps you have been dating Jane all this time, leading her to expect that you like people such as she, indeed leading her to expect a proposal from you; and instead, you turn around and propose to some total stranger. You may owe her an explanation. Or perhaps you promised your dear old Mum that you'd marry a fellow Seventh Day Adventist and now you've gone and proposed to a Buddhist, yet! There's no end of what might bring moral considerations into these matters. But my point is that *so far as it goes*, morality has no bearing on it: marry whom you like, and Justice will not blink an eye, though Prudence might turn around and quietly retch.

Is There Basic Discrimination?

Further reflection on the foregoing discussion of moral relevance raises the interesting question whether there really is any such thing as what I have implicitly identified as Basic discrimination. Nonbasic discrimination, we recall, is where there is something wrong with what you are doing to B *anyway;*

the fact that you do it to him because he is the possessor of some property (not common to all moral persons) which does not qualify him for that treatment is not needed in order to condemn the action in question. Basic discrimination, then, would be where your act of treating *B* worse than *C* is wrong, not because it is to do something to *B* which you have no right to do anyway, but because it unjustly discriminates between *B* and C. What we need here, evidently, is a principle calling upon us to do certain things to certain people if we also do them to certain others, but where there is in itself nothing wrong with doing it to anyone or no one.

Yet there seems something odd about this. Here is something I can do to someone, something which there is no inherent moral objection to doing. Call this act x. Often x will be some negative action, a *non*action such as not offering the person in question a job. There is also, we are assuming, *no* moral duty to do not-x, to refrain from x, to *anyone*. How, then, can it suddenly be unjust if I choose to do x to B, and not-x to C? Doing it, to anyone, is not wrong; nor is doing it, to anyone, a moral duty, required. Nobody has the right that I do it to him or refrain from doing it to him. How can it be that it is, under the circumstances, wrong to do it to *B* rather than C?

The most interesting current context, I take it, is employment. We have in general no obligation to hire anybody for anything; nor have we in general any obligation to refrain from hiring anybody for anything. We have, indeed, no duty to go into business in the first place. Yet it is widely supposed that if *A* hires *C* rather than *B* because *C* is, say, a male, or white, despite B's equal competence, then *A* has done *B* an injustice, and the law may properly descend upon *A* and make him toe the line of equality. Why? So interesting are these contexts that I propose to discuss them on their own for a few pages.

Public/Private

To begin with, we had better immediately take account of a distinction plainly relevant in this connection, namely the distinction between hiring in the public sector and private hiring. I mean this to be a conceptual distinction. Some might argue that the public sector is a fraud, or at any rate, that there ought to be no such thing: you name it and "the public" has no business doing it. Others might say the same thing about the private sector. I do not intend either to affirm or deny either view here. I only wish to point out that if we acknowledge a public sector, it is easy enough to see why discrimination there would be something to make a fuss about.

The reason is simple enough. Suppose there are services which any member of the public has a right to, vis-à-vis the public generally. He has that right, then, qua member of the public. Moreover, those offering it to him are also acting as agents of the public. Now, the public consists of *everybody. If,* then, there is some service to which one is entitled qua member of the public, clearly it will be wrong for any agent of the public to give it to *C* but withhold it from *B,* so long as both are members of the relevant public. If there is a limited resource which the public is to expend—medical services, say—it is held that this is a public matter, so that all and only the medically needy have a claim on it, and demand exceeds supply, then it is also plausible to hold that the resources ought to be proportioned equally to the need, or perhaps that we ought to maximize the public health, but in any case not on a basis which favors some irrelevantly distinguished group in society. In fact, the criteria of relevance will be quite clear: if there is some need N to which some service S of the public is to cater, then factors other than N are irrelevant when it comes to administering service S.

Prima facie, we also have a case for insisting that the agents administering S hire only on the basis of competence. If the idea is to maximize the satisfaction of N, then if applicant B promises to promote that goal better than C at the same cost, then the public would seem to have a right that B be hired rather than C. (The situation gets messy when we ask whether the public has the right that its servants reflect, say, the racial composition of the public they are to serve, particularly when perhaps the typical applicants from one readily distinguished group are less competent than those of some other, since now there will be a clash between considerations of efficiency, which the public has a right to, and the interest in an equal share of the action, which it may also have a right to. But we will not press these issues further here.)

What is important about the invocation of the public here is that it gives us a basis for nondiscrimination which again does not clearly show discrimination to be a *basic* injustice. For it seems, again, that if B can successfully claim to have been discriminated against in the public sector, there is also a claim on B's part to that which he was denied by virtue of the discriminatory act in question: in other words, it is *not* the case—contrary to hypothesis—that there is no obligation to hire at all, nor that there is no obligation to provide the service for which hiring is being done. On the contrary, the thesis is that the public has the duty to provide the service, and is also entitled to it, on a basis that is equal as between persons of one color and another, one sex and another, etc.

But this is not true of the private sector in general. In that sector, the assumption is that those who hire do so in pursuit of private gain, or perhaps some other sort of private satisfaction. There is no obligation to set up any business whatever, no obligation to offer any particular service, or any service at all. That somebody didn't get hired by you, a private employer, is prima facie not something he can complain about, since you have no obligation to hire anybody at all—neither that person nor any other. More interestingly, it is by no means clear that he can complain even if he was of superior competence as compared with his competitors. Since you have no obligation to hire at all, it is hard to see why you should have an obligation to hire the most competent. What if you don't care about competence? Perhaps you'd rather that your employees were attractive, or devout Catholics, or teetotalers, or males. So what? Again, it seems to me: if there is no right to a job at all, how can there be a right that people like you be hired rather than people like anybody else, if anyone is hired at all?

Again, there are certainly considerations of prudence; and no doubt some will see considerations of morality entering here too. Let us see, beginning in particular with prudence. We turn, briefly, to the question of the economics of discrimination. Too briefly, no doubt, but the matter can afford some instruction anyway.

Dollars and Discrimination

Let us first consider the matter on what are usually thought of as classical assumptions, viz., that everyone in the market is an economically rational agent interested in maximizing his dollar returns. (This assumption, as will be noted below, is unclear even if true; but one thing at a time. One good reason for starting with this assumption is that some people seem to think that discrimination is actually *caused* by the motive of gain.) Such agents will buy at the lowest price available for a given level of quality in the product, and will sell whatever they have to sell, e.g., their labor power, at the highest available price. If *A* wants an x and *B*, a black person, offers it to him at a lower price than *C*, who is white, then *A* will buy from the black person. (It should be noted that although, as I say, I will be questioning the above assumptions in some respects, there is plenty of empirical evidence that consumers, whether of labor or other things, will indeed buy from people they ostensibly despise if the price is right.)

Consider, then, the case of the Little Goliath Motor Company, a firm which makes no bones about its basic purpose: profit. And consider any position in this firm, call it P, forwarding some function, F, within this noble enterprise. The primary purpose of making money will determine both which subordinate functions will be values of F and, together with an understanding of how F fits in with the rest of the operation, the criteria of better and worse performance at P. The more efficiently per unit of pay F is fulfilled, the lower will be the firm's cost per unit, or the higher the quality, or some mix of the two; in either case it will do better on the market, being able to sell cheaper or higher quality goods than the competition, if the latter don't do as well on these scores. Applicants for P, therefore, will rationally be judged by those criteria.

Enter another classical assumption, viz., that such factors as race and sex make no difference to efficiency on the part of employees. (Again, it is an assumption which is often certainly false to fact, but, again, one thing at a time.) On this assumption, the people down at Little Goliath will not do well to have any interest in the race or sex of their applicants. For imagine what happens if they do. They begin, let us suppose, preferring males or whites. Preferring here means that they will hire them instead of females or blacks (or whatever). Now this presumably means that they will hire a less efficient white male at the same wage as they could get a more efficient black or female for the job at hand; which is equivalent, economically speaking, to paying more for an equally efficient one. On classical assumptions, what happens next? Well, the more persistently enterprising Universal Motor Co. up the road will begin to hire females and blacks, doing equally good work, for lower wages; it is in a position to do this, since the Goliath people insist on turning away perfectly good females with an interest in taking the best-paying job they can get. If this keeps up, and if, as our assumptions dictate, motor car purchasers are interested in quality for price rather than the color or sex of those who put the product together, then we shall expect the Universal people to do well, and the Goliath people to do badly.

Perhaps a case at a somewhat classier level will be still more perspicuous. Most firms, we are told, much prefer males to females for executive positions; and we are also told that this is in fact sheer prejudice, females being equally capable. Under the circumstances, we should expect cagey firms to be soon staffed, in their higher reaches, with high-powered women at half the pay which their competitors have to offer to their all-male staffs. If all firms were rational and our assumption about the relative abilities of the sexes correct, we should eventually see executives of both sexes at the same salaries more or less everywhere.[4]

The moral is generalizable: if the criterion of discrimination in hiring is that criteria other than those relevant to job performance are used for the sorting of candidates, then in free-market conditions, with economically rational consumers, the nondiscriminating firm will be better. Discrimination does not pay. It is, indeed, economically irrational.

Might things go severely otherwise? Might the assumptions be badly wrong? The situation is unclear. We can certainly imagine cases in which consumers are not out to maximize their returns. If consumers insist on buying grapes picked by unionized labor, we are into another ball game: not that store owners really *mind* customers who prefer paying more to paying less for the same goods, but it is all slightly puzzling. Likewise, it is possible that people would want to know whether the soap they buy was wrapped by lily-white rather than ebony hands—possible, but unlikely. More likely, of course, is discrimination in service industries where the customer comes into direct contact with the supplier. People might like black waiters and butlers better than white ones, or pretty stewardesses better than plain though efficient ones, or whatever. In all such cases, economies will not erode what might strike many people as discrimination. It will instead lead to the members of favored classes being better off than members of unfavored ones; and whether, for instance, wages in given industries will tend to equalize in a longish run is imponderable. But it should certainly be noted that there is no clear tendency toward *reinforcing* preexisting patterns of social discrimination, as such, as anyone who has recently attempted to procure the services of Bill Cosby or Leontyne Price will be acutely aware.

It is also essential to point out that the most scandalous cases in the past have been anything but cases of free market operation. Black slavery in the American South was not, in the usual sense of the term, a free market institution. Slave traders may have competed against each other, but the slaves themselves, obviously, did not own their own labor, and were not free to haggle about wages. Neither was the situation in South Africa, where wage differentials between black and white workers were reinforced not only by law, but by unions.[5]

I should like to explore this aspect of the matter much further, but space does not permit. Instead, I wish to turn to another crucial matter, closely related to that just discussed and, I think, offering perhaps the most puzzling challenge of all to those who think that there is a clear and straightforward underlying principle behind current attitudes about discrimination.

The Purposes of Firms

Competence is assessed by the criteria relevant to performance of the function which the position in question is to serve. Which functions are to be served depends in turn on the ultimate purpose of the firm in which the position is situated. Some firms are out to make money, but not all. Let us address ourselves to a couple of relevant cases. One of my favorites, for starters, is a small nonprofit organization known as the Ecuadorian Friendship Society. The E.F.S. has as its purpose the forwarding of friendship among Ecuadorians, and this purpose is not notably served by hiring, say, Bolivian janitors and secretaries, or even French chefs. We may well imagine that the management down at the E.F.S. will substantially prefer less competent Ecuadorians to more competent Bolivians when screening applications for those and other positions, right up to vice president depending, no doubt, on the condition of its finances. But who is to say that the firm is acting irrationally in such practices? After all, it might be argued, given the purpose of this particular firm, that it is *not* efficient, looked at from the higher point of view, to hire Bolivian secretaries, however efficient they may be qua secretary. Under the circumstances, the hiring of Bolivians, however competent, is less than utterly friendly.

Another of my favorites among these specialized nonprofit establishments is the Black Muslim Church of America, which may be presumed to look considerably askance at applicants of the Occidental persuasion for positions in their clergy, however eloquent and dedicated. The point, again, may be made that given the purposes of the firm, what would otherwise be discriminatory is legitimate, indeed efficient and thus mandatory. Thus it may be argued that these firms do not really violate the canon of hiring only on the basis of relevant competence: competence, as I say, is dictated by the purposes of the organization.

At this point, two questions loom before us. Both should tax us mightily, I think. The first point may be furthered by bringing up another example dear to my heart: the Irish-Canadian Distilleries Corporation. This amiable organization lets it be known to all and sundry that although it is happy to turn an honest dollar, it also has a pronounced interest in maximizing the percentage of persons of Irish descent amongst its employees, even if this should cut into profits a bit. For its purpose is not simply to make money—this, they imply, is a motive reserved for the low of mind, such as the denizens of the Highlands. It is, rather, to be a sort of marginally profitable Irish-Canadian Friendly Society, a high purpose for which, indeed, its commercial product is peculiarly suitable. Its otherwise inefficient hiring practices, when viewed from this higher perspective, turn out to be perfectly efficient after all, and therefore, on the standard view which seems to prevail about what is "morally relevant," quite free of any taint of discrimination.

The second question follows naturally enough, viz.: what's so great about efficiency, anyway? Why not accuse those firms which hire exclusively on the basis of competence of discriminating unjustly against the incompetent? Why should competence be thought a "morally relevant characteristic"? It is not, incidentally, thought to be so when it comes to such elementary matters as the right to vote, or indeed, to stand for Parliament. From the point of view of the employer, of course, competence is highly desirable. So indeed is it from the point of view of the consumer. But why should only that point of view count? Aren't we supposed to be adumbrating an impartial standard of justice?

Advertising of Positions

One possible account of the injustice thought to be inherent in discriminatory hiring, and to some extent applicable in other contexts as well, is that those who are excluded for apparently irrelevant reasons have been dealt badly with because their expectations, engendered by the advertisement for the position or other description of the opportunity regarding which the discrimination has taken place, have been disappointed. An applicant may well say, "Look, I've come all this way, taken all this time and trouble to get this job interview, and now you tell me that no X-ians will be considered. Why didn't you say so in the first place?"

Complaints of this kind, where applicable, may certainly be well-taken, and sometimes could be a basis for a claim of compensation. If you have flown from Los Angeles to New York for the job interview, only to find that you were never even considered for the position, the firm certainly owes you your considerable expenses for the trip. But so far as the general issue of a basic right to nondiscrimination is concerned, it is surely too weak to do the job many people feel there is to be done. For one thing, it would be hard to specify the number of factors on the basis of which a candidate might be rejected in any satisfactorily general way. After all, if there is just one job and many candidates, several are going to be disappointed, however excellent the reasons for their rejection. And more generally, it is surely not true that the case against discrimination, in the minds of the many who think it a major context for social concern, would always be settled just by wording advertisements appropriately. The claim is that it's wrong to impose the condition that No Irish Need Apply, however well advertised that condition may be. We shall have to look elsewhere to find any deep principles against discrimination. (Nor should it be assumed a priori that we will succeed.)

Current Practice

It is perhaps not entirely out of order to ask whether our current practices in this area make all that much sense, taken in large. For one thing, it does seem as though discrimination is in fact quite all right when practiced by the allegedly downtrodden against the allegedly mighty majority (though the term 'majority' has come to have a somewhat nonliteral usage, in view of the fact that, e.g., white Anglo-Saxon males must by now make up rather a small percentage of the Canadian or American populace, and women an appreciable majority). And do we not tolerate, indeed expect and encourage, discrimination as between members of our own family and others when it comes to the distribution of various economic and social benefits, including jobs, education beyond what is provided by the public, and many other benefits?

Another area in a more public quarter has to do with the matter of nationalism. At one time, discrimination on grounds of nationality was one of the standard bad examples, along with discrimination on grounds of sex, race, and religion. But recently, one hears less about nationality, perhaps for the reason that every government so flagrantly violates any principle along this line. Not only public employers, but also employers in the private sector, are routinely required to discriminate very strongly against citizens of other countries (in Canada, this is true even of immigrants, whom employers are often required to rank second to citizens for employment). Goods made by foreign firms are, of course, routinely discriminated against by means of tariffs and other restrictions. Even the freedom to marry foreigners has been abridged by some nations, and immigration restrictions having this effect are not uncommon.

I have already mentioned churches in connection with employment. But the existence of organizations with special purposes seem quite generally to raise a question about the intent of nondiscrimination principles; for do not organizations routinely distinguish between members and nonmembers, persons who share their goals and persons who do not? And why on earth shouldn't they—indeed, how could they not do so? But that is just the point. A clear principle distinguishing between all these myriad cases of intentionally prejudicial bestowing of important benefits and the ones popularly frowned upon as discriminatory is what we need and, it seems to me, do not have.

A Note on Utilitarianism

Those who have felt that nondiscrimination is a basic right have often, I think, supposed that it is a right which exceeds the reach of utilitarianism. Partly for this reason, it is of some interest to observe that, while it is, if the foregoing arguments are as strong as I am so far persuaded they are, extremely difficult to find a plausible deep principle going beneath the level of utilitarian considerations, it is not difficult to give a pretty plausible account of our practices and currently professed principles in utilitarian terms. For one thing, the distinction between private and public in the hiring arena, which figures strongly in the foregoing, does not have all that much status for the utilitarian. From his point of view, one might say all activities are "public" in the sense that the public has a legitimate interest in how they are carried on. If there is to be a private sector at all, from that point of view, it is because the public interest is served better by making some things private. That the wealth of society is promoted by private enterprise, if true, is certainly important and creates a presumption in favor of private enterprise; but then, in cases where it is not so promoted, the utilitarian has no scruples about putting it back in the hands of the public. And if some other important public interest besides wealth comes into the picture, then the utilitarian will simply consider whether this other interest is sufficient to outweigh the lost prosperity resulting from catering to it, if indeed that is what would happen.

What other utilities might be at stake? Prominent among them, surely, are two, or perhaps two sides of a single one. First, there is the sheer fact that those discriminated against feel badly done by. If the public is upset by a certain practice—or indeed, if a smallish minority is upset by it, given that it is upset enough—then that creates at least some presumption in favor of altering the practice. And secondly, it is fair to argue that discriminatory practices, particularly in areas of such substantial concern to people as hiring, are socially divisive, as was noted above. If sizable groups of people are clamoring for advancement, while others characteristically are preferred in those respects, even at some cost in efficiency, then the tendency will be for bad feeling to exist between the groups in question, and we may expect trouble. The fact that we can't identify, in principle and in general, any characteristics and range of practices such that the doing of those things to people with those characteristics and the nondoing of them to people without them is fundamentally wrong doesn't matter all that much; if we can deal with the situation pretty effectively with rather vague and unsatisfactorily messy principles, that is better than ignoring the problem.

It is to be expected, if utilitarianism is our guide, that there will be no stable list of discriminanda such that nondiscrimination principles would always be stated in terms of them, nor any particular social context, such as hiring, where the wrongness of discrimination is permanently to be abhorred. It will depend on social conditions. Fifty years from now, perhaps some quite new contexts, new discriminanda, will be where the focus of concern falls. And if we are interested in capturing current "intuitions" and predicting the way things will go, this aspect of utilitarianism seems likely to stand us in pretty good stead.

But there are some shortcomings. Naturally, the basic status of utilitarianism itself is one of them. Nor is it evident that the whole job to be done is to account for current practices; and if currently held beliefs are what are to be accounted for, then there is the widespread feeling that the right to nondiscrimination does not wait upon social interest for its confirmation to consider: is that part of what is to be accounted for, or isn't it? More importantly, however, is that it seems to me questionable what the real outcome of utilitarianism is on such issues. To see this, we need to distinguish between two views about the operation of utilitarianism, or perhaps about its application. We might call these the "crude" versus the "sophisticated" form. The crude variety, which I have tacitly appealed to above, has it that we weigh any old interest, however derived. If interests in strawberry jam count, and interests in Mahler symphonies, so do interests in wife beating, in keeping up with the

Joneses, and in one's neighbors all being attired in identical seersucker suits. The sophisticated type, however, does not easily allow such interests to count, or discounts them as compared with others. If interests in others' having such-and-such interests count, and if interests in others having such-and-such relations to oneself count equally, that seems to make way for the kind of objections to utilitarianism trotted out in the standard textbooks and introductions to philosophy. And the difficulty is that it seems that the kind of interests catered to in nondiscrimination principles are of that kind. In order to get very much weight behind the thesis that social utility will be further enhanced by A's electing to have B work for him rather than C, despite the fact that he'd prefer to have C, we have to attach a good deal of weight to the intensity of B's feelings of indignation at not being equally considered by A, and more weight to the fuss which will be caused by the objections of B's cohorts, etc. If, on the other hand, we simply attend to what appears to be the fact, that whichever A hires, A will be doing that person a favor, but if he hires the one he likes he will in addition create more utility for himself, then it is unclear that we should allow the further fact that B doesn't like the situation to count.

It is characteristic of utilitarianism that once one sees that there are competing sources of utility to take into account, and these are not easily estimated, the argument could be taken either way. And often, the very utility being counted is due to the preexisting moral beliefs of the persons involved. If B had the attitude that A has a perfect right to hire whomever he pleases, there wouldn't be the various political utilities to which the argument of crude utilitarianism appeals. And this means that utilitarianism may not be of much use in this matter after all.

And a Note on Contractarianism

One of the most important theoretical bases for social philosophy to have been taken seriously in recent times, as well as times past, is the suggestion that the principles of justice are the principles for the structuring of society which would be accepted by rational individuals on a long-term basis, or perhaps an impartial one. Indeed, I would be inclined to argue this way myself. But some who have been of this persuasion have evidently supposed that principles of nondiscrimination are among those which would most fundamentally be opted for in this way; and unfortunately, I fail to see that this is obvious.

Presumably a main source of the view that nondiscrimination would have such a status is the fact, which is not in dispute here, that the fundamental principles chosen would be, so to speak, color-blind (and sex-blind, etc.). Unfortunately, as has been in effect argued above, this is very far from supporting the very strong principles which are here being questioned. For it is one thing to say that the fundamental principles of morality will not favor any groups as compared with any other (except, of course, that it will disfavor those who don't comply with them), and quite another to say that those principles will require individuals not to favor other individuals on the basis of sex, color, race, religion, taste in wines, or whatever, when it comes to doing good things for them. When we are contracting for general rights, after all, we are contracting to give up certain liberties. The strategy of contractarianism is to pick out those liberties which we are better off giving up, and thus to argue that the rational person will be prepared to do so, in exchange for certain benefits which cannot be had without giving up those liberties. In the case of the liberty to kill, or in general to inflict harms on people, it is plausible to argue that the advantage of being free from such depredations at the hands of others will outweigh, in any even modestly longish run, the disadvantage of giving up the liberty to commit them oneself. But it is a different story when what is at issue is how one is to dispose of one's various positive assets, one's capacity to benefit others. Here it is *not* plausible to argue that every rational person *must* find it to his or her advantage to forgo the liberty to decide who will be the beneficiary of such activities, in return for the benefit of being assured of having an equal chance, along with others who differ in various respects, of winding up as the beneficiary of some other people's similar activities.

It has been the habit of Rawls and of theorists persuaded by his general views to speak rather vaguely about opportunities for realizing the benefits which one's 'society' has to offer. The trouble with this, as Nozick was at pains to argue, is that it seems to assume that society is a kind of organized club with certain rather specific purposes which all members in good standing must be interested in promoting, and having a variety of assets at its disposal for the promotion of these purposes. But since this is fairly obviously not so, and fairly obviously therefore not something which we can simply assume, it is clear that one would have to argue for the claim that everyone ought to look at it that way. And I don't see how such an argument is to go through in general. But in 'general' is what we are talking about here. It is not to the point to observe that many people would see advantage in so viewing the matter; for manifestly some would not, and given that that is so, there is surely no prospect of a general agreement, reaching to all rational persons, on the point.

Even if we suppose that some progress along that line is possible, there is a further problem about the relevance of our results to the present issue. Suppose, for instance, that we can make some kind of case for, say, an assured minimal income for all—already an extremely implausible assumption. But still, although that would, by the reasoning in the foregoing, provide the basis for nondiscrimination in the administration of the program for securing that minimum to all, it does not seem possible that it would provide a basis for nondiscrimination as between candidates for very high-paying positions, or even most positions. Presumably the minimum must be set somewhere below the average income from employment, and then we have the question of why everyone's entitlement to this minimum should carry with it an entitlement to nondiscrimination at any of the levels above it.

Most contractarian arguments about social minima and the like in any case run up against another problem. If people were so interested in security, including the particular kinds of security which nondiscrimination laws provide, why wouldn't they buy into insurance which provided that kind of security? Or form clubs whose members would agree to boycott those who practiced the types of discrimination they wished to avoid? Why, in short, are the kinds of benefits which nondiscrimination presumably provides of a type which justifies coercive methods for seeing to it that all persons avoid practicing the types of discrimination in question—not only those who do see it as a benefit, but also those who see it as just the reverse? Given contractarian premises, one would have thought that if one has one's choice between enabling some good to be brought about by voluntary efforts among those who want it and a system of imposing it by force, if need be, on all alike, the former would be preferable. When we disagree, the rational thing for us both to do is agree to disagree—not agree that something called 'society' will declare one of us out of bounds and impose the other's view on him willy-nilly.

A Note on Logic

The principal argument in the foregoing effort to establish that the foundations of our attitudes toward discrimination are insecure and obscure has been of the following general form: we do not (it is admitted) have any obligation to do anything of the kind in question—appointing to a position, say—to anybody at all; so why do we have an obligation not to do it to one person rather than another? If I don't owe *anybody* a certain benefit, x, how is it that I can owe it to everyone that if I do give it to some person other than he, it will not be because he has certain properties but rather because he has certain others? If I owe it to no one at all, then why can't I give it to whomever I please, since the option is to give it to nobody whatever?

The question arises how we are to formulate the principle thus implicitly appealed to. Very generally, no doubt, the idea is that found in Hobbes, to the effect that "Obligation and Liberty . . . in one and the same matter are inconsistent."[6] However, there is the question of specifying the "matter" in question. Perhaps it is the case that even though I have no obligation to do x to A or to B, I have an obligation to do it to A in preference to B if at all, because in doing x to B I would not simply be doing x, but also something else, y, which is forbidden. The trouble is, though, that in the foregoing I have argued that the cases in which there clearly is this other description of my act, this other fact about it, in virtue of which it is obligatory on me not to do it, we have what I called "nonbasic" discrimination, and this, I observed, doesn't seem to be sufficient to account for standard attitudes and practices on this subject. Were it the case that, in declining to give the job to A, one also hit him over the head or heaped insults upon him, that would be wrong; but that is not the behavior at issue. It is felt that it is wrong to decline to give it to A at all, if A is in fact "better qualified" than B and one simply prefers to have B for extraneous reasons such as that one simply likes B, or people like B in certain respects, better than A or people like A in certain respects.

A slightly formalized representation of the principle behind the argument would go, perhaps, something like this:

(1) A's preferring B to C in context H consists in A's doing x to B rather than to C, if at all.

(2) A's being obliged to prefer B to C in context H = A's being obliged to do x to B rather than C, if at all.

(3) A's not being obliged to do x at all = A's not being obliged to do x to any person whatever, for any reason; i.e., there is no class of persons such that A is obliged to do x to any member of that class.

(4) Context H involves some purpose, P, such that pursuit of P would give a reason to prefer B to C.

(5) But A has no obligation to pursue P at all. (If P were obligatory, then A would have some obligation to do x to someone, if available. But by hypothesis, A has no such obligation.)

(6) Therefore (by 5), A has no obligation to prefer anyone to anyone with respect to x; and hence not to prefer B to C.

If this is right, then it also appears that there is no such thing as obligatory basic nondiscrimination. If we were obliged to prefer one person to another vis-à-vis doing of some act x, that would imply that we had some obligation to do x, or pursue some purpose such that x promoted it, though other acts y could be done instead, or in general to perform kinds of acts of which x was an example.

Do we think this to be so? I am hard put to decide, but let us consider a few examples. Many of us would accept a general obligation to treat our children equally, for instance: if we have some limited resource money, for instance, which we can devote to promoting their welfare, we feel some obligation to divide that resource equally, or in such a way as to promote their respective welfares equally. True: but it is also true that we have an obligation to promote their welfare at all. How much is, of course, not entirely easy to say, but suppose that we say we are to promote each child's welfare maximally within some limit. If we have this for each of them, and the resources are only sufficient for some level short of what we would ideally like, then it is readily concluded that we should split the resource more or less equally, or aim at equal welfares. But if we had no such obligation at all, it is hard to see how any of them could reasonably complain if he or she were always passed over in favor of others.

In general, it seems to me that the claim to equal treatment rests on an assumption that there are equal claims to that kind of treatment; and hence, that there are claims to that kind of treatment. The right to equal opportunity, in particular, rests on an assumed right to opportunity. In the absence of the latter, it is hard to see how we can make much sense of the former.

A Note on Prejudice

One final matter should be mentioned. Very often, certainly, treatment of different large groups that is markedly unequal in the various respects we have in mind when we talk of 'discrimination' is based on beliefs about the relative merits of those different groups. When those beliefs are without foundation, we bring in the notion of 'prejudice', of judging people's merits before we actually know the relevant facts—if any. The subject of prejudice invites special comment; and doubtless some, though I think not all, of the prevailing beliefs about discrimination are accounted for on the basis of their relation to it. The following observations seem especially pertinent here.

First: we must bear in mind that not all discrimination will be due to prejudice. Perhaps Brown doesn't believe that all X-ians are shiftless, immoral, or whatever: he may simply not much care for X-ians, or he may care for members of his own race (etc.) more. There is a difference between an attitude based on an unreasoned or baseless belief, on the one hand, and on no belief at all, on the other.

Second: when the attitudes in question are based on beliefs, those beliefs are, of course, capable of being rationally appraised. Now sometimes, as we ought to recognize, they might be based on pretty decent evidence. It may not be obvious that the different races, sexes, etc., do have the same degree of allegedly relevant properties. Possibly it is a matter on which reasonable people may differ. Where this is so, it is at least clear that one cannot convict, say, an employer who turns out to employ a quite different percentage of X-ians from that which X-ians bear to the whole population, of discrimination straight off. Perhaps the X-ians are a lot better, or a lot worse, at that sort of job than the average other person. (Obviously there might still be discrimination, for perhaps the employer follows a policy of not even considering non-Xians, when in fact a modest percentage of them are better at the job than a lot of X-ians. This raises further questions, prominent among them being how much trouble an employer could reasonably be required to go to to test persons directly rather than going by obvious qualities, such as sex, which are quite well correlated with them.) At any rate, the point is that we cannot assume a priori that various abilities and whatnot are distributed in a population independently of the popular discriminanda; it simply isn't an a priori matter.

And finally: even where it is quite clear that prejudice is at work, there are two questions to raise about it. In the first place, there is the question whether it is right to persecute people for their beliefs. We do not do so, or at least we profess to believe that we have no right to do so, in the case of religious beliefs, even though those beliefs are always, strictly speaking, baseless, and even though they often lead to very substantial kinds of discriminatory treatment. In the second place, and more important at least in practice, there is the fact that once the foundations, or lack of them, of a belief are out in the open where critics can assail them, it is not easy to maintain that belief with a perfectly straight face for very long. Why should we assume so readily that the proper way to deal with actions based on beliefs we think are baseless, illogical, or confused is by making laws against those actions? We can hardly think that generally appropriate. Do we not, after all, have a pretty well-grounded suspicion that most people's practical beliefs are baseless, illogical, and/or confused? (Including, it will doubtless turn out, most of our own?) And are we not agreed that one does not properly outlaw the entertaining of that belief—that in fact the proper way to deal with it is to *refute* it, much to the psychic stress of the person who holds it?

At the risk of being embarrassingly obvious, I would just note that if we were to take seriously the suggestion that it is unjust to hold baseless beliefs, then any principle of freedom of religion would evidently have to go by the boards. Most religions, after all, are almost self-consciously mysterious, and do not even pretend to offer sound reasons, persuasive to any rational being, for holding their main tenets. For all that, these beliefs are obviously dangerous. It takes little investigation of history to see that any number of wars, including perhaps most of the messier ones, have been fought partly or wholly on religious grounds. If the sort of prejudices often leading to discrimination are a public menace, surely religion is even more so. Yet which tenets of liberalism have pride of place over religious freedom?

It may be urged that there is a difference between allowing someone to hold a belief and allowing him to act on it. Anyone seriously urging a strong principle of freedom of thought or of speech needs to make such a distinction, since otherwise he will find himself in the embarrassing position of having to allow any degree of iniquity whenever the agent in question does it on conscientious grounds. In those cases, of course, we need to establish the iniquitousness of the acts in question on independent grounds; and by and large, my argument in this chapter has been that it is unclear that we have such grounds. Meanwhile, it in any case remains that employers frequently cannot be said to have clearly unreasonable grounds for their discriminatory beliefs; and when this is so, it is difficult to see how we could proceed against them on the ground that their beliefs were, as we in our wisdom have decreed, false. And on the other hand, we do allow people to act on their religious beliefs, within broad limits, and those beliefs don't have nearly so much to be said for them as some of the beliefs on which prejudices are based.

There is one particular kind of prejudice supporting belief of which we may make a special case. This is the kind which consists in holding that certain groups of people are, without further explanation, "morally inferior." A belief so expressed might, of course, be an empirically based one, to the effect that the incidence of certain standardly recognized types of immoral behavior is greater in that group than in others—which in any case, of course, would not in fact justify across-the-board discrimination against members of that group. But the case I have in mind does not involve an explicable belief of that kind. It consists instead of simply holding that the group in question is not morally deserving of normally good treatment or of ordinary rights. Such a belief, we may certainly agree, is not only unintelligible but certainly immoral. It is unintelligible because it requires that there be a special, empirically undetectable property or set of properties that render their possessors eligible for inclusion in the moral community, and it is in principle erroneous to suppose that there is any such feature or features. And it is immoral because it would make it impossible for an accused person to defend himself against the "charge" of "inferiority" of that kind, even though its purpose is to justify the kind of treatment that is only properly administered to persons guilty of genuinely immoral behavior. But as with the kind of beliefs discussed previously, it must again be pointed out that persons engaging in that kind of treatment of others without a supportable charge of that kind are themselves guilty of violating the rights of others. What is wrong with the behavior in question is not that that is its motive, and it is unclear that the motive in question *adds* to the iniquity of the behavior. But certainly the spreading of such "beliefs," since it *can* only be used to promote evil behavior, may be condemned strongly enough.

Summary

The thesis of this chapter is that the case for regarding discrimination, properly so called, as an injustice has not been clearly supported in western thought, despite its enormous impact on western practice. "Discrimination properly so called" marks an essential distinction here, for as we have seen, much discriminatory behavior, termed 'nonbasic' in the foregoing, is undoubtedly wrong, and yet not wrong by virtue of being discriminatory: killing or injuring people who are innocent of any morally sustainable crime is wrong, whatever the motive. But that leaves a great deal that is "properly so called," where the discrimination consists only in treating some people less well than others, and doing so for a reason that is not morally relevant, in the strong sense of that term in which a morally relevant distinction morally requires a corresponding distinction in treatment. Not giving one person rather than another a job in a company of which you are the owner, and where your reason for preferring the other has nothing to do with competence at that job, is an example. What is anomalous about classifying such behavior as unjust, I have argued, is that there seems to be no *duty* to give anyone the job, in general; how, then, can it be unjust not to give it to one person rather than another? That is the central puzzle, and it seems to me to remain unanswered.

Cases can be made for the wrongness of what is ordinarily called discrimination on indirect grounds having to do with social harmony and the like. But such cases, unlike what can be said in the case of nonbasic discrimination, run up against a serious barrier, viz., the principle of liberty. To require persons to perform all sorts of actions despite the fact that the actions they might instead prefer are not literally harmful to anyone is surely to violate their liberty. It has been assumed throughout that that is a serious point against any requirement or prohibition, and perhaps some would be inclined to deny that it is. Arguing against those people would get us into another essay, and thus I let the case rest at this point.[7]

Notes

This essay was originally composed in the summer of 1977, and after many presentations and discussions, was published in Deborah Poff and Wilfrid Waluchow, eds., *Business Ethics in Canada* (Scarborough, Ont: Prentice Hall Canada, 1st ed., 1987; 3rd ed., 1999), 270-87. Reprinted with permission by Pearson Education Canada.

1. See also chapter 4.

2. In private conversation with G. A. Cohen.

3. Henry Sidgwick, *The Methods of Ethics,* 7th ed. (Indianapolis: Hackett, 1981), 379.

4. The first version of this paper was written in the late 1970s; thirty years later, when the present book goes into press, my example is very false to fact. I have read (but cannot verify) that although women in the very highest reaches of corporate life are still fairly rare, women in middle management positions are not only frequent, but may even have reached the majority portion.

5. Again, I remind the reader that this paper was written in the heyday of apartheid in South Africa.

6. Hobbes, *Leviathan*, ch. 14 (New York: E. P. Dutton, Everyman Library, 1950), 107.

7. I have readdressed these matters, and restated my main views about them, in four further published treatments: Jan Narveson, *Moral Matters* (Peterborough, Ont.: Broadview Press, 1993; 2nd ed., 1999), 301-16; Marilyn Friedman and Jan Narveson, *Political Correctness—For and Against* (Lanham, Md.: Rowman & Littlefield, 1995), 77-96; Jan Narveson, "Fair Hiring and Affirmative Action," in Wesley Cragg and Christine Koggel, eds., *Contemporary Moral Issues* (Toronto: McGraw-Hill Ryerson, 4th ed., 1997), 313-25.

Chapter 13

Collective Rights?

Introduction

The question addressed here is whether there are any collective rights. I am inclined to answer this in the negative; but the main challenge is to give a reasonably clear sense to the notion of 'collective rights'. My negative answer will then be defended from a general viewpoint utilizing what we may call a kind of "individualism." Some are inclined these days to reject a priori anything with that label. I shall have something to say later on that inclination. Individualism, as I shall explain, by no means implies that there are no group rights in *any* sense that may reasonably be given to that term. Very much the contrary. A careful explication is needed.

A Normative Question

I certainly will not argue that the whole idea of a collective right is nonsense. If it were, then there would be no normative question whether there are collective rights. Consider, for example, an argument that went as follows: "It makes no sense to talk of collective rights; therefore we should not recognize any." But if it made literally no sense to talk of them, what is it whose recognition we should not engage in? I argue that we can well understand what a collective right is, just as we can understand what someone is saying who insists that rocks have rights. It is precisely because we can understand it that we can understand the inimical implications of such theses, and should reject them. The negative answer I propose is conceived in response to a normative question.

Individualism and Groups

It is really essential to be clear what we are and are not rejecting here. In holding that there are no collective rights, I certainly do not hold that no groups have rights in any sense. Quite the contrary. Moreover, as we shall see, I accept that there are, in some senses we may reasonably attach to the term, *irreducible* groups. But I do wish to maintain, nevertheless, that because individual rights are all the rights there basically are, all the *legitimate* group rights there are derive from rights of individuals. All individuals are members of various groups, and virtually all individuals attach at least some normative significance to some of the groups of which they are members. On the other hand, all individuals are also members of an indefinitely large number of other groups to which they attach no significance whatever, e.g., the group of persons within an inch of their own height and persons whose last names contain exactly one 'k'. We might try to demarcate groups from mere "sets" of individuals for this purpose,[1] perhaps without begging any questions. In any case, not all groups in any familiar sense of that term will qualify for collective rights status, on anybody's view.

I point this out in order to emphasize an important disparity. To proclaim, as I certainly wish to do, that all individuals whatsoever have certain important rights, and have them just because they *are* (more-or-less normal) human individuals, is not, I would hope, bizarre or implausible on anyone's view. But to proclaim that all groups, or even just those groups that are not "mere sets," have rights simply as such would be bizarre. All proponents of collective rights, I take it, would want to maintain only that *some* collectivities would have them. That is important. For it at least suggests that those who want to protect certain collectivities by extending rights to them don't really think that collectivities as such need, or deserve, or are the sort of things that are "naturally endowed with" rights. And it suggests that there is going to be some way of getting at those cases in which the proponent wants to defend collective rights that may be more persuasively formulated in terms that don't really require recourse to rights of collectives per se. We shall see.

Rights

Well, what are rights? To attribute a right to someone or something is to say that there is something about that person or thing such that in virtue of that, some moral agents have duties concerning it. Rights are duty-creating properties.[2] (Later I will also use a by-now familiar distinction between 'negative' and 'positive' rights.) The expression 'duties concerning it' is meant to leave this open and also allow the case where A ends up with a duty to B by virtue of a right of C.

This definition is neutral as between moral and legal claims. A right is the same sort of thing in either context. Moral rights entail moral duties; legal rights entail legal ones. But I do believe that what people call "legal rights and duties" are *nonfundamental*. It is sometimes the case that we have a certain (moral) duty by virtue of having a certain legal requirement placed on us. If, as some claim, there is a duty to obey the law, it would be a moral duty, not a legal duty in the sense that phrase would have if it had the same conceptual structure as 'moral duty'. The claim that it is a "legal duty" is either uninterestingly pleonastic, or a very misleading way of asserting the moral duty in question. We will be concerned here exclusively with moral considerations; but these importantly include the issue of whether we ought to have laws protecting this or that collectivity by giving them enforceable legal rights. It will be noted that I ignore in this chapter, or reject, some distinctions pressed by various legal theorists, notably Wesley Hohfeld.

Two Notes about Rights

I shall make two points related to the familiar Hohfeldian distinctions. First, the curiously popular alleged distinction between a "liberty" right and a "claim" right is bogus, at least in contexts of fundamental normative inquiry.[3] The former is supposed to be the right you have when it is only the case that it is not wrong for you to do the thing in question, whereas the latter asserts, supposedly in addition, that somebody has the duty to let you do it, or perhaps to help you do it. But the notion that someone of whom it is merely true that it is *not wrong* for him to do x has, thereby, a *right* to do x makes no sense. Such a person, insofar forth, does not as yet have any sort of right, period. The notion of rights is vacuous if it has no normative implications for anyone's conduct in relation to the right holder. If its being not wrong for you to do something is compatible with my forcibly preventing you from doing it, for instance, then there is no point in describing this status of yours as that of having a "right" to do it. You simply don't, possibly because there are no rights here.

To take a familiar supposed example: does the player running down the field have a right to make a touchdown? Surely nobody has the duty to prevent people from preventing him from doing that? Wrong. He does have that right, against everybody in the world, in precisely that sense—except, of course, members of the other team. Obviously *they* are not under a general duty to allow him to make that touchdown. Against them our right holder has only the right to *try*, in certain specific ways, to make that touchdown. Yet they too have certain duties along this line. Even they are not permitted, for instance, to mow him down with a machine gun before he crosses the goal line. What *they* have the right to do is to use a certain specified range of methods of stopping him; and they do have that right in my sense: that is, nobody else may intervene to prevent them from utilizing those methods, though of course the opposing team may take measures to prevent them from succeeding. But then, they don't have the right to succeed—only to try.

Secondly, I deny that there are two fundamentally distinct notions involved in speaking of rights to *do* and rights to *have*—rights to *things*.[4] To have a right to a thing is to have the right to do various things *with* or *about* it. Moreover, having a right to do something is equivalent to having a partial property right in the self which does that act. In the remainder of this chapter, I shall generally use the language appropriate to doing, but this is not to be construed as implying the need for a different treatment concerning rights of ownership.

Confusion is compounded when people suppose that "liberty rights" in the sense of rights to do are merely "liberty rights" in the above-rejected pseudo-sense of 'rights' that consist merely of negations of 'ought-nots', that is, supposed "liberty-rights" as distinct from "claim-rights." To be a right is to be a claim-right: it is to be a basis for a claim against (some or all) others, namely that those others refrain from something (negative) or do something (positive) in relation to your actions.

When we discuss collective rights, then, what we shall want to know is always precisely the same thing as when any rights of individuals are in question: namely, are we constrained from preventing, or perhaps constrained to assist, this collectivity doing whatever it is claimed to have the right to do?

Morals Are Essentially Group-Related

A further background point of importance. Many theorists think that there is something specifically social, group significant, in the very idea of morals. I am one of those. Or more precisely, I take it that what we are *interested* in here under the heading of moral rules are essentially rules of (and for) human groups, groups of persons. Morality (or anyway, if you prefer, the branch of it that I consider here) is social: the morality of a society is a set of rules, requirements, and ideal paradigms of behavior (virtues) which is, as I have put it elsewhere,[5] informal and expected to be universally reinforced and inculcated in *and by* all members of the society. This in no way contradicts the individualist outlook, however. In my view, the right basic morality for any society is one that reinforces and inculcates rights of individuals, namely, the right of individuals to do whatever they please within the limits imposed by the same right of all others. Rights are inherently social in their administration and, in a sense, in their foundations and origin. In the view of us individualists, it is the content of morals that is individual.

The Idea of Rights of Collectives

As I shall be explaining, there is no problem about saying that someone has a right on account of his membership in a certain group or "collectivity." But there are problems about claiming that certain collectivities, *as such*, have rights. Michael McDonald joins the issue directly in drawing "a distinction between a group's having a right and its members having that right."[6] Just so. Let us consider. If a collective had a right, against whom would it be a right? Who would have duties toward it? We may usefully divide the possibilities into two sets: (a) members and (b) nonmembers.

Regarding (a), it is of course perfectly clear that members of groups often have duties toward other members of the group in virtue of their being members of it: the duties of membership, say. And various specific duties of one member to another might be affected by their membership, in important ways. However, if the collective *as such* had a right over members of it (for example, to observe its rituals, respect its history and traditions, or whatever), then we would have to ask whether these were duties that members could disavow by, for instance, leaving the group. If so, one must really be thinking of these as obligations one assumes upon becoming a member, even if membership was due to birth. And in that case, to whom are they really owed? Surely they must be owed *to other members*. If one supposes instead that they are owed "to the collectivity as such," then there is a problem. For how could a collectivity as such ever either impose or release one from any such obligations? Since collectivities do not have minds and cannot act, that would seem not to make any sense. In which case, it is also hard to see how one could ever be released by it no matter what one did, if one ever had these duties in the first place. The collectivity would become a sort of metaphysical slave master to whom members were bound without recourse. Free persons should surely reject this.

Regarding (b) there is, for one thing, the same kind of problem about non-members. Suppose that the actual members of that collective all ceased their membership: e.g., that a certain tribe of Indians decided, for some reason, to disband and simply amalgamate with the surrounding society. To whom would we now owe the duties entailed by the supposed rights of this collectivity? And in any case, why would we owe them to anyone at all? Why, in other words, would we ever rationally recognize the supposed rights in question?

McDonald gives an example: "Think of a club having the right to your repayment of a loan in contrast with each of the members of the club individually and severally having the right."[7] Agreed: we may certainly think of this. So let us think. In the first place, we must now recognize an important point made by Michael Hartney, that such entities as clubs, corporations, and so on are, legally speaking, "fictitious person[s], separate from all the persons making up the sociological group."[8] And, as Hartney convincingly argues, when we owe things to such "persons," we owe them neither to the several members nor to the collectivity associated with it. The way in which a group's being a "legal person" is "fictitious" is that the law imputes a unity to the group in question that can only literally belong to the organisms we know as individual persons. Only individuals literally think, decide, act. When groups are treated for certain purposes as though they too think, decide, and act, then we apply categories to them whose legal or moral implications for actual individuals need to be spelled out. In order to enjoy such a status a group must be organized in a suitable manner. Otherwise if we, say, owed the club some money, we would have no idea how to pay it, i.e., no idea which actual individual could take money "on behalf of" the club, as we say. And when States have rights, this shows not that collectivities have rights but rather, as Hartney quite properly argues, that States are not collectivities. States are, instead, legal persons.

These are useful fictions. But if we ask what they are useful for, my answer is that they are useful only for the various purposes of individuals, if at all. The State, for example, is pointless, quite useless, if it does not function so as somehow to advance the welfare or well-being of the various individuals who compose it, and perhaps of other individuals who deal with it in various ways. To regard the State as literally a person, with a welfare or illfare of its own to consider, in complete logical independence of any persons whatever, would be to create a moral and metaphysical muddle of a pernicious kind. In saying such things, of course, I am taking sides on significant normative issues. There is, as I say, no purely logical problem in *attributing* rights to all sorts of odd entities. But in such cases, the normative implications of such ascription should be rejected, because the premises on which the duties flowing from them are founded are false. But the reasons for finding them so are normative, not "logical."

Values and Collectivities

It does make perfectly good sense to value such things as traditions and histories. Travel in foreign lands, reading works of history or anthropology, talking with natives, all reveal interesting cultural possibilities that one might find delightful or admirable, horrifying or instructive, and so on. We might be moved, for instance, to contribute to a fund for preserving some of these customs and ways of life. People sometimes describe this sort of process in rights-and-duties language: "We owe it to these noble people not to let the memory of their deeds disappear without a trace," etc. But of course we don't literally owe it to that "people" in the sense in which we might owe our neighbor his lawn mower back after borrowing it. Nobody may incarcerate us for failing to fulfill this duty. What may happen is that the tradition in question dies out, and this may be too bad. Those of us who feel that way will do well to take steps to keep their deeds in memory, e.g., by erecting memorials and writing about them. But that's it.

Methodological Individualism

Individualism, in the present context, is primarily a view about the social sciences. It says, as against "holism," that individuals, facts about them and states of them, rather than any sort of "social wholes," are the explanatorily basic entities in social science. What makes such a view plausible are two things.

First, there is the fact that social wholes, collectivities and so on, in some fundamental sense *consist* of individuals, and not vice versa. However much truth there is in the claim that individuals, in turn, are social creatures and could not exist "on their own," the very meaning of this claim and the very descriptions of any processes by which this dependence is explicated will be in terms of individuals relating to each other in innumerable ways, individuals being born and inheriting this and that from their parents or others in their group, developing various ties of affection and sympathy with fellow group members, and so on. The idea that social wholes are ontologically distinct entities in their own right seems to make no sense. Whereas, the idea that there might (for awhile!) be Robinson Crusoes or isolated Neanderthal members of

Homo sapiens does make sense, even though it scarcely ever happens. The rarity or nonexistence of cases of isolation and the pervasiveness of substantial relations to others is an obvious truth that needs to be emphasized here because of its *irrelevance* to individualism, whether methodological or normative. For it is widely said that individualism presupposes that people are "atoms" or "Robinson Crusoes." The fact is so far otherwise that were people isolated as said, there would be no need for, because no subject of, moral or legal philosophy.

Second, and much more germane to the present purpose, there is the point that only individuals can make decisions, can literally have values, literally engage in deliberation and reasoning: and the subject matter of morals is how entities capable of doing those things should do them. Facts about group decisions and actions are logically contingent on the occurring of acts of communication and responsive behavior among individuals, who establish chains of command and other patterns of behavior responsive to the behavior of others. We sometimes say that groups behave in ways that are contrary to or distinct from the behavior of their component individuals, but again, these claims are contingent on the individuals in that group being complex beings, able to exhibit consciously intended behavior in one direction while the side effects of that behavior, multiplied in many examples, make for a group pattern different from what any individual intended. The classic argument of Adam Smith about the "invisible-hand" effects of market behavior is a perfect case in point. Rather than showing that group behavior is utterly irreducible to individual behavior, it illustrates just the opposite.

Even though individualism as I understand it would seem to be virtually trivial, bearing it in mind can be helpful in warding off misconceptions or sillinesses. Here's an example. In a book I'm currently reading, a demographer is quoted as saying that the sudden and dramatic increase in the number of teenagers in the U.S. in the early 1960s resulting from the 'baby boom' of the late 1940s caused the capacity of the society to deal with the "socialization" tasks regarding teenagers to be "almost literally swamped." Yet a doubling of the number of teenagers in the whole United States meant, in fact, merely that each of a large number of families had one more teenager to cope with than typical families did earlier or later (the previous average having been roughly one). Since every family that has any children at all who survive to maturity faces similar tasks in the case of each of its children, and since having two teenagers around is hardly the sort of eventuality that would throw typical parents into desperation, the image of 'the resources for coping with socialization tasks being swamped', when "reduced to" the particular facts that are actually being so summarized—that is, when clearly understood—turns out to be quite underargued by the fact cited. The fact is that the phenomenon in question would have had essentially zero impact on those resources had they consisted, as they did in almost all societies everywhere before, mainly in familiar family structures. (As a matter of fact, the teen "wave" consisted of a proportionately much smaller number of individuals than was typical a century earlier.)

Facilities such as YMCAs, churches, and public schools might, of course, be pressed by such a "wave." But when such facts are pointed to as explicating the claim in question, they make us understand which sorts of individuals are affected, and how, by the mass phenomenon in question, rather than illustrating how loose talk of "social" phenomena must be understood in an irreducible way. Only a politically organized society that insists on trying to provide publicly managed resources, such as schools, can intelligibly be described as being "in danger of being swamped" by this sort of increase. Were society an organism, then a doubling of the size of, say, its right forearm over a period of two weeks would no doubt have presented a problem of "swamping" its resources. But it is not an organism, and claims of that kind are automatically in need of rethinking and analysis because it is not—rethinking which in many cases, such as this one, eviscerate the original claim.

This must be followed with one cautionary note. Too many people still seem to think that individualism in social theory consists in the view that all social facts are explicable on the basis of the sort of behavior patterns that could be displayed by a Robinson Crusoe: i.e., that the existence of a huge human environment in close contact with an individual nevertheless makes no difference to the latter's behavior. The sheer statement of this view should be enough to dispose of it, of course; but also to dispose of any idea that methodological individualism presupposes or entails it. Social theory *is* the study of interaction among people and the difference various sorts of it makes to them. That the subjects of interaction are individuals, then, implies nothing about the relation between social behavior and nonsocial behavior, what little there is of the latter.

Liberalism

What about 'liberalism'? This is primordially a *political* view, though it is easy enough to identify the analog in moral theory. Politically speaking, liberalism holds that rulers ought to rule in the interests, and only the interests, of the ruled, these being their interests as seen by those persons. The thesis could be (and often is) stated in terms of the "good" of individuals, but this runs a danger. The ruler could well rule for what *he* conceives to be the good of his subjects, but suppose that those subjects will have nothing to do with it? Then that ruler is not being a liberal, but rather, in one sense of that term, a "conservative," or in Raz's term a 'perfectionist'. The liberal holds that the appropriate values to employ in dealing with Jones are Jones's values (and, of course, the values of those his behavior affects), not someone else's. This is true both for the government and for individuals, such as Jones, themselves. So when Jones deals with Smith, Jones will need to have regard for Smith's values.

Liberalism consists, then, in holding that we may not overrule people's values as being, simply, the wrong values for them to have. Any overruling must be done on the basis of the impact of the behavior of some, in response to their values, on others, as affecting them in ways significant according to the latter's values. We may suggest to others that this or that would be better for them; but we may not, in principle, act on the suggestion in their cases unless we succeed in getting the suggestion accepted by them.

In so saying, I admit, the terms 'liberal' and 'liberalism' are employed in a sense perhaps remote from that current among many of today's social thinkers. In today's world, the values to be promoted among many segments of the population are those assessed by social workers, social "scientists," and politicians—which means the values *imputed* to the poor by, approximately, the middle class and/or the intellectual class. Still, this possible change in usage is surely aberrant. The nouveau liberal, I believe, still *claims* that her usage really does capture the values that the poor, etc., really do embrace, even though those poor, etc., need the help of the social scientists and so forth to see this. But I shall leave it at that for the present.

Liberal Individualism

To be a liberal is certainly to hold that government and, more generally, any social institutions possessed of coercive power, should use that power only in order to promote the goods of the individuals who compose that society (or of individuals everywhere). But liberals, so conceived, can differ about how this is to be done. In particular, we must distinguish those who think there are fundamentally *positive* rights from those who deny this. This distinction, between "negative" and "positive" rights is important, and we pause here to give a brief explanation.

A "negative" right is one imposing only negative duties on others: namely, duties not to do various things; in particular, negative rights entail duties not to do what would prevent the right holder from doing what she is being said to have a right to do, or from doing with her property what she thereby has the right to do with it. A "positive" right, by contrast, is one that entails positive duties, that is, duties to do and not merely to refrain. Such duties will in general be duties to help the right holder (to some degree that would have to be further clarified by the theorist) and provided that the right holder both wants and in some sense needs the help in question. Take two relevant kinds of examples, the right to health and the right to security. A right to bodily health may be a negative right, a right that others not damage or impair the state of health of the right holder. But it might also be asserted to go beyond that, and be a right that others *repair* damage suffered by the right holder. A right to security of person may be a negative right, that others not damage or in various ways constrain the person in question. But it may be also (and usually is asserted as) a positive right, a right that others provide facilities for ensuring the security of persons, e.g., police forces. In both cases, note that when we talk of rights we are, or at any rate I am, here talking of coercively enforceable rights. If one has a right, whether negative or positive, then one may take measures to enforce it (just *how* enforceable is a further question for moral consideration, not dealt with here). But a positive right to coercion is a right that others exercise some coercion, where needed, on behalf of one's right; a negative right is merely a right that others refrain from preventing one, or one's agents, from using coercion.

Now, the kind of liberals I mean to distinguish from those to be favored here are those (almost everyone these days) who are ready to compel some members of society to promote the good of other members (always, of course, under the rubric of "society as a whole") in various ways, e.g., through taxation to support welfare legislation and schools. And some of those are ready to indulge in a good deal of social science support for such programs of types that look awfully "nonindividualistic." But others, more distinctively liberal individualists, wish to stand up for "the individual" in some more robust sense. They hold that we in general ought to allow individuals to do what they wish, follow their own chosen ways of life, even when others don't like them or don't go along with those ways. They will hold that individuals have rights that operate as "trumps," which apply even when the general good as a whole is perhaps not on balance promoted by upholding the right in question on a given occasion. Such liberals may even hold that we should encourage such things, e.g., by publicly promoting opportunities of various kinds. And many pay a lot of attention to "fairness" and are interested in upholding or promoting "equal opportunity" and suchlike, say by proposing "affirmative action" programs. At some point, individualism is strained by doctrines of the latter kind, so popular in present times. It becomes a rather fine question where such liberalism leaves off and other theories (conservative, perfectionist, or collectivist, for example) begin.

Radical Liberal Individualism

The view taken in this chapter may be described by the term 'radical liberal individualism', which may now be given a fairly clear sense. It consists in interpreting the force we are to attribute to individuals' values in a yet narrower manner: it ups the ante by holding that the only legitimate collectively imposed norms are those concerned to protect individuals from each other, thus to permit them, so far as possible, each to realize their own destinies, pursue their own goals, limited only by the rights that accrue from the similar right of others. The radical liberal holds that nobody—not even the middle class!—may be coercively required (or require anyone) to do anything essentially on the ground that it would benefit some *other* person (e.g., the "poor"). All such benefiting must proceed from the voluntary activity of the person conferring the benefit; neither the recipient nor anyone else may properly force him to supply it.

Finally, we will bring in the term 'Libertarian' to identify the theorist who holds that we can only explicate the radical individualist program in terms of property rights. Liberty = Property. I believe, in fact, that radical individualism makes no sense without libertarianism, and that to hold that individuals may do as they please is necessarily to hold that they may do so with bits of the external world that they have in one way or another come to involve in their activities. Indeed, to hold to individual liberty is to hold that individuals are their own owners: that they, and not others, may direct the motions of their own bodies and minds. It is the concern of this chapter to explore the bearing of such a general outlook on the specific subject of collectivities. Nevertheless, a little must be said.

Why Be a Liberal Individualist?

People have assorted interests, goals, values (hereinafter I shall use the term 'interest' indifferently for all of these). These interests define their lives for them, humanly speaking, and their pursuit constitutes those lives. Many or perhaps nearly all of those interests are derived from their lives in various communities, often from one particular community: the one they grew up in. Most or all of those interests are also social in the sense that the things they wish to pursue, the things they value, involve others—particular others or groups of others, no matter. It is his adherence to these which, in "defining his life," as I put it, enable him or anyone to assess the rationality of his actions and decisions. For him there is nothing else; yet, obviously, it is *his* rationality that we are talking about.

But he relates to all sorts of other people, who share to infinitely varying degrees his particular values: some very close persons may share them quite fully, while others, who may be physically near but psychologically at downright planetary distances, share them scarcely at all. Yet there they all are, and he must somehow deal with them. In former times, I note, this might have been false: many people in the world would remain throughout his life completely unknown and sealed off; he would, quite simply, *not* "have to deal with them." Those times, I take it, are past. How is he best to do so?

The libertarian view may, I believe, be defended broadly as follows. These other people, being people as well as he, assess their actions in terms of *their* various values. The accepting and pursuing of one's assorted values being the stuff of our lives, we cannot but be interested in not having them thwarted, trampled on, and so forth, by others. But also we must reserve the right, as it were, to value-changes without notice. These two, I think, are the sources of our interest, as individuals, in a right to liberty, that is, in not being prevented by others from doing the things we are bent on doing. We are all the same in this respect. And this does not presuppose any fundamental respect for others, any sharing of their values, or even any prior inhibitions about treating them in whatever way suits us in terms of our own values. It doesn't presuppose it—but, argues the Libertarian, to adopt an attitude of respect for the liberty of others in exchange for their respect for one's own is one's best bet among moral theories. We will join with willing others in pursuing some of our projects; and regarding all other persons, those who do not share our projects, we ask only that they not take what we have, interfere with our lives, and we similarly will refrain from interfering in theirs. The policy is live and let live. It is also "You scratch my back, I'll scratch yours." But it is not "My back needs scratching—so you scratch it or I'll shoot!"

The General Principle of Liberty, as I shall call it, gives everyone the right to do whatever she or he pleases. Since to be a right is to be a status generating duties, namely those in which respecting rights consists, it follows that everyone's duty is to respect everyone else's liberty. We may somewhat misleadingly say, following Mill, that the sum of our fundamental moral duty is not to "harm" others; but what is meant by 'harm'? Too much, or alternatively not enough, has been imputed to this notion to let it stand uninterpreted. On the view being advanced, we "harm" others in the relevant sense when we interfere with their liberty. We can do this by abusing their bodies in assorted ways, without their consent; we can also do it by abusing their property, that is, using it in ways contrary to those intended and desired by them, and without their consent. We can do it by threatening them with harm if they don't refrain from engaging in activities which, of themselves, do not involve any such invasions of others.

The rights envisaged in this idea consist entirely of what have at last come to be recognized with some (though not yet enough) clarity as "negative" rights, in the sense explained above. Positive rights, by comparison, require us to devote our energies to certain specific sets of pursuits rather than others—other ones that we would prefer to engage in—whether we like it or not. They cut into liberty; that is to say, into that space of performable actions compatible with others' action-spaces. Now, negative rights require us *not* to devote our energies to certain things, indeed: but this requirement is the minimum compatible with having liberty in a social environment, where all of us have the inherent capacity to interfere with each other without limit. If we make the Principle of Liberty our sole fundamental source of restrictions, we capture the maximum possible socially reinforcible liberty for each. Those who wish to "promote" and "foster" general liberty by trying to make a positive right of it are, we argue, misguided: by turning liberty into a coercively enforced *social goal,* they defeat it rather than promote it.

Freedom of Association

The *Canadian Charter of Rights and Freedoms*, though like all political documents not free of its share of muddles, nevertheless accepts the central core of the libertarian program when it tells us that "*Everyone has the right to life, liberty and security of the person* and the right not to be deprived thereof except in accordance with the principles of fundamental justice," (my emphasis). This latter proclamation is found way down in section 7; but plainly it could have—and should have—stood as a general preamble to the whole, for it implies all of the freedoms that actually precede it. Thus, everyone is declared to have the following fundamental freedoms: (a) freedom of conscience and religion; (b) freedom of thought, belief, opinion and expression, including freedom of the press and other media of communication; (c) freedom of peaceful assembly; and (d) freedom of association. It also promises us rights of "Mobility"—specifically, to "enter, remain in and leave Canada," and to "move to and take up residence in" and "pursue the gaining of a livelihood in" any province. Never mind the questionable provisions for various "positive" freedoms that more or less invade the foregoing: for the present, the point is that freedom of association is explicitly recognized as among fundamental freedoms.

That it should be so is obvious on our view. Plainly if A and B may do as they please, then they may do it together, if that also pleases them. But this is a right, and not a requirement. As a right, it imposes on the rest of us a duty to respect it, namely, by not forcibly breaking up associations other than those that are conspiracies against the rights of others. But as a right, it also does not impose on us any positive duty, e.g., to help keep the association together, or to subsidize it, or even to approve of its activities, let alone to celebrate it or to promote its purposes.

One of the rights of individuals, then, in the view of us individualists, is the right of association. It is, we saw, one of the "fundamental freedoms" specified in the Charter. A number of individuals may associate freely for any legitimate purpose, where "legitimate" purposes are here taken to be simply those purposes the pursuit of which does not as such conflict with anyone else's rights. This makes one type of group the very paradigm of a legitimate group: the voluntary association, or "association" for short, associated for any purpose that does not violate the rights of those outside the group.

Now, associations are voluntary in two important but distinct senses: (1) they contain only people who deliberately *join* the group, and (2) everyone who is a member has the right to *leave*, though the group could properly impose some conditions on the manner of leaving. This distinction is of major significance for our subject, as we will now go on to see.

Four Sorts of Collectives

To explore our subject of collective rights, it is vital that we distinguish between at least two kinds of groups, two kinds of collectives: roughly speaking, Voluntary and Involuntary ones. The distinction is too rough, though, and we must make some immediate refinements. We will distinguish four sorts from the present perspective:

(1) Groups that are *fully voluntary*, where the members deliberately and intentionally join the group in question, becoming members by engaging in specified acts having that effect, and where they may leave at any time (subject perhaps to minor restrictions inherent in the group's rules, as accepted by their members upon joining).

(2) Then there are two kinds of *partially voluntary* groups. One type is groups that one can join freely but *cannot leave freely*, such as "til death do us part" marriages, and perhaps certain religious orders or fraternities. The Mafia comes to mind as a case to worry about.

(3) Groups that one *cannot join freely* but may leave (more or less) freely, such as one's state or other political division and, perhaps, one's tribe.

(4) And finally, there are groups that are *fully involuntary*: one is, say, born or conscripted into them, and one either cannot leave at all (e.g., one's race) or leaves only at the behest of others (e.g., slaves).

1. Fully Voluntary Groups

When entry and exit are both voluntary, the purposes, methods, activities, and internal structures of such groups may, I believe, be anything the members like (with the usual essential provision that those purposes, etc., not impinge negatively on the rights of others). For example, their internal structures need not be democratic.[9] They can have any amount of internal hierarchy and stratification you please, up to and including ones that involve elites and dictatorships. In some cases, the dictator will even be regarded as sacred by the members: the Roman Catholic Church perhaps exemplifies (or at least used to exemplify) many of these characteristics, and I take it that it is a perfectly legitimate organization, even if some people might personally prefer that its membership were empty.

2. Entry-Voluntary Groups

What about groups where entrance is voluntary but exit is not? An interesting case in point here is that tiny group consisting of one married couple, as the situation was prior to liberal divorce laws. Should we countenance groups whose members swear to remain together "until death do them part"? Are those violations of our general right of liberty?

Such groups pose a very different issue from the category of involuntary-entry groups, for one might certainly argue that taking on irreversible lifelong duties is a possible undertaking which individuals should be free to engage in. The main question with them, I suggest, is: who is to enforce the conditions? Prior to liberal divorce laws, the State took a major hand in this, depriving the absconding partner of assorted rights. This, I suggest, was wrong. On the other hand, if we leave it up to the couple themselves to make the arrangements that enforce their marriage contract, then we should, I think, have no fundamental objection. People may morally commit themselves for life; to forbid this would be paternalism. But one looks with concern on this category. How intolerable must membership become before we are inclined to judge that perhaps the individual's original commitment was made in a moment of unthinking enthusiasm? The pressure to relax divorce laws was immense. Whether the relaxation in question was unwise is difficult to judge. But the negative consequences of this particular liberalization are especially born by unwitting victims: children, especially, but also women whose ex-husbands have reneged on their agreed separation payments.

But other exit-involuntary groups would not have those particular side effects. And where none such exist, the libertarian must be fairly reluctant to intervene on behalf of the joiner who subsequently changes his mind. Nevertheless, the onus would in general be against any set of individuals forcing others to remain in association with them. Genuinely exitless organizations will be hard to countenance for anyone concerned for liberty.

3. Entrance-Involuntary but Exit-Voluntary Groups

Next, and considerably more interesting for present purposes, is the group to which entry is not voluntary, but exit is. For example, there is the group of native Ontarians: you might be born an Ontarian, and this automatically makes you an Ontario resident, whether you like it or not. At first and for quite some time, you presumably don't think of it at all; and by the time you do, you may well have acquired a fairly strong attitude toward being Ontarian. Not very many Ontarians have the same sort of attitudes toward being an Ontarian that, say, the typical Briton does toward being British. Still, the development of such attitudes is typical. Moreover, I would think they are healthy and, in moderation, to be encouraged. It is a sad thing to be a member of some cultural or even political grouping while entertaining a continuing attitude of disaffection and perhaps of distrust toward it.

More interesting than these, for our purposes anyway, is the case of the Cree Indian, say. Here again, one is born into the tribe. But as I understand it, one can, and may, leave it. That is, it is both possible to divest oneself of tribal membership, and doing so is permitted by the tribe. What are we to say of such groups, on my individualistic view? The answer, I suggest, is that whenever we have a native who does not take advantage of a right of exit that she knows is available, then we presume that her membership is voluntary. Members of tribes have sometimes had some pretty rigorous practices imposed on them by virtue of their membership. They may blanch at these, but they don't regard them as reasons for leaving. We have no business intervening to change tribal practices so long as they occur with the evident approval of members (and, of course, so long as they are not significant negative spillover effects on the persons and properties of those outside the tribe).

When a liberal surveys such groups, she will often have conflicting feelings. For the internal structures and practices of some such groups is quite illiberal. For example, one hears of unsanitary puberty rites in which members are disfigured. There is a tribe in Canada, I have heard, which had the interesting practice of removing one finger per defunct husband from one hand of the surviving widow, as a sign of respect. Even such draconian practices, I believe, are nevertheless not occasions for forcible outside intervention, unless the widow in question is denied any right to leave. Some might argue that a widow in a tribe is in no position to *address* the question whether on the whole continued membership, including subscription to the practice in question, outweighs the utility of removing herself. In some sense, I am sure, this is true. She was brought up in tribal values and ways of thinking and these make it, one supposes, immensely unlikely that she will prefer leaving the tribe to having one finger removed. Nonetheless, she may take the option of making an internal fuss, and *then* there is a good deal to be said on behalf of external intervention in the form of support for her point of view to the tribal authorities (which are ones we assume she accepts). We may suppose that the tribe insists, in which case what we would be in a position to insist on in return is that the woman at least have the right to leave the tribe in order to avoid this disfigurement. What we may not do, however, is simply insist that the tribe abandon this "barbaric" practice.

Here if anywhere the "irreducibility" thesis becomes highly plausible. To 'define' tribal membership in terms that presuppose no group involvement would, I suppose, be very difficult—indeed, practically (whether or not theoretically) impossible. Yet to define group involvement otherwise is quite easy, operationally speaking. We know fairly well when someone is or is not a member of the Inuit or the Cree, even though neither we nor the Cree can define Cree-ness. Thus the moral individualist can get a fairly clear grip on these cases. And the grip in question is, I should think, rather favorable to the contemporary who wants to protect the rights of tribes and such. So do I: for in doing so, we protect the rights of their members. A member who considers that his very being is bound up with the tribe is a person whose interests cannot be respected without extending respect to tribal ways, so far as they bear on his case.

My general conclusion is that when a group is exit-voluntary, its right to engage in its various practices, including weird or, in our view, questionable practices is clear. Outsiders making war or otherwise forcibly intervening in the affairs of such groups is in general unwarranted.

4. Fully Involuntary Groups

At the opposite end of the spectrum we have groups whose membership is not voluntary at all, such as the group of caucasians. We are stuck with our basic skin color, like it or not, and more generally with our genetically determined characteristics. One's biological sex is, near enough, another case in point (slightly complicated by the possibility of sex-change operations, to be sure). It is, of course, a basic thesis of the liberal individualistic point of view that groups of this sort may not feature essentially in any rights and duties. There are no special rights, and no special duties, of white people, or of black people, or of women or of men, for example, *simply as such*. The black man who holds his fellow black man to be under a sacred duty to support and defend his fellow blacks is, I submit, in the wrong. That is to say—and this is all there is to saying these things—the rest of us (including his fellow black people) should *not* uphold the impositions that would flow from such a right.

I would hope that this thesis is also pretty widely accepted. I don't think it is universally accepted, and this worries me. We shall return to some of these worries below.

Nothing said here is intended to deny that people might *assume* obligations and duties toward members of such groups, nor that they sometimes should do so. Siblings, for instance, should and normally do hold each other in more affection and regard than miscellaneous strangers. It is sad and, one might say, unnatural if they do not. But still, should some falling-out or some native disinclination for each other crop up, the rest of us cannot reasonably demand that they nevertheless hold each other in affection and regard. Siblings don't have a *right* to each other's affections. Affection just isn't the sort of thing that can be commanded or required, just like that. Civility and respect, yes: affection and enthusiasm, no. A good family, like a good community, will inspire such attitudes, and the value of them and of groups united by them is so great that we should surely be concerned to foster them if we can. But that's very different from requiring and commanding, which is what is in question when we speak of rights.

Nor is this to deny that people might do well to supply considerable levels of reinforcement short of the coercive on behalf of such things as family ties. To have no regard for a brother, even if he turns out pretty badly, is something we would do well to look askance at. Where coercion leaves off and inducement begins is not, to be sure, so easy to say. But the case of the libertarian applies to what is on one side of that line, and not what is on the other. We are certainly free to admire or deplore many things that we are not free to make laws about.[10]

Rights and Public Policy

Rights are coercively reinforcible: that's a core part of the idea of rights. When you have a right, you have something normatively potent. It may be that available enforcement procedures are hopelessly inadequate to defend your right against its actual sources of threat in the circumstances, and when that's so, having the right will not be worth much, one might say. But that doesn't mean you don't have it.

Part of the thrust of the liberty proposal is that involuntary methods of enforcement are put very much in question. Even if the institutions of the law hold that we have such-and-such a right, the fact that citizens generally will be *required* to support this renders the legislators' moral position regarding them at least problematic. Unless they can be quite sure that *all* citizens would voluntarily support the procedure in question, then some people's liberty rights are, in the view I am supporting, violated. More to the point, governments cannot simply make things right or wrong by say-so, by decree. When a government makes it a crime for a citizen to advertise his wares in a certain language, for example in the interests of "language rights," what it is doing is, in my view, simply wrong. It has no business doing any such thing.

Similarly, no group, no collectivity, has the (positive) "right to exist" against the outside world at large. All voluntary groups whose purposes and activities are innocent in the senses considered certainly have the right not to be interfered with, but no group can maintain that others must help it to remain in existence if its own members do not have enough interest to support it; nor does it have the right to forcibly impose duties on its *own* members to do that. Members can leave if they don't like it, and if all do, then the group ceases to exist, and that's that. If others are unhappy about this, as some are at the disappearance of species of birds, then let them ante up support for those groups. And if that is still not enough, then that is, again, that.

Conclusion

Are there "collective rights," then? In the main sense in which this question is currently under discussion, I believe that the answer is in the negative. There are plenty of collectivities whose members' rights would be violated if we were to interfere with them. But there are none who may require anyone outside, or who may forcibly impose as a duty on any fundamentally unwilling insiders of the group, to keep the group in being or keep it operating at a level above some particular threshold or at some kind of level of activity equal to that practiced by other groups, and so on. Groups worthy of our respect are so because their members are worthy of respect, and the respect consists in letting them live their lives as they see fit. Groups worthy of something more, such as our admiration and support, must do worthy and admirable things to earn it. To be sure, many have done just that.

Notes

This essay was published in *Canadian Journal of Law and Jurisprudence* 4, no. 2 (July 1991), 329-45. My thanks to the editors of that journal for permitting its reproduction here. My thanks also to several discussants at a meeting of the Canadian branch of the International Society for Social and Legal Philosophy at which several of the papers in that volume were presented.

1. The suggestion is due to Michael McDonald.

2. In, especially, *The Libertarian Idea* (Peterborough, Ont: Broadview Press, 2001; formerly Temple University Press, 1989), at 122-30.

3. This analysis is due, in recent print, to Joseph Raz; see *The Morality of Freedom* (Oxford: Clarendon Press, 1986), 166. I adopt his formulation only because it seems to me a particularly perspicuous way of stating what I have long employed in my own work. See, for instance, Jan Narveson, *Morality and Utility* (Baltimore: Johns Hopkins Press, 1967), 204-5.

4. See Wesley Hohfeld, "Fundamental Legal Conceptions as Applied in Judicial Reasoning," *Yale Law Journal* 23 (1913-14), 16-34.

5. See Wesley Hohfeld, "Fundamental Legal Conceptions as Applied in Judicial Reasoning," *Yale Law Journal* 26 (1916-17), 710-720.

6. Michael McDonald, "Should Communities Have Rights? Reflections on Liberal Individualism," *Canadian Journal of Law and Jurisprudence* IV, No. 2 (July 1991), 217-38.

7. McDonald, "Should Communities Have Rights?" 218.

8. Michael Hartney, "Some Confusions Concerning Collective Rights," *Canadian Journal of Law and Jurisprudence* 4, no. 2 (July 1991), 305.

9. I have argued this in "Democracy and Economic Rights," *Social Philosophy and Policy* 9, no. 1 (1992), 29-61.

10. This paragraph was motivated by a discussion with Michael McDonald.

Chapter 14

The Drug Laws

More Nails in the Coffin of American Liberalism

Introduction: The War on Drugs

The drug law situation in North America, and to a considerable extent elsewhere, constitutes a topic that it is difficult to discuss dispassionately. The reach of those laws has been expanded and their means of enforcement intensified over many years, culminating in a period in the late 1980s that has become known as the "War on Drugs." The result of all this activity is probably well known to most readers of this chapter. The prison population of the United States today is, I understand, the highest in the world in relation to population, with close to 1 percent of the entire population behind bars—and even that figure is kept artificially low by the capacity of the prison system; most American prisons are desperately overcrowded already, almost all of its judicial systems are under such pressure that over 90 percent of arrests are now settled by plea bargaining instead of trials, and a very high percentage of arrests lead to no imprisonment at all, or to much reduced sentences relative to what the law would normally call for. All of·this tremendous increase in prison populations and law enforcement is a direct or indirect result of the drug laws. Conservatively, well over one million people are in prison right now either because they have been caught possessing or selling drugs, or for crimes committed in the course of attempting to obtain or supply them. The total number of arrests for drug law violations, we are told, was 1,126,300 in 1993, up from 1,066,400 in 1992. According to the Federal Justice Statistics Program, the average incarceration sentence length imposed on Federal drug offenders increased from 47 months in 1980 to 82 months in 1992. And the amount of taxed money spent on drug control programs increased from $1.5 billion in fiscal year 1981 to $13.3 billion in fiscal year 1995.[1]

It should be a matter of astonishment that in America, the supposed bastion of liberalism, there is an enormous prison population of persons who are guilty of no crime of violence against their fellows. In the course of this chapter,

I shall suggest that there is nothing astonishing about it—but plenty to deplore.

There is said to be a good deal of earnest discussion of the drug laws, and a few public figures have made a splash by suggesting that perhaps they should be considerably modified. But no elected or appointed officials have gone so far as to suggest that they should be dropped altogether. That position is reserved for cloistered academics such as myself—people who have little to lose by communicating radical views to their fellow eggheads.

Nevertheless, that is the position I will be taking in this chapter. I will not merely be "taking" that position, though; I will argue for it. I thus engage in an extremely old-fashioned project: trying to defend a concrete social policy or measure on the basis of general, abstract considerations that are claimed to be rationally compelling. America is of all places in the world the country whose political legacy should incline it to listen sympathetically to arguments such as the one I will give. Despite this, my arguments are based on premises that have nothing particularly modern about them, going back, as they do, to Aquinas and Hobbes.

Failure

Though the fundamental argument is abstract, the facts about drug enforcement and drug use are plain enough. On any remotely rational appraisal, what they tell us is that the war on drugs, in general and in particular, is a failure. The consequences of making drugs illegal so enormously outweigh any relevantly evil consequences of leaving the decision whether to take them up to the individual people for whose welfare our governments supposedly exist that it is difficult to see what there is left to argue about, no matter what you think of drug taking. This should surprise few: we've been through it all before in the prohibition era, during which thousands of people were killed and many more imprisoned due to the laws against alcohol production, distribution, and consumption, and yet the gross consumption of alcohol apparently increased. It is a moot point whether the gross consumption of all drugs has increased in very recent years, but there is no question that during the entire era of drug prohibition it has increased enormously. And in any case, one does not pronounce a pogrom against the performance of activity X to be legitimate by noting that the pogrom has in fact reduced performance of X.

I will argue in this chapter that there is no justification for the drug laws, and an enormous weight of reasons against them. Indeed, I find it difficult to see how anyone could contemplate the statistics cited at the outset and yet say, with a straight face, that there is any serious room for questioning the absurdity and evil of these laws. On the empirical front, it is hard to see how it could be more obvious that the War on Drugs is a dismal failure—at least, if it was supposed actually to be aimed at "defeating" drugs. And on the conceptual front, which is the only fundamental arena in which to defend them, I shall be pointing out that to engage in drug prohibition is to deny virtually every basic tenet of liberalism. Americans have wrung their hands about dropping the atomic bomb on Japan, about getting involved in Vietnam, and many other things. (One may be forgiven for mentioning abortions and alcohol—both of which were also forbidden by law with hugely evil consequences.) The evils resulting directly or indirectly from the drugs laws approximate those of Vietnam and the atomic bomb to date, but public hand-wringing about these evils seems to be virtually nil. Wars on other people, it seems, are cause for impassioned complaint, but wars against our own citizens are no problem. This ought to be regarded as an outrageous attitude even if it weren't absurd on top of it.

What Is Law For?

But I am a philosopher, not a politician, and my main interest is in getting at the truth about the morality of law. My question is whether our governments should be doing the sort of things they have been doing in regard to the taking of drugs. This of course raises the most basic question: what should governments be doing at all—if anything? It has become fashionable to suppose that this is an extremely deep question, inherently insoluble and thus forever disputable; and this because the relevant concepts, such as justice, are, to use a current buzzword, "essentially contestable."

Frankly, I think that is an evasion. The most fundamental principles of decent government are fairly obvious and readily demonstrable to the ordinary intellect. The problem is not what governments ought to be doing, but why they aren't doing it very well, and why they are doing so many other things instead—whether, indeed, they are inherently capable of doing what they ought to be doing at all. The drug laws are, for this purpose, a locus classicus. I shall proceed first, then, to the argument for my "radical," though perfectly mundane conclusion, that the proper business of government—if it has any proper business—is advancement of the common good of its people, as *those people themselves* see that good.

Liberalism

Let's first talk about the State. States, especially the modern state, and above all, the particular modern states that you and I live in, are very special entities. They are not clubs, or even neighborhood associations, nor are they supermarkets. The societies they govern are very large collections of people who live in various particular, quite sizable, geographic areas. A lot of those people were born there, and those who moved there from elsewhere did so for quite a diverse range of reasons. Taking the expression literally, these people have very little in common. Unlike the chess club or the local branch of the Seventh Day Adventists, they did not come together for some specific purpose. They do all hope to live well, and as well as possible. But they do not share a common view about what "living well" consists in or how to attain it. They differ enormously in things like religion, education, "culture," and interests both large and small, as well as in other respects such as height, skin color, personality, and many more. Yet here they all are, jostling together, encountering one another in streets, marketplaces, parks, workplaces, and more indirectly via TV sets or on the pages of newspapers. One might put it this way, without serious exaggeration: if there's one thing they have in common, it's difference.

Some differences matter more than others, of course. What is particularly important about the diversity we encounter among persons is that they each have their own sets of values, on the basis of which they judge both themselves and others' actions. And so, if somebody proposes some value as appropriate for ordering the public, it is always appropriate, in this context, to ask: "According to whom?" And then, "Why does that person get to tell us all what to do?"

Turn now to the agencies known as "governments." These have a distinctive feature: they are, whenever they deem it necessary, armed, and they claim a right to be so, and to be able to use these arms to enforce uniformities—laws—applying to the set of citizens over which they claim jurisdiction.

Some will no doubt insist that this is too weak: they will say that governments not only *claim* this right but that they actually *have* it. But to say that is to go beyond the surface facts of the matter. It is obvious that governments claim to have authority; but, if it is true, it must be shown that their claims are correct. Even the word 'authority' contains enough ambiguity to make the point. Is authority something that governments just simply do have, as if it were a matter of fact, demonstrated by such facts as that a great many people *think* they do and concede it, and that it says they have it on various documents? Or is it something more open to question, something you have to earn on the basis of some general, normative criteria that might not actually be met very well, or at all? And does the failure to live up to those criteria imply that their claimed authority is nonexistent or at least in question?

The answer to this last question, though, is surely beyond serious dispute. Everyone—certainly everyone likely to read this chapter—is ready to point to certain historic cases of evil governments, such as the Nazi regime in World War II Germany. And we all accept that even supposedly decent governments sometimes make unjust laws, laws that should never have been made. We even think that there are some laws made by our own governments that we, the citizens, ought not to comply with if we can possibly help it. And you probably hold many laws in contempt in practice, whatever you say if quoted in the newspapers. You probably sometimes walk across a street against a red light; if you are like most people, you probably exceed the speed limit a bit in your cars and think nothing of doing so. If you exceed it quite a lot, you probably are quite conscious of doing so—in the sense of devoting considerable attention to the question of whether there are police around who might give you trouble for it. But you likely lose no sleep over the question whether what you are doing is morally permissible. If you are any of the above people—and statistically, almost all of you are—then you are the people I want to talk to. For you agree that the question of what governments should be doing is discussable, and that sometimes what they do isn't what they should be doing. Fascism as a political philosophy is, I trust, dead, at least among serious thinkers.

Well, what should governments be doing? What should they be doing, that is, in light of the fact that a political society is not like the chess club, or your local church? The chess club is easy: we are all in it to promote the playing of chess, we all have a clear idea of what people who play chess are trying to do, and so the policies of the chess club make sense to us or, if not, the criteria of criticism relevant to them are very clear indeed. But governments aren't chess clubs; indeed, they aren't clubs at all. Membership in the United States or Canada is not a function of having paid your dues and joined with a bunch of others in the common pursuit of some defining purpose. It is, rather, living in a certain geographic area and hoping to live a good life there, a better one, if possible, than what you could manage by moving to any other area you might live in instead. This you do by exerting yourself on behalf of that end. You aren't alone; there are lots of other people also attempting to do well, *none* of whom have exactly your profile of aims.

When you think about it, most of them don't have even approximately that profile. Some people, for example, might well have the idea that being "high" is a major part of the good life. Others, such as myself—boringly "straight" on matters like this—are probably quite unable to understand what you see in it; just as we likewise do not understand what you see in your religion of choice, or your preference for calamari, or your taste in spouses, or the music of The Rolling Stones. Nevertheless, here we are, and what are we going to do? In particular, at what point, if any, are we going to resort to force against our neighbors? When do we sic the cops on them? (And when do we allow that they can sic them on *us*?)

There is an answer to this which, I suggest, is the liberal answer, and moreover, the right answer. To get at this, I first have a look at a (the?) classic view about Law.

Law

St. Thomas Aquinas, monk of the Roman Catholic Church and (despite that disadvantage, as we non-religious types are inclined to put it) great philosopher, long ago formulated an analysis of the idea of Law which, so far as I can see, is right on the beam. A law, said he, is an "ordinance of reason [enforceable by punishments] for the common good, promulgated by the whole community or, on its behalf, by him who has care of the community."[2] Most of the features on St. Thomas's list are pretty obvious. Law is intended to apply to the whole community over which it has authority, and is legislated and promulgated by a government which claims to represent, and at least to apply to, the community. But two need special comment. One is that a law has to be rational, reasonable. Some laws pretty obviously are not, such as the famous one in nineteenth-century Tennessee decreeing that the value of pi would henceforth be exactly 3 1/7. Nevertheless, it is surely correct to say that if a law is unreasonable, that is a relevant criticism of it. Of course, that brings up the question what makes a law reasonable, and that brings us directly to the other, closely related, subject, namely, the specification of the purpose of law: to promote the *common* good.

The Common Good

Laws make a claim to be reasonable, and that relates, I think, to one central, essential component: that laws are for the common good of the community to which they apply. Aquinas has a special view of the the good of the community, stemming from his religious commitments. He did not realize the incipient liberalism in his analysis, but he had the right tiger by the tail. What he was right about is that the common good of the whole community is the standard by which any legislated law, and more generally any act whatsoever of persons purporting to be acting in the capacity of "ruler" of a community, is to be judged.

Well, why is it? There's a simple answer. Law asks all of us to obey, and in obeying, to do things that we may not like doing. It had better give us a reason for doing so, if it is to maintain its claim to "authority." But that reason had better be a reason *for me* to obey. The fact that a law benefits somebody else is something about which I can't be expected to be terribly concerned. But if law benefits us *all*, it promotes the common good, because that's what we mean by the "common good," and so if something affects the common good, then it *does* matter to you, whoever you are, because you are one of the people affected by any such thing. Every individual has at least *an* interest in the common good—though, to be sure, that interest may very well not seem to him to outweigh the sum of his other interests on this or that occasion.

There are three points to take very seriously regarding this very sensible requirement.

First: the good to be sought is that of the community, and *not* that of the ruler or rulers, a point about which St. Thomas is delightfully clear. In fact, the essence of bad rule is precisely rule that aims at the advancement of the ruler rather than that of the people. Good government, by contrast, is government in the interests of the governed. Period. What this means is that if the operation of government should in any way redound to the interest of those who govern, that can be justified only by showing that the advantage in question is necessary for the promotion of the good of the *ruled*. Of course, the good it happens to do for the ruler may come to him not in virtue of his being the ruler, but rather insofar as he is a fellow member of the community, like the rest of us. Rulers, in other words, can only be benefited by the function of ruling insofar as that benefit comes under another hat, the same hat we all wear: just folks, trying to do the best we can. Of course this suggests a problem: in assessing his own interest, the citizen who happens also to be a ruler may easily confound the two—the special interests that he can satisfy only by his exercise of the power to rule, and his interests as a mere citizen, also satisfiable by proper exercise of the power to rule, but as such satisfiable by whoever rules, whether it be someone else or himself.

This observation is of particular importance when we contemplate the subject of *interpersonal power*—the capability of getting others to do what one wants by exercising coercion over them. Power is one of the notorious objects of desire of many people, for reasons that are understandable enough. To secure our future good, says Hobbes, we engage in a "perpetual and restless desire of Power after power, that ceaseth only in Death."[3] Persons in ruling positions have powers that the rest of us do not, and one of the inevitable temptations of office is to protect and enhance one's own power, irrespective of its tendency to promote the good of those being ruled. Yet such power is, strictly, a trust from *us*—it's not the property of the power-holder to do as he pleases with. No challenge to the designer of constitutions is more difficult or more important than that of curbing these desires, harnessing political ambition to the public good. The drug laws, I shall be suggesting, are perhaps today's number one case in point.

Second: what is good and bad is commonly, and plausibly, thought by reflective people to be quite variable and subjective; and we all, including the unreflective, are accustomed to encountering disagreement when we make value judgments on various matters. Those disagreements are notoriously difficult to resolve, in a great many cases. Indeed, it is still by no means clear that there is any way genuinely to resolve many of them, and there is no reasonable alternative to regarding many disputes about values as matters of taste, about which, as the old maxim has it, there is "no disputing."

We should modify that: there is plenty of disputing, of course, but the point is that there is no *reasonable* dispute—that is, no *publicly compelling* set of considerations that simply decide the issue by invoking rational criteria obvious to all. Disputes are always being "settled," of course, to the satisfaction of one party, by criteria that the other party doesn't accept. But that isn't quite what we should have in mind by the term 'settle'. Any such settlement cannot count as rational; it is imposed, and the deciding factor in the settlement is simply the power of the party able to do the imposing.

Third: it is also perfectly clear that people will, because they must in the end, be guided by their *own* sense of values. The rational person tries to do the best he can, as he sees that "best"—not as someone else sees it, unless he should judge, for reasons of his own, that that other person's judgment may be superior to his in the case at hand. At some level, the idea of being literally ruled by someone else doesn't make any sense. Insofar as it does, it's because person A *decides* to take orders from person B. Rational action is action to do your best by what *you* see to be the appropriate criteria of valuation.

If we take these three points seriously and accept the central idea of the Thomistic proposal, then we will see, I suggest, that they commit us to *political liberalism*. Liberalism is the view (a) that government should, as Aquinas's formula specified, be used exclusively for the benefit of the governed, *and* (b)—what was not seen by Aquinas, no doubt because of his commitments to Catholicism—that the assessment of benefit is fundamentally to be made by those very people themselves. Each person is to be regarded as being the ultimate authority on what is good for himself. To govern well, then, is to govern in a manner conducive to the good of all those governed, as understood by each person in the whole group—not as understood by their leaders, or the majority, or your particular club or faction.

Legal Positivism?

Legal philosophy over the past many decades has been very much preoccupied with the question whether law is to be defined my (that is, Aquinas's) sort of way, or whether a "neutral" definition, incorporating no normative criteria at all, should be employed. As the use of such phrases as 'bad law' suggests, there is an obvious need for such a "neutral" definition. Why, then, should we bother with normative characterizations at all?

The short answer is that if you have no notion of what the law is for, then the belief that law *should*, nevertheless, be *enforced*, is nonsensical. It would be like arguing that since guns are excellent for killing people, we should therefore approve of killing people. Yet definitions of law, no matter how neutral, are invariably proposed by those who think that putting people in jail, and the like, for "disobeying" those laws is—as Aquinas noted—*part of the idea*. Legal Positivism, which is the doctrine that law is essentially definable without essential use of any normative notions, almost inevitably is accompanied by legal Conservatism—the view that law *as such* ought to be enforced by authorities and obeyed by citizens.

On my more reasonable view, whether a law should be obeyed or enforced depends entirely on its merits—which of course is a normative notion. Those who wish to maintain that it "should" be obeyed and enforced in the absence of any merits whatever are, so far as I can see, espousing a nonsense position. Those who think that maybe law had better have some merit must then face up to the question of just what "merit," in the case of things like law, might consist in. And in particular, whether there must not be merits that are centrally connected with the function of law in a community; in which case, they will find themselves driven back to Aquinas's idea, like it or not.

When it comes to normative legal philosophy, in short, Legal Positivism is either a cop-out or a semantically buttressed version of fascism.

Peace

Given this, a serious problem looms: under the circumstances, how *can* there be any such thing as a "common good" for law to try to promote? A serious question indeed, and probably as much as anything thought to be the major stumbling block for "natural law" theories of law, and for that matter for liberalism. But those who stumble before this challenge do so because they have looked in the wrong direction. There is indeed an answer to it, and a conclusive one.

In a way, Aquinas's definition biases us a bit in the wrong direction, prompting us to look for some "positive" good, beneath the surface of people's desires—chocolate (or maybe vanilla? or Catholicism?) for all! Trouble is, some are allergic to chocolate (or Catholicism), and others just don't like it. However, if we think about it a bit more, we soon see a plausible glimmer of light in another direction. Of course there is no common good, if by this you insist on meaning Chocolate for All. Nevertheless, there is a common evil, an evil that is peculiar to communities, and peculiarly a function of what is in fact common to people: namely, *interpersonal violence*. All of us are inherently susceptible to damage at the hands of our fellows, and this is damage reckoned in terms of our own pursuits of our own interests, for it diminishes or altogether stops such pursuits.

The absence of interpersonal violence is peace, and the common good, accordingly, is *peace*—as Aquinas himself noted, but as Thomas Hobbes later brought to the center of the discussion. "Seek peace, and follow it," says Hobbes, adding that if you can't get it, then you are entitled to use "all the helps and advantages of War."[4] In what way is peace a "common" good? That is: how is it "common," and why think it a "good"? There are clear answers to both. What makes peace a good is that you are now free to exert yourself, to spend your time and energy doing what you think best. Peace won't get you those things, to be sure—it merely allows you to try to get them. (But maybe you can only get them by war? We'll discuss that in a moment.) However, if you aren't at peace—if people are busy trying to kill you, say—then you won't be able to get any of those other things done, and if, as there's an uncomfortably good chance will be the case, they actually succeed in killing you, then you won't even be able to pursue war, let alone any other good, any further. Peace can reasonably be equated with life, actually. And it can also be aligned with prosperity.[5] People at peace spend their time bettering their situations, and in the process are motivated, in nearly all cases, to co-operate with selected others in doing so; this leads, characteristically, to an increase in prosperity—on terms set by each for her own case. Such co-operation, again, presupposes peace, at least among the co-operators.

What about the "commonness" of peace? Note that if A is at peace with B, then B is at peace with A. There is no way to have unilateral peace: peace is a situation obtaining between two or more persons, and it takes both to instantiate it. However, this is understating the matter. The philosophical interest of peace is that, prima facie, it makes both of the peaceful parties better off than either will be if they instead resort to war. That is an important and substantial claim. It is also a very plausible one. And it is also our only hope. It is why governments are morally required to prefer peace to war. That in turn stems from their obligation to prefer policies on which all can agree to policies on which they necessarily cannot—for example, policies that presuppose or declare that some people are inherently superior to others. Or, by the way—a subtler case of precisely the same thing—policies declaring or presupposing that they are all *equal* in respects in which they obviously may not be, which is the currently favored way of fostering community strife in what are claimed to be "liberal" communities.

I.e., Liberty

What all this suggests is another way of putting the fundamental common value of a community: freedom, or liberty. Socially speaking, to be free, or at liberty, to do x is for nobody to stop you doing x when you try. The formula for peace and that for liberty are basically identical: don't make war! Which is to say: don't aggress against others (unless they in turn are aggressing against yourself or yet others). More specifically, don't intervene in someone else's affairs without that person's say-so.

In order to be able to interpret either, we need, then, an understanding of what belongs to whom—a matter widely regarded as difficult and contentious. But it isn't so very hard to see either. To aggress on someone, to make war on that person, is to force him to do something other than what he is doing and prefers to do, in the status quo situation. The sum of what we prefer is, in effect, our life—*our* life, our own pattern of desired activity, as distinct from any other life there may be. What makes a pattern ours is simply that we do it, we choose it, in the absence of compulsion by others—though, of course, characteristically with a good deal of assistance and influence by selected others. (It is a peculiar modern conceit to suppose that if others influence you, then they ipso facto coerce you. That is a totally incoherent thought, when you think of it; it would deprive us of the power to agree with anyone about anything, for example.[6])

Thus, there are three cases to consider:

First, where we choose, prefer, and decide to act in a situation in which nobody else is around, nobody else is concerned, or at any rate, nobody else is affected either for better or worse (in, as is always understood hereinafter, their own view of what is better or worse).

Alternatively, there are some others "around," and we then have two sub-cases.

Second, where they don't mind, or positively welcome our activity.

Third, where our interests are such as to disrupt what others are trying to do, thus creating conflict, frustration, strife, damage, pain, and the like.

Liberalism disapproves of actions carrying out the third sort of interests. When, if ever, are such actions legitimate? That is the question of the justification of the State, whose actions inherently require some or all to do things they might prefer not to. And part of the answer is clear enough. We may, certainly, take actions that would otherwise be wrong in order to ward off the would-be depredations of others. Of course this requires that we be able to distinguish who is the aggressor and who is the defender.

Property

A further implication of the preceding is worth special note here. Consider those cases in which the pattern of activity of those we disrupt is established before we ever got on the scene. In such cases, as our analysis implies, newcomers who "invade and despoil," to use Hobbes's phrase, are in the wrong. Those who got there first have primacy in regard to the materials of their activity. It is this that especially leads to the idea of private property—that which particular people have the right to use without asking anyone else, and to use which others must have the assent of the owner.

The most perspicuous example of "getting there first" is one's native powers and equipment, such as our bodily (and, if different, psychological) parts—arms and legs, hearts and minds. We were, after all, born with these and they constitute *us*: it is logically impossible for anyone else to have "gotten there first." Nevertheless, there they are, and anyone else who proposes to make use of them contrary to the wishes of the person they constitute is an aggressor in the relevant sense. Your claim to yourself is founded on nothing more than the fact that you *are* yourself. But that, obviously, is enough—how, indeed, could there possibly be a better basis for regarding something as yours?

We bridge out to the external world from this natural beginning by, simply, using what we have and what we find. So, to respect someone else's activity, to take up a noninvasive stance, is to refrain from interfering with her use of whatever she happens to be using, and undertook use of, so long as she did so without thereby invading others.

Respect for personal liberty, therefore, leads straight to the basic idea of private property. Once we have property, the rules are simple: respect others' property rights! When you yourself acquire anything, you are to do it either by finding or inventing it yourself, or by making an arrangement with someone who has it—buy it, or persuade him to give it to you, for instance. But we get to the property idea in the first place by seeing the wisdom of peace, which commits us to refrain from forcibly undoing or blocking the activities of others, so long as those activities do not in their turn consist in invading and blocking others.

There is no other way, no coherent system for reconciling the pursuit of different interests that also recognizes no standard of appraising fundamental interests external to the person whose interests they are. If we don't respect people's property, we don't respect people. They may be, of course, and very often are, glad to share it with others, or to sell it, or to give it away to what they see to be worthy recipients. But with regard to those things, their word is law. Any other social principle guarantees war of one kind or another. Such as, we may as well add, the War on Drugs.

Why Liberty?

Critics often ask, "Why regard liberty as the ultimate value?" For example, Rasmussen and Benson, whose excellent book on the drug war is my source for much information on this matter, tell us that "the libertarian position that freedom is the ultimate value is not subject to debate; it is a belief that cannot be logically refuted."[7] If that were literally true, then liberty versus force would be in the same conceptual position as chocolate versus vanilla—you have to just take your pick, there being no basic reasons operating to influence choice in this area. But that account gets the reasons for liberty fundamentally wrong.

To begin with—literally, since nothing can be more fundamental than this point to our area of investigation—liberty in society is *not* an "ultimate value" at all; it is, rather, a necessary condition for doing anything. You do x, whatever x may be, only if nobody stops you from doing it. It is, indeed, the only basic "value" of a proper *political* constitution—the only properly basic political value, because the only one that is a common good; but it is so precisely because it itself is *not* a "basic value" of any individual person. Liberty (for oneself) is required no matter what one's basic values are; it is not hitched to any particular one or any particular subset of them.

Second: *of course*, then, the importance of liberty in society can be logically discussed, and if it is "irrefutable," that is only because the case for it is so strong—not because there can be no "case" from the nature of the subject. My argument above is an explanation, a genuine argument, explaining why liberty should have pride of place in the general community. There is nothing else that can appeal to everyone, but it appeals to everyone precisely because it is not an ultimate value. It's not chocolate versus vanilla all over again. Both the lovers of chocolate *and* the lovers of vanilla need liberty if they are to have any hope of pursuing and enjoying their different tastes in the great community, which contains people of all persuasions—not just lovers of chocolate and vanilla, but also of raspberry and banana, Shostakovich, tennis. And marijuana. Liberty is the only solution to the problem that we all have when we find ourselves crossing paths in the great community.

Illiberal Interests

Are there any particular sort of interests we simply must have in order to be at peace with each other? No; but there are certain motivational profiles, as we might call them, that you cannot have, profiles which militate against peace, and which therefore cannot be tolerated in a liberal community. The ones that make peace essentially impossible are those which are such that *in order to satisfy the defined desire, someone else must be dissatisfied in some respect*. Obvious examples are malice, hatred, rivalry, envy, jealousy, sadism, aggression, meddlesomeness, and in general the love of interpersonal coercive power. All these, and many more—the recognized social vices, generally speaking—have the important feature that they defeat the common good, so far as they go.

Therefore, no proper law can be accepted whose object is to promote one or some few or however many persons' interests *at the expense of others*. To do so is to promote the good for one or some citizens by promoting the bad for other(s). From the public point of view, indeed, the satisfaction of any of these profiles in my third category isn't a good at all: it is, rather, an evil, tending to the defeat of the public good. No law may cater to the tastes of some people at the expense of the rest—to advance the good of some by imposing costs on others. No law may decree that The Good is chocolate and not vanilla, or that the citizen shall acknowledge Vishnu rather than Allah, or Allah rather than Jehovah, or any god rather than none.

Liberal Goods

There are, on the other hand, innumerable goods that have the highly attractive feature that they may be secured for one or more persons without thereby adversely affecting anyone else. These we may call the "liberal" goods: liberal, because they are goods acknowledged to be such by the persons whose goods they are, *and* because they are compatible with the public peace, maintenance and promotion of which, on the liberal view, is the sole rationally acceptable purpose of political agencies. The "liberal" view is, simply, everybody's view.

Having said this, we now have a potential problem. We must distinguish, namely, between two sorts of claims about types of goods along the lines we have just been pursuing. On the one hand, we may talk about a certain sort of good "as such"—what's true of it insofar as it is of the kind in question. Pleasure, for instance, is a subjective entity: it takes place in the experience of a given person, and there is no logical connection between that person's experiencing it and anyone else's doing so. It is, indeed, a prime example of a "liberal good" in the sense just discussed. Yet it can easily enough happen that A's pleasure is got at the expense of B: some sources of pleasure for person A are such that the actions A undertakes in order to promote that pleasure are inherently at the expense of another: sadistic pleasures, for example, are so called because they are pleasures taken in another's pain.

Risk

But in other cases, the fact that the attainment of a good for A has imposed a cost on B is not inherent in the very idea of the good A tries to attain, but just a matter of fact, a foreseen or unforeseen effect of the effort to secure that good. For example, unbeknownst to A, his activities affect the atmosphere, say, or create a risk for some people. These side effects are called "externalities" (more precisely, "negative externalities"—for of course actions can and often do have positive externalities, side effects on others welcomed by those others; but positive externalities are, obviously, not a problem here), because they are external to the doings of the parties to the transactions in question. In principle, the way you handle these is clear enough: find the set of people thus affected, and negotiate a suitable set of compensations or restrictions so that the results are mutually acceptable to all concerned. Once this is done, those actions too are rendered consistent with the common good.

In some other cases, though, the claim will be that if A does x, which is innocent enough taken by itself, yet as a result A will be more likely to do y, which is not. You eat spinach, and lo!—you are seized by the desire to punch people up. In cases like these, we have a problem. For many people who do x will not go out and do y. And even in the case of those who do, surely, there is the thought that they might try exercising some self-control. Instead of blaming the spinach, we might put our finger on the morals of the assaulter. The claim that it was the *spinach* that did it may be a cop-out. Insofar as the effects are foreseeable, indeed, it certainly is. Taking responsibility for our own actions is a fundamental category: to act is to choose, and to have a morality is to have an idea which things are to be chosen and which not. Choices are ours, not someone else's. Knowing what he does, the responsible person will refrain from taking spinach, since punching people up is plainly the sort of thing that a liberal community can and must rule out. What we penalize this aggressor for is not the taking of spinach, but the punching up of peaceable citizens.

Liberty, Risk, and Compensation

Suppose that doing X brings with it a probability of p that some negative effect, E, on someone else will ensue. May we then, irrespective of the particular *value* of p, declare x to be illegal? We may not. Insofar as we make x illegal, we declare war on the doers of x: we impose a cost on those who do x. Whenever x does *not* produce E, imposition of this cost is wrongful, and justice requires that any such costs not be imposed; if they are, compensation is in order to those upon whom they are imposed. If the cost imposed on some is equal to or less than the cost of the expected disutility of E to others, then is it justified? Indeed not. We may not deal with evils to Jones by incarcerating Smith. In that case, the law, insofar as it punishes people for doing x as such, is in the wrong. Law is said to be a blunt instrument, and indeed it is. But blunt instruments, because they are blunt, need to be aimed with precision; neither the law nor anyone else may just go bashing about, as the wielders please. Moreover, it is quite possible to impose the penalties only for E itself: when persons do X and E does in fact ensue, then X's perpetrator owes compensation to the victim(s) of E. This might well be covered by, say, an insurance policy.

In any case, there is a responsibility upon the authorities to analyze X, with a view to seeing whether it is really X, as such, that carries the risk of E, or only some subcategories of X. Drivers who have travelled hundreds of thousands of miles at speeds well in excess of the posted limits, yet have caused no accidents in which any other persons were injured, cannot plausibly be thought to be imposing, by their driving, significant risk on others. Speeding fines and threats to suspend driver privileges on public highways, when imposed on such persons, are simply unjustified; public authorities enforcing speed limits in such cases are not promoting the public good of safety, but rather the nonpublic good of seeing to it that others drive at certain speeds rather than others—in short, imposing chocolate on some who prefer vanilla. Likewise with all other regulations and laws imposing costs on persons for doing what, in the actual circumstances in which they do it in the particular case in question, does not in fact inflict significant risks on others, even though in some *other* circumstances it might.

Despite the technical-sounding exposition of the above point, this is no fussy little exercise in abstract theory. I suggest, in fact, that no single source of modern tyranny exceeds this one in today's erstwhile liberal democracies.

Fraudulent Externalities

We have an externality of a type relevant to liberal government and eligible for controlling measures when someone's pursuit of a liberal good has a side effect that blocks someone else's pursuit of some liberal good. I play the trumpet, which I enjoy, and you in the apartment next door hear it through the thin walls, thus destroying the quiet, which you enjoy. Owing to the laws of nature and the circumstances, we can't both achieve, at the time, our respective goods, despite the fact that both are inherently perfectly OK. We must find a solution that respects the rights of both: a "hardware" solution, such as a soundproof wall, paid for mainly by the one who makes the noise; or a "software" solution in which we coordinate schedules and practice times to minimize unwanted noise for you, and unwanted silence for me.

But now imagine that although I still play the trumpet, the walls are perfectly soundproof. However, you are annoyed at the sheer knowledge that I play it: you don't approve of playing the trumpet, or of my taste in music, or for that matter of the particular way in which I play the instrument. Is this, too, to be regarded as an 'externality'? No. Not, at any rate, in the sense in which externalities are a concern of the liberal. For now, the interest *you* profess is incompatible with *my* liberty. If you have views about what I should be doing, then if I do anything else, I of course dissatisfy this supposed interest of yours. Some who consider themselves liberal at this point propose that you sit down with your copy of the *Nichomachean Ethics* and acquire the proper knowledge of the Mean in regard to dealing with your neighbors. The supposedly bad effects I visit on you are only such because of your attitudes toward me, or toward people in general. In your view, they should all be doing such-and-such, even though it would be perfectly possible for some or all of them to do so-and-so with no disruption of the peace. And if they aren't, then—well, then what? The answer, in too many cases, is Kill 'em! Which brings us to the drug laws.

Drugs and Wars

Turning our attention, now, to the subject of our inquiry, where do drugs fit into the liberal scheme of things? The prima facie answer is easy to see. Drugs affect the user, essentially, and they do not essentially affect anyone else. Their essential effect on the user—the one on account of which they are called "drugs," and because of which they are sought after by those who seek them—is to put that individual into a certain state of mind, of feeling or sensation, known as "getting high." This feeling seems to be much enjoyed by many people, and in some cases it is not only enjoyed, but life can seem pretty miserable without it. So it goes. It is not difficult to think of other things with the same general profile. Love, for example. Or gourmet cuisine. Learning to contain our involvements so that they don't take over our lives, and to cope with their side effects, is part of the discipline of life for anyone, applying as much to the drugtaker as to anyone else.

A lot of us, encountering persons who are "on drugs" or reading about various cases, or perhaps even as a result of personal experience dabbling in them, conclude that the drug experience is one to avoid; but a lot of others come to quite the opposite conclusion. Perhaps us straight folks have it wrong: maybe we'd be better off with an occasional, or even a fairly frequent, high. Or perhaps the drug takers are wrong: they'd be better off drug-free. And then again, perhaps we are both right: for some people, drug-taking really is better, and for others it really is worse. In the nature of the case, if we were to enter into a discussion of the merits of these different relations to drugs, neither of us is likely to make very much headway with the other. At the most basic level, it's chocolate versus vanilla, and there's no accounting for tastes.

Tastes are, it seems to me, as nearly as anything can be, a matter of intrinsic values. The goodness of a certain experience, to the experiencer, is underivative, basic, self-evident. My claim that you'd be better off not taking drugs would be pretty high-handed, since I know nothing about the effect of drugs on myself, let alone their internal effects on you; whatever else, I certainly can't know better than you whether you *like* those effects.

If I insist, nevertheless, that you "are" better off, and propose to do something about it—especially if I propose to put you in jail to think it over or force you onto a "treatment" program to "free you" of this bad habit—then I am evidently setting myself up as an authority over you—presuming to be able to run your life better than you can yourself. That is the essence of illiberalism.

Perhaps you are not in fact very good at running your life, and you do need help. Perhaps we all do. It does not follow that the right place to get it from is the one appointed by the servants of a democratically elected government. We are allowed to choose our doctors, our priests, our confidantes, our psychiatrists. The idea that this is the proper work of Society, understood to imply that it is the proper work of a particular set of administrators politically selected in that society, has nothing to be said for it.

St. Thomas Aquinas thought it was perfectly all right to coerce heretics into abandoning their heresies. Nobody's perfect. It has taken a long time for today's liberal countries to embrace the only reasonable solution to the problem of conflicting religions, though that solution is remarkably simple: namely, to declare a *right* to freedom of religion. The question that arises here is how much longer and how many more lives will it take to embrace the similarly reasonable solution to the drug problem: namely, to establish freedom in this area as a *right*, something others may not take away from A just because they disagree with A about what makes a good life.

The Externalities

As I pointed out, the essential, or defining, characteristic of drug taking is its effects on the taker. But as previously observed, it is quite possible, nevertheless, for logically nonessential effects to go along with the essential ones. It is possible that drugs carry with them genuine externalities: perhaps taking drugs makes you tend to go out and shoot people, or rob banks or commit rape. Or maybe it adversely affects your driving. It is likely, I gather, to affect your efficiency at some jobs. But are these good grounds for prohibition of drugs? The short answer is no.

It would be difficult to deny that they *could* be. If everyone who took drugs were suddenly seized by an irresistible impulse to go out and rape people, we would certainly be reasonably tempted to make them illegal, and to suppose that this would be for the public good. But in that case, the proposed laws would be made on the basis of an empirical claim. It would only be justified if some such claim were literally true, for one thing—it's not enough that someone *claims* it's true—in particular, not enough that some official, especially some official in an agency with an interest in expanding its bureaucratic empire, makes that claim. And it's particularly suspicious if the person who makes that claim has a strong interest in its being accepted by the public. (In this particular case, by the way, the claim—that drugs invariably provoke violence—is obviously false. Millions of peaceable citizens take drugs frequently, without appreciable effect on their peaceability, except perhaps in the sense that they make them nearly somnolent.)

All such claims are empirical, and any that are put in unguarded form as flat generalizations are false, just like the one imagined in the preceding paragraph. At most a few people, if any, are affected in ways such as that one. That is not enough to prohibit anything that isn't already prohibited—murder, for example. Murder, indeed, is a very good example for the point being made here. Many murders have been committed in the name of one or another religion, but that is not sufficient to justify making religion, or those religions, illegal. We have to do a lot better than that. One can blame alcohol for very much more evil than all of the known drugs, I understand; yet prohibition of alcohol was attempted and, not surprisingly, failed. Those who commit murders and other wrongful acts under the influence of alcohol are certainly culpable, but they are culpable because of the wrongful acts, not merely because they have consumed alcoholic beverages.

The political climate of recent times—though it differs only in degree from that of earlier ones—seems to display the idea that if we can blame some evil, of whatever degree, on something, then it is worth *any* cost to prevent or control the latter. This is an outrageous and absurd idea. No rational person regards life like that. We take out insurance against major risks, but we are not willing to pay an unlimited amount for it. And the reason we aren't is, simply, that it *isn't worth it*. And when I propose to pay for my insurance by sticking a gun to my neighbor's head and making *him* pay, then I compound the absurdity with injustice.

Suppose that there is a one in ten thousand chance that if somebody takes some substance, that person will as a result do some evil he would not otherwise have done. In order to prevent this eventuality, we send 350 people to jail for five years. Suppose that those 350 would have committed no crimes whatever themselves, had they been left alone. What, then, is the net balance sheet? Someone's life is saved, and 350 lives have been seriously damaged or ruined. Now suppose, in addition, that among those 350, a dozen or so end up dead due to the kindliness of prison conditions, or from having gotten in the way of a bullet fired by some drug dealer in order to defend himself from the police or some other drug dealer, or fired by the police themselves who were aiming at some drug dealers, as they supposed: then the cost of saving that one life has also risen to include several lives.

That is exactly how things now stand, as far as I can see: several lost lives for every life we save, hundreds of lives damaged or ruined—and all for the sake of what? The answer, in the main, is this: we like chocolate and they like vanilla. The genuine violence spawned by the drug situation is almost entirely a function of the illegalization of drugs; what residual violence can be attributed directly to their effects is, of course, already illegal anyway, and drug takers who also are thereby stimulated to violence may and should be punished for the violence they do—leaving it to them to get the message that perhaps they had better think twice about taking drugs. But the millions of people who could and do take drugs without such effects are not sacrificial lambs that we should feel free to line up at the altar of a "war on drugs." Not, that is, if our governments are what they are thought to be: organizations devoted to serving the interests of the public, that is, of the people they rule over.

To be sure, wars have been fought for even worse reasons.

In voting for legislators who come up with laws like this, people suppose themselves to be defending themselves and people they hold dear from threats of some kind. What is the perceived threat in the case of drugs, and what causes them to think that such threats actually exist? To these questions there are two closely connected answers.

First, many people evidently suppose that drugs really do lead to behavior that would be seriously threatening. The image of the crazed drug taker raping one's daughter, crashing into one's car, stealing from the company till, and so on, holds many a mind in a vicelike grip, supplementing the basic aversion to a way of life one doesn't understand and doesn't approve of. In addition, one imagines one's own children being corrupted by drugs, becoming addicts, abandoning cherished values and losing the disposition to continue one's genetic line or the family business, or religion, and so on.

Second: the reason why these fears are present in the average mind in North America is because that mind has been *told*, day in and day out, by various officials, supplemented by willing popular media organs of the day, that these are serious problems.

If we want the truth about drugs, we cannot expect to get it by listening to law enforcement officials. After all, the war on drugs provides a good living for a lot of people. Not only is there the usual good level of pay and excellent job security that goes along with government employment, but you get to do awful things to people, and for doing them you get a pat on the head from your superior instead of the lengthy jail sentence that is the lot of the people you incarcerate—or would be the lot of any private individual who acted the same way. Indeed, the main addiction involved in the war on drugs is the addiction to power—power over hapless citizens, exercised by persons operating in an atmosphere of virtual license.[8]

Negative Effects of Drug Wars

The main objection to the drug wars is an objection in principle, and not a quibble about statistics or a disagreement about assorted empirical matters. The objection is that they are wars fought *in the wrong cause*, a cause that has no place in a society devoted to the common good. But it is instructive to see what the further effects are—further, that is to say, in addition to literally millions of imprisonments on what amount to arbitrary charges. Fortunately, we have the results of much research to fill us in. This is well summarized and synthesized in Rasmussen and Benson's work.[9] The most important single side effect of interest to us is one that runs diammetrically counter to one of the principal official motivations behind drug laws. The claim is that drugs promote violent crime, and so in order to control this, we must make drugs illegal and enforce those laws effectively. The facts are quite another matter. In the first place, the principal promotion of any violence due to drugs stems from the very fact that they are illegal. Were they legal, suppliers of drugs would have no need of guns to defend themselves from zealous law enforcers, nor to defend their "turf" from other dealers. As has often been noted, the number of liquor store dealers who die from shootouts with other liquor store dealers or with the police is somewhere around zero. In the Prohibition era, of course, it was quite another matter. The War on Drugs is the Prohibition era moved to a new time and context, except that the effort and expenditure involved is immensely greater, and the results even less impressive.[10]

There are other and more sinister unintended side effects. Benson and Rasmussen point out that the tremendous increase in arrests which result from the drug laws further overcrowds our already overcrowded prisons. Budgets don't permit building more prisons fast enough, and somebody has to go—that is, to be paroled early or just not incarcerated in the first place. And who do the "law enforcement" officials prefer for this purpose? Not those evil drug-takers, indeed. Instead, it is the truly violent criminals, the hardened ones, that get out early so as to let the druggies in. Moreover, the system is easy on young people who merely commit violent crimes and theft, and hard on ones who, it is claimed, set themselves down the road to crime by taking drugs.

> Juveniles . . . are very myopic. They consider only the immediate costs and benefits of actions. When they learn that there are no real costs associated with committing crimes—even when they are arrested—because as first-time and even multiple-time offenders they get off with no real punishment, they tend to focus only on the personal benefits of the crime.[11]

The result is an enormous increase in the rate of violent crime, while the nonviolent drug users take up the available prison space. "In fact, as a direct consequence of getting tough on drugs, scarce criminal justice resources have been diverted away from the control of non-drug property and violent crimes."[12] And besides, they're easier pickings. Why take chances trying to track down real criminals when you can round up nonviolent druggies instead?

The war on drugs makes life worse for everybody. Though it alleges that it is out to protect the public, what it does is to greatly increase the number of attacks on innocent persons by law enforcement officials themselves. These are crimes, indeed—but, since they are sanctioned by the law and committed by people with badges, they are accounted OK. And then it greatly increases the amount of genuine crime, violent crime, both by devoting law enforcement effort to catching potheads when it could instead be devoted to catching and punishment serious criminals, as well as by causing an enormous increase in the price of drugs, thus motivating the criminal entrepreneur to engage in this now high-profit, because high-risk, activity. This is a singular track record, certainly not equalled by the worst days of Prohibition.

There are special further twists to drug law enforcement. The law doesn't distinguish much between those with a teeny bit and those with several pounds; if it finds any at all, it can deprive people of their cars, yachts, etc., with virtually no recourse available, even if the owner is entirely innocent. It is easy for zealous law enforcement officials to plant evidence on unsuspecting citizens. Suspected persons may be strip-searched without warrant, and in familiar ways exposed to violence from police officers. And so on. In short, you, the ordinary citizen, are *less safe* because of the drug laws, whether you use drugs or not. You are more likely to be murdered by a hardened criminal let out of prison early because there isn't enough room to accommodate both him and the junkies; more likely to be caught in a cross-fire between police and drug dealers, or one drug dealer and another, more likely to have your house raided by officials owing to mistaken address, and immensely more likely to be the victim of some official with a grudge against you or an interest in increasing his arrest quota. Meanwhile, of course, you are paying for all this—to the tune of $200 per family on average last year. (I'm not inventing these figures.[13])

And just to top it off, the use of these drugs has not decreased, but by and large enormously increased after the onset of the drug laws and harsher enforcement of same. It is debated whether recent increases in severity reduced the number of users: are there now only 15 million, or are there still 30 million? In the nature of the case, things like that can't be known with precision. But there is no question but that the number of drug users in, say, the 1930s was trivial by comparison with the present figures.

Legalizing drugs would greatly reduce their price. Would it increase their use? That is rather a moot point. Evidence from European countries with more rational drug policies than ours suggests that usage would decrease in the longer run, and not much increase in the shorter one. There is a good reason for this. Drugs don't do much for most people, and they do some unwanted things. You are likely to be much less productive, and thus much less employable, if you take drugs very much. The picture of drugs as "addictive," which we are fed constantly by authorities, has less to it than in the case of alcohol—or workahol, for that matter; but in any case, this is all beside the point. For the objection to legalization of drugs, that it might result in more people taking them, obviously begs the fundamental question, which is: whose life is it? If we but allow the consequences of their actions to be borne *by the persons whose actions they are* we will then be able to see the difference responsibility will make. Indeed, it is not overly enthusiastic to suggest that the reason why we have a drug "problem" is almost entirely because drugs are illegal.

It is worth mentioning one further aspect of the subject, which no doubt is by far the foremost in many minds: what about kids? If drugs are totally legalized, won't children be able to get them? And are we not reasonable to try to protect them from this "scourge"? One fallacy in this is the assumption that drug laws do protect children. Does the reader seriously think that his or her teenager couldn't obtain drugs if they wanted to? The recent Academy Award winning movie *Traffic* depicted, effectively in part because so plausibly, the daughter of the top drug enforcement official getting high with her friends, frequently and without, it seems, serious fear of apprehension. It is illegal for persons under 21 or so to buy cigarettes or alcohol over the counter. What percentage of such children smoke and drink? There is no greater absurdity in contemporary policy studies than to suppose that X will cease because X is made illegal. If X is a bad thing for your kids, what you as a parent need to do is to show this to your children, and to show, most especially by your own example, that the thing to do is to refrain from X. Schools, boy scout troupes, and so on, can take effective means toward reducing the likelihood that their members take drugs. Making drugs illegal won't do it. What it will do, however, and for certain, is to bring enormous misery on a great many innocent people. Nobody has the right to try to protect his or her children by doing such things.

And why, in the end, are drugs illegal? Because some people think that everybody should prefer chocolate, and because some few people in positions of power find it in their interest, and within their power, to *make* them illegal. This has nothing to do with the only reasons for having government in the wider community. Wars do not do much for promoting peace, and wars on innocent people, such as the war on drugs, are a more salient case in point for this maxim than most wars on other countries.

How did America go from being a nation in which individual liberty was extolled above all else, and whose constitution appeared to enshrine this in the law, to a nation in which the government routinely takes the role of Supernanny, only with guns and prisons instead of finger smacks and withheld dessert? That is a fascinating question, no doubt. The point of this chapter is merely that it in fact has made that transition in the largest way, and to the ill of many millions of people.

But, gosh—think of all those exciting cops-and-robbers movies we have because of the drug laws! I admit I can't answer that one.

Notes

The essay was composed for a conference held at the State University of New York at Buffalo, 1995. It has not been previously published.

1. Figures are from *Crime in the United States: 1994, FBI Uniform Crime Reports* (Washington, D.C.: U.S. Government Printing Office, 1995), 216-17.

2. For the scholarly, it's found in *Summa Theologica*, sect. 90, x: The Essence of Law, 4th Article, William Baumgarth and Richard J. Regan, eds., *Saint Thomas Aquinas on Law, Morality and Politics* (Indianapolis: Hackett, 1988), 17.

3. Hobbes, *Leviathan* (New York: E. P. Dutton, Everyman Library, 1950), 79.

4. Again for the scholarly, that is his First Law of Nature, developed and stated

in *Leviathan,* chapter 14 (New York: E. P. Dutton, Everyman Library, 1950), 106-18 . Significantly, Hobbes argues that this is the origin of all the other laws, too.

5. Aquinas, sharp observer that he was, also listed prosperity as another of the great objects for rulers to pursue. See *On Kingship,* in Paul E. Sigmund, ed., *St. Thomas Aquinas on Politics and Ethics* (New York: Norton, 1988), 29.

6. No contemporary discussion of the difference between threats and offers, coercion and assistance, is more penetrating, to my knowledge, than the work of Michael Rhodes, currently found in his Ph.D. dissertation for SUNY, Buffalo, under the title, "A Nonevaluative Analysis of Coercion" (1994). Dr. Rhodes summarizes his analysis in "The Nature of Coercion," Jan Narveson and Susan Dimock, eds., *Liberalism: New Essays on Liberal Themes* (Dordrecht, Netherlands: Kluwer Academic Publishers, 2000), 221-33.

7. David W. Rasmussen and Bruce L. Benson, *The Economic Anatomy of a Drug War* (Lanham, Md.: Rowman & Littlefield, 1994).

8. A balanced collection is found in Rod L. Evans and Irwin M. Berent, eds., *Drug Legalization: For and Against* (La Salle, Ill.: Open Court, 1992). The bias, however, of the supporters of drug laws is unmistakable: all of them take it that the fact, if it is one, that those laws do or would reduce the incidence of drug use is a sufficient justification of those efforts. If, as here, you deny this, it is hard to see how there can be anything to be said for the War on Drugs.

9. *The Economic Anatomy of a Drug War.*

10. See Mark H. Moore, "Actually, Prohibition Was a Success," Evans and Berent, 95-98. The reduction of alcohol use during prohibition was considerable, but hardly sensational; in the case of "hard" drugs, it is very difficult to believe that their use is not far more widespread now than it would have been had it never been illegal.

11. *The Economic Anatomy of a Drug War,* 204.

12. *The Economic Anatomy of a Drug War,* 205.

13. $14 billion/250 million x 4 (average family).

Chapter 15

Children and Rights

The Point of View of This Essay

Let's begin by laying some theoretical cards on the table. Contemporary moral philosophy in applied areas such as this is typically expounded in intuitionistic terms. This or that principle is appealed to on the ground that it sounds good. Why we should accept it is not considered a useful subject for discussion. I have long rejected intuitionism, especially as a device for solving problems. It is perhaps a device for stating them, yes. But until we know why a given principle should be accepted, we aren't much better off than if we hadn't bothered with it at all. And we may be worse off, for we may then think we know when we do not.

I know of only one general approach to moral theory that is fully non-intuitionist—full-blooded Hobbesian contractarian theory. The principles of morals, according to this view, are what amount to rational, or reasonable, agreements, made by the people whose behavior is to be directed by those principles. Moreover, the sense in which they are rational is not some cooked-up moralized sense. It is, simply, that the output of a course of deliberation that is rational is that the selected course of action has the best chance of realizing values actually held by the agent. Those values, of course, need not be and in the first instance cannot be "moral" values. Morality is an output, and what makes it rational is the same as what makes any action or decision rational: it best fills the bill specified by one's general set of values, *whatever they are.* 'Whatever they are' is very strong stuff. What do we do about the preferences of the sadist, for example? There is an easy answer. It is probably too easy, but it will do. The preferences of the sadist, like any other preferences, motivate certain kinds of actions. Those actions would have effects on others which are what motivate the others to get into this moral philosophy game in the first place. And what they motivate those others to do is, of course, object.

Now, the rational social contract is agreement from rational consideration of options. The sadist's option leads to war, to put it somewhat dramatically. Wars are counterproductive for all parties. Nobody wins a war. (Real wars are sometimes won; this is to say that one of the parties comes out comparatively less badly off than the other. My point is that both could do better; wars always accomplish less than could be achieved in some other way.)

The Specialness of Children for Ethics

However, children raise a special problem—*very* special. For the "social contract" is among moral agents, and very young children are not moral agents. The rights of nonagents ("moral patients," we may call them) are a function of agreements *among agents*. We agents must consider *our* interests when we ask whether some proposed patient should be regarded as having moral rights, or something of the kind. If the patient is also an agent, of course, she will consider the situation from the perspective of her own interests, as well, including how she will interact with others, and vice versa. But if the patient is not also an agent, there is no a priori reason why other agents should consider things from the point of view of that patient's interests. Agents interact with other agents; but with patients, they only act. Or rather, agents may indeed be affected by patients, and often are. But affection is just that. It is a matter of contingent fact whether a given patient affects a given agent, and how. And it is, in the present case, not just logical contingency. People are in fact affected very differently by different patients. Down through the ages, adults have slaughtered infants, abandoned them, occasionally eaten them, and certainly neglected or ignored them. It is not obvious, to put it mildly, that all adults love all children.

Upholders of children's rights may think they reject this, or may even in fact reject it. But rejection is useless. "We *know* what you believe," say those who don't share their views—"now, pray tell me why should *I* agree with it?" A familiar answer to this, indeed, the only answer we usually in effect get, is this: "because *my* side is accepted by the majority, and *we* can beat you up!" If it is thought that children don't get "enough" rights by some, perhaps they should ponder the implications of majoritarianism in ethics. And then, perhaps, they will get serious and try to find some real answers to the questions we are investigating here.

Children and the Public Good

What is the common, or public, good as it emerges from contractarian theory? There is a ready and plausible answer: it is the Paretian-constrained web, or collage, of private good. We people generally should allow any good realized by anybody that is not got at the expense of any other moral agent. People, in short, should be free to promote their own goods, as they see them, except only insofar as such promotion entails the frustration of others, pursuing their own and often different goods.

Another way to put it is also Hobbesian: that the common good is, in general, peace. I don't hit you, you don't hit me. I don't impose on you, you don't impose on me. No one, indeed, imposes on anyone: all human relations are to be such as are agreed to by all concerned, given their interests, abilities, and situations. In the special case of relations between one person and the family of another, we need to remember that the bond between typical parents and their own children is very strong. One way to hit someone, in the relevant sense, is to attack her children. To damage a child is to damage the interests of its parent, and the aggressor will have the parent to answer for it.

Prior to their becoming moral agents themselves, with interests to be considered in their own right, children are, prima facie, the "property" of their parents, insofar as they are anybody's. But this may make it sound as though parents may do absolutely as they like with their children. However, the impression is wrong. There isn't any property that owners may do *absolutely* as they like with, for they must always respect the rights of others.

Should we say that children aren't anybody's? I think not, though of course the answer that they are is risky. Being nobody's suggests one or the other of two things. It may suggest having no connections, no rights, no status. Or it may suggest being just another human being, with the usual rights of adults. Neither is very satisfactory, on reflection. A child to whom no one has any duties or special responsibilities seems likely to be soon a goner—unless, of course, he has parents or parental figures near to hand who have a loving concern for him.

There would seem to be the following possibilities in this regard:

(1) Children belong to society at large. Their direction is to be overseen by social agencies, the Central Committee for Children.

(2) Children should be under the special direction of someone, but that someone is The Best Person for the Job—by some criterion other than that of being its parents.

(3) Children should be under the special direction of their parents. (And where there are none? In the case where the child has been abandoned, or his parents are dead, then next-of-kin have first refusals, and after that, the first persons who want the child enough to bring it up, or perhaps the ones who bid the most for the right to direct it, etc. The latter idea segues into idea [2] above.)

I think that (3) is the correct view; it is also the de facto normal procedure, to be sure, but that isn't why it's right. What's right about it is, first, that views of the first type are illusory, and basically fraudulent. And, second, that the arrangement has several powerful things going for it that are hardly capturable in any other way.

In the standard case where the child does have parents and those parents intentionally brought the child into existence, the overwhelming argument for recognizing those parents as having the right to the direction and overseeing of those children is the same as the argument for recognizing any producer of a good as the owner of that good: it exists because that person exerted himself to bring the thing into being, and did it for reasons which will be frustrated if it is taken from him. Not so to recognize his rights in this regard creates a disincentive to that kind of creative activity. That is what is wrong with the socialist outlook in general: production is by individuals, though usually acting in concert with others, by various voluntary arrangements, and the producer does it for reasons of his own, reasons which a general public or a social institution have no business second-guessing.

Then there is the fraudulence hinted at in (1). A social decision-making system will stick the child with what amounts to another set of parents, this time ones who are very likely to be worse than the originals, especially because they lack the motivation (namely, parental love) that holds in the standard case. I call this 'fraud' because the socialist view sounds as though it pretends to do something else, something inherently better at that.

On the contrary: a public procedure will generate much heat, but it is a mirage to think that there is a "public view" about this sort of thing from which assured better parenting will emerge. Instead, there is at most a majority view, and precious little reason for thinking that that will be *better* than some minority view, or the view of some individual persons. And in the end, it is some individual persons, selected at what amounts to random, who will be brought in, for better or (more likely) worse anyway.

In what sense do children "belong" to their parents? Normally, if A has created x, then A has the right to do what he likes with x, including destroy or neglect it. If an infant's moral status is that of a created thing, things don't look promising for rights for that infant. It will no doubt be said that, for instance,

> The obligations and rights of the parents derive from their act of creation. These are default rights and obligations which can be modified by contract, but they are not established by contract, but derive from natural law or the universal ethic.[1]

But the arrangements made between a creator and any other persons regarding use of what he has created are normally by contract. Where does the idea of a "natural law" bearing on this matter come from, anyway? If it is said that natural law is, well, *natural*, don't you see?—then the reply may well be: "Oh, really? Well, I'm afraid I *don't* see." This is exactly what the people facing laws or strongly reinforced mores limiting their freedom of action in relation to children will say, unless we can do better than that.

So we'd better try to do better than that. To do so requires sorting out the following:

(a) the parents' interests in their children
(b) impinging societal interests
(c) the child's own emerging interests

These are distinct, and can be at odds. The puzzle is to find the right mix and to explain why it is right for the purpose.

(a) Almost all parents, at least among us residents in technologically advanced, comfortable contemporary parts of the world, are keenly interested in the welfare of their offspring. If this were true of all parents, and not merely virtually all, we would perhaps have no problem. Or wouldn't we?

Well, firstly, there is the fact that parental interests of this description are not their only interests. Parents may be keenly interested that their children will continue a family tradition that may be both useless and irksome to the child, or even harmful—even fatal. Or they may have other aspirations for the child, not shared by it, and not approved or looked on kindly by other people in the community.

And secondly, there is the question whether we all agree on what constitutes welfare. We all want to be in good health, and want our children to be so too; but health is not our only value, nor even the only component in our welfare. A child might be in physically excellent health but demoralized or neurotic, for example; and things its parents does that put it in that condition, and put it there intentionally too, might be regarded as promoting its welfare by them but not be so regarded by some others.

Apart from those two important sources of difficulty, we must also have a very hard look at appeals to sentiment in general. We hardly need the authority of Kant to persuade us that morality is not, at least in any simple way, to be founded on sentiment—especially when the sentiments are other-directed. And the problem cases will be those parents who do not love their children, are little or not at all concerned for their welfare, and yet have other plans for them.

(b) The question then becomes this: when and why should the sentiments of other people regarding a given child be able to override the sentiments of the child's own parents? A plausible answer, prima facie, is, never. To answer this, we need to look beyond sentiments of that kind, and look instead to the interests of others, apart from the emotional interest they may take in others. This is, in short, related to the issue of tuism and nontuism in social theory.

The issue of tuism has tended to be addressed as if it were ontological, or alternatively as if it were a basic issue about rationality. In assessing what is practically rational for agent A, according to one view of the matter, we should look only at what conduces to those of A's interests which are specifically directed *at A*, as definably independently of their bearing on other people. That view seems to me untenable. If person *A* is interested not only in himself but in various other people, then *A* will rationally assess his actions in light of their probable effects on those people as well as himself. To take an example very much at the heart of the present inquiry, parents characteristically take a strong interest in their children. It matters very much to parent *B* that *B*'s children do this or that, and that they not do certain other things. We say, plausibly enough, that *B* is disposed to "sacrifice her interests" to those of the child. But while this is in a way very true, it is clear that what *B* sacrifices are only interests in *B*'s *independently characterizable* interests. *B* may make do with less food than she would like in order that her child have more, for instance. But does she see this is practically unwise? Quite the contrary. Her interests reach to her children, and even where those interests conflict with her narrowly assessed interests in herself, they do in fact outweigh the latter so far as she is concerned. And if we are describing the practical reasoning of B, what is true "so far as she is concerned" is what is true, period.

So it is simply wrong to claim that rationality consists in advancing only a subset of one's interests, namely those taken in oneself as an independently existing person. Most people do not "exist independently," and certain other people matter to them, and matter enough that they will not assess their interests independently.

Nevertheless, the proposal that we should not count a person's tuistic interests has a point, and an extremely important one. That interest has to do with morals, not psychology. While people may be terribly interested in what happens to other people, it hardly follows that whatever promotes the interest in question should be regarded as morally acceptable. In particular, an individual's interests in harming others are not. Insofar as what I want to do is to make you worse off, what I want to do has no moral weight at all.

To affirm this is, of course, to take a moral stance: namely, the stance of classic liberalism. Hobbes and Locke, Kant and Mill, all affirm that the basic principle of morals, or more precisely of the part of morals consisting of prohibitions on behavior, prohibits behavior that is directed at lowering the utility of others. Or, in the recent version of David Gauthier, people are to refrain from advancing their own situations *by* worsening the situations of others. A negatively tuistic interest is one that, by definition, can *only* be advanced by worsening the situation of the other person at which it is directed. So such interests stand generally condemned by liberal moral theory.

There is, of course, the basic question of why we should be classic liberals. But there is a basic and good answer to that question. Morals is a sort of general rational agreement among us all. We will all buy into that set of general directives, addressed to all, which will leave us all better off, in our own view of what makes us better or worse off, than alternative general sets. Since negatively tuistic interests, uniquely, have the feature that they necessarily violate that restriction, it is irrational to accept a morality that sanctions actions directed at the worsening of some other person's self-regarding interests, as such; and more generally, of actions that can be seen to have such effects even if not specifically intended to do so. So much is, one might insist, moral common sense. Thus Hobbes's "First Law of Nature" enjoins us to seek peace, and only when it is not forthcoming to resort to war. And Locke's famous "Law of Nature" has it that "no one ought to harm another in his Life, Health, Liberty or Possessions."[2] The point of these is the same. However interested we may be in other people having this or that predicate hold of them, the fact that *they* regard that as adverse to their own interests constitutes a normally decisive block against our pursuit of those interests. When dealing in tuistic interests, we must deal by negotiation and agreement. What *A* does to *B* must be such that *B* is agreeable, or at least not averse, to *A*'s doing it to *B*.

Classic liberals have disagreed, at least on paper, concerning the basic reasoning behind the classic liberal restriction on the pursuit of our interests. Kant regarded it as a synthetic a priori form of reason. Locke appealed, rather irresponsibly, to God. Only Hobbes, I think, has it right. People generally have a large repertoire of powers, but these, in all standard cases, include the power to make life worse for others. We all have this, we can all use it, and it is contrary to everyone's interest that others do so. The short of it is that reasonable people will adjust their relations to others so as to take due account of that fact. The "due account" that, in the abstract, fills the bill is the liberal prohibition on the pursuit of negatively tuistic interests, and more generally of engaging in action contrary to the narrowly construed self-interests of others.

But all of this has to do with the self-control of rational agents. And the problem is that children aren't exactly such agents. But to say just that is, firstly, to misstate, or at least to state misleadingly, the situation. Even quite young children exhibit rationality, after all, and perhaps we should say that even infants do. That point leads us to my third question, which will be pursued below. Meanwhile, we should restate the problem. It is not quite that children aren't rational agents; it is, more nearly, that they are not fully competent rational agents—that their repertoire of powers makes them appreciably less than equal to adults in respect of the exercise of control over others. Infants are at the mercy of others, quite totally; toddlers are pretty nearly so; children of elementary school age are considerably so; and so on up to full adulthood. The terms of reference of this project are (inevitably) not precise. Which level of competence are we envisaging here?

No fact is more basic about children than that they grow up, and "up" means emerging into adulthood and joining the rest of us as standard members of society. The very term 'child' is applied to a phase of a human career, not to the whole: children are not a subset of people in the same sense as males or aboriginals or schoolteachers are. To be a child is to be a human being who is not yet an adult. We are undoubtedly not clear just what we mean by 'adult', but we are quite sure that it is meaningful to say that x is an adult and that y is a child; in standard cases the difference is clear enough so that we may, for example, rely on motorists to understand the point of a traffic sign with a picture of children on it, warning them to watch out for their presence.

We can perhaps both generalize and make more precise the sort of problem we are addressing here by saying that *insofar as* people are less than fully competent in the sense in which normal adults are so, others must somehow care for them, and the question is, which adults and to what ends? Some of the less than competent will be elderly persons, or those with severe psychological problems or diseases affecting the nervous system, and so on. But in the present chapter, we are focusing only on the case of the child, and more narrowly yet, only on the case of the "normal" child. Our question is what adults must do in relation to children. We ask this against the background, as noted above, that, first, children have parents who normally continue to be around after their birth, and normally have a very substantial motivation to look after them and bring them up to operational adulthood, and, second, that some parents may botch the job, either for reasons of lacking normal motivation or normal competence at child rearing.

When they are not so, one option is nevertheless to do nothing. We shall, on this view, say that children are, simply and totally, in the charge of their parents, and that's that. If the child suffers as a result, that is tough luck for it, but no skin off the backs of the rest of us.

In fact, it is not quite clear what this option really amounts to, and quite clear that we should have serious doubts about it insofar as it does seem to be clear. Most especially, it is pretty obvious that it may indeed be some "skin off our backs" how a given set of parents deal with their offspring. They might well grow up to be thieves, murderers, liars, rapists, and assorted scoundrels, and if they do, it will certainly mean skin off the backs of some other people. The thought certainly suggests itself that we should insist that parents raise their children in such a way as to have them emerge into adulthood as peaceable people, unlikely to do damage to others. We may put this aspect of the matter thus: that people should raise their children in such a way that those children do not become burdens on others—not live, in adulthood, at the net expense of other people.

It is a natural thought that perhaps we could do better than that. Perhaps we could insist that parents raise their children so as to be "productive": that is, that their relations with others are such as to leave at least some of those others better off than they would be in the absence of those newly grown up former children, while leaving no others worse off. But if by 'insist' we mean that the rest of us get to force parents to do that, then we must resist the temptation. True, the standard will usually be met; indeed, I think it would almost always be, if no pressure is applied to meet it. But intervening to compel such performance will certainly be counterproductive. Compulsion may indeed be applied to avoid worsening the lot of others, but not to bettering. We better each others' lots when we engage in cooperative activity, not by cracking whips over people.

A further thought also suggests itself, of course: some children will be born with unfortunate conditions—paralysis, and any number of other things may be there from the start or early on, regardless of our efforts. An important side issue here is whether parents have a duty to see to it, where possible, that their children will not be born with such maladies, insofar as that is predictable. But while it is an important side issue, it is a side issue, and we must leave it on one side in this inevitably brief discussion. In any case, some children will be born with such misfortunes. Parents will of course be anxious to do what they can for such cases. But many philosophers will also insist that society in general has the duty to care for unfortunate children; some would say, more specifically, that we all have the duty to do what we can to make their situations more nearly "equal" to the rest.

Such proposals, bizarrely popular at present, have one major disadvantage: total inability to explain *why* the rest of us have this onerous duty. The egalitarian view is not only arbitrary, but also counterproductive. Of course it is not the parents' fault—usually—when this happens but, nevertheless, it is *their* activity, not others' that led to their children being born thus. It most assuredly isn't anyone else's fault either, if fault it be; but then, the rest of us (in the typical case) did nothing at all to bring it about. Catering to the unfortunate is the work of charity, not justice, and any parent of such children should be grateful for the help of others. They are also quite likely, indeed almost certain, to get it, people being the way they are—namely, helpful.

But as I say, we must leave that topic on one side. The question is what social interests are relevant to framing the role of parents. My answer is the interest in not being harmed, damaged, or in general, worsened, by the activities of others. This totally reasonable end justifies some control over parenting activities. But, in the typical case, not very much. Parents can and should be held responsible for any antisocial behavior on the part of their children, and for that reason it behooves the parent to avoid irresponsible parenting; under which we may include cruelty, utter laxity, and disciplinary inconsistency. This is a substantial result indeed. But it also brings us abruptly to face the third question for this analysis: the bearing of the child's own emerging interests.

(c) When children are born, they are in a state of nearly total incompetence, by adult standards. Everything must be done for them, and no expectations on them are reasonable. But while they are born that way, they don't long remain so. It soon becomes clear that this little being has a mind of its own. The question is, how much does that count? How soon, and to what extent, ought parents to regard their children's wishes as having the same kind of moral weight that our own do?

True, some philosophers evidently think that adults' wishes have very little if any moral weight anyway, so that my question regarding children is merely academic. An assumption of this chapter is that they are wrong about that. But while they are, there nevertheless remains a very difficult question about the lengthy period during which the child is slowly becoming an adult. Is there some rational way to allocate responsibility and rights, so that when there are conflicts of will between parent and child, we can say who should win at which times?

Let's first make a distinction that will surely loom pretty large in any such discussion: between sheer bodily protection and nurturing in health, on the one hand, and liberty of action in the narrower sense on the other. Children soon, as I say, begin to have wills of their own. When they do, on which sorts of occasions do parents have the right to thwart those wills? Consider, on this point, the following divisions:

(a) They may be thwarted when their chosen actions will make for damage to other people. This, of course, is elementary.

(b) They may be thwarted when their chosen actions will make for damage to themselves.

(c) When their preferred actions would leave them less able to live their lives well, on any plausible account of what living a human life amounts to, after they become adults;

(d) When their preferred actions would leave them less able to live their lives well—not on just *any* plausible account of what living a human life amounts to, after they become adults, but on *their* account;

(e) When their preferred actions would leave them less able to live their lives well, on their *parents'* preferred view of how they should live their lives;

(f) When their preferred actions would leave them less able to live their lives well, on their *community's* preferred view of how they should live their lives.

Among these views, I take it that (a) is elementary. It represents the minimal moral training of children that every parent owes to the rest of the world. Perhaps (b) is less elementary than (a), but it is scarcely less so. And virtually every parent will be sensitive to this one—it is, more than anything else, where the term 'paternalism' comes from. But already problems arise. Suppose that some damage to the child results from what their parents see as either economically necessary, or as required by their religion, and so on. Thus, Christian Scientists will prevent their children going to doctors for certain purposes, when the consequence for the child is certain death. Here we have an out-and-out conflict between (b) and (e).

A major question about (c) is how much it differs from (f). This will of course depend on the community, and it also depends on the plausibility of Communitarianism. Since I reject the latter, and take it that different communities might have not only varying, but varyingly plausible, views about the good life, I take it that we can pry the two apart. And if we can, then I think that (f) can be marginalized. We could defend inculcation of community ethics into our children on the ground that they will, after all, have to live with those people. But that is quite different from taking the community mores as authoritative even above the child's own view of his future, if he has one, and the parents', if they have one.

It seems to me that the most important and fundamental issue here has to do with parental versus children's aspirations for the child. Are parents morally required to let their children live their lives according to their own lights? I take it that at very early ages, there isn't much data: two-year-olds do not typically have long-term aspirations, even if they can give voice to them. But plenty of children do have such things by the time they are of elementary school ages, and of course when they become teenagers, they rather often do. And these are sometimes in considerable conflict with the views that their parents entertain.

Two kinds of conflicts need to be distinguished here. First, a parent might have a different view than his child regarding what is good for the child. But, second, a parent might conceivably have in mind a certain life or future for the child that is not a view about what is "good for the child," at least in the narrowest sense, but rather is good for the family, or the community, or god, or whatever.

The view that children "belong to" their parents, in some quite strong sense, is the one that may be thought to generate support for parents over their children in a quite thoroughgoing way. Such, for example, was the inference Susan Moller Okin drew[3] from a Lockean premise, to the effect the parents make or create their children, just as a farmer makes or creates his grain crops. If A makes x, doesn't x belong, then, to A? But what parents "make" or "create" is only a human organism. They do not make or create the person this organism by and by becomes, and of course when it becomes a full-fledged adult, Locke will insist, along with libertarians and most of us, that any duties to parents as such terminate. The interesting question is not whether adults are the property of their parents—obviously they are not—but whether children's relation to parents is such that parents have a real right to exercise major control over the child's future.

Now, no one can really determine a child's future. But parents can do a lot to make it much more likely that a child's future will be of one kind rather than another. In a peasant environment in Vietnam or central Africa or many other places, children will go to work early on agricultural chores, and by the time adulthood comes along, that child is all but certain to become and remain a peasant, like his father, for the rest of his life. In a much less constrained way, academic parents often have academic children, musicians' offspring are often musicians, and so on.

There need be nothing the least morally problematic about this. The child's family lives in a certain way, does what it does, and the child naturally falls in with it. If enthusiasts for egalitarianism were right, of course, this would be very problematic indeed. Children often emerge from childhood into an adulthood the general shape of which is practically preordained, and often the life in question is not much like the favored model of contemporary academic philosophers. On the contemporary egalitarian view, a society ought to show a range from assistant professor to full professor—neither more nor less. If a lot of people are slogging away at life below the assistant professor floor, then society is at fault and there's injustice to rectify. Likewise, if some few individuals manage to earn more than full professors, that too shows evidence of some serious disease in the social organism. For philosophers who buy into this view of society, almost all of the lives lived by people from prehistory until now have been due to injustice—society is simply shot through with it.

Now, I am not persuaded that the average midwestern farm boy or farm girl in the agricultural communities in which I spent my early childhood had much interest in becoming professors, and I doubt that any of them lost much sleep over the alleged injustices they were suffering. I doubt also that any of their parents saw anything objectionable in trying to bring their children up prepared to cope with the many problems besetting those who try to make a living from the soil. On the other hand, few objected very strongly (though some objected a bit) to having their children bussed into town to go to school several hours a day, there to learn, or at least to be exposed to, a good deal of information of whose utility they were skeptical, and of whose very meaning they were probably often unsure. People are pretty malleable and accommodating, on the whole, and for a great many people the questions I'm raising here are literally "academic." They would be a lot less so, though, if the state also tried to tell them which religion to practice, and to inculcate some rival one in their children. And in some individual case, we may be sure, there was objection to their children professing to be interested in taking up a way of life very, very different from the one they were brought up to.

So now the question is: which of these two things should we say?

(1) That it is a parental duty, enforceable by their fellows, to refrain from trying to broaden the child's horizons and instead confine it to what they see as the straight and narrow. This I take to be the view of many Islamic and many other conservative societies.

(2) That it is a parental duty, enforceable by their fellows, to expose their children to alternative ways of life, alternative religions, and educational efforts that might open their minds to other possibilities

besides the ones they know. This I take to be the view of contemporary liberals, in the modern, North American sense of the term.

The correct view, I suggest, is *neither*; and in so saying, I suppose, I am going pretty strongly against the received wisdom among contemporary theorists on this matter. But in part that is because I don't think there is any straight and narrow in life, and so, apart from the minimal moral requirements that I set down at the outset, I wouldn't really know how to go about contraindicating the first. I have a fair idea what it is like: I live on the edge of a Mennonite community, considerable elements of which do, they think, have this clear idea of what is straight and narrow, and are quite concerned to keep their children on it—without, I think, a great deal of success, but we'll return to that. But how can we not sympathize with those parents who have a vision of the future for their children and are strongly concerned with realizing it for them? Children are, after all, a big investment in trouble and expense, and it is hardly surprising that people would like to see a return on their investment.

But two things should temper their strivings. First, there really is a good chance that their children simply won't find the proffered life to their liking, in one or another of several ways. And in this likely event, the parent who is determined to march his child down a set path is likely, first, to generate resentment and unhappiness in the child. And does the parent really want *that*? Even if he does, it is easy to see why the community doesn't want it, and shouldn't. Happy people make better neighbors, better friends, better business associates, and in general better assets to their communities.

Second, this man is very, very likely to fail. I hardly need to go into detail about the many ways in which a growing child can flout its parents' wishes about almost anything. But also, when they grow up, they will, after all, have it within their power to do something else, and at that point, the just community must side with the right of the now-grown child to do his own thinking and live his own way. Accordingly, any parent who sets himself in this direction needs, as we may put it, a good talking-to.

Children are, of course, going to take over the world. That's just the way things are, and few parents would want it otherwise. But it's quite another matter to say that they should get it now, while they're still children. It's also quite another matter to say that children, as a matter of natural right or something of the sort, simply belong to the community.

The philosophy of children is the philosophy of parenting, and parents too have rights, on any reasonable view of the matter. Parenting has, needless to say, major responsibilities; but it also has major rewards and presents major opportunities. A rational view of morals will leave parents largely in charge, to be shown right or wrong when their children emerge into the world as fellow grown-ups.

Parents' basic duty regarding their children, stemming from their relations with their fellows, is extremely clear: to bring up their children in such a way that those children will not be enemies of their fellows, and if possible not be burdens on them either. But beyond that, parents have wide scope.

For example, they may want to get into homeschooling. Or they may just want to let their children grow up, so far as possible, in the directions they find themselves wanting to go. I know of at least one parent whose home-schooling consists in precisely that; her children seem to be doing well, by conventional standards, despite their complete lack of conventional schooling. Modern communities' presumption in marshaling children into schools with a more or less standardized array of subjects, most of which the students aren't much interested in, strikes me as remarkably unpromising. But in any case, parents ought not to be bound to fall in with the scheme, and certainly not to pay large tax bills to support it.[4]

A great deal of information about life outside the home can and usually does reach modern children through television. Parents surely have the right to regulate this tendency—but in both directions. They should be able to give their children very wide latitude, or conversely to refrain even from owning a TV.

Socialization by peers is crucial to some aspects of child development, and in any case likely to be a great source of enjoyment to almost any child. Again, parents have the right to regulate that—though their duty to keep their children from becoming menaces to their fellows will sometimes require, and not merely permit, intervention in their social spheres. And in general, in many areas of life, parents rightly have a good deal of say—and in general, in my view, are well advised to exercise it rather little, and that discreetly.

Of course, the most important thing that a parent can do for a child is something that can't be converted into a duty at all: to love that child, fiercely and wisely. We philosophers would do well never to lose sight of that point. But that comes from within; there isn't much that the rest of us can do if it's lacking, except suffer the consequences.

Conclusion

The case for a generally liberal, and thus contractarian, point of view on morals precludes taking the easy route to a view of children's rights. If morals are by agreement, it can only be among those who can agree and keep agreements, and very young children do not qualify. On the other hand, children become adults, and do so over a considerable period. Not surprisingly, evolutionary forces have arranged that most parents have a strong instinct to protect and nurture their children. Somewhat surprisingly, there are many exceptions to that. And least surprisingly of all, modern life with its richnesses and complexities is not what evolution had in mind in making all these arrangements. Without relying on instinct or intuition, we can still see that children become adults for better or worse, and what we want is that it be better and not worse. So we of course have some say in how people may bring up their children. But above the baseline of nonviolence and respect for others, there is much latitude in which children can develop to live the wide range of lives they will acquire interests in. The fact that children are the offspring of particular people, with many interests and intentions in conceiving and rearing them, makes a strong case for parental priority in most matters; the rest of society ought to be pretty reticent to take a hand in children's upbringing. First the parents, and then the children themselves, should have priority in deciding what children are to do. These conclusions, I hope, are pretty obvious. For the day-to-day substance of childrearing, relevant books, magazines, television programs, and back-fence discussions available to all are of more value than the writings of theorists.

Notes

This paper, previously unpublished, stems from many sources, including readings at the University of Helsinki and at Bowling Green State University in autumn 1990, the Canadian Philosophical Association meetings, 1991 at Queen's University, Kingston, Ontario, and in another version at the conference on children at the University of Western Ontario, March 2000. I am grateful to discussants at those and several other places.

   1. This was said by a contributor to a web discussion whose identity I have lost track of.

   2. In Section 87 Locke refers to "his Property, that is, his Life, Liberty and Estate." See Locke, *Second Treatise on Civil Government*, in P. Laslett, ed., *Two Treatises of Government* (Cambridge, U.K.: Cambridge University Press, 1960), 323. Later still, in Section 123, he refers to "their Lives, Liberties and Estates, which I call by the general Name, *Property*," Laslett, 350.

   3. Susan Moller Okin, *Justice, Gender, and the Family* (New York: Basic Books, 1989), especially chapter 4, "Libertarianism: Matriarchy, Slavery, and Dystopia." The main argument of that chapter, and more generally of the book, cannot, I think, be taken seriously, though the fact that it has been suggests that common sense does not play the role in philosophy that one might hope.

   4. The further insoluble problem about arranging public school curricula so as to respect the rights of every parent motivated a discussion, my contribution to which was "Liberalism and Public Education," *Interchange* (The Ontario Institute for Studies in Education, Toronto) 19, no. 1 (March 1988), 60-69.

Chapter 16

Natural Resources, Sustainability, and the Central Committee

The Argument about Resource Scarcity

Few topics have been of more concern in recent applied and political philosophy than that of natural resources and their supposed scarcity. Both the naturalness and the scarcity of such resources are central features that tend to dictate thinking about them. But almost all the thinking in question is wrong, and its effect on social policy is enormous and disastrous. That is the burden of this chapter, which is mainly a matter of conceptual housekeeping.

Involvement in the area of resources is inevitably in part empirical, to be sure. But the main impetus to recent bad work in the area is due to conceptual, not empirical factors. To appreciate this, let me sketch a general type of argument that is ubiquitous in discussions of environmental issues. I will therefore call it the Standard Argument. It is set up as a syllogism, though elaboration in particular instances might make it a good deal more complicated.

(1) Major Premise: There is some natural resource, R, such that continued human life (or some such thing) depends on R.

(2) Minor Premise: There is only just so much R. Reason: R, after all, is finite, is it not? There are just so many tons, or barrels, of R.

(2a) Therefore, R is *scarce*.

(3) Conclusion: Humanity (or, The World, or whatever—adjust to suit political context) is headed for trouble, unless We, *collectively*, Do Something.

I intentionally cast the conclusion in a fairly vague form, and insert variables requiring specification into the premises. But while the result is fairly vague, its intent isn't. For present purposes, what matters is that the Conclusion is understood in such a way that the remedies envisaged—the "somethings" which "we" must "do"—require public, and specifically political, action. Global resource problems are taken to be public in a sense of that term that is incompatible with letting individual people and voluntarily acting groups of people carry on as before. And that is why this subject is essentially a political one. The question is not the scientific or technical one: "How long will this or that last?" Rather, the question is whether the situation calls for political rather than voluntary, individual action.

If the argument were serious, everything would depend on the choice of values of several specific variables and what the theorist proposes to make of them. At any rate, the main message here is that construal of the variables in such a way that (3) is actually supported is, as I shall show, all but impossible. The argument, taken seriously, is worthless, certainly in today's circumstances, and probably in almost all.

To begin with, consider the variables in the first premise. Here are some familiar variants of that premise:

(1a) replace 'continued human life' by 'human life at level L'

(1b) replace 'continued' with 'indefinitely continued' or even 'eternally continued'

(1c) specify the duration and the population level in some more or less precise way: 10,000 years and 20,000,000,000 people? 500 years and 8,000,000,000?

It obviously makes an enormous difference how one specifies these variables. Consider the first one. Is it sensible to talk of "catastrophe" if the claim is that not everyone could afford a Rolls-Royce? Presumably not: starvation and disease are the sorts of things that we would suppose to be in question if "global catastrophe" is the subject. But it is very easy for the agenda to switch, subtly or otherwise, from concern about starvation to concern about "poverty," as measured, for example, by official Canadian and American criteria. In the morning paper, I see a hand-wringing article about local poverty, there being families of four in the writer's vicinity making less than $27,000 annually—this in a world where the median income is a bit more than a twentieth of that figure. But if the concern about sustainability in the face of resource exhaustion is really about getting the whole world up to American and Canadian middle-class living standards, the complainer should just say so; that simply isn't what it sounded like, and not something the lack of which very many people are going to rate as a "catastrophe." By that remarkable standard, after all, the world has been below "catastrophe level" for the past ten thousand years and will no doubt continue to be so for at least a few more centuries, come to that.

Again: *how far* into the future are we looking? Civilization of a sort has been with us only a few thousand years so far. Eventually, we suppose, the earth itself will disappear: the sun will burn out or will turn into a supernova, vaporizing the earth in an instant; or earth will become too cold for human habitation; whatever. Environmentalism cannot be concerned with such remote eventualities. Concern about resource scarcity, if it is to have any practical significance, focuses on far less of the future than that: a century or a few centuries, say. And then there is the problem, for any thesis of catastrophism, that our knowledge of how to meet whatever challenges may come up is constantly on the increase, a point we will return to frequently in this chapter. This makes the future beyond a few decades or so impossible to speculate usefully about.

Feeding the Billions

Let's start by asking what plausible examples of R might possibly be thought to make the argument work. Historically, one example has gotten most of the attention until very recently—food. The concern of alarmists about population has almost always been that mankind will face a shortage of food. There is only so much land, they will point out, and on the other hand, the inherent tendency of population is to expand in geometric fashion; so, they argue, we could eventually become so numerous that there won't be enough land to grow enough food for all those people and thus there will be massive starvation, and as the starvation begins to set in, or even before, there will be a catastrophic breakdown of civilized society as a Hobbesian state-of-nature war for the limited food supply sets in–that sort of thing. Overpopulation scares have been a regular stock-in-trade of intellectuals for thousands of years. Even Plato thought that overpopulation would soon be a problem, and of course the idea was given a major push on the accelerator by Thomas Malthus, who quantified the idea by proposing that whereas mankind could increase food supply "arithmetically," population tends to increase geometrically. Ere long, the geometric curve will break away from the arithmetic one, said he, and then doom-time is on the near horizon.

For all such arguments, it is assumed, the evils *must* set in sooner or later and it's just a question of when. The assumption is that this is basically an empirical matter, the only serious question a strictly empirical one, the answer to which is calculable: just so much of X, so many to divide it among, this much needed by each, and so this is how long X will last—though of course it could last a lot longer if we rich folks would just scale down our materialistic demands a good bit. It is a tempting set of assumptions, and very few haven't succumbed to their lure, including the present author in earlier days.

But we were all wrong.

The Concept of Resources

The first conceptual question is: just what is a "resource"? Are resources the sort of thing such that it is a basically empirical question whether mankind will "have enough" of? Bear in mind that all humans, everywhere, ever since the dawn of time and into the indefinite future, have faced and will continue to face scarcities. We would all like to have more of something or other, and often it is quite clear that we're going to have a considerable problem availing ourselves of that "more." But the problem we're addressing here is the global one: not, is this or that person or this or that small group faced with a fairly definite, near-future problem, but rather, is Humanity faced with a collective, global problem over a longer run? The two sorts of question are enormously different.

To see why and how they are so different, we must turn our attention to the idea of "resources." We use such an idea in all sorts of contexts. We can talk of material or intellectual or spiritual resources, of monetary, pianistic, or artistic resources, and so on, and the things in question might be used in any number of ways. Considering this range of uses for the concept, we might well ask whether there is a clear common element. As often happens in philosophy, we are likely to find necessary conditions, and possibly sufficient conditions, but it is extremely difficult indeed to find necessary and sufficient conditions. Still, we can be confident about this: a "resource" is a means, whatever else it is (and it is always something else; a lump of coal can have its aesthetic attractions). Being a means implies, of course, that there is an end to be served, relative to which the utility of the means is to be assessed. And it must be an end that is capable of being realized in varying degree. So it will always make sense to ask whether our resources are "equal to the task," whether we will have "enough" for the purpose in question. It makes *sense*, yes: but it requires information about the extent of the resources at hand, and that raises the possibility that the supply can be expanded, with more or less effort. And then, as we will now see, things get very tricky very quickly.

The question of global resources has been raised almost exclusively as being concerned with one broad sort of means—what we may call "material resources," specifiable not only in quantitative terms, but specifically the sort of quantities relevant to matter: tons of this, cubic feet of that, bushels of wheat, and so on. Latterly, however, people also talk of "human resources" and clearly that will not lend itself so readily to such measurement. Moreover, talk of human resources will be a bit puzzling and oblique to the usual discussions because of the fact that people, broadly speaking, are not just means but, in a philosophically proprietary sense, ends: the well-being of people, especially, is what these discussions are all about. Or if not, the theorist who thinks otherwise needs to tell us more, and to explain. From the point of view of the cow, the farmer who feeds and milks it is a resource; but for us, for present purposes, the cow is the resource, and the farmer would mainly be considered the caretaker of that resource, and in part an instance, or the repository, of some of the ends being promoted.

All this is right enough, but the fact remains that people *are* resources. Our bodies and minds are resources to ourselves as well as the locus, somehow, of our ends, and other people's skills, even their personalities, may be resources to us. Above all, the knowledge that we and others discover is a resource in a perfectly real and straightforward sense.

Resources: Three Conceptual Components

After this rather general discussion, we must now be a little more specific. When something is said to be a "resource" for humans, a conceptual complex is being invoked, not a simple, unitary notion. There are three quite distinguishable components to it.

First, there is the end being served by it. Food, for example, is a resource for human life because it keeps us alive and fuels our bodies, enabling them to do the sorts of things we want to do. We have other ends to which food would be quite useless, in any direct sense, though food is always indirectly relevant, since we will be dead if we go very long without it. And while it can be conjectured that there is some sort of ultimate ends toward which we all aim, the sort of thing we normally have in mind by 'ends' differ enormously among people, and moreover are changeable with time.

Second, there is *stuff*: whatever discoverable substances serve the end in question. In the main, for present purposes, the means in question is material, the sort of thing that can be measured in bushels or tons. Stuff is the usual referent of the term 'resources' in almost all current discussions, the only one of the three that tends to be had in mind when the subject of resources comes up.

Third, however, and perfectly generally, a component is required whose necessity is easily, and very largely, overlooked. This is, in the broadest sense of the term, *technology*, "know-how." It consists in the knowledge that enables those who use the stuff mentioned in our second category to do so in such a way as to promote the ends mentioned in the first. Not much thought is required to see the necessity of knowledge, or skill, provided we allow the notion to range widely enough so as to cover not only the sort of knowledge we acquire from books, but also skills that might only be developed by practice, and even genetically programmed instinctive responses, such as the tendency of newborn infants to suckle. (It does not matter for present purposes whether it really is an example, in the end—perhaps it is in some way "learned"; the point is that even if it is not learned, it is still a bit of know-how, without which the infant is likely to be in very tough shape.)

Listing these three components makes it clear that a situation of claimed resource scarcity can be met in three ways:

(1) We might stop being interested in the end it's needed for, and get interested in something else which doesn't have the same shortage problem; or just grit our teeth and make do with less of it—turning down the thermostat in our home heating system, for instance.

(2) We can try to find more of the stuff that is thought to be in short supply.

(3) Or, we can think up new ways to use the old stuff for the same purposes, that don't require as much of it; or new ways to create the stuff out of something else, previously undreamed of; or ways to utilize different stuffs that are not in short supply.

There is a social mechanism for sorting these responses out: the pricing system. In a free market, those who own various amounts or sources of those resources can raise prices, thus imposing a sort of rationing scheme. Some will pay those higher prices and go on as before, but others will be unwilling to buy as much at the higher price. Higher prices provide an incentive for various people to respond in the ways listed in (3).

What this chapter will point out is that when we take proper account of point (3), we will realize that it is *impossible*, in principle, to *know* that the world is genuinely facing a long-term scarcity situation to which the only possible response is the first, and that it is difficult to see why central committees created to control the use of any given material resource would ever be justified.

Why Resource Estimates Are Difficult

Now consider the task facing the theorist who wants to proclaim that humanity is headed toward a resource crisis of some kind. He will have to show us that the human race, at the time in question (presumably now), is such that it requires such-and-such an amount of R, and that the amount of R actually available is, say, just about that much, and no more, or only somewhat more. But can we expand the supply of R? If he says not, he will need to explain why this is unlikely or impossible. To do that, he will have to show us that the further stuff, S, out of which R is to be made is also limited, such that we will not be able to expand the supply of R to meet demands. But can he do that? As we will see, in almost all cases the answer is a simple no. In a few, the answer is a somewhat more complex no.

Consider. In order to show that, he needs to establish not only that the world has just so much S, but also that there is no way to make more R than a fundamentally inadequate amount, so that mankind will inevitably be deficient in R at the time in question. If you have been following this discussion carefully, it may already have occurred to you that the information such a theorist would need for his thesis is not so easy to come by. If so, you are right. It is not only not so easy, but for theses at the level of philosophical generality we are especially interested in here, it is *impossible*. So long as the conversion of material stuff into things we want is mediated by knowledge, there simply is no way to know that anything is relevantly in irremediably short supply.

Let us see why, first by considering some relevant examples. The most obvious material resources relevant to the present subject will be food and water, and then air, and then something not so obviously material—temperature environments at the rather narrow spectrum compatible with longer-term human functioning. People can freeze, or burn, they can die of thirst or hunger, they can choke. Food and water are material as they stand, and the best candidate for the scarcity-theorist's purposes, so let's look especially at them. But the need for a fairly constant ambient temperature brings up the subject of keeping warm enough in cold climates, or cool enough in hot ones, and that, especially in the contemporary world, brings us to the subjects of shelter and, in the main, heat, and thus energy, and so, fuel. Conceivably fuel could be in short supply, and then a lot of us, especially in places like Canada, where the author lives, could face an unpleasant prospect of freezing. Maybe.

Recycling, Natural and Otherwise

Let's look first at food and water. Water has an important feature that is going to make our scarcity theorist's project a bit complicated, at the least. For when we drink water, the fact is that we *don't* "use it up." It is not true, except in the very short run, that when people use water, it ceases to exist. Instead, it comes back: we drink, but we sweat and we urinate; we take a bath, but the water merely gets dirtier, rather than disappearing. It vanishes into thin air, but then, the air sheds it as rainfall. Nature goes to work on the results, and by and by 100 percent of the original water is here again, potentially available once more for human use. When as a material stuff can be reused, a scarcity thesis has to have it that the *rate* at which we use it, and the number of users, is such that it won't turn back into reusable form soon enough to keep all those people from dying of thirst, or whatever. And how is the theorist going to do that? Take a metropolitan area facing a drought: a very large percentage of the water running through a given consumer pipeline is not used for drinking but for washing clothes, carrying away human and other wastes, watering the lawn, and so on. We can reduce the rate at which we use water for those other purposes to quite a remarkable degree; in a serious case, devices for catching the runoff, cleaning it quickly, and recycling can be employed. The tribesman in the Sahara dons his heavy robe, reducing the rate at which he turns water into sweat and enabling him to survive on a remarkably modest supply of fresh water. One can multiply examples endlessly.

In any case, next there enters technological improvements, which speed the rate of recycling. The astronaut in her spaceship lives in a special environment: all the air she breathes, all the water she drinks, and even much of the food she eats, is ingeniously reprocessed and recycled on the spot. Of course most people aren't astronauts, but then, quite ordinary people, indeed all of us, inevitably and necessarily recycle, without being aware that it is happening. All the water we use goes down the drain or evaporates, eventually to return as rainfall. The astronaut merely speeds up the process. There is no inherent reason why it couldn't be speeded up for us all, if it came to that—as to a considerable degree it is, in one way or another.

The situation is similar for food. The Malthusian evidently assumes that humans can only grow just so much food, that they need a given minimum of land to do so, and thus that, with a bit of simple arithmetic, we can infallibly conclude that by and by, burgeoning mankind will be unable to sustain itself. But any farmer can tell him that his premises are wrong. Different areas, with different soils and different weathers, support amazingly different levels of food output, given the right sort of care and attention. And at this point, once again, technology, this time of the agricultural variety, comes into play in a major way. The same land that used to grow a handful of nuts when nature alone was responsible, and thirty bushels of wheat when a hardworking seventeenth-century farmer was in charge now grows a hundred bushels under the watchful eye of an ingenious farmer with a computer. What's more, vast new areas come under cultivation that were reckoned to be hopeless wasteland at one time. And then, just to make life for the overpopulation theorist really difficult, there is the interesting fact that we can actually grow many sorts of plants without using any land at all. Technologies for doing so are not just on the drawing board, but are in place and in use at this very time.[1] Those technologies were undreamed of a century ago. By definition, we do not know what new technologies lie in the future. But we do have very good reason for expecting new ones to come along, and no reason to think that none will.

At this point, we can move to the empirical facts for a moment, just to confirm that the above points are no fussy little academic exercise. Indeed, the Malthusian's case comes a complete cropper when we contemplate the modern world. For at the very time when it has undergone a major increase in population, it has increased its food supply even more. By the 1990s, with twice the people it had in the 1930s, the average number of calories per person is higher by more than a quarter.[2] Geometrically increasing population has gone hand in hand with geometrically increasing food supply, but with food supply winning rather than losing in the process. Garrett Hardin was, and is, just wrong.[3] The world is not an overcrowded lifeboat now, and in fact never was. Lifeboat situations happen on lifeboats, sometimes, and have happened, very rarely, in a few villages or limited regions here and there. But those limited situations have little to do with the world food situation. Moreover, modern technology of other types now steps in to solve these local problems. We have the food, and with cargo planes, helicopters, Land Rovers, and the rest of the panoply of modern transport devices, we can feed anybody, anywhere, any time—provided the local governments of the intended recipients will allow us to get to the threatened people. It is those governments, in fact, that have been the only serious obstacle to the complete elimination of resource-type scarcity situations. But obviously that problem is not the type that shows a scarcity of the relevant resources.

Is there any reason to think that this process must stop? The short answer is no. It is obviously impossible, in principle, for anybody to *know* that it will, because it depends on the expansion of human knowledge, and that is fundamentally unpredictable. It is in the nature of information to expand. What we already know doesn't disappear as we seek more knowledge—it accumulates. So while we can't predict in detail what we will discover, since we must first discover it to do that, we can confidently predict that there is no way to go but up. And since there is no reason to expect people to cease being interested in improving things—quite the reverse—we have every reason to expect knowledge to grow at least at the rate it has been growing over the past few centuries. That doesn't prove that we can never have a global crisis, but it does mean that predictions that we will are hugely implausible, short of certain knowledge of major exogenously originating catastrophes—large asteroids headed straight this way, say. And even then, since we are certain, in the present state of astronomical knowledge, to have at least a few years to find some way to avoid the collision, it is very doubtful that we would even be able to know that. But in any case, asteroids and volcanoes are not what these discussions are about. They are concerned instead with the probability that we will run out of this or that in normal use, under realistically normal conditions, in fairly foreseeable real time—decades, for instance. Such predictions are baseless at present, and there is no reason to have more confidence in them for longer runs. Just the reverse, in truth: what we really have reason to expect is a great increase in the number of alternative ways of doing any given desirable thing, alternative materials and processes.

To firm this point up empirically, consider food production per acre. Is there some knowable limit to the number of calories we can extract from a given amount of land? Even in the mid-1960s, by the best available methods of the day, the amount of land required to sustain one average human was down to about 28 square meters.[4] At that rate, the entire world's populace could have been fed from an agricultural area the size of the American state of Minnesota. But that was over three decades ago. By now, remarkable agricultural techniques such as hydroponic farming have come into use. With that technique, a single acre of surface area can raise enough food to feed 500-1,000 people, and with real food, such as tomatoes, not funny stuff like ground fish meal. The surface area required to feed the whole world at that rate would be on the order of the state of New Hampshire, or about 1/5,000th of the world's land area. Moreover, that surface need not be literally on the land: multilayered hydroponic surfaces are perfectly possible.[5] How many stories tall do we make our agricultural factory? The sky being the limit, it is obvious that it has become pointless to discuss the question any more. There is no practicable limit to the size of human population that can currently be fed. In realistic terms, *there simply is no such thing as the "carrying capacity" of the earth.*

But in addition, and not really surprising, there is no reason to expect that we will have an incredibly large population anyway. The earth's numbers are in fact not increasing very fast any more, as birthrates plummet (again, contrary to the Malthusian supposition) in all of the better-off countries of today's world, and most of the not-so-well-off ones too. For that matter, the increase in population of the world in the twentieth century was due much more to increased life expectancy than to high birthrates.[6] Some population experts, indeed, are beginning to think that absolute decline in the earth's population is fairly likely by roughly midcentury.[7]

Malthus's two requirements, in short, are both wrong. The world's population does not tend to increase without limit, and exponentially, until some external force stops it; and the food supply can increase very rapidly with increasing population.

General Pointers about Productivity

The example of food supply and population is only an example, if a major one, but it well illustrates the general point: you can't predict how much in the way of valued human output we can get from a particular lot of natural stuffs. You cannot do so because of the other two components of the notion of resources. Either the demand for the sort of product that resource is used in changes, or production increases as a result of new developments in technology, or, usually, both. Indeed, everything depends on technology. But technology continually improves and the relevant details about its future expansion are not even in principle predictable. Will we run out of steel? Certainly there is no reason to think so. But if there were, by the time natural iron ore ever got really scarce, what alternative materials will be found that are strong enough to support tall buildings? Even cars and framing members of many buildings are already being made substantially from other materials, such as plastics and aluminum. No one could have predicted the rise of plastics two centuries ago, or even one; and no one now can predict what kind of exotic materials we will use in the future. Those new materials, in turn, are often made from natural resources that are hugely plentiful. Carbon fiber, for example, is made from basic materials that are essentially inexhaustible.

Scarcity, then, is always a function of three things, not just one. First, there is the purpose to be served. Which particular bits of matter are employable for a given purpose is, obviously, determined by that purpose—we will only use what we are interested in using. Second is know-how: we may use Stuff x at first, then discover Stuff y, then learn to fabricate Stuff z, and so on, for any given purpose, as we learn more of the technology by which natural stuffs can be transformed into the products in question. And third is the quantity of whatever stuffs are required. Let's consider that one now.

Material Resource Estimates

This last item is the only one most discussions ever mention, though it is the least important of the three, so far as scarcity predictions are concerned. But when it comes to trying to estimate how much of a given sort of natural material there "is," we again encounter a fundamental role for technology, and this again upsets all relevant calculation. How do we estimate the amount of stuff of the kind in question *in the whole world*? For any given kind of stuff, it is to be presumed, anyhow, that the globe contains, at any given time, a certain definite amount of a given natural kind of stuff. That is the premise—sole premise—of the general scarcity argument. But finding out what that amount is turns out to be a very tricky and uncertain business. It is sobering to see the range of estimates that have been made for various stuffs over the past few decades. Thus in 1974, there was estimated to be enough copper left in "known reserves" to last the world a mere 45 years. However, at the same time the U.S. Geological Survey's estimate of "ultimate recoverable resources," at the then-current rate of consumption, gave a figure of 340 years. But that estimate shrinks to insignificance compared to an estimate of the total amount of copper probably present somewhere in the earth's crust, derived from samplings: that figure is 242 *million* years.[8] As copper gets more difficult to extract with what are presently regarded as conventional methods, we can turn to less conventional ones, such as extracting it from seawater. But there is simply no basis for talking about an ultimate scarcity of copper. And the same is true for other natural stuffs.

In the case of bulk natural stuff such as oil or coal, the technology of extraction will be a major factor. To take a historically interesting example, a journal reported in the early 1970s, when it was fashionable to claim that the world was on the point of running out of oil, that estimated reserves were down to something like thirty years. But astute oilmen pointed out that this estimate was based on gravity-fed pumping. Yet it was already known at the time that if you used a recently developed technique, which involved forcing oil to the surface under pressure, you multiply that estimate by about ten. Then we have to consider the matter of new exploration, undersea sources, conversion from oil shales and tar sands, and finally, use of alcohol distilled from grains. Taking all this into account, there simply is no way to produce a sensible estimate of the world's resources of petroleum, natural gas, and other fuels. In 1970, it was said that production of oil in the world would peak in 1990. But by 1990, the price of crude oil had dropped by nearly two-thirds relative to 1970—an odd phenomenon if supplies were really getting low. (Updating things, the latest estimate of total known extractable oil in the world would last, at present rates of consumption, about *800* years.[9] No one thinks that estimate will remain solid—but of course, it has nowhere to go but up, since it concerns actually found oil sources.)

Extraction technology is only one factor. Next are the uses of the materials. Of course those are determined by the demand factors mentioned first. But in addition, given the same general uses, technological progress enables us to do more with less. The amount of iron ore required to make a car is far less now than in 1905 and could drop to zero. The amount of gasoline required to move an automobile at 60 mph has been cut by over half since 1950. The story can be repeated indefinitely. What it all adds up to is that there is, absolutely, no sufficient basis for any claim that "we are running out of resources" to the point that human consumption of them needs to be curtailed over and above the natural adjustment of the market, if we are to survive or maintain our standard of living. The whole idea that something of that sort might be true is muddled, depending on a simpleminded argument whose basic premises are wrong and whose conclusion does not follow.

And that is just the point. In very local circumstances, it is obvious that we can have critical shortages of something we desperately need—water in the Sahara, for instance. But if we broaden our scope ever so modestly, the situation changes, and when we broaden it to the global level, it changes totally and irretrievably. There is really no subject left. Shortages of this and that are a constant in human life, from birth to death. Each one of us could always use a little more, or perhaps a lot more, of something or other. But there is no underlying irremediable shortage of raw material, natural stuff, driving all this. At any given time, the basic shortage is of ingenuity. There are ways, in all likelihood, to do whatever it is we want to do, or to do it better, and there are people around who, given the chance, will find them. Their contribution to knowledge will spread, and before too long most of us will be doing that something.

Freedom's Controls

Individual people around the world live in a huge variety of ways, utilize a great range of resources, and face a great range of particular problems, many of which are reasonably described as having to do with scarcity. Of course, many of those scarcities are very far removed from the sorts that prophets of doom have in mind. Love, for example, is rarely abundant: most of us could use a bit more, or maybe a lot more. But if we confine ourselves to the general type that this discussion is concerned with, that still leaves plenty of problems.

When particular people encounter particular problems of supply, how do they attack them? Sometimes they increase their efforts to produce things that the individual in question can produce on his own hook. Often they will go out and buy what is needed, if they can afford it. But suppose they can't? Then they will have to alter their consumption patterns, or find ways to do what they want without the now scarce items. If a lot of people face the same scarcity problem, that will at least in the short run lead to an increase in prices from those who can supply them. And those increasing prices may prompt other producers to take the opportunity to increase their incomes by getting into the business of extracting, or of making, or making alternatives to, the needed items (or likely both).

The prospect of making money by devoting efforts in this area is a powerful incentive to hard work and ingenuity. Where the chips will fall when they do this is impossible to predict in detail. A new discovery might multiply tenfold the supply of materials of the type needed for this purpose, or it might alter drastically the sort of material that can be effectively utilized. Which of these responses will prevail? It is impossible to say, in general; everything depends on particular profiles of consumer interest, and the findings of particular people possessed of particular kinds of ingenuity. The world we live in has had ample experience with all these kinds of responses to scarcity. The result, in the longer term, is a general decrease in the prices of natural stuffs of all kinds, a general decrease in the prices of all sorts of consumer goods and services, and an increase in wages for many kinds of work.

All these responses amount to controls, though not of the kind that bureaucrats and prison guards are fond of. Price exerts its control in the best possible way: by allocating products in the direction of those who judge their use of these things of sufficiently importance to justify the expenditure required. The owners of natural resources are out to make a living, and will presumably charge the highest prices they can manage in the process. Yet not one has the kind of arbitrary, dictatorial powers that would be wielded by a cabinet minister or policeman. We all make up our minds, given a particular set of constraints and tastes; and we then do, according to our lights and our time and energy, our best. Everyone has the same basic type of rights—the right to do whatever he or she, in his or her own judgment, thinks best to do with a certain set of items, namely the ones come by in the course of voluntary relations with other people. The question is whether initiatives by governments to "defend" the environment are sufficiently well grounded to override these efforts of particular people.

What would it take for them to be so? Attributing property rights to people provides them with substantial resources for protecting themselves if they should need protecting. You can't assault my lungs, my backyard, my car, or anything else that is mine; nor I yours. If property rights are in place and defended, then big companies may not assault them any more than small ones or individuals.

Individual people of larger means, or sizable associations such as business firms, may be in a position to make people an offer for properties or services that is attractive enough to induce them to sell. But if they don't want to sell, they do not have to, and no privately acting persons can legitimately coerce them into doing so. Individuals' property rights are fairly often violated by private theft or assault. They are far more often and more effectively assaulted by governments of all kinds. And environmental initiatives would do this even more than most other programs. The governments which initiate those programs agree that individuals assaulting, invading, and damaging other individuals, including their property, is wrong. The question is whether governments' own actions are any better—or are they, perhaps, a great deal worse, viewed in the large scale that they inevitably involve?

Defenders of such programs may say that when governments take such measures, they are *not* really violating people's individual rights, even though the effect on the individual in question is the same: uniformed agents or bureaucrats behind desks rather than stocking-hooded men taking what used to be one's own, without asking and without compensation.

When, then, is it wrong to invade? What are the limits of property rights? There are many opinions about this, and not a few people appear to think that it is nothing but a matter of opinion. Presumably those of the latter view do not bother to read papers such as this, but all others will be interested, one would think, in knowing which views are better than which. I shall argue that normal property rights of individual people will handle virtually every situation of concern in this area, and do so much better than political methods with their elected deliberative bodies and lavishly empowered regulators presuming to make these sorts of decisions better than individuals themselves. That is especially because the premise on which central control is predicated is invariably false.

At a minimum, I presume, it will be agreed that one may not use one's property to inflict damage, harm, or loss on others, including their properties. It might be thought but a short step from there to the conclusion that people may not use their property to "harm the environment." But that odd locution is very far from signifying a short step. Considerable bits of the environment *are* owned by people. Fields and forests, yards and mines, some lakes and streams, are owned by individual people; and the proscription against harm to others extends, of course, to all that. But some environmentalists, as they are called, claim that *in addition to*, or perhaps even *instead of* those damages, we should acknowledge a category of damage to the environment *itself*, harm to nature as such. Those who say that are trading on a misunderstanding. The environment itself is not a person or personage; it has no interests, no will, no say in the matter. There isn't anyone around who can have such a "say" except us people, the only entities that can communicate with each other at the level necessary to understand and make decisions about requirements, duties, and values in this or any area. If some people want to endow trees with rights, we will have to ask how and why they propose to do this.

And what is there to say on the matter? If someone is interested in trees, then the fact that action x would damage some tree will be of interest to that person. But trees can be mine or yours or somebody else's. They do not have any independent moral standing, they can't speak up for their supposed interests. The only way in which the others of us can be expected to respond to claims that nonhuman entities have moral standing on their own hook is as assertions that *we*, somehow, have an interest *in the tree*—we love trees, just as we might love children or Mozart symphonies. The trouble is, though, that "we" might or might not share that attitude toward trees, and of course different people will differ. Property rights sort this out: the person who first begins to use the tree in some way has preference over all others, who must ask him for permission to use it, and who must also persuade him that he should "save" it rather than, say, turning it into firewood or pulp for paper. The decision, though, is up to the owner, not the rest of us. We don't own it, and he does. And the claim that the decision is up to *the tree itself*, so that no human *can* rightly own it, indulges in hocus-pocus. Suppose that property owners ask their trees what they think, and take silence by way of answer as acquiescence in their own proposed uses of them. How does the proposed savior of the trees know that trees don't *prefer* being turned into cabinets or houses? Needless to say, he does not.

The concern for trees is often put in terms of conservation: stop using trees, or we'll run out of them. But this runs up against the same fact as holds in agriculture. The fact is that people can take care to grow more trees, and they have an interest in doing so, trees being valuable, and so they do—to the point that many more trees are grown than harvested each passing year. Not using trees in order to keep trees from disappearing is exactly the wrong policy: it is our use of trees that prompts people to grow so many of them.[10]

Until some other human's interests is brought relevantly into the case, as one who is positively or negatively affected by someone's actions regarding some nonhuman item, there simply is no case. The supposition that there is enters as an excuse for attacking the lives and properties of other people—but it's a trumped-up excuse. It's not that the rights of humans "come first": it's that they exhaust the field. Nothing else has any rights or any standing against people in general; rather, it is particular people who have rights against other particular people. Those include rights to use or exercise decision-making power over the use of things.

So an environmental legislator must show, in order to justify some intervention that would damage the property of many people, or undermine their ability to use it as they would, that his continued use of it threatens someone else's rightful interests in some way. And this, of course, can easily happen. Do I put smoke in your lungs? Then you have a case: they are your lungs, and I do not get to use *them* however I wish. Do I poison your crops or your drinking water? Again, you have a case. Do I exhaust the available supply of x, including your share of it? Then you have a case—but the case you have is contingent on your demonstrating that you do have a share of X, as well as that I have done something to it. Once you establish that, you of course may sue me for doing this, and recover the damage I do. This is not how the environmental initiatives of the Central Committee proceed, however. The claim is not that some property owner is harmed; it is, rather, that a nebulous entity, "mankind," is harmed or even that the trees or canyons or whatever are *themselves* "harmed." This is a kind of claim that has no rational standing.

The only credible way to proceed, then, is to argue that individuals' being permitted to make their own decisions about particular bits of the environment will not only lead to evils, but to evils that those affected can do nothing to remedy. Remember, what has to be meant is that this is true regarding such few bits of the environment as those individuals have thus far managed or might in the future manage to obtain from others by suitable purchases, and which their owners are already required to refrain from using in such a way as to damage other persons or their properties. But how is that to be shown, if the others affected by one's uses of those bits find nothing to complain about on their own account? If Jones uses his property to poison Smith or Smith's trees or water supply, and so on, then of course Smith, as we have noted above, may indeed complain and require redress from Jones, and is likely to do so. On the other hand, to accuse Jones of murdering his own trees when he chops them down to make a parking lot or a house is to invert the relevant values, and to attack Jones's autonomy.

Sometimes, indeed, the pattern of use makes it difficult to locate the individuals who are harmed. Large-scale pollution, for example, might affect many people who cannot identify the particular polluter responsible. For such cases, work will have to be done to locate the patterns of pollution. But that is not all. For to talk thus is to assume that pollution is *necessarily* bad. Now of course the term is typically used in such a way that we only call something "pollution" if it is bad for someone. However, this tendency serves to obscure the issue. Consider, for example, various sorts of smoke or exhaust fumes. The claim that these "pollute" is not true by definition. To establish that smoke X pollutes is to establish that X impedes someone's breathing, or causes some other identifiable harm to someone. But whether X does do that depends on many things.

Prominent among those is the *degree* of the kind of alteration of the air caused by the purportedly polluting activity. Humans are such that tiny amounts of what would otherwise be poisonous are not so, and are even, sometimes, good or even essential to life. Is carbon dioxide a "poison," as one often sees said? Well, for one thing, it is the very breath of life for those same trees we were talking about above. And it is obviously not poisonous all by itself: the air we all breathe is and always has been composed partly of that gas, and we all exhale it constantly. The external atmosphere could possibly have too much of this trace gas in it, but how much is "too much"? There is at present no case for the claim that the earth's atmosphere has too much of it;[11] it has in the past sometimes had a good deal more than now, and the slight increase sustained during the past fifty years or so appears to be having a highly beneficial effect on the growth of plants, including trees.

The point is that no substance is just as such, irrespective of quantity, a poison. It is always a matter of degree. So how is that to be decided? Two components are required. One is scientific work, to see how this or that quantity affects the human body. But the other is a judgment by individuals to the effect that those effects are or are not inimical to their interests as they see them.

Someone might prefer more pollution and lower prices of the items whose manufacture causes it, to less pollution and higher prices, or to a life devoid of the items that cause it.

But it is characteristic of environmental initiatives by governments that they require the making of decisions of the latter kind on behalf of individuals. On what grounds? The assumption is that they know better than those individuals what is good for them. Is this a reasonable assumption? Certainly there are familiar cases in which we would accept that A knows better than B about certain things that are important for B's well-being. Doctors often know that their patients have condition x, y, or z, and what the consequences will be for them if they don't do something to fix it. But having assembled this knowledge and transmitted it to the patient, they normally, and rightly, leave the decision to the patient. This is so even when the affliction in question is lifethreatening. A patient might prefer an earlier death to a cancer operation, and the patient's word on the matter is decisive.

But environmental initiatives don't adhere to that model. The individual isn't asked. It might be said that he is asked en masse, as it were, at the polls. But this is not a very good answer. Voters merely elect representatives—they don't, or rarely do, vote for or against programs, referendum-style. In either case, they almost never have the information required for a rational decision. The congressman or M.P. decides on their behalfs, it seems. But elected representatives are very far from having the competence that physicians do, for one thing; and for another, as we have just noted, they act on behalf of people without any further consultation—in marked contrast to doctors, who do.

More importantly, elected politicians, like nonelected ones, have the usual interests of persons in power: they want to expand it, to solidify it, and of course to reap various rewards associated with it. The last thing any politician wants to be told is that nothing needs to be done by the government. And so there is a systematic, deeply entrenched bias toward reading the facts so as to yield a conclusion favorable to more action. Since civil servants and elected representatives have far more access to the public ear than any dissidents, the prevailing mentality will in general be favorable to activism by government, within only the broad and crude limits imposed by democracy.

It is characteristic of some environmental problems, and claimed of all of them, that they can only be handled by mass means, and that since they involve public goods problems, individualistic, market methods are inapplicable. That is conspicuously not true of natural resources, though it is arguable in regard to pollution. Pollution problems, to be sure, can be viewed as resource problems by stating them in terms of the availability of clean air and the like—though it is clear that it's not a matter of being about to run out of air or water, now or any time. Rather, it's a matter of the quality of air declining, or the quantity of good-enough air. And there we have to note that the life expectancy of the world's population has been increasing mightily in this century, despite all (with the exception of AIDS effects in large parts of Africa—but that's a problem having nothing to do with air or water quality). Thus, it must either be the case that air quality hasn't been declining, or that it has not declined seriously enough to make a net negative difference to life expectancy. Even in the worst-case scenario of nineteenth-century industrialized Britain, life expectancy increased dramatically throughout the century. Doubtless much of that increase was due to the very products whose factories emitted the pollutions, as well as to the home-heating levels that enabled people to be healthier even while they made the air worse for everyone in the neighborhood. Given what we know now, people's choices at the time look wise—much wiser than shutting down all the factories and turning people back to primitive agricultural life.

So the question about cleanup measures is whether they are worth the cost, and there is a clear likelihood that the answer is in the negative. In the case where the purpose of the cost is to "save the forests" or bring the level of air pollution from some already very low figure to near zero, the answer is that it is not. Aggressive "environmentalism" is a waste of a very large amount of money in the short run, and self-defeating in the longer run.

To those who say, "It's only money" the reply is: "Speak for yourself!" And this environmentalists rarely do. High officials in the environmental activist organization Greenpeace, we are told, commanded incomes on the order of those enjoyed by high-ranking officials in large corporations. Ordinary people's plans for their lives are devoted considerably to spending their incomes in the best ways. Taking those incomes from them, via taxation and regulation, reduces their ability to run their lives as they would like. Assaults on incomes are assaults on the people whose incomes they are. To treat those incomes lightly is to treat those people lightly.

Sustainability

'Sustainability' has become, as they say, a buzzword nowadays. Whole departments in universities are devoting themselves to the subject; like 'global warming' the word is used in a self-evident manner, as if it simply referred to a problem, one that is just there, awaiting solution. The question whether there is any genuine reason for the effort in question or whether it even makes sense doesn't seem to be welcome. Yet it is obviously the most basic question to ask. What's odd is that it is a question that individual people ask quite often and quite relevantly: if we retire now, can we live (well enough) on the income? Are the days of Chateau Lafitte numbered? But what they ask are all sorts of different questions, and any legislator attempting to help some of them out with their problems will do so at the expense of others with different problems.

The last examples discussed above illustrate, of course, the extreme relevance of the question, What is it that is to be "sustained"? But in truth, it hardly matters, because whatever it is, the people interested in that will, in the first place, likely be interested not merely in "sustaining" but in increasing and improving. The psychology and ideology of sustainability are devoted to keeping heads in the sand, refusing to consider possibilities for development, and maintaining a nanny-like stance toward the sustainability-preacher's fellows. For what the proponent of sustainability wants to do above all, as it turns out, is to require other people to get off the gravy train, tighten their belts, make sacrifices—not to go out and improve things by finding new and better ways to

do the things people like to do, nor, indeed, to allow those who do have
ambitions to do just that to get on with it. The idea seems to be that doing that
will further increase the rate at which we are using up precious and irreplaceable
resources.

Once one sees the flaws in the general thesis of resources limitation, the case
for concentrating on "sustainability" has nothing to sustain it. People who have
done no serious homework on the matter aver that we cannot go on like this,
using up iron, copper, what-have-you. In fact, we can go on like this for so long
that there is no point in thinking about it. Once you get more than a few decades
or so into the future, technological developments become unforeseeable; yet
technology is what it all depends on. Technology enables us to have
automobiles, and then to have millions and millions of them, plus roads to
drive them on and, even, places to go in them that are worth going to. The idea
that "sustainability" is a major global issue rapidly crosses the threshold of the
absurd when the role of technology is injected properly into any scenario where
the question is raised.

People who do claim there is such a problem need to be asked what their
proposed time-horizon is. As noted above, current known sources of oil,
standard and nonstandard, are enough to "sustain" us for 800 more years of
consumption at current levels.[12]   But there is no reason to think that we will
continue to consume at those levels: more, or less, is much likelier than the
same. But eight centuries is far, far beyond the threshold of foreseeability. The
builders of Chartres Cathedral, visionary as they were, could not have had the
faintest idea what would be perfectly routine in the twentieth century; but most
of the intervening millennium was one of abysmal technical ignorance by
modern standards. Consider the number of very bright people working on all
things technical at present, and then consider how much we know even now,
and the fact stares us in the face: no one can say, to even the roughest
approximation, how we will be doing what a thousand years from now, or even,
in innumerable respects, one hundred.

The charming slogan of the Canadian Green Party at one time had it that
"We do not inherit the earth from our parents, we borrow it from our children."
But those who intone such slogans have not contemplated the facts, for in any
sense in which that is true, those children are getting a terrific rate of return on
their capital: the earth they get from us will be one that they will have a hitherto
undreamed-of stock of knowledge about how to use—all courtesy of us, their
parents and grandparents. Barring war, genuine external catastrophes, or politics
even worse than those to which we have already been subjected, the earth they
inherit will be a far more comfortable, healthy, and interesting place than the one
their parents and grandparents had to put up with. Sustainability is not the
problem they will mostly be confronted with: rather, it will be the challenge of
how best to spend their lives given a range of options to choose from that are
currently inconceivable. But the political factor is quite another matter. The
politics of saddling current earthlings with huge and onerous debts, all payable
to the bureaucrats and environmental policemen who enforce them, is by far the
greatest obstacle to the progress that is plainly possible. There isn't any
question at all that politics can put a stop to growth, including the growth of

technology. It will be fascinating to see how well it succeeds in that. But as to natural and inherent limits to growth, of a sort requiring clamping down on people in their use of resources, the case is closed. For all practical purposes, there are no resource-type limits.

Notes

This essay owes its life to three things: my participation in the now-defunct Committee on Health and Safety of the Royal Society of Canada over several years after my election to it in 1989; my discovery, due to an acquaintance who has faded into memory, of the writings of Julian Simon; and the popularity in the philosophical profession of the very views that are so resoundingly refuted in Simon's and many other books and articles. My first publication on these matters was "Is There a Problem about Overpopulation?" a guest editorial in *Risk Abstracts* 9, no. 1 (March 1992), 1-10. Versions of it have been presented at various meetings, including the Ontario Philosophical Society, Carleton University, 1991, the Canadian Philosophical Association, 1997, the Center for Philosophic Exchange at the State University of New York College at Brockport, April 1994, and the Center for the Study of Ethics in Society at Western Michigan University, Kalamazoo, Michigan, in November 1994. Both the latter presentations were published, the former in *Philosophic Exchange* nos. 24-25 (1993-94), 39-62, the latter, somewhat updated and improved, in their Papers Published by the Center 8, no. 3 (March 1995). It was also presented during my stay as the Lansdowne Lecturer at the University of Victoria in April 1996. I am grateful to audiences from those and many more occasions for useful, and in some cases slightly frightening, discussion. Finally, there is the chapter "Morals and the Environment" in *Moral Matters* (2nd edition, Peterborough, Ontario: Broadview Press, 1999), 197-228.

1. Julian Simon describes one in *The Ultimate Resource II* (Princeton, N.J.: Princeton University Press, 1996), 100-101.

2. "By these figures [those of the UN Food and Agricultural Organization and its predecessors], the global per capita calorie availability rose by nearly 30 percent between the 1930s and the late 1980s. For the less developed regions . . . per capital foods supplies are thought to have risen by nearly 40 percent." Nicholas Eberstadt, "Population, Food, and Income: Global Trends in the Twentieth Century," in Ronald Bailey, ed., *The True State of the Planet* (New York: Free Press, 1995), 28.

3. Garrett Hardin, "Lifeboat Ethics: The Case against Helping the Poor," *Psychology Today* 8 (1974-75), 38-43, 123-26.

4. Colin Clark, *Population Growth and Land Use* (New York: St. Martin's Press, 1967), 157.

5. Simon, *The Ultimate Resource II* , 100-104.

6. Eberstadt, "Population, Food, and Income," 8.

7. Nicholas Eberstadt, "World Population Prospects for the Twenty-first Century: The Specter of 'Depopulation'?" in Ronald Bailey, ed., *Earth Report 2000* (New York: McGraw-Hill 2000), 63-84, especially, 81.

8. Julian Simon, *Population Matters* (New Brunswick, N.J.: Transaction Publishers, 1990), 73.

9. Jerry Taylor and Peter Van Doren, "Soft Energy versus Hard Facts: Powering the Twenty-First Century," in Ronald Bailey, ed., *Earth Report 2000* (New York: McGraw-Hill, 2000), 121.

10. See Roger A. Sedjo, "Forests: Conflicting Signals," in Bailey, *The True*

State of the Planet, 177-210, esp. 189, detailing the excess of net tree growth over removals in the U.S. since 1952; the same general story holds for the other major wood producers. The Amazon is an exception, owing to the policies of the Brazilian government, but not actually a very important one; the world situation is one of net growth.

11. See Bailey, *True State of the Planet*, 426-27, showing that the incidence of CO_2 in the earth's atmosphere leveled off after 1979.

12. Taylor and Van Doren, "Soft Energy versus Hard Facts."

Bibliography

Anscombe, Elizabeth. "On Frustration of the Majority by Fulfilment of the Majority's Will." In *Collected Philosophical Papers, Vol. III: Ethics, Religion, and Politics*. Minneapolis: University of Minnesota Press, 1981.

Aquinas, Thomas. *Summa Theologia*. Selections in William P. Baumgarth and Richard J. Regan, S.J., eds., *Saint Thomas Aquinas on Law, Morality, and Politics*. Indianapolis: Hackett, 1988.

————. *On Kingship*. In Paul E. Sigmund, ed., *St. Thomas Aquinas on Politics and Ethics*. New York: Norton, 1988.

Aristotle. *Nichomachean Ethics*. In Richard McKeon, ed., *Basic Works of Aristotle*. New York: Random House, 1941.

Arnold, Scott. "Why Profits Are Deserved." *Ethics* 97, no. 2 (January 1987): 387-402.

Avery, Dennis. "Saving the Planet with Pesticides: Increasing Food Supplies While Preserving the Earth's Biodiversity." In Ronald Bailey, ed., 49-82, *The True State of the Planet*. New York: Free Press, 1995.

Baier, Kurt. *The Moral Point of View*. Ithaca: Cornell University Press, 1958.

Bailey, Ronald, ed. *The True State of the Planet*. New York: Free Press, 1995.

Barnett, Randy. *The Structure of Liberty*. New York: Oxford University Press, 1998.

Barr, Nicholas T. *The Economics of the Welfare State*. 3rd ed. Stanford, Calif.: Stanford University Press, 1998.

Barry, Brian. *The Liberal Theory of Justice*. Oxford: Clarendon, 1973.

Braybrooke, David. "Utilitarianism with a Difference: Rawls' Position in Ethics." *Canadian Journal of Philosophy* 3 (December 1973): 303-31.

Buchanan, Allen. *Ethics, Efficiency, and The Market*. Totowa, New Jersey: Rowman & Allanheld, 1985.

Canadian Charter of Rights and Freedoms. Government of Canada: Part I of the Constitution Act, 1982.

Clark, Colin. *Population Growth and Land Use*. New York: St. Martin's, 1967.

Cohen, G. A. *Karl Marx's Theory of History*. Princeton, N.J.: Princeton University Press, 1978.

————. "The Labor Theory of Value and the Concept of Exploitation." *Philosophy and Public Affairs* 8, no. 4 (Summer 1979): 338-60.

Cowan, Robin, and Mario Rizzo, eds. *Profits and Morality*. Chicago: University of Chicago Press, 1995.

Dahl, Robert A. *On Democracy*. New Haven, Conn.: Yale University Press, 1998.

Dancy, Jonathan. *Moral Reasons*. Oxford: Blackwell, 1993.

Danielson, Peter. "The Rights of Chickens." In John T. Sanders and Jan Narveson, eds., 171-94, *For and Against the State*. Lanham, Md.: Rowman & Littlefield, 1996.

Dworkin, Ronald. "What Is Equality?" *Philosophy and Public Affairs* 10, nos. 3 (Summer 1981): 171-94, and 4 (Fall 1981): 283-346.

———. "In Defense of Equality." *Social Philosophy and Policy* 1, no. 1 (Autumn 1983): 24-40.

Eberstadt, Nicholas. "Population, Food, and Income: Global Trends in the Twentieth Century." In Ronald Bailey, ed., 7-48, *The True State of the Planet*. New York: Free Press, 1995.

———. "World Population Prospects for the Twenty-first Century: The Specter of 'Depopulation'?" In Ronald Bailey, ed., 63-84, *Earth Report 2000*. New York: McGraw-Hill, 2000.

Engels, Friedrich. "Speech at the Graveside of Marx." In Robert C. Tucker, ed., 681-82, *The Marx-Engels Reader*. New York: Norton, 1978.

Evans, Rod L., and Irwin M. Berent, eds. *Drug Legalization: For and Against*. La Salle, Ill.: Open Court, 1992.

Ewin, R. E. *Virtues and Rights*. San Francisco: Westview, 1991.

Federal Bureau of Investigation. *Crime in the United States: 1994, FBI Uniform Crime Reports* (Washington, D.C.: U.S. Government Printing Office, 1995).

Feinberg, Joel. "Justice and Personal Desert." In Joel Feinberg, ed., 55-94, *Doing and Deserving*. Princeton: Princeton University Press, 1970.

Fiske, Milton. "History and Reason in Rawls' Moral Theory." In Norman Daniels, ed., 53-80, *Reading Rawls*. New York: Basic Books, 1974.

Frank, Robert. *Choosing the Right Pond*. New York: Oxford University Press, 1985.

Friedman, David. "Anarchy and Efficient Law." 235-54 in John T. Sanders and Jan Narveson, eds. *For and Against the State*. Lanham, Md.: Rowman & Littlefield, 1996.

Friedman, Marilyn, and Jan Narveson. *Political Correctness—For and Against*. Lanham, Md.: Rowman & Littlefield, 1995.

Gauthier, David. "Justice and Natural Endowment: Toward a Critique of Rawls' Ideological Framework." *Social Theory and Practice* 3, no. 1 (Spring 1974, but published in 1975): 3-26. Also reprinted in *Moral Dealing*, 150-70.

———. "Reason and Maximization." *Canadian Journal of Philosophy* 4, no. 2 (March 1975): 411-33. Also reprinted in *Moral Dealing*, 209-33.

———. *Morals by Agreement*. New York: Oxford University Press, 1986.

———. *Moral Dealing*. Ithaca: Cornell University Press, 1990.

George, Robert P., ed. *Natural Law Theory*. New York: Oxford University Press, 1992.

Gibbard, Allan. "Natural Property Rights." *Nous* 10, no. 1 (March 1976): 77-86.

Gospel According to St. Matthew, The New Testament.

Gould, Carol. *Rethinking Democracy*. New York: Cambridge University Press, 1988.

Green, Leslie. "Who Believes in Political Obligation?" In John T. Sanders and Jan Narveson, eds., 1-18, *For and Against the State*. Lanham, Md.: Rowman & Littlefield, 1996.

Grunebaum, James. *Private Ownership*. London: Routledge & Kegan Paul, 1987.

Gwartney, James D., and Richard L. Stroup. *What Everyone Should Know about Economics and Prosperity*. Vancouver, B.C.: Fraser Institute, 1993.

Hardin, Garrett. "Lifeboat Ethics: The Case against Helping the Poor." *Psychology Today* 8 (1974-75): 38-43, 123-26.

Hardin, Russell. *Morality within the Limits of Reason*. Chicago: University of Chicago Press, 1988.

Hare, Richard M. *Moral Thinking.* Oxford, U.K.: Clarendon, 1981.

Hartney, Michael. "Some Confusions Concerning Collective Rights." *Canadian Journal of Law and Jurisprudence* 4, no. 2 (July 1991): 293-314.

Hobbes, Thomas. *Leviathan.* New York: E. P. Dutton, Everyman Library, 1950.

Hohfeld, Wesley. "Fundamental Legal Conceptions as Applied in Judicial Reasoning." *Yale Law Journal* 23 (1913-14): 16-34.

———. "Fundamental Legal Conceptions as Applied in Judicial Reasoning." *Yale Law Journal* 26 (1916-17): 710-20.

Honoré, A. M. "Ownership." In A.G. Guest, ed., 107-28, *Oxford Essays in Jurisprudence.* Oxford, U.K.: Oxford University Press, 1961.

Hume, David. *An Inquiry Concerning the Principles of Morals.* Indianapolis: Bobbs–Merrill, Library of Liberal Arts, 1957.

———. *Treatise of Human Nature.* London, U.K.: Oxford University Press, 1955.

Hunt, Ian. "A Critique of Roemer, Hodgson, and Cohen on Marxian Exploitation." *Social Theory and Practice* 12, no. 2 (Summer 1986): 121-71.

Jasay, Anthony de. *Before Resorting to Politics.* Cheltenham, U.K.: Edward Elgar: The Shafetesbury Papers 5, 1996.

Kirzner, Israel M. "The Nature of Profits: Some Economic Insights and Their Ethical Implications." 22-47 in Cowan and Rizzo, *Profits and Morality.* Chicago: University of Chicago Press, 1995.

Klosko, George. "The Natural Basis of Political Obligation." *Social Philosophy and Policy* 18 no. 1 (Winter 2001): 93-114.

Lester, Jan. *Escape from Leviathan.* New York: St. Martin's, 2000.

———. "Market-Anarchy, Liberty, and Pluralism." In John T. Sanders and Jan Narveson, eds., 63-80, *For and Against the State.* Lanham, Md.: Rowman & Littlefield, 1996.

Locke, John. *Second Treatise on Civil Government,* In P. Laslett, ed., *Two Treatises of Government.* Cambridge, U. K.: Cambridge University Press, 1960.

Mack, Eric. "The Self-Ownership Proviso: A New and Improved Lockean Proviso." *Social Philosophy and Policy* 12, no. 1 (Winter 1995): 186-218.

———. "Gauthier on Rights and Economic Rent." *Social Philosophy and Policy* 9, no. 1 (Autumn 1992): 171-200.

MacLeod, Alistair. "Equality of Opportunity." In J. Narveson, ed., 370-78, *Moral Issues.* Toronto: Oxford University Press, 1983.

Macpherson, C. B. *Democratic Theory.* Oxford: Clarendon Press, 1973.

Marshall, John. "The Failure of Contract as Justification." *Social Theory and Practice* 3, no. 4 (Fall 1975): 441-60.

Marx, Karl. *Preface to The Critique of Political Economy.* New York: International Publishers, 1970.

———. *Communist Manifesto.* In Robert C. Tucker, ed., 469-500, *The Marx-Engels Reader.* New York: Norton, 1978.

———. "Critique of the Gotha Program." In Robert C. Tucker, ed., 525-41, *The Marx-Engels Reader.* New York: Norton, 1978.

———. *Capital,* Vol. I. Selections. In Robert C. Tucker, ed., 294-438, *The Marx-Engels Reader.* New York: Norton, 1978.

Mayo, Henry B. *Introduction to Marxist Theory.* New York: Oxford University Press, 1960.

McBryde, William Leon. *The Philosophy of Marx.* London: Hutchinson, 1978.

McDonald, Michael. "Should Communities Have Rights? Reflections on Liberal Individualism." *Canadian Journal of Law and Jurisprudence* 4, no. 2 (July 1991): 217-38.

Mill, John Stuart. *Utilitarianism, Liberty, and Representative Government.* London: Everyman's Library, J. M. Dent & Son, 1968.

Mitchell, William C., and Randy T. Simmons. *Beyond Politics.* Boulder, Colo.: Westview, 1994.

Moore, G. E. *Principia Ethica.* Cambridge, U.K.: Cambridge University Press, 1954.

Moore, Mark H. "Actually, Prohibition Was a Success." In Rod L. Evans and Irwin M. Berent, eds., 95-98, *Drug Legalization: For and Against.* La Salle, Ill.: Open Court, 1992.

Narveson, Jan. "Pacifism: A Philosophical Analysis." *Ethics* 75, no. 4 (July 1965): 259-71.

———. "Utilitarianism and Formalism." *Australasian Journal of Philosophy* 43, no. 2 (May 1965), 58-72.

———. *Morality and Utility.* Baltimore: Johns Hopkins University Press, 1967.

———. "A Puzzle about Economic Justice in Rawls' Theory." *Social Theory and Practice,* 4, no. 1 (Fall 1976).

———. "The How and Why of Universalizability." In Nelson Potter and Mark Timmons, eds., 3-46, *Morality and Universality.* Dordrecht, Netherlands: Reidel, 1981.

———. "Rawls and Utilitarianism." In H. Miller and W. Williams, eds., 128-43, *The Limits of Utilitarianism.* Minneapolis: University of Minnesota Press, 1982.

———. "Marxism: Hollow at the Core." *Free Inquiry* (Spring 1983): 29-35.

———. "On Dworkinian Equality" and "Reply to Dworkin." *Social Philosophy and Policy* 1, no. 1 (Autumn 1983): 1-23, 41-44.

———. "Equality vs. Liberty: Advantage, Liberty." *Social Philosophy and Policy* 2, no. 2 (Fall 1984): 33-60.

———. "Michael Sandel's *Liberalism and the Limits of Justice.*" *Canadian Journal of Philosophy* 17, no. 1 (March 1987): 227-34.

———. "Have We a Right to Non-Discrimination?" In Deborah Poff and Wilfrid Waluchow, eds., 270-87, *Business Ethics in Canada.* Scarborough, Ont.: Prentice Hall Canada, 1st ed., 1987; 3rd ed. 1999.

———. "Liberalism and Public Education." *Interchange* 19, no. 1 (March 1988): 60-69.

———. *The Libertarian Idea.* Philadelphia: Temple University Press, 1988. Republished, Peterborough, Ont.: Broadview, 2001.

———. "Collectives Rights?" *Canadian Journal of Law and Jurisprudence* 4, no. 2 (July 1991): 329-45.

———. "Democracy and Economic Rights." *Social Philosophy and Policy* 9, no. 1 (1992) 29-61.

———. "The Justification of Private Property by First-Comers." Not currently published; available from the author.

———. "Is There a Problem about Overpopulation?" Guest Editorial in *Risk Abstracts* 9, no. 1 (March 1992): 1-10.

———. "Resources and Environmental Policy." *Philosophic Exchange* nos. 24-25 (1993-94): 39-62

———. *Moral Matters.* Peterborough, Ont.: Broadview, 1993. 2nd ed., 1999.

———. "Resources and Environmental Policy." *Papers Published by the Center For the Study of Ethics in Society* 8, no. 3 (March 1995). Kalamazoo, Mich.: Western Michigan University, 1995.

———. "Deserving Profits." Mario Rizzo and Robin Cowan, editors. *Profits and Morality*, (University of Chicago Press, 1995).

Narveson, Jan, and Marilyn Friedman. *Political Correctness—For and Against*. Lanham, Md.: Rowman & Littlefield, 1995.

———. "Fair Hiring and Affirmative Action" In Wesley Cragg and Christine Koggel, eds., 313-25, *Contemporary Moral Issues*. Toronto: McGraw-Hill Ryerson, 4th ed., 1997).

———. "Liberty, Equality, and Distributive Justice." In Larry May, Christine Sistare, and Jonathan Schonsheck, eds., 15-37, *Liberty, Equality, and Plurality*. Lawrence, Kansas: University Press of Kansas, 1997.

———. "Libertarianism vs. Marxism: Reflections on G. A. Cohen's *Self-Ownership, Freedom and Equality*." *Journal of Ethics* 2, no. 1 (1998): 1-26.

———. "Property Rights: Original Acquisition and Lockean Provisos." *Public Affairs Quarterly* 13, no. 3 (July 1999): 205-27.

———. "Liberal/Conservative: The Real Controversy." *Journal of Value Inquiry* 34, nos. 2-3 (September, 2000): 167-88.

Narveson, Jan, and Susan Dimock, eds. *Liberalism: New Essays on Liberal Themes*. Dordrecht, Netherlands: Kluwer Academic Publishers, 2000.

———. "Morals and the Environment." In *Moral Matters*, 197-228, 2nd ed., Peterborough, Ont.: Broadview, 1999.

———. "Morality: Force and Reason." Read at Ontario Philosophical Society meetings, Kingston, Ont., October 1997.

Nielsen, Kai. *Equality and Liberty*. Lanham, Md.: Rowman & Allanheld, 1985.

Norman, Richard. *Free and Equal*. Oxford, U.K.: Oxford University Press, 1987.

Nozick, Robert. *Anarchy, State, and Utopia*. New York: Basic Books, 1974.

Okin, Susan Moller. *Justice, Gender, and the Family*. New York: Basic Books, 1989.

Olen, Jeffrey. *Moral Freedom*. Philadelphia: Temple University Press, 1988.

O'Rourke, P. J. *All the Trouble in the World*. New York: Atlantic Monthly, 1994.

———. *Eat the Rich*. New York: Atlantic Monthly, 1998.

Parkinson, G. H. R., ed. *Marx and Marxisms*. Royal Institute of Philosophy Lecture Series #14. Cambridge, U.K.: Cambridge University Press, 1982.

Pence, G. E. "Fair Contracts and Beautiful Intuitions." *New Essays on Contract Theory—Canadian Journal of Philosophy* Supplementary Volume 3, ed. Kai Nielsen and Roger Shiner (1977): 137-52.

Poff, Deborah, and Wilfrid Waluchow, eds. *Business Ethics in Canada*. Scarborough, Ont: Prentice Hall Canada, 1st ed., 1987; 3rd ed. 1999, 270-87.

Rasmussen, David W., and Bruce L. Benson. *The Economic Anatomy of a Drug War*. Lanham, Md.: Rowman & Littlefield, 1994.

Rawls, John. *A Theory of Justice*. Cambridge, Mass.: Harvard University Press, 1971.

———. "Fairness to Goodness." *Philosophical Review* 84 (October 1975).

———. "Distributive Justice." In Peter Laslett and W. G. Runciman, eds., *Philosophy, Politics, and Society, Third Series*. Oxford: Blackwell, 1967, 65.

Raz, Joseph. *The Morality of Freedom*. Oxford: Clarendon, 1986, 166.

Reiman, Jeffrey. "Exploitation, Force, and the Moral Assessment of Capitalism." *Philosophy and Public Affairs* 16, no. 1 (Winter 1987): 3-41.

Rhodes, Michael. "The Nature of Coercion." In Jan Narveson and Susan Dimock, eds., *Liberalism: New Essays on Liberal Themes*. Dordrecht, Netherlands: Kluwer Academic Publishers, 2000, 221-33.

――――. *A Nonevaluative Analysis of Coercion.* PhD dissertation for SUNY, Buffalo, New York, 1993.

Ridley, Matt. *The Origins of Virtue.* New York: Viking Penguin, 1997.

Rizzo, Mario, and Robin Cowan, eds. *Profits and Morality.* Chicago: University of Chicago Press, 1995.

Ross, William David. *The Right and the Good.* Oxford, U.K.: Oxford University Press, 1930.

Sandel, Michael. *Liberalism and the Limits of Justice.* New York: Cambridge University Press, 1982.

Sanders, John T., and Jan Narveson, eds. *For and Against the State.* Lanham, Md.: Rowman & Littlefield, 1996.

Sanders, John T. "The State of Statelessness." In John T. Sanders and Jan Narveson, eds., 255-88. *For and Against the State.* Lanham, Md.: Rowman & Littlefield, 1996.

――――. "Justice and the Initial Aquisition of Private Property." *Harvard Journal of Law and Public Policy* 10 (1987): 367-400.

Schmidtz, David. "The Lockean Proviso." In Schmidtz, *The Limits of Government.* Boulder, Colo.: Westview, 1991, 17-26.

Sedjo, Roger A. "Forests: Conflicting Signals." In Ronald Bailey, ed., 177-210, *The True State of the Planet.* New York: Free Press, 1995.

Sher, George. *Desert.* Princeton, N.J.: Princeton University Press, 1987.

Sidgwick, Henry. *The Methods of Ethics.* London: Macmillan, 1961.

Simmons, A. John. *On the Edge of Anarchy.* Princeton, N.J.: Princeton University Press, 1993.

――――. "Philosophical Anarchism." In John T. Sanders and Jan Narveson, eds., 19-41, *For and Against the State.* Lanham, Md.: Rowman & Littlefield, 1996.

Simmons, Randy T., and William C. Mitchell. *Beyond Politics.* Boulder, Colo.: Westview, 1994.

Simon, Julian. *The Ultimate Resource II.* Princeton, N.J.: Princeton University Press, 1996.

――――. *Population Matters.* New Brunswick, N.J.: Transaction Publishers, 1990.

Taylor, Jerry, and Peter Van Doren. "Soft Energy versus Hard Facts: Powering the Twenty-First Century." In *Earth Report 2000,* ed. Ronald C. Bailey, 115-54, New York: McGraw-Hill, 2000.

Tucker, Robert C., ed. *The Marx-Engels Reader.* New York: Norton, 1978.

Vallentyne, Peter, ed. *Contractarianism and Rational Choice.* New York: Cambridge University Press, 1991.

Waldron, Jeremy. *The Right to Private Property.* Oxford, U.K.: Oxford University Press, 1988.

Waluchow, Wilfrid, and Deborah Poff, eds. *Business Ethics in Canada.* Scarborough, Ont: Prentice Hall Canada, 1st ed., 1987; 3rd ed. 1999.

Williams, Bernard. *Ethics and the Limits of Philosophy.* Cambridge, Mass.: Harvard University Press, 1985.

Index

About the Author

Minnesota-born and raised, **Jan Narveson** received his B.A. from the University of Chicago, and his Ph.D. from Harvard. After two years at the University of New Hampshire, he moved to Canada and since then has been professor of philosophy at the University of Waterloo in Ontario, Canada. He is the author of more than two hundred papers in philosophical periodicals and anthologies, mainly on ethical theory and practice, and of four previous published books: *Morality and Utility* (1967); *The Libertarian Idea* (2001); *Moral Matters* (2nd ed., 1999); and, with Marilyn Friedman, *Political Correctness* (1995). He is also the editor of *Moral Issues* (1983), and, with John T. Sanders, of a volume of essays by thirteen philosophers, *For and Against the State* (1996), and is on the editorial boards of several philosophical journals. He was also elected as a Fellow of the Royal Society of Canada, and sat on its Joint Committee on Health and Safety. He is a frequent guest at colloquia and conferences around North America and in the United Kingdom. In his nonprofessional life, he is an avid classical concert goer, organizer of concerts presented by the Kitchener-Waterloo Chamber Music Society, board member of the Kitchener-Waterloo Symphony Orchestra for many years, music columnist for the *University of Waterloo Gazette*, and author of program notes for concerts by the Canadian Chamber Ensemble and other ensembles. He enjoys the company of his wife Jean and two children in their home in Waterloo.